THE RELIGIONS BOOK

Penguin
Random
House

DK LONDON

SENIOR EDITORS
Gareth Jones, Georgina Palffy

PROJECT ART EDITOR
Katie Cavanagh

US SENIOR EDITOR
Rebecca Warren

US EDITOR
Kate Johnsen

JACKET DESIGNER
Laura Brim

JACKET EDITOR
Manisha Majithia

JACKET DESIGN DEVELOPMENT MANAGER
Sophia MTT

MANAGING ART EDITOR
Lee Griffiths

MANAGING EDITOR
Stephanie Farrow

ILLUSTRATIONS
James Graham

PRODUCTION EDITOR
Lucy Sims

PRODUCTION CONTROLLER
Mandy Inness

original styling by
STUDIO8 DESIGN

produced for DK by
COBALT ID

ART EDITORS
Darren Bland, Paul Reid

EDITORS
Louise Abbott, Diana Loxley,
Alison Sturgeon, Sarah Tomley,
Marek Walisiewicz

DK DELHI

MANAGING EDITOR
Pakshalika Jayaprakash

SENIOR EDITOR
Monica Saigal

EDITOR
Tanya Desai

MANAGING ART EDITOR
Arunesh Talapatra

SENIOR ART EDITOR
Anis Sayyed

ART EDITOR
Neha Wahi

ASSISTANT ART EDITORS
Astha Singh, Namita Bansal,
Gazal Roongta, Ankita Mukherjee

PICTURE RESEARCHER
Surya Sankash Sarangi

DTP MANAGER/CTS
Balwant Singh

DTP DESIGNERS
Bimlesh Tiwary, Rajesh Singh

This American Edition, 2018
First American Edition, 2013
Published in the United States by
DK Publishing 1745 Broadway,
20th Floor, New York, NY 10019

Copyright © 2013, 2018
Dorling Kindersley Limited
DK, a Division of Penguin Random House LLC

23 24 10 9 8 7 6
054–192230–Nov/2018

Published in Great Britain by
Dorling Kindersley Limited.

A catalog record for this book is
available from the Library of Congress.
ISBN: 978-1-4654-7646-3

DK books are available at special discounts
when purchased in bulk for sales promotions,
premiums, fund-raising, or educational use.
For details, contact: DK Publishing Special
Markets, 1745 Broadway, 20th Floor, New York,
New York 10019 or SpecialSales@dk.com

Printed and bound in UAE

For the curious
www.dk.com

MIX
Paper from
responsible sources
FSC™ C018179

This book was made with Forest Stewardship
Council ™ certified paper — one small step in
DK's commitment to a sustainable future.
For more information go to
www.dk.com/our-green-pledge

CONTRIBUTORS

SHULAMIT AMBALU

Rabbi Shulamit Ambalu MA studied at Leo Baeck College, London, where she was ordained in 2004 and now lectures in Pastoral Care and Rabbinic Literature.

MICHAEL COOGAN

One of the leading biblical scholars in the United States, Michael Coogan is Director of Publications for the Harvard Semitic Museum and Lecturer on the Old Testament/Hebrew Bible at Harvard Divinity School. Among his many works are *The Old Testament: A Historical and Literary Introduction* and *The Illustrated Guide to World Religions*.

EVE LEVAVI FEINSTEIN

Dr. Eve Levavi Feinstein is a writer, editor, and tutor in Palo Alto, California. She holds a PhD on the Hebrew Bible from Harvard University, and is the author of *Sexual Pollution in the Hebrew Bible* as well as articles for *Jewish Ideas Daily* and other publications.

PAUL FREEDMAN

Rabbi Paul Freedman studied Physics at Bristol University and Education at Cambridge. Following a career in teaching, he gained rabbinic ordination and an MA in Hebrew and Jewish studies at Leo Baeck College, London.

NEIL PHILIP

Neil Philip is the author of numerous books on mythology and folklore, including the Dorling Kindersley *Companion Guide to Mythology* (with Philip Wilkinson), *The Great Mystery: Myths of Native America*, and the *Penguin Book of English Folktales*. Dr. Philip studied at the universities of Oxford and London, and is currently an independent writer and scholar.

ANDREW STOBART

The Rev. Dr. Andrew Stobart is a Methodist minister. He studied Christian theology to the doctoral level at the London School of Theology and Durham and Aberdeen universities, and has taught and written in the areas of theology, church history, and the Bible, contributing to Dorling Kindersley's *The Illustrated Bible*.

MEL THOMPSON

Dr. Mel Thompson BD, M.Phil, PhD, AKC was formerly a teacher, lecturer, and examiner in Religious Studies, and now writes on philosophy, religion, and ethics. Author of more than 30 books, including *Understand Eastern Philosophy*, he blogs on issues of religious belief, and runs the "Philosophy and Ethics" website at www.philosophyandethics.com.

CHARLES TIESZEN

Dr. Charles Tieszen completed his doctorate at the University of Birmingham, where he focused on medieval encounters between Muslims and Christians. He is currently a researcher and adjunct professor of Islamic studies, specializing in topics related to Islam, Christian–Muslim relations, and religious freedom.

MARCUS WEEKS

A writer and musician, Marcus Weeks studied philosophy and worked as a teacher before embarking on a career as an author. He has contributed to many books on the arts, popular sciences, and ideas, including the Dorling Kindersley title *The Philosophy Book*.

CONTENTS

HINDUISM
FROM 1700 BCE

BUDDHISM
FROM 6TH CENTURY BCE

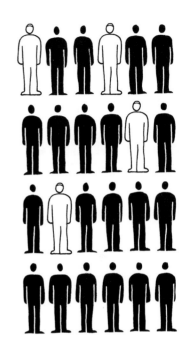

JUDAISM
FROM 2000 BCE

CHRISTIANITY
FROM 1ST CENTURY CE

ISLAM
FROM 610 CE

There is no simple definition of the concept of religion that fully articulates all its dimensions. Encompassing spiritual, personal, and social elements, this phenomenon is however, ubiquitous, appearing in every culture from prehistory to the modern day—as evidenced in the cave paintings and elaborate burial customs of our distant ancestors and the continuing quest for a spiritual goal to life.

For Palaeolithic people—and indeed for much of human history—religion provided a way of understanding and influencing powerful natural phenomena. Weather and the seasons, creation, life, death and the afterlife, and the structure of the cosmos were all subject to religious explanations that invoked controlling gods, or a realm outside the visible inhabited by deities and mythical creatures. Religion provided a means to communicate with these gods, through ritual and prayer, and these practices—when shared by members of a community—helped to cement social groups, enforce hierarchies, and provide a deep sense of collective identity.

As societies became more complex, their belief systems grew with them and religion was increasingly deployed as a political tool. Military conquests were often followed by the assimilation of the pantheon of the defeated people by the victors; and kingdoms and empires were often supported by their deities and priestly classes.

A personal god

Religion met many of the needs of early people and provided templates by which they could organize their lives—through rites, rituals, and taboos. It also gave them a means by which they could visualize their place in the cosmos. Could religion therefore be explained as a purely social artifact? Many would argue that it is much more. Over the centuries, people have defied opposition to their faiths, suffering persecution or death to defend their right to worship their God or gods. And even today, when the world is arguably more materialistic than ever before, more than three-quarters of its population consider themselves to hold some form of religious belief. Religion would seem to be a necessary part of human existence, as important to life as the ability to use language. Whether it is a matter of intense personal experience—an inner awareness of the divine—or a way of finding significance and meaning, and providing a starting point for all of life's endeavors, it appears to be fundamental at a personal as well as a social level.

Beginnings

We know about the religions of the earliest societies from the relics they left behind and from the stories of later civilizations. In addition, isolated tribes in remote places, such as the Amazonian forest in South America, the Indonesian islands, and parts of Africa, still practice religions that are thought to have remained largely unchanged for millennia. These primal religions often feature a belief in a unity between nature and the spirit, linking people inextricably with the environment.

All men have need of the gods.
Homer

As the early religions evolved, their ceremonies and cosmologies became increasingly sophisticated. Primal religions of the nomadic and seminomadic peoples of prehistory gave way to the religions of the ancient and, in turn, of the classical civilizations. Their beliefs are now often dismissed as mythology, but many elements of these ancient narrative traditions persist in today's faiths. Religions continued to adapt, old beliefs were absorbed into the religions of the society that succeeded them, and new faiths emerged with different observances and rituals.

Ancient to modern
It is hard to pinpoint the time when many religions began, not least because their roots lie in prehistory and the sources that describe their origins may date from a much later time. However, it is thought that the oldest surviving religion today is Hinduism, which has its roots in the folk religions of the Indian subcontinent, brought together in the writing of the Vedas as early as the 13th century BCE. From this Vedic tradition came not only the pluralistic religion we now know as Hinduism, but also Jainism, Buddhism, and, later, Sikhism, which emerged in the 15th century.

Other belief systems were developing in the east. From the 17th century BCE, the Chinese dynasties established their nation states and empires. There emerged traditional folk religions and ancestor worship that were later incorporated into the more philosophical belief systems of Daoism and Confucianism.

In the eastern Mediterranean, ancient Egyptian and Babylonian religions were still being practiced when the emerging city-states of Greece and Rome developed their own mythologies and pantheons of gods. Further east, Zoroastrianism—the first major known monotheistic religion—had already been established in Persia, and Judaism had emerged as the first of the Abrahamic religions, followed by Christianity and Islam.

Many religions recognized the particular significance of one or more individuals as founders of the faith: they may have been embodiments of god, such as Jesus or Krishna, or recipients of special divine revelation, such as Moses and Muhammad.

The religions of the modern world continued to evolve with advances in society, sometimes reluctantly, and often by dividing into branches. Some apparently new religions began to appear, especially in the 19th and 20th centuries, but these invariably bore the traces of the faiths that had come before.

Elements of religion
Human history has seen the rise and fall of countless religions, each with its own distinct beliefs, rituals, and mythology. Although some are similar and considered to be branches of a larger tradition, there are many contrasting and contradictory belief systems.

Some religions, for example, have a number of gods, while others, especially the more modern major faiths, are monotheistic;

There is no use disguising the fact, our religious needs are the deepest. There is no peace until they are satisfied and contented.
**Isaac Hecker,
Roman Catholic priest**

and there are major differences of opinion between religions on such matters as the afterlife. We can, however, identify certain elements common to almost all religions in order to examine the similarities and differences between them. These aspects—the ways in which the beliefs and practices of a religion are manifested—are what the British writer and philosopher of religion Ninian Smart called the "dimensions of religion."

Perhaps the most obvious elements we can use to identify and compare religions are the observances of a faith. These includes such activities as prayer, pilgrimage, meditation, feasting and fasting, dress, and of course ceremonies and rituals. Also evident are the physical aspects of a religion: the artifacts, relics, places of worship, and holy places. Less apparent is the subjective element of the religion—its mystical and emotional aspects, and how a believer experiences the religion in achieving ecstasy, enlightenment, or inner peace, for example, or establishing a personal relationship with the divine.

Another aspect of most religions is the mythology, or narrative, that accompanies it. This can be a simple oral tradition of stories,

or a more sophisticated set of scriptures, but often includes a creation story and a history of the gods, saints, or prophets, with parables that illustrate and reinforce the beliefs of the religion. Every existing faith has a collection of sacred texts that articulates its central ideals and narrates the history of the tradition. These texts, which in many cases are considered to be have been passed directly from the deity, are used in worship and education.

In many religions, alongside this narrative, is a more sophisticated and systematic element, which explains the philosophy and doctrine of the religion, and lays out its distinctive theology. Some of these

What religion a man shall have is a historical accident, quite as much as what language he shall speak.
George Santayana, Spanish philosopher

ancillary texts have themselves acquired canonical status. There is also often an ethical element, with rules of conduct and taboos, and a social element that defines the institutions of the religion and of the society it is associated with. Such rules are typically concise—the Ten Commandments of Judaism and Christianity, or the Noble Eightfold Path of Buddhism, for example.

Religion and morality

The idea of good and evil is also fundamental to many faiths, and religion often has a function of offering moral guidance to society. The major religions differ in their definitions of what constitutes a good life—and the line between moral philosophy and religion is far from clear in belief systems such as Confucianism and Buddhism—but certain basic moral codes have emerged that are almost universal. Religious taboos, commandments and so on not only ensure that the will of the God or gods is obeyed, but also form a framework for society and its laws to enable people to live peaceably together. The spiritual leadership that in many religions was given by prophets with divine guidance was passed on to a priesthood. This became an

essential part of many communities, and in some religions has wielded considerable political power.

Death and the afterlife

Most religions address the central human concern of death with the promise of some kind of continued existence, or afterlife. In eastern traditions, such as Hinduism, the soul is believed to be reincarnated after death in a new physical form, while other faiths hold that the soul is judged after death and resides in a nonphysical heaven or hell. The goal of achieving freedom from the cycle of death and rebirth, or achieving immortality encourages believers to follow the rules of their faith.

All religions, arts, and sciences are branches of the same tree.
Albert Einstein

Conflict and history

Just as religions have created cohesion within societies, they have often been the source—or the banner—of conflict between them. Although all the major traditions hold peace as an essential virtue, they may also make provision for the use of force in certain circumstances, for example, to defend their faith or to extend their reach. Religion has provided an excuse for hostility between powers throughout history. While tolerance is also considered a virtue, heretics and infidels have often been persecuted for their beliefs, and religion has been the pretext for attempted genocides such as the Holocaust.

Challenges to faith

Faced with the negative aspects of religious belief and equipped with the tools of humanist philosophy and science, a number of thinkers have questioned the very validity of religion. There were, they argued, logical and consistent cosmologies based on reason rather than faith—in effect, religions had become irrelevant in the modern world. New philosophies, such as Marxism-Leninism considered religions to be a negative force on human development, and as

a result there arose communist states that were explicitly atheistic and antireligious.

New directions

Responding to societal change and scientific advances, some of the older religions have adapted or divided into several branches. Others have steadfastly rejected what they see as a heretical progress in an increasingly rational, materialistic, and godless world; fundamentalist movements in Christianity, Islam, and Judaism have gained many followers who reject the liberal values of the modern world.

At the same time, many people recognize a lack of spirituality in modern society, and have turned to charismatic denominations of the major religions, or to the many new religious movements that have appeared in the past 200 years.

Others, influenced by the New Age movement of the late 20th century, have rediscovered ancient beliefs, or sought the exoticism of traditional religions with no connection to the modern world. Nevertheless, the major religions of the world continue to grow and even today very few countries in the world can be seen as truly secular societies.

Primal religions—so-called because they came first—were practiced by people throughout the world and are key to the development of all modern religions. Some are still active today.

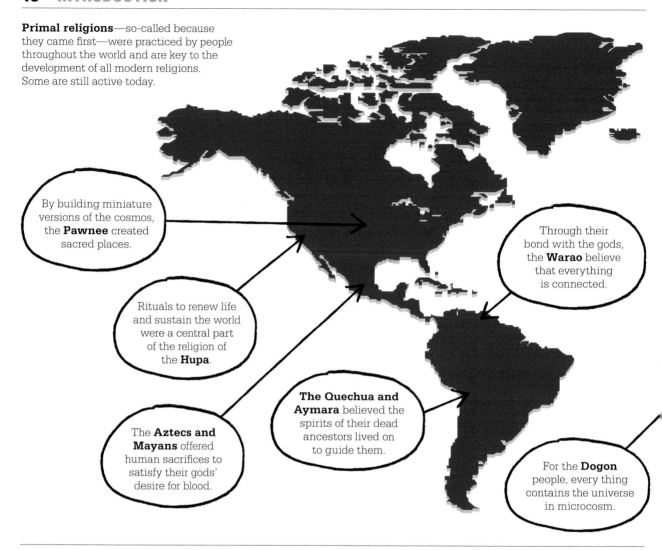

By building miniature versions of the cosmos, the **Pawnee** created sacred places.

Rituals to renew life and sustain the world were a central part of the religion of the **Hupa**.

Through their bond with the gods, the **Warao** believe that everything is connected.

The Quechua and Aymara believed the spirits of their dead ancestors lived on to guide them.

The **Aztecs and Mayans** offered human sacrifices to satisfy their gods' desire for blood.

For the **Dogon** people, every thing contains the universe in microcosm.

O ur early hunter-gatherer ancestors considered the natural world to have a supernatural quality. For some, this was expressed in a belief that animals, plants, objects, and forces of nature possess a spirit, in the same way that people do. In this animistic view of the world, humans are seen as a part of nature, not separate from it, and to live in harmony with it, must show respect to the spirits.

Many early peoples sought to explain the world in terms of deities associated with particular natural phenomena. The rising of the sun each day, for example, might be seen as a release from the darkness of the night, controlled by a sun god; similarly, natural cycles such as the phases of the moon and the seasons—vital to these people's way of life—were assigned their own deities. As well as creating a cosmology to account for the workings of the universe, most cultures also incorporated some form of creation story into their belief system. Often this was in the form of an analogy with human reproduction, in which a mother goddess gave birth to the world, which was in some cases fathered by another god. Sometimes these parental deities were personified as animals, or natural feature, such as rivers or the sea, or in the form of mother earth and father sky.

Rites and rituals
The belief systems of most primal religions incorporated some form of afterlife, one that was typically related to the existence of a realm separate from the physical world —a place of gods and mythical creatures—to which the spirits

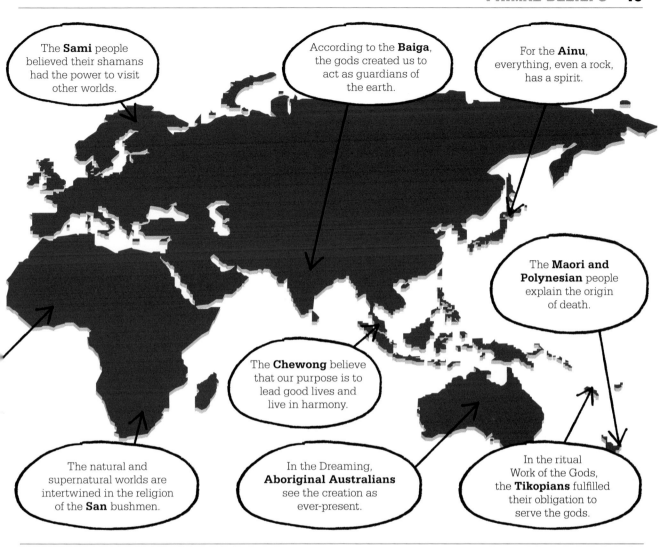

The **Sami** people believed their shamans had the power to visit other worlds.

According to the **Baiga**, the gods created us to act as guardians of the earth.

For the **Ainu**, everything, even a rock, has a spirit.

The **Maori and Polynesian** people explain the origin of death.

The **Chewong** believe that our purpose is to lead good lives and live in harmony.

The natural and supernatural worlds are intertwined in the religion of the **San** bushmen.

In the Dreaming, **Aboriginal Australians** see the creation as ever-present.

In the ritual Work of the Gods, the **Tikopians** fulfilled their obligation to serve the gods.

of the dead would travel. In some religions, it was thought possible to communicate with this other realm and contact the ancestral spirits for guidance. A particular class of holy person—the shaman or medicine man—was able to journey there and derive mystical healing powers from contact with, and sometimes possession by, the spirits.

Early peoples also marked life's rites of passage; these, along with the changing of the seasons, developed into rituals associated with the spirits and the deities. The idea of pleasing the gods to

ensure good fortune in hunting or farming inspired rituals of worship, and, in some cultures, sacrifices to offer life to the gods in return for the life they had given to humans.

Symbolism also played a key role in the religious practices of early cultures. Masks, charms, idols, and amulets were used in ceremonies, and spirits were believed to occupy them. Certain areas were thought to have religious significance, and some communities set aside holy places and sacred burial grounds, while others made buildings or villages

in the image of the cosmos. A few of these primal religions survive to the present day among dwindling numbers of tribespeople around the world untouched by Western civilization. Some attempts have been made to revive them by indigenous peoples who are trying to reestablish lost cultures. Although their belief systems may seem at first glance to be primitive to modern eyes, traces of them can still be seen in the major religions that have evolved in the modern world, or in the New Age search for spirituality. ■

UNSEEN FORCES ARE AT WORK

MAKING SENSE OF THE WORLD

IN CONTEXT

KEY BELIEVERS
/Xam San

WHEN AND WHERE
**From prehistory,
sub-Saharan Africa**

AFTER
44,000 BCE Tools almost
identical to those used by
modern San are abandoned
in a cave in KwaZulu–Natal.

19th century German
linguist Wilhelm Bleek sets
down many of the ancestral
stories of the San.

20th century Government-
sponsored programs are
set up to encourage San
peoples to switch from hunter-
gathering to settled farming.

1994 San leader and healer
Dawid Kruiper takes the
growing campaign for San
rights and land claims to
the United Nations.

The question of why human
beings first develop the
idea of a world beyond
the visible one in which we live
is complex. Motivated by an urge
to make sense of the world around
them—particularly the dangers
and misfortunes they faced, and
how the necessities of life were
provided—people in early societies
sought explanations in a realm
that was invisible to them, but
had an influence over their lives.

The idea of a spirit world is
also associated with notions of
sleep and death, and the interface
between these and consciousness,
which can be likened to the natural
phenomenon of night and day.

See also: Animism in early societies 24–25 ▪ The power of the shaman 26–31 ▪ Created for a purpose 32
▪ Living the Way of the Gods 82–85 ▪ A rational world 92–99

In this twilight zone between sleep and waking, life and death, light and dark, lie the dreams, hallucinations, and states of altered consciousness that suggest that the visible, tangible world is not the only one, and that another, supernatural world also exists— and has a connection with our own. It is easy to imagine how the inhabitants of this other world were thought to influence not only our own minds and actions, but also to inhabit the bodies of animals and even inanimate objects, and to cause the natural phenomena affecting our lives.

A meeting of worlds

The figures of humans, animals, and human-animal hybrids in Palaeolithic cave paintings are often decorated with patterns that are now thought to represent the involuntary back-of-the-retina patterns known as entoptic phenomena—visual effects such as dots, grids, zigzags, and wavy lines, which appear between waking and sleep, or between vision and hallucination. The paintings themselves represent a permeable veil between the physical and the spirit worlds.

It is impossible to ask the Palaeolithic hunter-gatherers of Europe about the beliefs and rituals that lie behind their cave paintings, but in the 19th century it was still possible to record the cultural and religious beliefs of the /Xam of southern Africa, a now-extinct clan of San hunter-gatherers who made cave paintings reminiscent of those of the Stone Age, for similar reasons. The spiritual life of the /Xam San offered a living parallel to the religious ideas archaeologists have attributed to early modern humans. Even the clicks of the /Xam San language (represented »

Since prehistoric times, the San have renewed their rock paintings, transmitting the stories and ideas they depict down the generations.

The Storm Bird blows his wind into the chests of man and beast, and without this wind we would not be able to breathe.
African fable

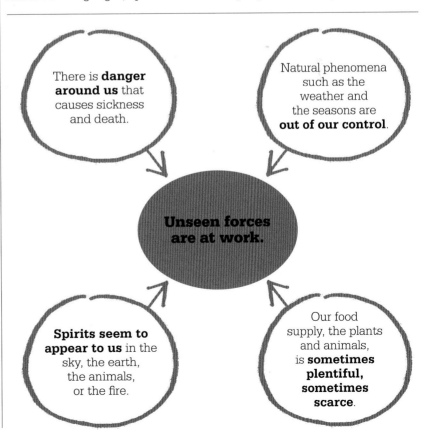

There is **danger around us** that causes sickness and death.

Natural phenomena such as the weather and the seasons are **out of our control**.

Unseen forces are at work.

Spirits seem to **appear to us** in the sky, the earth, the animals, or the fire.

Our food supply, the plants and animals, is **sometimes plentiful, sometimes scarce**.

by marks such as /, indicating a dental click rather like a tut of disapproval), are thought to survive from humankind's earliest speech.

Levels of the cosmos

The mythology of all San peoples is modeled closely on their local environment and on the idea that there are both natural and supernatural realms that are deeply intertwined. In their three-tiered world, spirit realms lie both above and below the middle, or natural, world in which humans live; each is accessible to the other, and whatever happens in one directly affects what happens in the other. Humans with special powers could visit the upper or sky realm, and travel underwater and underground in the lower spirit realm.

For the /Xam San, the world above was inhabited by the creator and trickster deity /Kaggen (also known as Mantis) and his family. They shared this world with an abundance of game animals, and with the spirits of the dead, including the spirits of the Early Race—a community of hybrid animal-humans, with powers to

shape, transform, and create. The /Xam believed that these beings were the first to inhabit the earth.

Elemental forces

In /Xam myth, elements of the natural environment were given supernatural significance or personified as spirits. Supernatural figures could take the form of the animals they shared their lands with, such as the eland (a type of antelope), the meerkat, and the praying mantis. The creator /Kaggen, who dreamed the world into being, usually took human form but could transform into almost anything, most often a praying mantis or an eland. While he was the protector of game animals, he would sometimes transform himself into one in order to be killed and feed the people.

The people of the Early Race were regarded with awe and respect, but not worshipped. Not even /Kaggen the Mantis was prayed to, although a San shaman such as //Kabbo (see box, facing page) might hope to intercede with /Kaggen to ensure a successful hunt. Because /Kaggen is a

> My mother told me that the girl [of the Early Race] put her hands in the wood ash and threw it into the sky, to become the Milky Way.
> **African fable**

trickster, many of the myths surrounding him and his family are comic rather than reverent; even the key myth of the creation of the first eland includes a scene in which an ineffectual /Kaggen is beaten up by a family of meerkats.

Important elemental forces and celestial bodies also became characters in stories that explained how they came to be, and why they behave in the way that they do. The children of the Early Race, for example, threw the sleeping sun up into the sky, so that the light that shone from his armpit would illuminate the world. It was a girl from the Early Race who made the stars by throwing the ashes of a fire into the sky of the Milky Way. Rain was not thought of as a natural phenomenon, but as a large animal. A fierce thunderstorm was a rain-bull, and a gentle rain was a rain-cow. Special people who had the power to summon the rain, such as //Kabbo, would make a supernatural journey to a full

Natural phenomena such as eclipses, possibly never before seen by any living member of the San, might be explained through tales passed down in their rich oral tradition.

A long time ago,
the baboons were little
men just like us,
but more mischievous
and quarrelsome.
African fable

waterhole to summon a rain-cow, and then bring it back through the sky to the place in need of water. There he would kill the rain-cow so that its blood and milk fell down as rain on the earth.

Rain was a vital necessity in the arid desert landscape in which the /Xam lived. It was essential to replenish the widely scattered waterholes that they moved between, and which were linked to each other by a complex web of story and myth, known as *kukummi* and similar to the Dreamings of the Australian Aborigines (pp.34–35).

Entering other worlds

Many aspects of the natural world described in /Xam stories feature the interaction of the supernatural beings with humans—how they have an interest in this world, and how humans can, in turn, act to influence and please them. All San peoples believe that the spirit realms are accessible, in altered states of consciousness, to those who have a supernatural potency, known as *!gi*, imparted to humans and animals by their creator. The trance dance is the key religious ritual in which the San

can use this power to access the spirit world, via trance, and launch their essential selves up through the top of their heads and into the spirit world. There, they may plead for the lives of the sick, and return with healing power so that they can drive out the arrows of disease fired by the dead from the other world.

The /Xam offered prayers to the moon and stars to give them access to spiritual power, as well as good luck in hunting. When /Xam people entered a state of altered consciousness, it was believed that they were temporarily dead, and that their hearts had become stars. Humans and the stars were so intimately linked that when a person actually died, "the star feels that our heart falls over [and] the star falls down on account of it. For the stars know the time at which we die."

After death, the links in /Xam belief between the worlds of human experience, of spirits, and of natural phenomena become even more apparent. The hair of a deceased person was believed to transform into clouds, which then shelter

Ascribing human traits to animals —for example, the inquisitiveness of the meerkat—is a mainstay of early myth, around which stories are woven about how the world came to be as it is.

humans from the heat of the sun. Death was described in elemental terms: the wind that exists inside every human being was said to blow away their footprints when they died, making the transition between the world of the living and the world of the dead a decisive one. If the footprints remained, "it would seem as if we still lived." ■

Kabbo's dream-life

Much of the information we have about /Xam San beliefs comes from a man named //Kabbo, who in the 1870s was one of several /Xam San released from prison into the custody of Dr. Wilhelm Bleek, who wished to learn their language and study their culture. They had been jailed for crimes such as stealing a sheep to feed their starving families. //Kabbo spoke of his waterholes, between which his family would move in the arid desert of the central Cape Colony, camping

some way from the water so as not to frighten off the animals that came to drink the brackish water. Wilhelm Bleek said of him: "This gentle old soul appeared lost in a dream life of his own," and in fact the name //Kabbo means "dream." The god /Kaggen was said to have dreamed the world into being, and //Kabbo had a special relationship with him; as a /Kaggen-ka !kwi, a "mantis's man" he was able to enter a dream state to exercise powers such as rainmaking, healing, and hunting magic.

EVEN A ROCK HAS A SPIRIT

ANIMISM IN EARLY SOCIETIES

IN CONTEXT

KEY BELIEVERS
Ainu

WHERE
Hokkaido, Japan

BEFORE
10,000–300 BCE Neolithic Jomon people—remote ancestors of the Ainu— live in Hokkaido, probably worshipping clan deities.

600–1000 CE Okhotsk hunter-gatherer people occupy coastal Hokkaido. Some of their ritual practices, such as bear worship, are seen later in the Ainu.

700–1200 Okhotsk culture blends with that of the Satsumon to create the Ainu.

AFTER
1899–1997 The Ainu are forced to assimilate into Japanese culture; many Ainu religious practices are banned.

2008 The Ainu are officially recognized as an indigenous people with a distinct culture.

Everything in the world **has a spirit**.

⬇

Even human beings are **simply containers** for a spirit.

⬇

Spirits are **immortal**.

⬇

The most important spirits are **the gods**.

⬇

Ceremonies, songs, and offerings give the gods status in the other world.

⬇

If we treat the gods well, **they will provide us with food**.

The word Ainu means "human being," and refers to the indigenous population of Japan, now living mainly on the island of Hokkaido. The Ainu have close cultural ties with other inhabitants of the north Pacific Rim—Siberian peoples (such as the Chukchi, Koryak, and Yupik) and the Inuit of Canada and Alaska. These peoples share, in particular, an animistic view of the world, in which every being and object that exists has a spirit that can act, speak, and walk by itself. They also believe that the spiritual and physical worlds are separated by only a thin, permeable membrane.

The Ainu consider the body to be simply a container for the spirit; after death, the spirit passes out of the mouth and nostrils, and arrives in the next world to be reborn as a *kamuy*, a word meaning both god and spirit. When the *kamuy* dies in the next world, it is reborn in this one. It will always reincarnate in the same species and gender—a man will always be a man, for example.

Kamuy can be animals, plants, minerals, geographical or natural phenomena, or even tools and utensils produced by humans. Because all spirits, even those of

See also: Living the Way of the Gods 82–85 ■ Devotion through puja 114–15

An Ainu chief performs a ceremony to honor the spirit of a slaughtered bear as it returns to the divine world, in a photograph taken in 1946.

inanimate objects, are considered immortal, after death a person's house may be burned to ensure that his or her *kamuy* will have a home in the other world; their tools and implements may also be broken (to release the spirits inside) and buried with the body, for use again in the next world.

The power of words

Some *kamuy* have roles in both the supernatural and human worlds. Kotan-kor-kamuy, for example, is the creator god, but he is also the god of the village, and may manifest himself on earth as a long-eared owl.

Humans and *kamuy* have a close relationship—so close that *kamuy* have been described as "gods you can argue with." The *kamuy* can be prayed to, using special carved prayer sticks, but the ritual relationship is based more on mutual respect and correct behavior than on worship. If someone has angered a god by carelessness or disrespect, they must conduct a ceremony to express their remorse. If, however, a person has treated a god with due respect and performed all the appropriate rituals, yet still receives bad luck, the Ainu can ask the fire goddess, Fuchi, to compel that god to apologize and make recompense.

In Ainu belief, even words are spirits, and the use of words is one of the gifts that humans have that gods and things do not. Words can be used to make bargains with both gods and things, and also to give pleasure to the gods. For example, the Ainu epic songs known as *kamuy yukar*, or "songs of the gods," are sung in the first person, from the perspective of *kamuy* rather than humans, and it is said the *kamuy* take delight in watching humans dance and sing the songs of the gods. ■

I also continue forever to hover behind the humans and always watch over the land of the humans.
Song of the Owl God

Spirit-sending rituals

Hunting rituals were central to traditional Ainu life and were used to appease the gods who visited earth disguised as animals. In return for offerings and rituals, the gods left behind the gift of their animal bodies.

After killing and eating a bear, the Ainu would perform the *iyomante* spirit-sending ritual. The spirit of the bear—revered as the mountain bear god Kimun-kamuy—was entertained with food, wine, dance, and song. Arrows were fired into the air to aid Kimun-kamuy's return to the divine world, where he would invite other gods to share the gifts of sake, salmon, and sacred carved willow sticks with which he had been honored on earth.

An *iwakte* spirit-sending ceremony was also held for broken tools and objects that had come to the end of their use.

SPECIAL PEOPLE CAN VISIT OTHER WORLDS

THE POWER OF THE SHAMAN

IN CONTEXT

KEY BELIEVERS
Sami

WHEN AND WHERE
From prehistory, Sápmi (formerly Lapland)

AFTER
10,000 BCE Ancestors of the Sami make rock carvings in the European Arctic.

c.98 CE The Roman historian Tacitus makes the first record of the Sami (as the Fenni).

13th century CE Catholic missionaries introduce Christianity, but traditional shamanism persists.

c.1720 CE Thomas von Westen, Apostle of the Sami, forcefully converts Sami to Christianity, destroying shamanic drums and sacred sites.

21st century Most Sami follow the Christian faith, but recent times have seen a revival of Sami shamanism.

Shamanism describes one of humankind's oldest and most widespread religious practices, based on a belief in spirits who can be influenced by shamans. These shamans, men or women, are believed to be special people who possess great power and knowledge. After entering an altered state of consciousness, or trance, they are able to travel to other worlds and interact with the spirits who live there.

Bargaining with the powerful spirits who control these other worlds is often a key aspect of the shaman's activities. For example, the shaman often requests the release of game animals (essential in some traditional societies) from the spirit world into this world, to gain insight into the future, or for remedies to cure the sick. In return, the spirits may ask humans (via the shaman, who acts as an intermediary) to make offerings to them or to observe certain rules and codes of conduct.

Shamans play an important role as healers of the sick; this role emphasizes that their journeys are not simply personal and private, but are undertaken primarily to

We believe in dreams, and we believe that people can live a life apart from real life, a life they can go through in their sleep.
Nâlungiaq, a Netsilik woman

alleviate suffering and hardship in the community. This function is reflected in some of the (now largely obsolete) terms that have been used to describe shamans, such as witchdoctors in sub-Saharan Africa and medicine men in North America.

In Europe, shamanism was a dominant feature of many societies from around 45,000 years ago up until the modern era. The Vikings, practiced a form of shamanic divination known as *seiðr* between

---

In worlds we cannot see, powerful **supernatural beings control** the supply of game and the weather.

These other worlds are **full of spirits**, too, as both humans and animals have **undying souls**.

There are some **special people who can visit the worlds** in which these spirits live.

These people can **enlist the help of the spirits** to ask for game or good weather for us, or cure us when we are ill.

See also: Making sense of the world 20–23 ▪ Animism in early societies 24–25 ▪ Divining the future 79

the 8th and 11th centuries; and shamanic elements appear in the medieval myths of the Norse god Odin, who hanged himself in an initiation sacrifice on the World Tree ("the axis of the universe").

In the 16th and 17th centuries, shamanic traces were evident in the Benandanti spirit-battlers (an agrarian fertility cult) of Friuli, Italy, and in the night-flying seely wights (fairylike nature spirits) of Scotland. In more recent times, the *mazzeri* dream-hunters of Corsica show clear shamanic influence.

Sami shamans

The longest recorded history of shamanism in Europe, however, is in northern Scandinavia, in the area now known as Sápmi (formerly Lapland). Here the Sami people, semi-nomadic reindeer herders and coastal fishers, maintained a fully shamanic religion into the early 18th century, which has been partially revived in recent decades. Their religion can be reconstructed from historical sources as well as

Mankind does not end its existence because sickness or some other accident kills its animal spirit down here on earth. We live on.
Nâlungiaq, a Netsilik woman

The Sami shaman's drum was used to make contact with the spirit world. Some of these drums survive, although many were burned by Christian missionaries.

from close comparison with related cultures in North Asia and the American Arctic.

Sami shamans, or *noaidi*, could inherit their calling or be chosen directly by the spirits. In some other cultures, those chosen to be shamans often experienced a period of intense illness and stress, as well as visionary episodes in which they might be killed and then brought back to life.

Sami shamans had helping spirits in the form of animals, such as wolves, bears, reindeer, or fish, whom they imitated when entering a trance. Shamans are often said to become the animal they imitate; this occurs through a process of interior transformation rather than by visible, exterior change.

Three things helped the Sami shaman enter a trance. The first was intense physical deprivation, often achieved by working naked in the freezing Arctic temperatures. The second was the rhythmic beat of the sacred rune drum (among similar peoples, such as the Yakut and Buryat, the drum is called

the shaman's horse); the drum was decorated with images of the world of the gods above, the world of the dead below, and the world inhabited by humans (the earth)— the three realms connected by the World Tree. The third way the shaman was helped to enter a trance was through the ingestion of the psychotropic (mind-altering) fly agaric mushroom (*Amanita muscaria*). After taking the mushroom, the shaman would fall into a trance and become rigid and immobile, as if dead. During this process, male Sami guarded the shaman, while the women sang songs about the tasks to be performed in the upper or lower realms, and songs to help the shaman find his or her way home.

Stories are told of Sami shamans who never returned from the other world, often »

In some Arctic cultures, animals are believed to have spirit guardians who protect them and ensure their well-being. Shamans have the power to negotiate with these guardians, on behalf of human beings, for the release of animals from the spirit world into the human world for hunting and fishing.

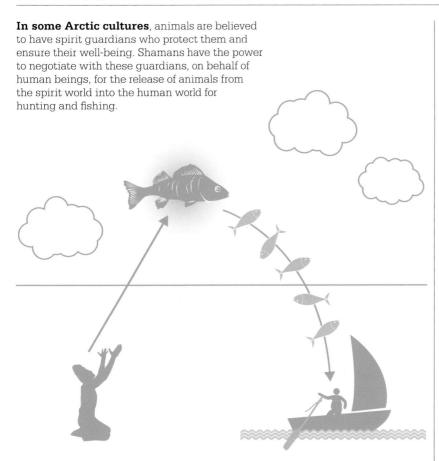

beliefs to the Sami. As well as subduing storms and acting as healers, they also mediated between the human world and the spirits of the earth, air, and sea. A shamanic seance was always held in subdued light, in a snow hut or a tent. The shaman would summon his helping spirits by singing special songs. After falling into a trance, he would speak in a voice that was not his own—most often in a deep, resonant bass, but sometimes in a shrill falsetto.

While in this trance state, the shaman could send his soul up into the sky to visit Tatqiq, the moon man, who was thought to bring fertility to women and good luck in hunting. If he was pleased with the offerings the shamans made to him, he would reward them with animals. When the moon was not visible in the sky, the Netsilik believed that he had gone hunting for animals to feed the dead.

Into the sky, under the sea

According to one Netsilik account, one day the great shaman Kukiaq was trying to catch seals from a breathing hole in the ice. He gazed

because those responsible for waking them with a spell had forgotten the magic words. One shaman was said to have been lost for three years, until the person acting as his guardian remembered that his soul needed to be recalled from "the coil of the pike's intestine, in the third dark corner." When the relevant words were spoken, the shaman's legs trembled, and he awoke, cursing his guardian.

Communicating with the spirits

Sami shamans were believed to fly to a mountain at the center of the world (the cosmic axis) before entering the spirit world, either above or below the mountain. They might typically ride on a fish spirit,

be guided by a bird spirit, and protected by a reindeer spirit. A journey to the upper world of Saivo would be undertaken in order to plead for game or for help of some other kind; a journey to the underworld of Jabmeaymo would be made to fetch back the soul of a sick person. This could only be done after the mistress of the underworld had been placated with offerings. The shamans were able to communicate with the spirits in the upper and lower worlds because their shamanic training involved learning the secret language of the spirits.

The Netsilingmiut (Netsilik Inuit) shamans—an Arctic culture, from present-day Canada (west of Hudson Bay)—had similar religious

Everything comes from Nuliayuk—food and clothes, hunger and bad hunting, abundance or lack of caribou, seals, meat, and blubber.
**Nâlungiaq,
a Netsilik woman**

Some Inuit in Gojahaven, northern Canada, have maintained a belief in shamans, who are thought to have a special relationship with the landscape and with the spirits who control it.

upward and realized that the moon was gradually moving toward him. It hovered above his head and transformed into a whalebone sledge. The driver, Tatqiq, gestured to Kukiaq to join him, and whisked him off to his house in the sky. The entrance of the house moved like a chewing mouth, and in one of the rooms the sun was nursing a baby. Although the moon asked Kukiaq to stay, he was anxious he would not be able to find his way home. So he slid back to earth on a moonbeam, landing safely at the very same breathing hole he had left from.

Sometimes, however, the Netsilik shamans would send their souls down to visit Nuliayuk (also known as Sedna), the mistress of sea and land animals, at the bottom of the ocean. Nuliayuk possessed the power to either withhold or release the seals on which the Netsilik depended for food and clothing. She therefore had great influence over them. When the Netsilik broke any of her strict taboos, she would imprison the seals. However, if the shamans ventured down to her watery underworld to braid her hair, she was usually appeased and would release the seals into the open sea.

The shamanic tradition of the Netsiliks lasted into the 1930s and 1940s. Within the Netsilik community, only the shamans (or *angatkut*)—who were protected by their own guardian spirits— were unafraid of the dangerous and malevolent spirits that filled the world. A Netsilik shaman might have several helping spirits. For example, the spirits of the shaman Unarâluk were his dead mother and father, the sun, a dog, and a sea scorpion. These spirits informed Unarâluk about what existed on, and beneath, the earth, and in the sea and sky. ∎

Au's mysterious shamanic illumination

The following account of shamanic illumination was given to the Danish explorer Knud Rasmussen by Au, an Iglulik Inuit shaman. Au recalled a period in his life when he sought solitude, was deeply melancholic, and would sometimes weep uncontrollably. Then, one day, a feeling of immense, inexplicable joy overcame him. He explained that in the middle of this fit of pure delight, "I became a shaman, not knowing myself how it came about. But I was a shaman." Thereafter, Au could see and hear in a completely different way: "I had gained my *quamaneq*, my enlightenment...it was not only I who could see through the darkness of life, but the same light also shone out from me, imperceptible to human beings, but visible to all the spirits of earth and sky and sea, and these now came to me and became my helping spirits."

Knud Rasmussen (1879–1933) spent many years documenting the culture of Arctic peoples during his journeys of exploration.

WHY ARE WE HERE?
CREATED FOR A PURPOSE

IN CONTEXT

KEY BELIEVERS
Baiga

WHEN AND WHERE
From 3000 BCE, Mandla Hills, southeastern Madhya Pradesh, central India

BEFORE
From prehistory The Baiga are thought to share a common ancestry with the Australian Aborigines.

AFTER
Mid-19th century British forest officials restrict sacred *bewar* agriculture. Food shortages follow; the Baigas say that the Kali Yuga, the age of darkness, has begun.

1890 A reserve that surrounds eight Baiga villages is demarcated where *bewar* is permitted.

1978 A Baiga development agency is established.

1990s More than 300,000 Baiga live in central India.

The Baiga are one of the indigenous tribal peoples of central India, collectively known as the Adivasis. The Baigas, who call themselves the sons and daughters of Dharti Mata, Mother Earth, believe that they were created to be the guardians of the forest—a task they have carried out since the beginning of time.

In their belief, Bhagavan, the creator, spread the world out flat like a chapati, but it flapped about and would not stay still. The first

You are made of the earth and are lord of the earth, and shall never forsake it. You must guard the earth.
Bhagavan the Creator

man, Nanga Baiga, and the first woman, Nanga Baigin, who were born in the forest from Mother Earth, took four great nails and drove them into the four corners of the earth to steady it. Bhagavan told them that they should take care of the earth to keep the nails in place, promising them a simple but contented life in return.

The Baiga followed the example of Nanga Baiga, hunting freely in the forest and considering themselves lords of the animals. Believing it wrong to tear the body of Mother Earth with a plow, they practiced a form of slash-and-burn agriculture known as *bewar* (although always leaving the stump of a saj tree for the gods to dwell in), moving every three years to a new patch of forest. However, 19th-century British officials opposed the Baiga's methods, forcing them to abandon their traditional axe-and-hoe cultivation and take up the hated plow. They were permitted to practice *bewar* only in the reservation of Baiga Chak in the Mandla Hills. ∎

See also: The Dreaming 34–35 ▪ A lifelong bond with the gods 39 ▪ Renewing life through ritual 51

WHY DO WE DIE?
THE ORIGIN OF DEATH

IN CONTEXT

KEY BELIEVERS
Maori

WHEN AND WHERE
**From prehistory,
New Zealand**

BEFORE
2nd and 3rd millennia BCE
Ancestors of the Polynesian
people spread across the
Pacific Ocean, possibly from
origins in Asia. Their ritual
practices and mythology
develop independently but
retain parallels across this
vast region.

Before 1300 CE The Maori
people settle in New Zealand.

AFTER
Early 19th century European
settlement begins. Some Maori
convert to Christianity.

1840 The Treaty of Waitangi
formalizes relations between
whites and Maori.

Today Around 620,000 Maori
are resident in New Zealand.

According to Maori belief, death did not exist at the beginning of the world but was brought into being following an act of incest. In one version of the Maori myth, the forest god Tane grew up between and separated his parents—Rangi, the sky god, and Papa, the earth goddess—because they forced him to live in darkness. He then asked his mother to marry him, but when Papa explained that this could not be, Tane shaped a woman from mud and mated with her.

The result of this union was a beautiful child—Hine-titama. She became Tane's wife, unaware that he was also her father. One day, however, she discovered the terrible truth, and descended in shame to the darkness of Po, the underworld; it was from this moment that humankind's descent to the realm of death began.

When Tane visited his wife, she told him, "Stay in the world of light, and foster our offspring. Let me stay in the world of darkness, and drag our offspring down." She then

The trees, plants, and creatures of the forest were believed by the Maori to be offspring of Tane, the forest god. Before felling a tree they therefore made an offering to the spirits.

became known as Hine-nui-te-po, the goddess of darkness and death. In an attempt to overturn the course of events and regain immortality on behalf of human beings, the trickster hero Maui raped Hine-nui-te-po as she slept, believing that after this act she would die, and that death would also cease to exist. But Hine-nui-te-po awoke during the attack and squeezed Maui to death with her thighs, thereby ensuring that mortality would remain in the world forever. ∎

See also: Preparing for the afterlife 58–59 ▪ Living the Way of the Gods 82–85

ETERNITY IS NOW
THE DREAMING

IN CONTEXT

KEY BELIEVERS
Australian Aborigines

WHEN AND WHERE
From prehistory, Australia

AFTER
8000 BCE The date ascribed to certain changes to the Australian landscape in Aboriginal oral tradition; this has been supported by geological evidence.

4000–2000 BCE Aboriginal rock art depicts the ancestral beings of the Dreaming; some experts estimate the earliest portrayals of the Rainbow Serpent to be even older, dating them to some 8,000 years ago.

1872 Uluru is first seen by a non-Aborigine, Ernest Giles, who called it "the remarkable pebble." European settlers give it the name Ayers Rock in 1873.

1985 The ownership of Uluru is returned to the Pitjantjatjara and Yankunytjatjara peoples.

In the Dreaming, the **ancestral beings shaped the land**.

↓

They **embedded their spiritual power** within the land.

↓

The **land is alive** with this power.

↓

The **power** of the Dreaming is **eternal and ever-present**.

↓

We can **access that power** and enter the eternal Now.

In the Australian Aboriginal tradition, the time of the creation was once called the Dreamtime, but is now referred to as the Dreaming. This term better captures the crucial element of Aboriginal faith—that the creation is continuous and ongoing, existing in the real, eternal present, as opposed to the remote past. It also accords with the Aboriginal belief that the Dreaming can be accessed through acts of ritual, song, dance, and storytelling, and through physical things such as sacred objects, or paintings on sand, rock, bark, the human body, and even canvas.

Myths of the Dreaming, called Dreamings, tell of the ancestral beings, who are known as the

See also: Making sense of the world 20–23 ▪ Created for a purpose 32 ▪ The spirits of the dead live on 36–37 ▪ Living the Way of the Gods 82–85

Uluru holds great spiritual power, according to Aboriginal tradition. It is said to be the heart of the ancestral beings' Songlines, whose signs may still be seen in the great rock's features.

First People or "the eternal ones of the dream," and their role in creation. Aboriginal tradition tells how these beings awake in a primal world that is still malleable and in a state of becoming. They journey across the land, leaving sacred paths known as Songlines, or Dreaming tracks, in their wake. As they go, they shape human beings, animals, plants, and the landscape, establishing rituals, defining the relationships between things, and changing shape back

We say *djang*…
That secret place…
Dreaming there.
**Gagudju elder
Big Bill Neidjie**

and forth from animal to human forms. Finally they transform themselves into features of the environment including stars, rocks, watering holes, and trees.

The living land

Dreamings are thus intimately tied to natural features such as hills, rocks, and creeks, as well as the Songlines themselves. Aboriginal peoples revere the topography of Australia as sacred because it offers evidence both of their spiritual ancestors' wanderings, and of their bodies. The Gunwinggu tribe describes the land as being infused with the ancestral beings' *djang* (spiritual power): it is this that gives it its life and its holy power.

This sacred topography converges on Uluru, a sandstone rock formation in the Northern Territory, the center from which all the Songlines are said to radiate. Uluru is venerated as a great storehouse of *djang*, the navel of the living body of Australia.

Aborigines consider the land to be both their inheritance and responsibility, and so they nurture it, and the Dreamings accordingly. While they may be mortal, the *djang* of their ancestral beings lives forever, and is forever in the now. ▪

The origin of Uluru

According to one legend, before the Uluru rock existed, the Kunia, or carpet-snake people, lived there. To the west lived the Windulka, or mulga-seed men, who invited the Kunia to a ceremony. The Kunia men set out, but, after stopping at the Uluru waterhole, they met some Metalungana, or sleepy-lizard women, and forgot about the invitation. The Windulka sent the bell bird Panpanpalana to find the Kunia. The Kunia men told the bird they could no longer attend since they had just gotten married. Affronted, the Windulka asked their friends the Liru, the poisonous-snake people, to attack the Kunia. During a furious battle, the Liru overcame the Kunia, who surrounded their dying leader, Ungata, and sang themselves to death. During the battle, Uluru was formed. Three rock holes high on Uluru mark the place Ungata bled to death, and the water that spills from them is Ungata's blood. It flows down to fill the pool of the Rainbow Serpent, Wanambi.

OUR ANCESTORS WILL GUIDE US
THE SPIRITS OF THE DEAD LIVE ON

IN CONTEXT

KEY BELIEVERS
Quechua Indians

WHEN AND WHERE
From prehistory, central Andes, South America

AFTER
From 6000 BCE *Ayllu*, or extended communities, develop in the Andes.

3800 BCE Corpses are mummified and revered as sacred objects.

c.1200 CE The Inca Empire is established.

1438 The Inca Empire expands across the central Andes, reaching its peak in 1532.

1534 The Empire collapses after the Spanish Conquest.

21st century Catholicism has been institutionalized across this region since the colonial era; however, most present-day Quechua blend elements of Christianity with their traditional beliefs.

We **inherited the land** from our ancestors.

→

The **spirits of the ancestors** are enshrined in the land.

↓

If we do this, the **land will feed us** and the **ancestors will guide us**.

←

Both the ancestors and the land must be **fed with blood and fat**.

The religion of the Andean highlands can be said to be, in essence, a cult of the dead. This tradition of reverence for the ancestors stretches back to long before the short-lived empire of the Incas—the culture for which the region is best known—and has lasted to the present day.

Just one of many Quechua-speaking Andean peoples, the Incas rose to dominate much of modern-day Peru, Ecuador, and Chile, and parts of Bolivia and Argentina in the 13th century. As they extended their empire, they imposed a culture that in many ways resembled that of the Aztecs of Mesoamerica (pp.40–45), who were their contemporaries. It revolved around worship of their own supreme deity, the sun god.

However, beyond the Inca capital of Cuzco, with its priests, rituals, and golden artifacts, the common people, whom the Incas called the Hatun Runa, persisted with a cult of ancestor worship and earth worship that dated back to prehistoric times. This survived the mighty Inca Empire when, in the 16th century, it was utterly destroyed by Spanish conquistadors led by Francisco Pizarro.

See also: Making sense of the world 20–23 ▪ Created for a purpose 32 ▪ Sacrifice and blood offerings 40–45 ▪ Devotion through puja 114–15

People of the mountains

Since before recorded time, Andean peoples have organized themselves into *ayllus,* extended family groups or clans, each attached to a specific territory. Within these groups, they worked the land, shared resources, and worshipped at their *huacas*, or animistic earth shrines. The focus of worship was to pray to the earth to feed them—vital assistance in a mountainous region where farming was a harsh and laborious process. Running parallel to their entreaties to the earth was a belief that, just as the land had nurtured their ancestors, it would, with the intercession of those departed spirits, continue to nourish them.

Each *ayllu* mummified and worshipped the bodies of its dead, believing that the ancestors would help maintain the cosmic order and ensure the fertility of the land and the animals. The bodies were wrapped in weavings and placed in rock mummy shrines (*chullpa machulas*) facing the mountaintop. Once desiccated by the freezing, dry air, the mummies would be paraded around the fields during rituals to make the crops grow. Meanwhile, priests or diviners at the *huacas* and grave shrines offered up coca leaves, blood, and fat, believing that if the spirits of the land and the ancestors were fed, they would in turn feed the people.

An enduring power

In the 17th century, Christian missionaries burned many Andean mummies to quash what they saw as pagan beliefs. However, some mummies have survived, and the modern Quechua believe them to be the first beings or ancient ones. The *chullpa machulas*, now just niches in the rocks, remain sacred shrines at which contemporary diviners still sprinkle blood and fat, believing this to infuse the sites with life and energy. Some groups, such as the Qollahuayos Indians (see box, below) may burn coca leaves there, wrapped in bundles of llama wool. The graves are believed to retain their power, even without the mummies that once occupied them. The Feast of the Dead, on

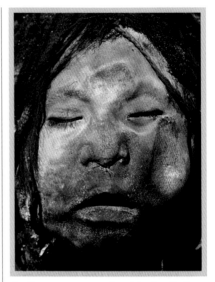

An Inca mummy of a girl who died five hundred years ago is still preserved; the ancestors are revered and have a central role among Andean peoples.

November 2—marking the end of the dry season and the beginning of the rains, when crops can be planted—remains a focus of the Andean year, when the dead are ritually invited to revisit the living, and to take a share of the harvest. ▪

The dead visit us and assist us in our work. They provide many blessings.
Marcelino, Kaatan elder

A mountain and a god

The Kaata of modern Bolivia, who live northeast of Lake Titicaca, form one of nine *ayllus* of the Qollahuayas Indians. The Kaata have a historic reputation as fortune-telling soothsayers; in the 15th century, Kaatan diviners carried the chair of the Inca emperor, an honored task. The power of these Qollahuaya ritualists was thought to derive from the graves of their ancestors on Mount Kaata. In addition to the ancestral graves on the mountain, Mount Kaata itself is venerated as if it were a human being—a kind of super-ancestor—and is also ascribed physical human attributes. The highlands are regarded as the head, with grasses as hair, a cave for a mouth, and lakes for eyes; the middle region is the torso, with heart and bowels identified; and a pair of ridges on the lowest reaches are the legs. The mountain is a living being that gives the Kaata both sustenance and guidance.

WE SHOULD BE GOOD
LIVING IN HARMONY

IN CONTEXT

KEY BELIEVERS
Chewong

WHEN AND WHERE
**From 3000 BCE,
Peninsular Malaysia**

BEFORE
From prehistory The
Chewong are one of the 18
indigenous tribes of Peninsular
Malaysia collectively known as
the Orang Asli—the "original
people". Each tribe has its
own language and culture.

AFTER
1930s Europeans first
encounter the Chewong;
contact with Chinese and
other Malay ethnic groups is
also very restricted until this
time because of the tribe's
remote forest location.

From 1950s Chewong come
under pressure to assimilate
themselves into mainstream
Malay society and convert to
Islam; many choose to retain
their traditional practices.

Most societies have
developed a system
of morality based
on an appeal to notions of human
goodness, reinforced by sanctions
from religious and social authorites.
Very few cultures have existed
where ideas such as crime and
warfare are unknown, but the few
that have been found have been
tribal peoples eking out a hunter-
gatherer existence in the rainforest.
One such tribe is the Chewong of
Peninsular Malaysia, whose first
contact with Europeans was in
the 1930s. They now number
around 350 people.

The Chewong are nonviolent
and noncompetitive; their
language has no words for war,
fight, crime, or punishment. They
believe the first human beings
were taught the right way to live
by their culture hero Yinlugen Bud
—a forest spirit who existed before
the first humans. Yinlugen Bud
gave the Chewong their most
important rule, *maro*, which
specifies that food must always
be shared. To eat alone is regarded
as both dangerous and wrong.
Only by looking after the entire
population in a spirit of fairness
and sharing can the group hope
to survive. The Chewong believe
that violation of their moral code—
by not sharing food, by showing
anger at misfortune, by expressing
anticipation of pleasure, or by
nursing ungratified desires—will
have supernatural repercussions
such as illness, or physical or
psychic attack, either by a tiger,
snake, or poisonous millipede, or
the *ruwai* or soul of the animal. ∎

Human beings should
never eat alone. You must
always share with others.
Yinlugen Bud

See also: Created for a purpose 32 ▪ The burden of observance 50
▪ The Five Great Vows 68–71

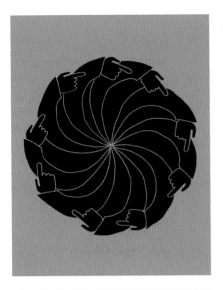

EVERYTHING IS CONNECTED
A LIFELONG BOND WITH THE GODS

IN CONTEXT

KEY BELIEVERS
Warao

WHEN AND WHERE
From 6000 BCE, the Orinoco Delta, Venezuela

BEFORE
From prehistory The Warao are one of the largest indigenous groups in the Latin American lowland.

AFTER
16th century Europeans first encounter the Warao and compare their settlements with similar structures in Venice, giving Venezuela ("little Venice" in Spanish) its name.

From 1960s Environmental degredation in the region affects local fisheries and displaces tribespeople to the cities; some are converted to Catholicism.

2001 More than 36,000 Warao people are registered as living in the Orinoco Delta area.

L iving in the environment of the Orinoco Delta, where the land is divided into countless islands by a network of waterways, the Warao tribe see the world as flat—the earth is just a narrow crust between water and sky. They believe that Hahuba, the Snake of Being—the grandmother of all living things—is coiled around the earth, and that her breathing is the motion of the tides. Their various gods, known as the Ancient Ones, live on sacred mountains at the four corners of the earth, with the Warao living at its very center. In villages under the particular protection of one of the gods, the temple hut also contains a sacred rock in which the god dwells.

Divine dependence
The Warao gods depend on humans to nourish them with offerings, especially tobacco smoke; in return, the Warao depend on the gods for health and life. This lifelong bond with the gods is established as soon as a baby is born. The child's

In Warao myth, the Bird of Beautiful Plumage is believed to provide supernatural protection to children. A child that dies is said to be claimed as food by spirits of the underworld.

first cry is said to carry across the world to the mountain of Ariawara, the God of Origin, in the east; in return, the god sends back a cry of welcome. Soon after a baby is born, Hahuba, the Snake of Being, sends a balmy breeze to the village, to embrace the new arrival. From that point on, the baby becomes part of the complex balance between natural and supernatural that forms the web of Warao daily life. ◼

See also: The Dreaming 34–35 ▪ The spirits of the dead live on 36–37 ▪ Symbolism made real 46–47 ▪ Man and the cosmos 48–49

THE GODS DESIRE BLOOD

SACRIFICE AND BLOOD OFFERINGS

IN CONTEXT

KEY BELIEVERS
Aztec, Mayan, and other Mesoamerican peoples

WHEN AND WHERE
3rd–15th century CE, Mexico

BEFORE
From 1000 BCE The Mayan civilization begins its slow rise, reaching its peak—the Classic Mayan period—between the 3rd and 10th century CE.

From 12th century CE The Aztec empire is established.

AFTER
1519 CE The Aztecs, whose population numbers 20–25 million, are overthrown by Spanish forces under the conquistador Hernán Cortés.

1600 CE Forced conversion to Catholicism and exposure to European diseases destroy the Aztec civilization and reduce the population to around one million.

T he sacrifice of animals and humans has been a feature of many religious traditions around the world, but the idea of ritual sacrifice was particularly important to societies in the ancient civilizations of Mesoamerica, notably the Mayans and the Aztecs.

The Mesoamerican peoples inhabited the area from present-day central Mexico through to Nicaragua. The Mayan civilization (which peaked c.250 CE–900 CE) preceded and then coincided with the Aztec civilization, which reached its height around 1300–1400 CE. Aztec culture drew on the Mayan tradition, and the two peoples had several deities in common; they went by different names but shared characteristics.

A reciprocal gift of blood

The Mesoamerican cultures believed that blood sacrifice to their gods was essential to ensure the survival of their worlds, in a tradition of ritual bloodletting that dated back to the first major civilization in Mexico—that of the Olmecs, which flourished between 1500 and 400 BCE. In legends, the gods themselves had made tremendous sacrifices in forming the world, which included shedding their own blood to create humankind; therefore they desired similar sacrifices of blood from humanity in return.

Sacrifice and creation

The power of blood and the necessity of sacrifice are central to the Aztec creation myth. The Aztecs believed that the gods had created and destroyed four earlier eras, or suns, and that after the destruction of the fourth sun by flood, the god of the wind, Quetzalcoatl, and his trickster brother, Tezcatlipoca, tore the goddess (or god in some versions) Tlaltecuhtli in half to make a new heaven and earth. From her body grew everything necessary for the life of humankind—trees, flowers, grass, fountains, wells, valleys, and mountains. All this caused the goddess terrible agony, and she howled through the night demanding the sacrifice of human hearts to sustain her.

Further cosmic acts of creation followed, all requiring sacrifice or blood offerings. One relief shows

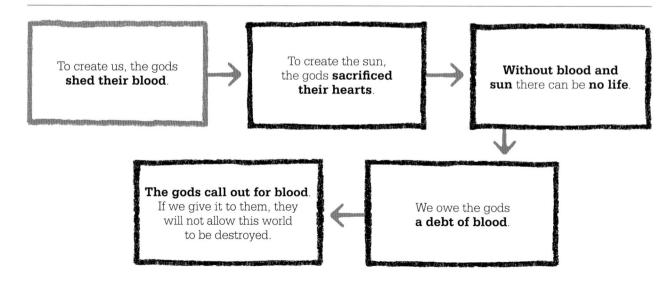

To create us, the gods **shed their blood**.

To create the sun, the gods **sacrificed their hearts**.

Without blood and sun there can be **no life**.

We owe the gods **a debt of blood**.

The gods call out for blood. If we give it to them, they will not allow this world to be destroyed.

See also: Created for a purpose 32 ▪ A lifelong bond with the gods 39 ▪ The burden of observance 50
▪ Renewing life through ritual 51 ▪ Beliefs for new societies 56–57

You have yet
to take care of bleeding
your ears and passing a
cord through your elbows.
You must worship. This
is your way of giving
thanks before your god.
Tohil, Maya god

Victims of Aztec human sacrifice
were typically prisoners of war, and,
when in combat, Aztec warriors sought
to capture rather than kill in order to
ensure plentiful offerings for the gods.

the first stars being born from
blood flowing from Quetzalcoatl's
tongue after he had pierced it.
Most notably, the creation of the
fifth sun required one of the gods to
cast himself into a funeral pyre.
Two gods, Tecuciztecatl and
Nanahuatzin, vied for the honor,
both immolating themselves;
Nanahuatzin became the sun and
Tecuciztecatl the moon. The other
gods then offered their hearts in
order to make the new sun move
across the sky (the offering of
hearts is a recurring theme in
Mesoamerican myth and ritual).

Humanity's gruesome debt

Both the Mayans and the Aztecs
were bound to their gods by a blood
debt from these acts of creation that
could never be repaid. After
Quetzalcoatl descended to the
underworld and retrieved the bones
of former humans (remains from the
four previous eras), the gods ground
them into a fine meal flour. They
let their own blood drip onto the
flour to animate it and created
a new race of people—people
whose hearts could in turn satisfy
the gods' own need for blood.

In Mesoamerican myth,
each period of 52 years was seen
as a cycle, the end of which could
spell the end of the world. Human
sacrifice could be used to appease
the gods and persuade them not
to bring an end to the present
age—that of the fifth sun. The
Mayans believed that blood
sacrifice was necessary for the sun
to rise in the sky every morning.

The Aztecs' sun god,
Huitzilopochtli, was locked in
an ongoing struggle with darkness
and needed to be fortified by
blood in order for the sun to
continue in its cycle. Thus
the continued existence of
the Mesoamerican world was
seen as extremely tenuous, and
in need of constant support
through acts of sacrifice.

Bloodletting for the gods
took two forms: autosacrifice
(self-inflicted bloodletting) and
human sacrifice. Both Mayans and
Aztecs took part in autosacrifice.
Mesoamerican nobles had what
was seen as the privilege and
responsibility to shed their own
blood for the gods. This involved
piercing their flesh with stingray
spines, obsidian knives, and, most
often, with the sharp spines of the
maguey (agave) plant. Blood was
drawn from the ear, shin, knee, elbow,
tongue, or foreskin. Autosacrifice »

> And this goddess cried many times in the night desiring the hearts of men to eat.
> **Saying of Aztec goddess Tlaltecuhtli**

> And when his festival was celebrated, captives were slain, washed slaves were slain.
> **Aztec hymn to Huitzilopochtli**

dates back to the Olmec people and continued after the Spanish Conquest of Mexico in 1519. Both men and women of the Mayan nobility took part—the men drawing blood from their foreskins, women from their tongues. They collected their offerings on strips of bark paper, which were then burned; through the smoke from these offerings, they communicated with their ancestors and the gods.

Sacrificial rites

Human sacrifice was far more common among the Aztec than the Mayans, who performed it only in special circumstances, such as the consecration of a new temple.

Aztec sacrifice usually involved cutting the victim's heart from his body. The heart was believed to be a fragment of the sun's energy—so removing the heart was a means of returning the energy to its source. The victim was typically held by four priests over a stone slab in the temple, while a fifth cut the heart from the body with an obsidian knife, and offered it, still beating, to the gods in a vessel called a *cuauhxicalli*, an eagle gourd. After the removal of the heart,

the body was rolled down the stairs of the pyramid-shaped temple to the stone terrace at the base. The victim's head was removed and the arms and legs might also be cut off. Skulls were displayed on a skull rack. Depending on the particular god being honored in the sacrifice, victims might be slain in ritual combat, drowned, shot with arrows, or flayed.

The scale of sacrifice sometimes reached immense proportions: for example, at the rededication of the Aztec temple of Huitzilopochtli, at Tenochtitlan, in 1487, around 80,400 victims were said to have been sacrificed to the god, their clotted blood forming great pools in the temple precinct. Even if a more modest estimate of 20,000 victims is accepted, this was still slaughter on a vast scale.

The Aztec ritual year was marked by sacrifices to various gods and goddesses. Although the gods could also be propitiated with

Descendants of the Mayans, the Tzotzil people were put to work on the Spanish colonists' estates, and fused their own beliefs with Christian forms of worship in a syncretic religion.

smoke from incense and tobacco, and with food and precious objects, blood was what they really craved.

Rituals and the calendar

The Mesoamerican year lasted 260 days, a calendar observed by both the Mayans and the Aztecs. At the end of each year in Aztec society, a man representing Mictlantecuhtli, the god of the underworld, was sacrificed in the temple named Tlalxicco, "the navel of the world." It is thought that the victim was then eaten by the priests. Just as human flesh sustained the gods, so by consuming a god (embodied in the sacrificial victim) a form of communion could be enacted. Less high-ranking celebrants ate figures made from dough, into which sacrificial blood was mixed. To break apart and consume these dough figures, known as *tzoalli*, was also to commune with the gods.

Such reenactment of the myths of the gods was a feature of Aztec belief and of annual rituals. During the main festival of Xipe

Tzotzil souls

The Tzotzil religion blends Catholicism with some non-Christian beliefs. The Tzotzil people maintain that everyone has two souls, a *wayjel* and a *ch'ulel*. The *ch'ulel* is an inner soul that is situated in the heart and blood. It is placed in the unborn embryo by the gods. At death, this soul travels to *Katibak,* the land of the dead at the center of the earth. It stays in *Katibak* for as long as the deceased person had lived; but it lives its life in reverse, gradually returning to infancy, until it can be assigned to a new baby of the opposite sex.

The second soul, the *wayjel*, is an animal spirit companion that is shared with a wild animal, or *chanul,* and kept in an enclosure by the ancestral Tzotzil gods. The human and the animal spirit have a shared fate—so whatever befalls the human is replicated in the animal spirit and vice-versa. The animal spirits include jaguars, ocelots, coyotes, squirrels, and opossums.

Totec, the flayed deity, a priest impersonating the god donned the flayed skin of a sacrificed captive. As the skin tightened and tore away, the impersonator emerged like a fresh shoot growing from the rotting husk of a seed, representing growth and renewal. Other Aztec sacrifices honor the importance of corn, their staple food. Every year, a young girl representing Chicomecoatl, the maize goddess, was sacrificed at harvest time. She was decapitated, her blood poured over a statue of the goddess, and her skin worn by a priest.

Conquest and absorption
When Spanish invader Hernán Cortés and his conquistadors landed in Mexico in 1519, the Aztecs are believed to have mistaken him for the returning god Quetzalcoatl, partly because Cortés' hat resembled the god's distinctive headgear. They sent the Spaniard corn cakes soaked in human blood, but their offering failed to appease the "god," and the Aztec civilization, just four centuries old when Cortés landed, was destroyed by the Spanish.

This Aztec stone sun calendar places a depiction of the sun within a ring of glyphs representing measures of time, reflecting the Aztec preoccupation with the sun.

In contrast, the Mayan culture did not suffer the same annihilation, possibly because the Mayans were more widely dispersed. In southern Mexico, even today the Tzotzil people, descendants of the Mayans, retain many elements of the old culture and religion, including the 260-day calendar.

The Tzotzil religion is a blend of Catholicism and traditional Mayan beliefs. The people's homeland, in the highlands of Chiapas in southern Mexico, is dotted with wooden crosses. These do not just reference the Christian crucifix, but are thought to be channels of communication with Yajval Balamil, the lord of the earth, a powerful god who must be placated before any work can be done on the land. In their adaptation of the ancient beliefs, the Tzotzil people associate the sun with the Christian God and the moon with the Virgin Mary, and also worship carvings of Christian saints. ∎

At this feast [to Xipe Totec] they killed all the prisoners, men, women, and children.
Bernardino de Sahagún,
General History of the Things of New Spain

WE CAN BUILD A SACRED SPACE
SYMBOLISM MADE REAL

IN CONTEXT

KEY BELIEVERS
Pawnee

WHEN AND WHERE
From c.1250 CE, Great Plains, US

AFTER
1875 The Pawnee are relocated from their lands in Nebraska to a new reservation in Oklahoma.

1891–92 Many Pawnee adopt the new Ghost Dance religion, which promises resurrection for their ancestors.

1900 The US census records a Pawnee population of just 633; over the next four decades, traditional Pawnee religious practices dwindle and die out.

20th century The Pawnee Nation is mainly Christian, its people belonging to the Indian Methodist, Indian Baptist, or Full Gospel Church. Some Pawnee are members of the Native American Church.

The **world** and we ourselves were **created by Tirawahat**, the expanse of **the heavens**. He told us **the earth is our mother, the sky is our father**.

⬇

If we make **our lodges** to **encircle the earth and encompass the sky**, we invite our mother and father to live with us.

⬇

If we open our lodges to the east, Tirawahat can enter with the dawning sun. **Our lodges are a miniature version of the cosmos**.

The first sacred spaces of early religions were naturally occurring ones— groves, springs, and caves. However, as worship became more ritualized, the need to define holy places arose, and buildings designed for worship encoded the essential features of each religion.

On the other hand, buildings used for everyday activities often took on cosmic significance in cultures in which religious and daily life were intertwined. This was true of the earth lodges, or ceremonial centers, of the Pawnee, one of the Native American nations of the Great Plains. The Pawnee earth lodge had a sacred architecture, making each lodge a miniature cosmos as Tirawahat, the creator god and chief of all the gods, had prescribed at the beginning of time, after he had made the heavens and earth and brought the first humans into being (see box, facing page).

Four posts held up each earth lodge, one at each corner. These represented four gods, the Stars of the Four Directions, who hold up the heavens in the northeast, northwest, southwest, and southeast. The Pawnee believed that stars had

See also: Making sense of the world 20–23 ▪ Man and the cosmos 48–49 ▪ Living the Way of the Gods 82–85

The earth lodge was a mini-cosmos in the Pawnee tradition, and was constructed accordingly. This Pawnee family stands at an earth lodge entrance at Loup, Nebraska in 1873.

helped Tirawahat create them, and that at the world's end, the Pawnee would become stars.

The entrance to the earth lodge would be in the east, allowing the light of the dawn to enter. A hearth would be positioned in the center of the lodge, and a small altar of mounded earth in the back (the west). A buffalo skull would be displayed on the altar, which the spirit of Tirawahat was said to occupy when the first rays of sun shone on it in the morning. Through this skull, Tirawahat was said to live and communicate with the people. Sacred star bundles containing objects used for rituals, such as charts of the night sky, hung from a rafter above the skull. These were said to give each village its identity and power.

A world within a world

In winter, a domed sweat lodge would often be constructed inside the earth lodge, creating a second mini-cosmos. These sweat lodges, or steam huts, used for spiritual and healing purposes, were also sacred spaces. The heated stones used inside them were said to be ancestral "grandfathers," and were treated with great reverence. The hot stones were doused in water, and the steam produced was believed to be the breath of the grandfathers.

The first sweat lodge was, according to legend, made by the son of a bundle-keeper, as part of a ritual taught to him by guardian animals. As he performed the ritual he said, "Now we are sitting in darkness as did Tirawahat when he created all things and placed meteors in the heavens for our benefit. The poles that shelter us represent them… When I blow this root upon them, you will see a blue flame rise from the stones. This will be a signal for us to pray to Tirawahat and the grandfathers." ▪

The legend of Tirawahat

In Pawnee myth, after the creator god, Tirawahat, had made the sun, moon, stars, heavens, earth, and all things on earth, he spoke. At the sound of his voice a woman appeared. Tirawahat created a man and sent him to the woman. Then he said: "I give you the earth. You shall call the earth 'mother.' The heavens you shall call 'father'… I will now show you how to build a lodge, so that you will not be cold or get wet from the rain." After a time Tirawahat spoke again and asked the man if he knew what the lodge represented. The man did not know. Tirawahat said: "I told you to call the earth 'mother.' The lodge represents her breast. The smoke that escapes from the opening is like the milk that flows from her breast… When you eat the things that are cooked [in the fireplace], it is like sucking a breast, because you eat and grow strong."

Our people were made by the stars. When the time comes for all things to end, our people will turn into small stars.
Young Bull

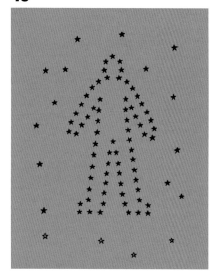

WE ARE IN RHYTHM WITH THE UNIVERSE

MAN AND THE COSMOS

IN CONTEXT

KEY BELIEVERS
Dogon

WHEN AND WHERE
**From 15th century CE,
Mali, West Africa**

BEFORE
From 1500 BCE Similarities
in oral myths and knowledge
of astronomy suggest that the
Dogon's ancestral tribes may
have originated in ancient
Egypt before migrating to the
region of present-day Libya,
then Burkina Faso or Guinea.

From 10th century CE Dogon
identity evolves in West Africa
from a mixture of peoples of
earlier tribes, many of whom
have fled Islamic persecution.

AFTER
Today The Dogon people
number between 400,000
and 800,000. The majority
still practice their traditional
religion, but significant
minorities have converted
to Islam and Christianity.

The Dogon people live in the Bandiagara plateau in Mali, West Africa, where they practice a traditional animist religion: for them, all things are endowed with spiritual power. Fundamental to Dogon religious belief is that humankind is the seed of the universe, and that the human form echoes both the first moment of creation and the entire created universe. Every Dogon village is therefore laid out in the shape of a human body, and is regarded as a living person.

Sacred and symbolic space

A Dogon village is arranged lying north to south, with the blacksmith, or forge, at its head and shrines at its feet. This layout reflects the belief that the creator god, Amma, made the world from clay in the form of a woman lying in this position. Everything in the village has an anthropomorphic, or human, equivalent. The women's menstrual huts, to the east and west, are the hands. The family homesteads are the chest. Each of these big homesteads is, in turn, laid out in the plan of a male body, with the kitchen as the head, the large central room as the belly, the arms as two lines of storerooms, the chest as two jars of water, and the penis as the entrance passage. The building reflects the creative power of the male–female twin ancestral beings, the Nommo (see facing page).

The hut of the *hogon*, the Dogon's spiritual leader, is a model of the universe. Every element of the hut's

Masked dancers perform the *dama*, or funeral ritual. This traditional Dogon religious ceremony is designed to guide the souls of the deceased safely into the afterlife.

See also: Symbolism made real 46–47 ▪ The ultimate reality 102–105

The **whole universe** was originally contained in an **egg or seed**.

⬇

Everything that exists **began as a vibration** in this egg.

⬇

The **form of man was prefigured** in the egg, and is also echoed in the form of the universe.

⬇

Everything, from the smallest seed to the expanse of the cosmos, **reflects and expresses everything**.

⬇

A village, or a homestead, or a hat, or a seed, can **contain the whole universe**.

The Nommo

The Nommo are ancestral beings worshipped by the Dogon. They are often described as amphibious, hermaphroditic, fishlike creatures who, acccording to myth, were fathered by the god Amma, when he created the cosmic egg. This egg was said to resemble both the smallest seed cultivated by the Dogon, and the sister star to Sirius—the brightest star in the night sky. Within the egg lay the germ of all things.

In one version of the myth, two sets of male–female twins, the Nommo, were inside the egg waiting to be born so that they could bring order to the world. But the egg was shaken by a vibration and one of the male twins, Yurugu, broke out of it prematurely, creating the earth from his placenta. So Amma sent the three remaining Nommo down to earth, and they established the institutions and rituals necessary for the renewal and continuation of life. But because of Yurugu's premature actions, the world was tainted right from the beginning.

decoration and furnishing is laden with symbolism. The *hogon's* movements are attuned to the rhythms of the universe. At dawn he sits facing east, toward the rising sun; he then walks through the homestead following the order of the four cardinal points; and finally at dusk he sits facing west. His pouch is described as "the pouch of the world"; his staff is "the axis of the world."

Cosmic meaning

Even the hogon's clothing represents the world in miniature. His cylindrical headdress, for example, is a woven image of the seven spiral vibrations that shook the cosmic "egg of the world" (see right). During a crisis, the chiefs gather around the headdress; the *hogon* speaks into it and upends it on the ground, as if the world itself has been turned upside down, ready to be restored to order by the god Amma.

The complex cosmic symbolism of the Dogon reflects outward from the cosmos, and then back in again to the headdress of the *hogon*, the shell of the world egg. Religion, society, cosmology, mythology, cultivation, daily life—all are intermeshed in every detail, and reflected in every action. ▪

For [the Dogon], social life represents the workings of the universe.
Marcel Griaule, anthropologist

WE EXIST TO SERVE THE GODS
THE BURDEN OF OBSERVANCE

Until Christianity arrived in Tikopia in the 1950s, all the residents of this small Pacific island devoted themselves to ritual for two weeks twice a year, as they undertook the Work of the Gods. At these times, they perfomed duties to propitiate the *atua*, spirits or gods, believing that they, in turn, would ensure plentiful harvests.

The Work of the Gods was a form of worship expressed as a system of trade between human and spirit beings. The Tikopians performed the rituals, and the gods granted the people the necessities of life. Moreover, the religion was structured so that many of the activities undertaken to please the gods—such as repairing canoes, planting and harvesting, and the ritual production of turmeric—were of economic value to the Tikopians. Offerings of food and kava (an intoxicating drink) made to the gods were consumed only in essence—leaving the actual food available for human consumption.

Taking part in the Work of the Gods brought status to individuals, and was perceived as a privilege. The rituals involved in this religion also underpinned key social and economic structures, and held Tikopian society together. ∎

A Tikopian man performs a dance with a canoe paddle: ritual dancing and drumming on canoes were part of the Work of the Gods.

See also: Making sense of the world 20–23 ▪ A lifelong bond with the gods 39 ▪ Sacrifice and blood offerings 40–45 ▪ Devotion through puja 114–15

OUR RITUALS SUSTAIN THE WORLD
RENEWING LIFE THROUGH RITUAL

IN CONTEXT

KEY BELIEVERS
Hupa

WHEN AND WHERE
**c.1000 CE,
northwestern California**

BEFORE
c.900–1100 CE Ancestors
of the Hupa arrive in
northwestern California from
subarctic regions to the north.

AFTER
1828 The first contact is
made with American trappers;
around 1,000 Hupa live in the
Hoopa Valley at this time, and
trade furs until the beginning
of the Gold Rush in 1848.

By 1900 The Hupa population
is reduced to about 500 as a
result of disease.

1911 The first modern Hupa
Tribal Council is formed.

Today More than 2,000 Hupa
live as a self-governing people
on their traditional lands.

Through their ritual songs and dances, the Hupa tribe of northwestern California believed they could renew the world, or "firm the earth," and revitalize the land to ensure sufficient resources for the coming year. One of their most important world renewal dances, held every autumn, was the White Deerskin Dance. The purpose of the dance was to re-create the actions of the the Kixunai, or First People, the Hupa's mythical predecessors.

By replaying the sacred narrative of the Kixunai, the Hupa hoped to tap into the powers of creation in order to safeguard the health of the people and guarantee abundant stocks of game and fish for the hunting season. During the dance, which lasted ten days, the elaborately decorated hide of an albino deer—a symbol of great wealth and status—was displayed. Participants paddled along the river in dugout canoes every morning and danced every afternoon and evening, holding deer effigies aloft on poles.

[The Kixunai] painted themselves and danced there one night. The next morning they danced again.
Hupa myth

The First People
The Kixunai were believed by the Hupa to be human in form but extraordinary in character. Whatever the Kixunai did became the predestined custom of the unborn Hupa race. So every detail of Hupa daily life was mapped out by the activities of the First People. According to Hupa belief, the Kixunai later scattered across the ocean, leaving only the mythical being Yimantuwinyai to assist people in their life on earth. ■

See also: The spirits of the dead live on 36–37 ▪ Beliefs that mirror society 80–81

Ancient Egypt is unified and the **Early Dynastic period** begins. A cult of a divine Pharaoh is established.

Tomb inscriptions known as the **Pyramid Texts**, the oldest known religious writings, suggest an **Ancient Egyptian** belief in an afterlife.

The pantheon of Greek mythology evolves in the **Minoan culture** of Crete.

The probable date of the foundation of **Zoroastrianism** in Persia, although this may have been as early as the 18th century BCE.

c.3000 BCE   **25TH–24TH CENTURIES**   **1700–1400 BCE**   **c.1200 BCE**

c.3000 BCE   **20TH–16TH CENTURIES**   **c.1600 BCE**   **8TH CENTURY BCE**

Celtic clans spread across much of Europe, each tribe having its own local deities.

In the **First Babylonian Dynasty in Mesopotamia**, a complex mythology is recorded in the Enuma Elish.

Scandinavian peoples begin to make figures of their gods and goddesses, and develop a recognizable **Norse mythology**.

According to legend, **Romulus** usurps his twin brother Remus to found the **city of Rome**.

The earliest civilizations emerged when scattered nomadic tribes began to settle in order to raise crops. Previously localized religious beliefs and practices evolved, and the beliefs of different tribes amalgamated around common deities and mythologies. Complex pantheons emerged, and an often sophisticated body of myths arose from the various strands that had come together, describing the role of the gods and mythical creatures in the workings of the world.

These more formal religions offered explanations for natural phenomena, such as the sun, moon, seasons, weather, and the gods' influence on them. They often included creation stories and tales of the interaction of gods and humans. It is clear from elaborate tombs left by the early civilizations, such as the Egyptians, that belief in an afterlife existed, and that rituals of death and burial played a major part in religion. As people settled in ever bigger communities, temples dedicated to the gods became focal points in the towns and cities.

Civilization also gave rise to various forms of written language, which allowed these stories of gods and creation to be recorded and embellished over the millennia. Religious inscriptions first appeared on the walls of tombs and temples in early civilizations, such as that of Egypt. Elsewhere, distinctive traditions were also taking shape as Indian, Chinese, Japanese, Norse, and Celtic folk religions were incorporated into the belief systems of the emerging nations.

Coalescing faiths

By about 1500 BCE, regional religious traditions were well established in many parts of the world, and new, more advanced, societies arose, requiring more elaborate belief systems. Some new religions also appeared, notably Zoroastrianism, which was arguably the first monotheistic faith, while the foundations of Judaism were also being laid down.

In India, the numerous local religious beliefs were incorporated into the Vedic tradition, based on ancient scriptures called the Vedas. This later became the pluralistic amalgam now known as Hinduism, but alongside this came Jainism, which placed more emphasis on a correct way of life than on the worship of deities, and Buddhism, which was arguably

The Greek poet **Homer** writes the *Iliad* and *Odyssey*, and **Hesiod** writes his *Theogony* (Origin of the Gods).

The Indian sage **Mahavira** establishes the **central tenets of Jainism**.

The classical period of the **Ancient Greek civilization** begins in the eastern Mediterranean.

The **Vikings** flourish, spreading their religion across northern Europe and in Iceland and Greenland.

8TH–7TH CENTURIES BCE   **599–27 BCE**   **5TH–4TH CENTURIES BCE**   **9TH–10TH CENTURIES**

6TH CENTURY BCE   **551 BCE**   **8TH CENTURY CE**   **13TH CENTURY**

The Chinese sage **Laozi** describes the *dao*, the way, and **establishes Daoism** in China.

Confucius, founder of Confucianism, is born in Zou, Lu State, China.

Two collections of **Japanese mythology**, the Kojiki and the Nihon Shoki, are compiled as a resource to support **Shinto** as national religion of Japan.

Icelandic epic poems describing **Norse mythology** are composed and recorded in the *Eddas*.

---

more a philosophy than a religion, as it concentrated on enlightenment without the need for gods.

This focus on moral philosophy was also prevalent in the religions that evolved in China and Japan. In the ordered society of the great Chinese dynasties, religion and political organization became intertwined. Daoism, proposed by the legendary scholar Laozi, advocated a religious way of life compatible with Chinese society. Confucius built on this to develop a new belief system based on a reinterpretation of respect for the hierarchy, and reinforced by ritual. Later, in Japan, traditional religions were unified to create the state religion, Shinto, which showed special reverence to ancestors and encouraged followers to connect with them through ritual practices.

By the 6th century BCE, the Greek city-states had been established, and classical Greek civilization was exerting a strong influence on the eastern Mediterranean region. Religion (although the Greeks did not have a specific word for it) was very much a part of life, and, although the gods were believed to live separately from the people, they were imagined to lead remarkably similar lives. The history of the Greek people, as interpreted by Homer in his epic poems, was also the history of their gods. The hierarchy of deities, with their very human lifestyles and tempestuous relationships, mirrored Greek society. As well as offering an explanation for aspects of the world, the deities gave reasons for the vagaries of human behavior, and with their help it was possible

to divine the future, choose auspicious times for action, and even defeat enemies. Most of the time they existed alongside people, unconcerned with human affairs, but, to keep them happy, the Greeks erected temples, performed rituals, and held regular festivals.

As the early civilizations rose and fell, many of their beliefs faded away, or were incorporated into the religions that replaced them; the pantheon of Greek mythology, for example, was absorbed into Roman mythology, and along with Celtic and other beliefs, into Christianity. Some religions, however, such as that of the Norse, were still practiced until the Middle Ages, and others, including Shinto, Jainism, Daoism, and Confucianism, have survived into the modern age. ■

THERE IS A HIERARCHY OF GODS AND MEN
BELIEFS FOR NEW SOCIETIES

IN CONTEXT

KEY BELIEVERS
Ancient Babylonians

WHEN AND WHERE
**c.2270 BCE, Mesopotamia
(present-day Iraq)**

BEFORE
5th millennium BCE The
Ubaidians settle in the fertile
valleys between the Tigris and
the Euphrates (Mesopotamia).

c.3300 BCE The Sumerian
people supplant the Ubaidians.

AFTER
c.1770 BCE Babylonian King
Hammurabi introduces laws
for governing Babylon.

c.1750 BCE The Babylonians
become the dominant people
of Mesopotamia, adapting
Sumerian religion to reflect
the power and authority of
Babylon's chief god, Marduk.

691 BCE Babylon falls to
the Assyrians; the myths
of Marduk are reassigned
to the Assyrian god Assur.

The god **Marduk kills**
the goddess **Tiamat** and
makes all the other gods
accept him as king.

↓

He then brings **order to
the universe** and creates
mankind to serve the gods.

↓

The **Babylonians
succeed the Sumerians**
and establish the city
of Babylon.

↓

King Hammurabi then
claims divine authority for
his rule and introduces
a code of laws.

↓

Both **Marduk and Hammurabi** assert their
supremacy over others by establishing…

↓

…a hierarchy of gods and men.

Mesopotamia, the area
of modern Iraq between
the Tigris and Euphrates
rivers, is often referred to in the
West as the cradle of civilization.
It was there that—in the Bronze
Age—small communities first
evolved into towns and cities.

As these larger settlements grew,
so did the need for new social
structures, a common culture, and
shared beliefs in order to unify
the population and reinforce the
political system. Religion not only
explained natural phenomena but
also provided a coherent mythology.

See also: Created for a purpose 32 ▪ Renewing life through ritual 51 ▪ Beliefs that mirror society 80–81 ▪ A rational world 92–99

Images of Babylonian soldiers lined the Ishtar Gate, which led to the city of Babylon. Effigies of gods were paraded from the gate to the city along the Processional Way.

In the 4th millennium BCE, the Sumerian people inhabited the region. The population of Sumer was concentrated in about a dozen city-states; each was ruled by a king, but political power was vested in the high priests of each city's religion. The Sumerians worshipped a pantheon of gods, including Enki, god of water and fertility, and Anu, god of heaven. When the Babylonians began to settle in Mesopotamia in the 3rd millennium BCE, they absorbed the Sumerians and their culture—including some aspects of their mythology—into their own empire. The Babylonian leaders used the Sumerian mythology to reinforce the hierarchy they established, which helped to assert their power over their own people and the supplanted Sumerians.

Babylonian religion

Central to the Babylonian religion was the epic creation story of the Enûma Elish, recorded on seven clay tablets. The sequence of events it relates had largely been adapted from earlier Sumerian mythology, but in this retelling featured Babylonian deities—in particular Marduk, son of the Sumerian god Enki and the rightful heir to Anu. The story tells of Marduk as the leader of a hierarchy of young deities, whose victory over the older gods, including the creator god, Tiamat (see box, right) gave him the power to create and organize the universe, which he ruled from his chosen home of Babylon. The Enûma Elish provided an obvious analogy to the takeover of Sumer and founding of Babylon, but Marduk's ascendancy over the other gods and his ordering of the world also served as a metaphor for the sovereignty of Babylonian kings and their authority to make and enforce laws.

A mark of kingship

To reinforce the idea of Babylonian dominance and to unify the empire, the Enûma Elish was recited and acted out in an annual New Year festival, known as the Akitu, which was held at the time of the spring equinox. This performance did more than mark the calendrical movement from one year to the next; it was a ritualized re-creation and reenergizing of the cosmos, which enabled Marduk to settle the destinies of the stars and planets for the year ahead. Both in its mythology and its ritual, the Akitu was fundamentally about legitimizing kingship; it was a public demonstration that the Babylonian monarch held his authority directly from the god. By recreating Marduk's triumph over Tiamat, the centrality of Babylon was also reaffirmed. ▪

The Enûma Elish

The Akitu ritual re-created the creation story of the Enûma Elish. This begins before time, when only Apsu (the freshwater ocean) and Tiamat (the saltwater ocean) exist. Apsu and Tiamat give birth to the primal gods, including Anshar and Kishu, the horizons of the sky and the earth, who themselves beget Anu, the god of the sky, and Ea (the Sumerian Enki), the god of the earth and water. The shouts of the young gods disturb Apsu and Tiamat's peace, so Apsu attempts to destroy them, but is killed by Ea. At the site of this struggle, the god Ea creates a temple for himself, which he names Apsu (after his father), where his son Marduk is born. To avenge her husband, Tiamat wages war on Marduk, and puts her son Qingu in command of her forces. Marduk agrees to fight Tiamat's army, if all the other gods accept him as king, with sovereignty over the universe. Marduk then kills Tiamat and Qingu, and brings order to the universe. From Qingu's blood he creates mankind.

I hereby name it Babylon, home of the great gods. We shall make it the center of religion.
Marduk, in the Enûma Elish

THE GOOD LIVE FOREVER IN THE KINGDOM OF OSIRIS
PREPARING FOR THE AFTERLIFE

IN CONTEXT

KEY BELIEVERS
Ancient Egyptians

WHEN
2000 BCE–4th century BCE

BEFORE
In predynastic Egypt
Bodies buried in the sand are preserved by dehydration; this may have inspired later mummification practices.

c.2400–2100 BCE Royal tomb inscriptions at Saqqara—the Pyramid Texts—suggest belief in a divine afterlife for the Egyptian pharaohs, promising the kings: "You have not died."

c.2100 BCE The first Coffin Texts—spells inscribed on the coffins of wealthy men and women—suggest that the afterlife is no longer reserved for royalty.

AFTER
From 4th century BCE The conquering Greeks adopt some Egyptian beliefs, especially in the cult of Isis, wife of Osiris.

We want to **live again after death**, as the god Osiris did.

⬇

If we imitate the mummification of Osiris by Anubis, we can **join Osiris** in the **realm of the dead**.

⬇

There, **Osiris will judge us**, and our hearts will be weighed against our sins.

⬇

If we are **judged worthy**, we will enjoy **everlasting life**.

The Ancient Egyptians left extraordinary tributes to their dead, such as the Great Pyramids, huge necropolises, underground tombs, and extensive grave goods and art, but it would not be true to say that they were obsessed with death. Instead, they were preparing for the afterlife.

All their mortuary rituals of embalming, mummification, entombment, and remembrance were aimed at ensuring new life after death. Egyptians wanted to live after their death as perfected beings in Aaru, the field of reeds, which was itself a perfected version of the Egypt they already knew.

Aaru was the domain of Osiris, lord of the dead. In it, the blessed dead gathered rich crops of barley and emmer wheat—abundant harvests that are joyously depicted on the walls of Egyptian tombs.

Egyptians believed that a complete person comprised a number of elements: the physical body, the name, the shadow, the *ka* (spiritual life force), the *ba* (personality), and the *akh* (the perfected being that could enjoy life in paradise). To ensure life in paradise, care needed to be taken of all these constituent parts.

See also: The origin of death 33 ▪ The spirits of the dead live on 36–37 ▪ Entering into the faith 224–25 ▪ Social holiness and evangelicalism 239 ▪ The ultimate reward for the righteous 279 ▪ Awaiting the Day of Judgment 312–13

Elaborate preparations for safe passage to the next world were at first reserved only for the nobility, as here, but later the promise of rebirth into eternal life was open to all Egyptians.

The body had to be preserved by mummification and buried with a set of funerary equipment, including jars containing the internal organs, in rituals that identified the deceased with the god Osiris. Reenacting the death and resurrection of the god prepared the deceased for the journey to the next world.

Every stage of mummification was accompanied by religious ritual. Embalmers enacted the role of the jackal-headed god, Anubis, who was the protective god of the dead; Anubis invented the mysteries of embalming in order to resurrect the slain Osiris. Embalming spells reassured the deceased: "You will live again, you will live forever."

The journey of the dead

The preservation of the physical body by mummification was important because it was to the body that the *ka* needed to return for sustenance. If the body was decayed, the *ka* would starve. The *ka* needed to take strength from the body to rejoin the *ba* in the afterlife. Together they created the *akh*, which would have to gain admittance to the afterlife.

The deceased then negotiated the path from this world to the next, and was led by Anubis into the Hall of Two Truths. Here, the heart was weighed in the balance against Ma'at, goddess of truth, symbolized by a feather. If the heart, heavy with sin, outweighed the feather, it would be gobbled up by Ammut, she-monster and devourer of the dead. If the scales balanced, the deceased could proceed to paradise, the gates of which were guarded by Osiris.

Important Egyptians were buried with a manual: the *Book of the Dead*, or the *Spells for Coming Forth by Day*. This guide taught the dead how to speak, breathe, eat, and drink in the afterlife. It included, crucially, a spell for "not dying again in the realm of the dead." ▪

The death of Osiris

The story of the death and resurrection of Osiris was the foundation myth that offered Egyptians the hope of new life after death—initially just for the king, but for all Egyptians by the Middle Kingdom period.

The god Osiris was said to have been killed by his jealous brother Seth, who cut his body into pieces and scattered them across Egypt. "It is not possible to destroy the body of a god," Seth said, "but I have done so." Osiris's wife Isis and her sister Nephthys gathered up the body, piece by piece, and the god Anubis embalmed it as the first mummy. Isis changed herself into a kite and, hovering over the mummified Osiris, fanned the breath of life back into him for long enough to conceive a child, Horus (who would avenge his father), before Osiris took his place as lord of the underworld.

O my heart...! Do not stand up as a witness against me, do not be opposed to me in the tribunal.
Ancient Egyptian Book of the Dead

THE TRIUMPH OF GOOD OVER EVIL DEPENDS ON HUMANKIND

THE BATTLE BETWEEN GOOD AND EVIL

IN CONTEXT

KEY BELIEVERS
Zoroastrians

WHEN AND WHERE
1400–1200 BCE, Iran (Persia)

BEFORE
From prehistory Many belief systems feature a destructive or mischievous god or spirit who is in opposition to a more benevolent deity.

AFTER
6th century BCE The Persian and Mede empires are unified; Zoroastrianism becomes one of the world's largest religions.

4th century BCE Classical Greek philosophers, including Plato, study with Zoroastrian priests; Aristotle is said to have considered Plato to be a reincarnation of Zoroaster.

10th century CE Zoroastrians migrate from Iran to India to avoid converting to Islam; they become the Parsis, the largest Zoroastrian community today.

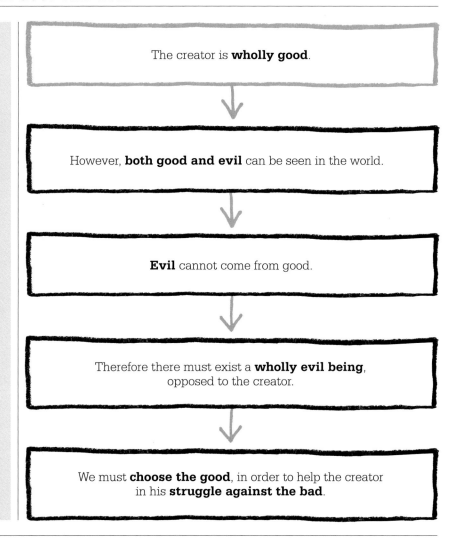

The creator is **wholly good**.

↓

However, **both good and evil** can be seen in the world.

↓

Evil cannot come from good.

↓

Therefore there must exist a **wholly evil being**, opposed to the creator.

↓

We must **choose the good**, in order to help the creator in his **struggle against the bad**.

Zoroastrianism is one of the oldest surviving religions, and one of the first recorded monotheistic faiths. It was founded by the prophet figure Zoroaster in ancient Persia (modern Iran).

Zoroaster's religion developed from the old system of Indo-Iranian gods, which included Ahura Mazda, lord of wisdom. In Zoroastrianism, Ahura Mazda (sometimes called Ohrmazd) is elevated to become the one supreme god, the wise creator who is the source of all good, and represents order and truth, in opposition to evil and chaos.

Ahura Mazda is assisted by his creations, the Amesha Spenta or bounteous immortals: six divine spirits. A seventh and less easily definable Spenta is the Spenta Mainyu, who is seen as Mazda's own bounteous spirit, and the agent of his will.

According to Zoroastrianism, the good Ahura Mazda has been locked in struggle with the evil entity Ahriman (also called Angra Mainyu, or destructive spirit) since time began. Ahriman and Ahura Mazda are regarded as twin spirits; however, Ahriman is a fallen being,

and cannot be considered Ahura Mazda's equal. Ahura Mazda lives in the light, while his twin lurks in the dark. Their struggle, as evil endlessly attempts to vanquish good, forms the entire body of Zoroastrian mythology.

Ahura Mazda battles with Ahriman using the creative energy of his spirit, Spenta Mainyu; the exact relationship between these three entities remains an unresolved aspect of the religion. Human beings, also Mazda's creation, have an important role in keeping disorder and evil at bay

See also: The end of the world as we know it 86–87 ▪ From monolatry to monotheism 176–77 ▪ Jesus's message to the world 204–207

> The goodness of the wise Creator can be inferred from the act of creation.
> **Mardan-Farrukh**

by using their free will to do good. Good thoughts, good words, and good deeds support *asha*, the fundamental order of the universe. *Asha* is seen as being constantly at risk from the opposing principle of *druj*, chaos, which feeds on bad thoughts, bad words, and bad deeds. The essential opposition is between creation and uncreation, with evil threatening at all times to undermine the ordered structure of the world.

The birth of Zoroaster, with his destiny to recruit humankind to the fight between good and evil, tipped the battle in favor of goodness. According to Zoroastrianism, it is good that will ultimately prevail.

A world made by goodness

Zoroastrianism tells that when Ahura Mazda wanted to create a perfect world, he made the Amesha Spenta and a spiritual, invisible world, which included a perfect being. The spiritual nature of this world was intended to foil Ahriman, who tries to attack it nevertheless. Ahura Mazda defeats Ahriman by reciting the holiest Zoroastrian prayer, the Ahunavar, which casts him back into the darkness.

Ahura Mazda then gives material form to his spiritual world. He creates one primal animal (a bull), and his perfect spiritual being becomes a human being, known as Gayomart (meaning mortal or human life). »

The symbol of Zoroastrianism, the Faravahar, is thought to depict a *fravashi*, or guardian angel. These protect the souls of individuals as they struggle against evil.

Zoroaster

It is not known exactly when the prophet Zoroaster (also called Zarathustra) lived, but c.1400–1200 BCE seems likely. Although his teachings draw on early Hindu texts such as the Rig-Veda, he regarded his religious insights into these texts as visions received directly from God. Zoroaster was already a priest among seminomadic, pastoral Iranians on the south Russian steppes when he began to preach the worship of Ahura Mazda. At first he found few followers, but he did convert a local ruler, who made Zoroastrianism the official religion of the Avestan people. However, it was not until the reign of Cyrus the Great, in the 6th century BCE, that the religion spread across the Persian empire.

Key works

4th century BCE Zoroaster's teachings are compiled in the Avesta, including the Gathas, 17 hymns believed to be Zoroaster's own words.
9th century CE The dualistic nature of Zoroastrian philosophy is laid out in detail in his *Analytical Treatise for the Dispelling of Doubts*.

The dissimilarity of good and evil, light and darkness, is not one of function but one of substance…their natures cannot combine and are mutually destructive.
Mardan-Farrukh

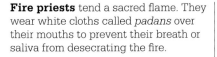

Fire priests tend a sacred flame. They wear white cloths called *padans* over their mouths to prevent their breath or saliva from desecrating the fire.

It is not long, however, before Ahriman recovers and renews his attack. He breaks through the sky in a blaze of fire, bringing with him starvation, disease, pain, lust, and death. He also creates demons of his own. Gayomart and the bull ultimately die, but upon their deaths, their semen spills on the ground and is fertilized by the sun. Ahura Mazda sends rain, which brings forth, from the seed of Gayomart, the mother and father of humanity: Mashya and Mashyoi. Meanwhile, the bull's seed gives rise to all the other animals of the world.

Because his perfect creation has been spoiled by Ahriman's destructiveness, Ahura Mazda sets a limit on time, which was previously limitless.

Evil and human will
In Zoroastrianism, all people are born good. The presence of Ahriman, an active principle of evil, explains why they may be tempted to do wrong. It also explains how evil can exist in the presence of a good god. Zoroastrian texts state: "What is complete and perfect in its goodness cannot produce evil. If it could, then it would not be perfect. If God is perfect in goodness and knowledge, plainly ignorance and evil cannot proceed from him." This is to say that Ahura Mazda cannot be responsible for the presence of evil in the world: the source of this is Ahriman.

The fact that Ahura Mazda has given humankind free will means that every moment of an individual's existence requires a choice to be made between what is right and what is wrong, and that it is our responsibility to choose good over evil.

This focus on moral choice makes Zoroastrianism a religion in which personal responsibility and morality are paramount, not only in conceptual terms but as practiced in day-to-day life. Human virtues

One good twin, one evil twin

In Zurvanism, a now-defunct branch of Zoroastrianism, Ahura Mazda is not the sole creator; he and Ahriman are the sons of a preexisting god, Zurvan (Time). This doctrine arose from the reasoning that, if Mazda and Ahriman were twin spirits (as texts said), they needed a progenitor. Zurvan, a neutral, androgynous god, sacrifices 1,000 of his years to create a son. But, as the end of the millennium approaches, Zurvan begins to doubt his power to produce a son. The evil Ahriman is born from his doubt, just as Ahura Mazda is born from his optimism. Zurvan prophesies that his firstborn will rule the world. Ahriman forces his way out first, declaring himself Ahura Mazda, but Zurvan is not deceived, saying, "My son is light and fragrant, but you are dark and stinking." And Zurvan weeps to think he has produced such an abomination.

Establish the power of
acts arising from a life
lived with good purpose,
for Mazda and for the lord
whom they made pastor
for the poor.
The Ahunavar Prayer

worthy of, and helpful to, Ahura
Mazda include truthfulness, loyalty,
tolerance, forgiveness, respect
for one's elders, and the keeping
of promises. Vices such as anger,
arrogance, vengefulness, bad
language, and greed are condemned
—and not only in this life.

Judgment and salvation

Zoroastrians believe that after
death, individuals will be judged
twice: once when they die and
once at a Last Judgment at the
end of time. The two judgments
will address, respectively, the
individual's morality of thought and
his or her morality of action. In both
cases, moral failings are punished
in hell. However, these punishments
are not eternal; they cease when
the person corrects their moral
failing in the afterlife—which,
once successfully accomplished,
is followed by the person going to
dwell with Ahura Mazda in heaven.

Zoroastrians gather to pray together.
This very moral religion is summed
up in the old Avestan phrase: "*Humata,
Hukhta, Hvarshta*"—"Good thoughts,
good words, good deeds."

Zoroastrian teachings tell that as
the end of time draws near, the
Saoshyant (savior) will arise
and prepare the world to be made
anew, helping Ahura Mazda to
destroy Ahriman. People will grow
pure and stop eating meat, then
milk, plants, and water, until at last
they need nothing. When all have
chosen good over evil, there will
be no more sin, so Az, the demon
of lust made by Ahriman, will
starve, turning on her creator.
Ahura Mazda will cast Ahriman
from creation through the hole that
Ahriman made when he broke
in. It is at this point that time
will be at an end.

Saoshyant will then raise
the dead, who will pass through
a stream of molten metal to burn
away their sins. According to
Zoroastrianism, the world will begin
again, but this time it will be a
world everlasting, free of taint.

The use of fire and molten metal
as a purifier in the Last Judgment
is reflected in the prominence of
fire in Zoroastrianism as a symbol
of sanctity. It is seen as the purest
of the elements. Ahura Mazda is
strongly associated with fire and

also the sun. For this reason,
Zoroastrian temples always
keep a fire burning, symbolizing
their god's eternal power. Some
temple fires have been kept
burning for centuries. Believers
bring offerings of wood (the only
fuel used), and fire priests place
these in the flames. Visitors are
anointed with ash.

The continuing struggle

The Zoroastrian idea of eternal,
opposing forces of good and evil
is a form of what philosophy
calls dualism. Another Persian
dualistic religion, Manichaeism,
was founded by the prophet Mani
in the 3rd century CE. Mani felt that
his Religion of Light completed
the teachings of Zoroaster, Buddha,
and Christ.

Like Zoroaster, Mani saw
the world as an eternal struggle
between the forces of good and
evil, light and darkness. This
was to have a profound effect on
Christian thinkers, and influence
medieval, heretical Christian cults
such as the Paulicians in Armenia,
the Bogomils in Bulgaria, and, most
famously, the Cathars in France. ∎

ACCEPT THE WAY OF THE UNIVERSE

ALIGNING THE SELF WITH THE DAO

The *dao*, or Way, is the **fundamental principle** of the universe.

The *dao* **sustains all things**.

The *dao* **remains unchanged**, while all else flows around it.

We must cease actions that interrupt this flow and **live simply, in harmony** with nature.

Through meditation and inaction we **accept the Way of the universe**.

The origins of Daoism are rooted in ancient Chinese beliefs concerning nature and harmony, but its first text, attributed to the philosopher Laozi, was written in the 6th century BCE —an unusually active time for ideas that also saw the emergence of Confucianism in China, both Jainism and Buddhism in India, and early Greek philosophy. Laozi's book, the *Daode jing* (The Way and Its Power) identified the *dao,* or Way, as the power or principle that underlies and sustains all things and is the source of order in the universe. Following the *dao*, rather than hindering or obstructing it, not only helps to ensure cosmic harmony, but also leads to personal spiritual development and a virtuous, fulfilled, and possibly longer life.

See also: Wisdom lies with the superior man 72–77 ▪ Physical and mental discipline 112–13 ▪ Zen insights that go beyond words 160–63

For life to run smoothly along the Way, we must attune and align ourselves with it, performing only those simple actions that maintain nature's inherent balance.

What it means to follow the *dao* is succinctly expressed in the more modern phrase, "going with the flow."

Action and inaction

The *dao* itself is eternal and unchanging. It is life that eddies and swirls around the *dao* and, to keep to its path, people must detach themselves from material concerns and disruptive emotions such as ambition and anger. They should instead live a peaceful, simple life, acting spontaneously and in harmony with nature, rather than acting on impulses from the self. This is the concept of *wu wei*, or inaction, inherent in the *dao*; as the *Daode jing* says, "the Way never acts, and yet nothing is left undone." In daily life, Laozi placed great emphasis on those virtues that encourage *wu wei*: humility, submissiveness, non-interference, passivity, and detachment.

The wisdom of Laozi came from long contemplation of the nature of the universe and its constituents, which in Chinese philosophy are yin and yang. Yin comprises all that is dark, moist, soft, cold, and feminine; all that is light, dry, hard, warm, and masculine is yang. Everything is made of yin and yang, and harmony is achieved when the two are kept in balance. In Daoism such balance is sought in mind, spirit, and body through practices such as meditation and t'ai chi: physical, mental, and spiritual exercises intended to balance the flow of qi, the life force, through the body.

Under the rule of the Han dynasty (206 BCE–220 CE), Daoist philosophy became a religion. Its meditative practices were thought to guide experts to immortality. In the *Daode jing* itself, the notion of immortality is not intended literally. Someone who completely accepts the *dao* reaches a plane above the material, and achieves immortality by detachment. But the statement that, for the sage, "there is no realm of death," was to be taken more literally by followers of the Daoist religion, who believed that actual immortality could be achieved through acceptance of the Way. ▪

My words are very easy to understand and very easy to put into practice, yet no one in the world can understand them or put them into practice.
Laozi

Laozi

The author of the *Daode jing* is said to have been a court archivist for the Zhou emperors who earned the name Laozi (the Old Master) because of his wisdom. The younger sage Kong Fuzi, or Confucius (p.75), is thought to have journeyed to consult him on religious rites. However, almost nothing is known for certain about Laozi. It is possible that he was not a historical figure at all, and that the *Daode jing* is in fact a later compilation of sayings.

According to legend, Laozi disappeared under mysterious circumstances; Confucius himself compared him to a dragon, which can ascend to heaven on the wind. The story goes that on witnessing the decline of the Zhou dynasty, Laozi left court and journeyed west seeking solitude. As he left, a border guard who recognized him asked for a token of his wisdom. Laozi wrote the *Daode jing* for him, and then traveled on, never to be seen in this world again.

Key works

c.6th century BCE *Daode jing* (also known as the *Laozi*).

THE FIVE GREAT VOWS

SELF-DENIAL LEADS TO SPIRITUAL LIBERATION

IN CONTEXT

KEY FIGURE
Mahavira

WHEN AND WHERE
From 6th century BCE, India

BEFORE
From 1000 BCE The concept of samsara, the cycle of death and rebirth, is developed by wandering ascetics of the *shramana* tradition in India.

AFTER
6th century BCE Buddha's enlightenment shows him the way to escape samsara.

From 2nd century BCE In Mahayana Buddhism, bodhisattvas—enlightened humans that remain on earth to help others—are revered.

20th century Jainism is recognized as a legally distinct religion in India, separate from Hinduism.

J ainism is the most ascetic of all Indian religions. Its followers practice self-denial in order to progress toward moksha, release from constant rebirth into this world of suffering. Jainism as we know it was founded by Mahavira, a contemporary of Buddha, in the 6th century BCE. However, Jainism takes a long view of its own historical development: it is said that it has always existed and always will exist. Within the faith, Mahavira is simply regarded as the most recent of 24 enlightened teachers in the current era. Jains believe each era lasts for millions of years and recurs in an infinite cycle of ages. These teachers are called

See also: The four stages of life 106–109 ▪ Escape from the eternal cycle 136–43 ▪ Buddhas and bodhisattvas 152–57 ▪ The ultimate reward for the righteous 279 ▪ The Sikh code of conduct 296–301

Life is an endless **cycle of reincarnation**.

Only by freeing ourselves of the **burden of karma** can we achieve enlightenment and be liberated from this cycle.

To do this we must **follow the example** of the great teachers who have achieved liberation, such as Mahavira.

If we follow this path, we too may eventually **achieve enlightenment**.

The path is set out in the **Five Vows** of nonviolence, truth-telling, chastity, not stealing, and nonattachment.

Images of the *jinas* or *tirthankaras*, the enlightened beings revered in Jainism, are used as devotional objects and as a focus for meditation while prayers and mantras are recited.

jinas, or more commonly, *tirthankaras*: "builders of the ford across the ocean of rebirth." By following the path of self-denial taught by the *tirthankaras*, Jains hope to free their souls from the entanglements of material existence. Without this hope, life is simply a continuous cycle of life, death, and reincarnation.

Personal responsibilty

Jainism does not recognize any deity, placing full responsibility on the actions and conduct of the individual. In order to adhere to a life of self-denial, Jain monks and nuns take what are called the Five Great Vows—nonviolence (ahimsa), speaking the truth (*satya*), celibacy (*brahmacharya*), not taking what is not willingly offered (*asteya*), and detachment from people, places, and things

(*aparigraha*). The most important of these vows is the practice of ahimsa, which extends beyond avoiding violence against human beings to encompass all animals, including the smallest organisms found in water or air. The other four Great Vows equip the monk or nun to follow the life of a wandering mendicant, dedicated to preaching, fasting, worship, and study.

Self-denial is central to Jainism. It is said within the faith that Mahavira himself went naked, having been so deep in thought at the start of his wanderings that he failed to notice when his robe snagged on a thorn bush and was pulled off. But in the 4th century CE, long after Mahavira's death, the extent to which self-denial should be practiced caused a schism in Jainism between the Shvetambara ("white-clad") and Digambara

("sky-clad") sects. Shvetambara monks believe that detachment and purity are mental qualities that are unimpeded by wearing a simple robe. However, Digambara monks go naked, believing that the wearing of clothes indicates that »

Having wisdom, Mahavira committed no sin himself, nor did he induce others to do so, nor did he consent to the sins of others.
Akaranga Sutra

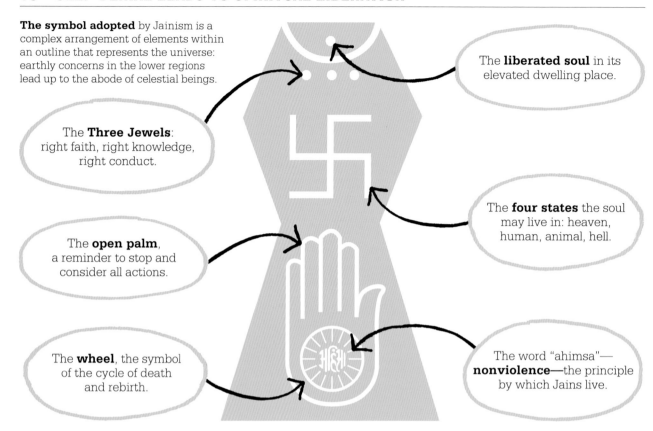

The symbol adopted by Jainism is a complex arrangement of elements within an outline that represents the universe: earthly concerns in the lower regions lead up to the abode of celestial beings.

The **liberated soul** in its elevated dwelling place.

The **Three Jewels**: right faith, right knowledge, right conduct.

The **four states** the soul may live in: heaven, human, animal, hell.

The **open palm**, a reminder to stop and consider all actions.

The **wheel**, the symbol of the cycle of death and rebirth.

The word "ahimsa"—**nonviolence**—the principle by which Jains live.

a person is not completely detached from sexual feelings and false notions of modesty. Digambara monks may not even carry alms bowls, but must receive food in their cupped hands. Digambaras also believe that liberation from rebirth is not possible for women until they have first been reborn as a man.

Living in the world

Lay Jains do not take the Five Great Vows, but they do take lesser vows that are similar: renouncing violence, vowing not to lie or to steal, embracing chaste sexual behavior, and avoiding attachment to material things. All Jains are strictly vegetarian, in line with the vow of nonviolence, and must not do work that involves the destruction of life. Some Jains will only use flowers that have already

fallen from the plant in their worship, arguing that to cut a living flower is an act of violence. Lay Jains may marry, but are expected to uphold the highest standards of behavior. In this, as in all things, Jains follow the path of the Three Jewels: right faith, right knowledge, and right conduct.

Sometimes there is said to be a fourth jewel, right penance: atonement for sins is important in Jainism. At the annual festival of Samvatsari, which follows an eight-day period of fasting and abstinence in the monsoon season, a full confession is made to family and friends of the sins of the past year, and vows are taken not to carry grudges into the new year. Meditation is important, too, and Jain daily rituals include 48-minute sessions of meditation, in which

the aim is to be at one with the universe, and to forgive and be forgiven for all transgressions. (Forty-eight minutes—one-thirtieth of a day—is a *mahurta*, a standard unit of time in India often used for ritual purposes.)

Other Jain virtues are: service to others, attention to religious study, disengagement from passion, and politeness and humility. Particular merit is gained by donating food to monks and nuns. All of these practices combine with the self-denial required by even laypersons' vows to reduce the karma (consequences of past deeds) which, the Jains believe, accumulates on the soul as a kind of physical substance. All karma, both good and bad, must be removed to achieve liberation. The idea is to progress gradually along the path of spiritual enlightenment, earning merit little by little, life by life. One of the Jain holy texts, the *Tattvartha Sutra*, sets out a sequence of 14 stages through which the soul must pass to achieve liberation: the first stage is called *mithyadrishti*, in which the soul is in a spiritual slumber; the final, 14th, stage is *ayoga-kevali*, which is populated by souls known as *siddhas*, who have achieved full spiritual liberation. This final stage is beyond the reach of lay Jains.

Forms of devotion

Jains may worship in a temple or at a domestic shrine at home. Jain temples are seen as replicas of the celestial assembly halls where the liberated *tirthankaras* continue their teaching. The adoration and contemplation of images of these *tirthankaras* is thought to bring about inner spiritual transformation. The simplest form of worship, also

Only monastic Jains who have fully embraced a life of austerity and detachment can hope to ascend the 14 steps to spiritual enlightenment.

I ask pardon of all living creatures. May all of them pardon me. May I have a friendly relationship with all beings.
Jain prayer

found in Hinduism, is called *darshan*, and involves making eye contact with the image of a *tirthankara*, often while reciting a sacred mantra. The fundamental prayer of Jainism is the Navkar, or Namaskar, Mantra. By reciting this mantra, *namo namahar*, the worshipper honors the souls of the liberated and gains inspiration from them in his or her own quest for enlightenment. ∎

Mahavira

The religious reformer Mahavira was born in around 599 BCE in northeast India as Prince Vardhamana, the son of King Siddhartha and Queen Trishala, who is said to have had many auspicious dreams during her pregnancy. According to Jain tradition, Mahavira was placed in the queen's womb by Indra, the king of the Vedic gods. Mahavira was allegedly so dedicated to nonviolence that he did not not kick in his mother's womb, in case he caused her pain.

At the age of 30, Prince Vardhamana left the palace to live as an ascetic, renouncing material comfort and devoting himself entirely to meditation. After 12 years he reached enlightenment and then became a great teacher, with the new name of Mahavira. Founding a large community of Jain monks and nuns (traditionally thought to be more than 50,000 in total), he molded Jainism into its current form. Mahavira died at the age of 72 at the town of Pava in Bihar, India, and is said at this point to have attained moksha (release from the cycle of death and rebirth).

VIRTUE IS NOT SENT FROM HEAVEN

WISDOM LIES WITH THE SUPERIOR MAN

IN CONTEXT

KEY FIGURE
Confucius

WHEN AND WHERE
6th–5th century BCE**, China**

BEFORE
From 11th century BCE
The Zhou dynasty redirect traditional Chinese ancestor worship toward the concept of a heaven, with the Zhou emperor as its representative.

6th century BCE Laozi proposes acting in accordance with the *dao* (the Way) in order to maintain universal harmony.

AFTER
From 6th century BCE
Confucian ideals of virtue and responsibility inform Zhou imperial rule and the political ideology of later dynasties.

18th century Confucius's meritocratic ideas are admired by Enlightenment thinkers who oppose the absolute authority of Church and State.

Confucius, as he is known in the West, was one of the first thinkers to systematically explore the notion of goodness and whether moral superiority is a divine privilege or is inherent in humankind and can be cultivated.

Born in the 6th century BCE in Qufu, in modern China's Shandong Province, Confucius was one of a new breed of scholars—in effect, the first civil servants—who became advisors to the Chinese court, rising from the middle classes to positions of power and influence on the strength of their own merit rather than through inheritance. In the rigidly class-stratified society of the day, this presented an anomaly, and it is this anomaly that lies at the heart of Confucius's thought.

The rulers of the reigning Zhou dynasty believed that they were given their authority directly by the gods, under the Mandate of Heaven, and that the quality of *ren* (or *jen*)—humaneness—was an attribute of the ruling classes. Confucius, too, saw heaven as the source of moral order, but he argued that the blessing of heaven was open to all, and that the quality

To govern by virtue, let us compare it to the North Star: it stays in its place, while the myriad stars wait upon it.
The Analects

of *ren* could be acquired by anyone. It is in fact the duty of everyone to cultivate the attributes that make up *ren*—seriousness, generosity, sincerity, diligence, and kindness. To practice these virtues is to uphold the will of heaven.

The *Analects*—sayings and teachings of Confucius collected by his pupils—established a new philosophy of morality in which the superior man, or *junzi* (literally gentleman), devotes himself to the acquisition of *ren* for its own sake—he learns for learning's sake, and is good for goodness' sake.

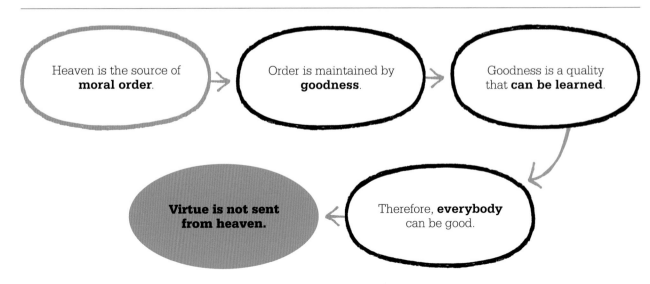

Heaven is the source of **moral order**.

Order is maintained by **goodness**.

Goodness is a quality that **can be learned**.

Therefore, **everybody** can be good.

Virtue is not sent from heaven.

See also: Living in harmony 38 ▪ Aligning the self with the *dao* 66–67 ▪ Selfless action 110–11 ▪ Man as a manifestation of God 188

Asked by a student to explain the rules to be followed by the seeker of *ren*, Confucius replied, "One should see nothing improper, hear nothing improper, say nothing improper, do nothing improper."

Confucius was concerned not simply with self-cultivation, but with the relations between people, and the proper way to behave in a family, a community, and a larger society. Confucius himself admitted students of all classes as his disciples, and fundamentally believed that virtue lay in self-cultivation rather than noble birth. Because of the rigidity of the prevailing hierarchy in China's feudal society, Confucius had to find a way to promote individual virtue without calling for a simple meritocracy. He did so by arguing that the virtuous man accepts and understands his place in the social order, and uses his virtue to fulfill his allotted role rather than to transcend it. "The superior man," he said, "does what is proper to the station in which he is; he does not desire to go beyond this."

Attributes of a wise ruler

As for the rulers, Confucius advised that rather than exercising their powers in an arbitrary and unjust way, they should lead by example, and that treating the people with generosity and kindness would encourage virtue, loyalty, and right behavior. However, in order to govern others, it is necessary first to govern oneself. For Confucius, a humane ruler was defined by his practice of *ren*; without it, he might forfeit the Mandate of Heaven. In many ways Confucius's idea of the perfect ruler echoes Laozi's concept of the *dao*: the less the ruler does, the more is achieved. The ruler is the stable center around which the activity of the kingdom revolves.

Rulers who took this advice to heart also found themselves in need of advisors and civil servants whose skill and trustworthiness »

Imperial authority in China was expressed through decisive rule that reinforced the notion of a stable power center; well-advised judgments were less likely to require revision.

Confucius

According to tradition, Confucius was born in 551 BCE in Qufu, in the state of Lu, China. His name was originally Kong Qiu, and only later did he earn the title Kong Fuzi, or Master Kong. Little is known about his life, except that he was from a well-to-do family, and that as a young man he worked as a servant to support his family after his father died. He nevertheless managed to find time to study, and became an administrator in the Lu court, but when his suggestions to the rulers were ignored he left to concentrate on teaching.

As a teacher he traveled throughout the Chinese empire, returning to Qufu at the end of his life. He died there in 479 BCE. His teaching survives in fragments and sayings passed down orally by his disciples and subsequently collected in the *Analects* and anthologies compiled by Confucian scholars.

Key works

5th century BCE *Analects; Doctrine of the Mean;* Great Learning

The Five Constant Relationships

Sovereign–Subject
Rulers should be benevolent, and subjects loyal.

Father–Son
Parents are to be loving, and children obedient.

Husband–Wife
Husbands are to be good and fair, and wives understanding.

Brother–Brother
Elder siblings are to be gentle, and younger siblings respectful.

Friend–Friend
Older friends are to be considerate, younger friends reverential.

were founded in the Confucian concepts of virtuous behavior; in 136 BCE the Han dynasty introduced new competitive examinations for the imperial civil service based on meritocratic Confucian ideals. In turn the Chinese concept of heaven acquired a distinctly bureaucratic tone, and by the time of the Song dynasty (960–1279 CE), heaven was seen as a mirror image of the court of the Chinese emperor, with its own emperor and a vast celestial civil service of lesser deities.

Despite his many references to heaven, Confucius did not believe his moral precepts were derived from the gods; instead he found them already existing in the human heart and mind. To this extent, Confucianism is more a humanistic system of moral philosophy than it is a religion; although even today, with some 5–6 million followers, the distinction between the two remains blurred. In Chinese popular religion, Confucius has joined the crowded pantheon of gods, but many of his followers revere him simply as a great teacher and thinker.

Building on ritual
The adoption of Confucianism as a religion stems largely from the fact that Confucius upheld the duty to practice rites and ceremonies that honored ancestors. This he saw as part of a wider imperative of loyalty to family and friends, and respect for elders—which Confucius defined in what he called the Five Constant Relationships (see left). Reciprocity plays a key role in these relationships, for Confucianism, at its heart, embodies the Golden Rule: do not do to others what you do not want done to yourself. Confucius believed that by honoring ties of love, loyalty, ritual, and tradition, virtuous thought, virtuous action, and respect, not

Confucius traveled and taught for 12 years, acquiring disciples in much the same way that the contemporary schools of philosophy were taking shape in the Ancient Greek world.

only could everybody be good, but society would be bound together in a positive and right-thinking way. By revering the ancestors and performing the correct rites in their honor, humans could maintain a state of harmony between this world and heaven. At the family level, such rites were an echo of those in which the emperors made sacrifices to their ancestors and confirmed the Mandate of Heaven under which they ruled.

Only he who is possessed of the most complete sincerity that can exist under Heaven can transform.
Doctrine of the Mean

Filial piety remains one of the most important Confucian virtues, and its ties and duties extend beyond death. Sons are expected to make offerings at their parents' graves, and to honor them at shrines in the home that contain ancestor tablets, in which the spirits of the elders are said to dwell. Even today, the key moment in a Confucian wedding is when the couple bow to the groom's ancestor tablets, thus formally introducing the bride to the ancestors of her husband's family in order to secure their blessing.

Confucianism evolves

It was during the Song dynasty that the scholar Zhu Xi (1130–1200 CE) incorporated elements of Daoism and Buddhism into Confucianism, creating an enduring religion that is also known as Neo-Confucianism. Confucius was not the first Chinese sage to contemplate the eternal truths, and Confucius himself claimed to have invented nothing, but merely to have studied the ideas of earlier thinkers, gathering them together in five books, known as the Five Classics. Under the Western Zhou dynasty, from 1050 to 771 BCE, scholars were highly valued at court, and in the 7th century BCE the so-called Hundred Schools of Thought emerged. Confucius lived in a time of philosophical ferment, but also of social change, as the power of the Zhou emperors declined and the whole social order seemed to be under threat. His focus on order and harmony emerged from a genuine concern about potential societal breakdown. The emperors

Respect for elders and ancestors is a core value of Confucianism: these young Chinese students are marking the anniversary of Confucius's birth by honoring his image.

Hold faithfulness
and sincerity
as first principles.
The Analects

Men's natures are alike,
it is their habits that
carry them far apart.
The Analects

of later dynasties such as the Han (206 BCE–220 CE), the Song (960–1279 CE) and the Ming (1368–1644 CE) recognized the value of Confucian ideals in maintaining social order, and Confucianism became the Chinese state religion. It was also a profound influence on daily life and thought into the 20th century, and was attacked during the Cultural Revolution for its social conservatism, but in recent years a

New Confucianism has emerged in China, blending Confucian ideas with modern Chinese thinking and Western philosophy. Although Confucius built his philosophy on existing concepts and practices, he was remarkable for his insistence that human beings are naturally good—only needing to be taught and encouraged, to be virtuous— and that this goodness is not confined to the aristocracy. ∎

A DIVINE CHILD IS BORN
THE ASSIMILATION OF MYTH

IN CONTEXT

KEY BELIEVERS
**Ancient Minoans
and Myceneans**

WHEN AND WHERE
14th century BCE, Crete

BEFORE
From prehistory Early
settlers, probably from western
Asia, leave evidence of rituals
and worship in caves on Crete.

c.25th century–1420 BCE
Goddesses are the primary
focus of worship in Minoan
Crete; many are associated
with serpents, birds, or bees.

AFTER
7th century BCE The Greek
poet Hesiod relates the birth
of Zeus to Rhea at Psychro
and his concealment from
the wrath of his father.

5th century BCE The Roman
Republic assimilates the
myths and iconography
of Zeus in its supreme
god, Jupiter or Jove.

Around 1420 BCE, the Minoan civilization of the island of Crete was conquered by the Myceneans from mainland Greece, and as the Greek invaders absorbed the culture of the Minoans, so indigenous Cretan and Greek myth became intertwined. The chief deity of the Minoans was a great mother goddess, who, in legend, gave birth to a divine son in the Diktaean cave above Psychro. This cave became her holiest shrine and no one, god or man, was permitted to enter. Once a year a fiery glow was said to erupt from the cave, when the blood from the birth of the divine child spilled over.

This child grew into a wondrous beardless youth or *kouros*, a demi-god who was often invoked in hymns to bring fertility and good fortune to humans each year.

The Dorian Greeks, who succeeded the Myceneans, gave the Minoan *kouros* the name of their own supreme god, Zeus, the deity who came to rule the classical Greek pantheon of gods that lived on Mount Olympus. Regarded as the place where Zeus's mother, Rhea, hid her baby from his jealous father, Cronus, the cave became one of ancient Greece's many sacred sites, or shrines.

Rhea may have been one of the names of the original, Minoan, great goddess, but in Greek myth, although she was the mother of gods, Rhea was not considered an Olympian goddess in her own right. Her divine child, on the other hand, was elevated in status to become the highest god of all, the father of all other gods. ∎

The infant Zeus, here painted by Carlo Cignani (1628–1719), was variously described in myth as being nursed by nymphs, a she-goat, or bees that lived in the Diktaean cave.

See also: Symbolism made real 46–47 ∎ Beliefs for new societies 56–57 ∎ The power of the great goddess 104

THE ORACLES REVEAL THE WILL OF THE GODS
DIVINING THE FUTURE

The ancient Greeks set great store by divination of the future, and the most valuable and influential sources of prophecy and wise counsel were the oracles, who were almost always women. The oracles would enter a trancelike state, during which the gods spoke directly through them. The gods' messages were sometimes unintelligible, but could be interpreted by priests. If offerings were made at the oracles' sanctuaries, or dwelling places (often caves), they would often provide more satisfactory responses.

Oracles could be consulted on any aspect of life, from personal matters, such as love and marriage, to affairs of state. Prophecies could also be used for political ends: Alexander the Great visited the oracle of the Egyptian god Amun after conquering Egypt in 332 BCE, and had his rule legitimized when the oracle recognized him as the "son of Amun." However, the number of oracles was limited, and this, combined with the fact that substantial offerings were often advisable, meant that personalized access to the gods became the province of the rich and powerful. A popular alternative was the service offered by seers or soothsayers, who, unlike the oracles, were prepared to travel—particularly useful for Greek armies on the move. These seers interpreted signs from the gods by methods such as dream analysis, inferring meaning from chance events, observation of birds, and deducing omens from animal sacrifice. ∎

The Sibyl, with raving lips… reaches over a thousand years with her voice, thanks to the god in her.
Heraclitus

See also: The power of the shaman 26–31 ▪ The African roots of Santeria 304–305 ▪ The Pentecostal Church 336

THE GODS ARE JUST LIKE US

BELIEFS THAT MIRROR SOCIETY

The gods take an active interest in our **domestic affairs**.

The gods take an active interest in our **public affairs**.

Household gods, **the penates**, reside in our homes and help provide for us.

The gods are just like us

Public leaders **consult the gods** about political decision making.

Political leaders can be given the status of gods.

Ancestor spirit gods, **the lares**, act as our guardians.

The pantheon of ancient Roman gods was largely adapted from that of other civilizations, notably the Greeks. As the Greek deities had done, the Roman gods lived, loved, and fought their battles in a way that mirrored the lives of the mortals and reflected their history. However, while the Greeks saw their gods as remote controllers of the universe, the Romans considered them to be an intrinsic part of their lives, and to have

See also: Beliefs for new societies 56–57 ▪ The assimiliation of myth 78 ▪ Living the Way of the Gods 82–85

a direct influence on every aspect of existence. They believed that divine aid was key to successful governance, and so worship, ritual, and sacrifice were incorporated into public ceremonies in order to ensure the cooperation of the gods. Public ceremonies also helped to strengthen the authority of the regime, and religious festivals, often involving public holidays and games, contributed to political unity. Religious and state life were interdependent, with priests forming a part of the political elite and leaders expected to perform religious duties. In time, individual rulers became associated, during their lifetime, with a particular god; some eventually became regarded *as* gods—either by being deified after death or even achieving divine status while they were still alive.

Cults and household gods

Various cults coexisted with the religion of the state. Some were devoted to a particular god— often one outside the conventional pantheon; sometimes the foreign god of a conquered people was invited to take up residence in Rome. For most Roman citizens, however, the local and household gods, the lares and penates, were the ones associated with everyday life. They were so interested in human affairs that their presence was everywhere; they were open to negotiation, and prayers to them often took the form of bargains: "I give so that you will give."

The foundation of religion for the Romans was the family. The paterfamilias—head of the family— was the spiritual leader and moral authority, who held legal rights over the property of the family and was responsible for its members in society. The home was sacred to the Romans, and the heart of the home was the hearth. The spirit of the head of the household presided over all the household gods, including the penates, the deities of the store cupboard, to whom a portion of each meal was offered on the flames of the hearth. ▪

The Roman gods had human characteristics; they are often depicted feasting, sleeping, or engaging in bawdy drunkenness.

The lares

Constituting a bridge between the public and domestic gods, the lares were typically guardian deities, whose function was to protect the livelihood of a particular area. While many homes had a shrine devoted to the local lares, their scope was broader than that of the household penates, and shrines to the neighborhood lares were often placed at crossroads, a symbol of home in its wider sense. The lares are thought to have evolved from earlier cults of hero-ancestors, or the spirits of ancestors buried in farmland, with their role as protectors of agriculture and livestock. In the Roman Republic, they came to be the guardians of businesses, transport, and communication. Lares were closely associated with local communities and everyday public life, and were very much gods of the plebians (such as soldiers, seafarers, farmers, and traders), rather than of the ruling class of patricians, complementing the major deities of the state religion.

At Rome as elsewhere, in order to understand the society of the gods, we must not lose sight of the society of men.
Georges Dumézil

RITUAL LINKS US TO OUR PAST

LIVING THE WAY OF THE GODS

IN CONTEXT

KEY MOVEMENT
Shinto

WHEN AND WHERE
8th century, Japan

BEFORE
From prehistory In Japan, animist belief in nature spirits blends with ancestor worship; the emperors claim to be descendants of the gods.

2nd millennium BCE In ancient China, just rulers are thought to be invested with divine authority.

6th century CE Buddhism reaches Japan and begins to attract followers.

AFTER
19th century Shinto becomes the Japanese state religion.

1946 The Japanese emperor renounces his divine lineage. Shinto is disestablished, but continues to be practiced.

Shinto is the indigenous, traditional religion of Japan. Some say that it is not so much a religion as a Japanese way of life, because it is so intrinsically linked to the topography of the land and its history and traditions. Its origins can be traced to prehistoric times in Japan, when animist beliefs, with their respect for nature and natural phenomena, prevailed.

As the universal belief system of an isolated island nation, Shinto had no need to define itself until it was challenged by the arrival of a rival religion, Buddhism, in the 6th century CE. The traditional Japanese beliefs lacked complex intellectual doctrines, allowing

See also: Making sense of the world 20–23 ▪ Animism in early societies 24–25 ▪ Beliefs for new societies 56–57 ▪ Devotion through puja 114–15 ▪ The performance of ritual and repetition 158–59 ▪ Jesus's divine identity 208

Great Japan is the Land of the Gods. Here the Deity of the Sun has handed on her eternal rule.
Account of the Righteous Reigns of the Divine Emperors

The **world was created by the gods** at the beginning of heaven and earth.

⬇

It is full of sacred energies, or **kami.**

⬇

Some kami are great **creative beings**, some are **natural forces**, some are the **souls of the ancestors**.

⬇

The kami **created our nation** and **shaped our culture**.

⬇

Rituals honoring the kami link us to our past.

Buddhism and also Confucianism to become influential in Japanese theology and philosophy. In response, the Japanese imperial court consolidated Japan's native beliefs with a name—Shinto— and in the early 8th century, at the request of the Empress Gemmei, the great Shinto texts such as the Kojiki ("Record of Ancient Matters") and Nihon Shoki ("Continuing Chronicles of Japan") were compiled. These books recorded the oral traditions of Japanese history and myth, alongside the lineage of the Japanese emperors, said to be descended from the gods. They also defined a body of ritual that has remained key to Shinto ever since—perhaps more so than belief. Shinto still permeates every aspect of Japanese life, and its rituals, in which purification plays a key role, are performed in both spiritual and secular situations—for example, to bring success and good fortune to sporting events, new car assembly lines, or construction projects. During these rituals, which carry a great weight of tradition, sacred beings called kami are prayed to and honored. The word Shinto literally means "Way of the Divine Beings," and Shinto is known in modern Japanese as *Kami no michi*, the "Way of the Kami."

The essence of everything
The word kami means "that which is hidden" and can be translated as god, spirit, or soul. However, in Shinto belief, the term designates not only a vast range of divinities and spirit beings, but also the spiritual energy or essence that is found in everything, and which defines that thing: kami are present, for example, as essences of natural phenomena (such as storms and earthquakes) and the geographical environment (rivers, trees, and waterfalls, for example). Mountains, especially Mount Fuji, are held to be particularly sacred.

As entities, kami include gods, goddesses, and the souls or spirits of family ancestors (*ujigami*) and other exceptional human beings. Shinto teaches that these kami occupy the same material world as people, rather than existing on a supernatural plane. They respond to prayer and can influence events. However, unlike the divine beings in many other religious traditions, » kami, although godlike, are not omnipotent: they have limitations and are fallible. However, not all kami are good—some can be evil or demonic. But in their more benign aspect, they possess sincerity and a will to truth, or *makoto*, and maintain harmony in the universe through the creative potency known as *musubi*.

Shinto's creator gods

According to the Kojiki, at the creation of the universe, the first three kami emerged. These included the Kamimusubi (divine/high generative force kami), which was too abstract to be a focus of worship. However, after several generations of formless kami, the major Shinto gods appear: Izanagi and Izanami, who created the world, or "invited it into being." Many Shinto myths are devoted to them and to the activities of their offspring, Susanoo, the storm god, Tsukuyomi, the moon god, and Amaterasu, the sun goddess.

The kami represent the creators of Japan, the very land itself (as the spirits of its natural features and natural forces), and those who have gone before—Japanese ancestors. The ritual worship of these sacred beings therefore confirms a powerful connection to Japanese history and tradition.

Shrines and temples

A harmonious relationship between kami and humankind is maintained by praying and making offerings at shrines and temples. On entering a shrine, a ritual of purification is performed. These rituals are central to Shinto, for which ideas of purity and impurity are very important. Shinto does not have a concept of original sin, but rather believes that human beings are born pure, only becoming tainted by impurity later. The sources of impurity are sin (acts within our control) and pollution (things beyond our control, such as disease or contact with death). These impurities, or *tsumi*, need to be ritually purified. Purification rituals may take a variety of forms, but ceremonial hand washing and mouth washing sequences are common to most.

Small shrines known as *kami-dona* are found in many Japanese homes, consisting of a small shelf displaying objects used to honor the ancestors and other kami.

As you have blessed the ruler's reign...so I bow down my neck as a cormorant in search of fish to worship you through these abundant offerings on his behalf.
Prayer to Amaterasu

Public temples and shrines may be as large as a village, or as small as a beehive. They are remarkable for their simplicity; many originated as sacred areas around natural objects such as trees, ponds, or rocks. Each Shinto temple has a gateless entrance called a torii, which usually consists of a pair of uprights and a crossbar. Typically, every temple also has a wall where worshippers may post wooden votive tablets that bear a message to the kami, asking, for example, for success in passing an exam or help in finding a suitable marriage partner.

Individual prayers at the worship hall of a Shinto shrine follow a set four-step process, after the initial ritual cleansing. First, money is put into an offering box. Next, the worshipper makes two deep bows before the shrine, then claps their hands twice, and finally, after concluding prayers, makes

Shinto priests may be male or female; their white-clad assistants, or *miko*, are often the daughters of priests. Traditional costumes emphasize Shinto's connections with Japan's great imperial past.

one last deep bow. In addition to prayer and offerings at shrines, Shinto has celebratory festivals known as *matsuri*, at which the kami are honored and important points in the agricultural year are marked, such as rice-planting in April. Correctly performed, Shinto followers believe that these rituals enable *wa*, the positive harmony that helps to purify the world and keeps it running smoothly.

Descended from the gods

The most revered Shinto temple is that of Amaterasu, the sun goddess, at Ise, on the Japanese island of Honshu. The simple wooden shrine has been rebuilt every 20 years for the last 1,300 years; the action of renewal is thought to please the kami. Most Japanese people aim to visit Ise at least once in their life.

The emperors of Japan were traditionally regarded as the direct descendants of Amaterasu (the first emperor, Jimmu, who took power in 660 BCE, was said to be her great-great-great-grandson), and this became official doctrine in the 7th and 8th centuries. The codifiying of Shinto at this time not only eliminated influences from

Rituals that please and propitiate the gods are among the oldest in history, and still reverently attended to by followers of Shinto. An offering of sushi to a fox-spirit or *kitsune* statue should result in a prayer being carried to Inari, goddess of plenty, and be rewarded with a fine harvest.

Buddhism, but also placed an emphasis on the superior status of the Japanese people in general. This was used, in turn, as the rationale for Japan's political and military ambitions, especially after the Meiji Restoration, which returned imperial rule to Japan in the 19th century.

The emperor and his court were obliged to carry out ceremonies to ensure that the kami watched over Japan and secured its success, a tradition that was maintained until the end of World War II. Shinto's standing in Japan was transformed, however, after the country lost the war and was forced to make

concessions to the Allies. Viewed by the occupying US forces as too militaristic and nationalistic, Shinto was disestablished in 1946, ceasing to be the official state religion. In the same year, Emperor Hirohito renounced his claim to divinity. But while today the emperor is no longer formally regarded as divine, the imperial ceremonies are still viewed as important. Shinto's strong emphasis on order and harmony; its regard for social norms, ritual, and tradition; and its respect for the emperor means that Shinto has maintained its role as the bedrock of conservative Japanese society. ■

Man by nature is inherently good, and the world in which he lives is good. This is the kami-world. Evil then cannot originate in man or in this world. It is an intruder.
Sokyo Ono

The origins of purification rituals

Purification rituals (*harai*) play a key role in Shinto and are believed to originate in a myth involving Izanami and Izanagi, the two creator gods. The female of this pair, Izanami, is fatally burned while giving birth to the fire god, Kagutsuchi, so she descends to Yomi, the land of the dead. Grief-stricken, Izanagi follows her there, but discovers that she has eaten the food of the underworld and is unable to leave. Izanami begs Izanagi not to look at her, but he lights a torch and discovers her rotting body crawling with maggots. He flees to the land of the living and bathes in the sea to purify himself. The message of the contaminating influence of the dead is clear: Shinto regards death as the ultimate impurity. For this reason, Shinto priests will not officiate at funerals, which means that most funerals in Japan are Buddhist, whatever the beliefs of the deceased.

THE GODS WILL DIE

THE END OF THE WORLD AS WE KNOW IT

A sense of doom runs through the Norse mythology of the Vikings, for everything in it leads up to one calamitous moment, in which two gods—Odin, the all-father, and the trickster, Loki—bring an age-old conflict between the gods and the giants to its terrifying conclusion. This is Ragnarok, the final battle, in which gods will die and the world will be utterly destroyed.

As punishment for having duped Odin's blind son, Hoder, into slaying his brother, Baldr, the shining prince of goodness, Loki was chained to three rocks for eternity. As he struggles to

---

Catastrophe and **violence** will signal the **beginning of the end**.

↓

The **barrier** between the worlds of the living and the dead **will be breached**.

↓

In a **mighty conflict**, the **gods** themselves **will die**.

↓

In the twilight of the gods, the **whole world** will be **destroyed**.

↓

But a **new world** will arise, with **new hope** for humanity.

See also: Making sense of the world 20–23 ▪ The battle between good and evil 60–65 ▪ Beliefs that mirror society 80–81 ▪ Entering into the faith 224–27 ▪ Awaiting the Day of Judgment 312–13

The gigantic wolf Fenrir, here swallowing Odin, was the offspring of Loki's liaison with a female *jötunn*, one of a race of giants at war with the gods.

free himself, the world will shake; trees will be uprooted, and mountains will fall. Loki will begin to regain his strength, and nature itself will start to go awry: a series of terrible winters, with snow, frost, and biting winds, will soon become constant, with no summer at all. There will be battles everywhere, brother fighting against brother, father against son, until the whole world is ruined. When the chained

god finally breaks free, the sky will split open, Loki's monstrous wolf-son Fenrir will swallow the sun, and Loki will lead an army of giants, monsters, and the dead from the underworld, in a ship made from the uncut fingernails of the dead.

Odin's army retaliates

Odin is the god of poetry and magic, but he is also the god of war and battle, and it is from the slain of the battlefield that he assembles his army of dead warriors, the Einherjar, to fight against Loki's underworld horde.

Norse mythology is quite clear, however, that even with this mighty army, the gods are destined to be defeated and destroyed in this conflict. Odin's son, the mighty god Thor, will be killed by the huge serpent Jörmungandr, and Odin will be devoured by Fenrir. Thor's brother Vidar will step forward and rip Fenrir in two by the jawbones, but it will not be enough to save either Odin or creation. The whole world will be destroyed by fire, and will subside beneath the sea.

Yet from this destruction a new world will be born, as a new land rises from the sea. One man and one woman, Lifthrasir and Lif, will survive the destruction. From them a new race of humans will be born. As for the gods, Odin's sons Vidar and Vali, and Thor's sons Modi and Magni, will be the only survivors of the battle. They will be joined by the slain Baldr the beautiful and his blind brother Hoder, who were tricked by Loki—both freed at last from the underworld. ▪

The sun turns black, earth sinks into the sea, the bright stars vanish from the sky.
The Eddas

The Viking heaven

Vikings who died of natural causes faced the dismal prospect of Hel, the cold, damp realm of the dead. Only Vikings chosen to die in battle by Odin's valkyries (a race of warlike, supernatural females), or those selected for sacrifice, could cross the rainbow bridge to Asgard, home of the gods. Half of those who had died in battle belonged to the goddess Freyja and went to the meadow, Fólkvangr, to be seated in her hall. Women who died heroic deaths may also have

been eligible. The other half of slain warriors belonged to Odin, and they spent the afterlife in Valhalla, the hall of the slain, roofed with shields. There they fought each other all day, but arose unhurt at night to feast on the meat of a magical boar and drink the mead milked from a magical goat. This was to prepare them for the day when they would march from Valhalla to fight for the gods in the final battle of Ragnarok.

Fallen warriors were burned on a pyre, as decreed by Odin. Weapons, food, and tools were burned with them for use in the afterlife.

Vedic tradition
begins to develop
in India, with ritual
offerings made
to the gods.

Brahmanic ideas
emerge, based on the
concept of Brahman,
the supreme power.

Mahavira becomes
a major figure
in establishing
Jainism.

The poet **Valmiki**
writes the Sanskrit
epic the *Ramayana*.

1700 BCE   **6TH CENTURY BCE**   **6TH CENTURY BCE**   c.**500–100** BCE

1200–900 BCE   **6TH CENTURY BCE**   **6TH CENTURY BCE**

The **four Vedas** are
written. These are the
oldest Hindu scriptures
and most ancient
Sanskrit texts.

The first of the
Upanishads is
written, offering a
philosophical approach
to religion.

Siddhartha
Gautama, later
known as **Buddha**,
is born into a
Hindu family.

Although Hinduism could arguably be called the oldest of living religions, the term itself is a relatively modern one, which gives a misleading impression of a unified faith with a single set of beliefs and practices. Hinduism can trace its origins to the Iron Age, but it is in fact more a convenient umbrella term covering most of the indigenous religions of the Indian subcontinent. Although these religions share some characteristics, they vary greatly in practice and encompass a wide range of different traditions. In some of these traditions, the faith has remained substantially unchanged since the earliest times.

While more than three-quarters of the population of India identify themselves as "Hindu," today the definition of such a range of loosely connected faiths is as much sociopolitical as religious. The word "Hindu" (which shares its roots with the name of the River Indus, and of India) essentially means "Indian." It distinguishes the native religions from those introduced to the country, such as Islam, and newer breakaway religions such as Jainism and Buddhism.

The difficulty of defining Hinduism was summed up in an Indian High Court ruling in 1995: "… the Hindu religion does not claim any one prophet; it does not worship any one god; it does not subscribe to any one dogma; it does not believe in any one philosophic concept; it does not follow any one set of religious rites or performances; in fact, it does not appear to satisfy the narrow traditional features of any religion or creed. It may broadly be described as a way of life and nothing more."

Common beliefs
However, certain ideas have remained central to virtually all strands of Hinduism, in particular the notion of samsara (the cycle of birth and rebirth of the atman, the soul) and the associated belief in the possibility of moksha, or release from this endless cycle. The key to achieving moksha is encapsulated in the word dharma, which is variously translated as "virtue," "natural law," "right living," or simply "appropriateness."

Inevitably, this is subject to a number of interpretations, but three main ways of achieving moksha have emerged, collectively known as the *marga*. These are *jnana-marga*

The **Yoga Sutras**
—the key texts
of Yoga, a school of
Hindu philosophy—
are compiled.

Adi Shankara
establishes the
non-dualistic Advaita
Vedanta school of
Hindu philosophy.

Sri Ramakrishna
emerges as a leading
figure in the Hindu
reform movement.

Mahatma Gandhi
combines religion
and politics in his
peaceful opposition
to injustice and
discrimination.

2ND CENTURY BCE **788–820 CE** **1836–86** **1869–1948**

2ND CENTURY BCE **6TH CENTURY CE** **1526** **1788–1860**

The *Mahabharata*,
including the **Bhagavad-
Gita** ("Song of the Lord"),
offers role models
for Hindus.

Bhakti—a Hindu
movement with an
emphasis on personal
devotion—develops.

The Islamic
Mughal Empire is
founded, ruling
parts of India until
the arrival of the
British Raj in 1858.

The German
philosopher **Arthur
Schopenhauer** begins
to incorporate Indian
beliefs into his
Idealist philosophy.

(knowledge or insight), *karma-
marga* (appropriate action or right
behavior), and *bhakti-marga*
(devotion to the gods). The *marga*
allow scope for a very wide range
of religious practices to suit the
different traditions, including
a variety of rituals, meditation,
yoga, and everyday worship (puja).

Concepts of god

Virtually all branches of Hinduism
accept that there is a supreme
creator god, Brahma, who with
Vishnu (the preserver), and Shiva
(the destroyer) form a principal
trinity, the Trimurti. However,
many traditions have their own
pantheons, or add local and
personal deities to the mix.
Confusingly, even the three major
gods (and a lot of the minor ones)
often appear in different guises.

And so, while it may seem that
Hinduism is a polytheistic religion,
in many traditions, it is truer to say
that adherents have a belief in a
Lord God, who is complemented
by the many minor deities who
have special powers or carry
particular responsibilities.

Sacred texts

The different Hindu traditions
have all been shaped by the four
Vedas, a collection of ancient
texts composed between 1200
and 900 BCE. The Brahmanas,
commentaries on the Vedas, and
later the Upanishads, provided a
theoretical underpinning of the
religion, while other texts—notably
the two Indian epic poems, the
Mahabharata and the *Ramayana*—
expanded on history, mythology,
religion, and philosophy.

One of the main characteristics of
these Hindu traditions is tolerance.
As a consequence of invasion, first
by the Greeks under Alexander the
Great, and later by Muslims and
Christians, Hinduism has adapted
and accepted some influences.

However, while some reform
movements emerged as a result of
colonial influences, collectively
labeling these connected religions
as Hinduism gave them political
clout and a focus for nationalism.
This came to a head in the
struggle for Indian independence
in the 20th century, with Mohandas
Gandhi famously advocating the
Hindu weapons of nonviolent
resistance and civil disobedience,
and thereafter establishing an
independent India in which all
religions are not only tolerated
but embraced. ∎

THROUGH SACRIFICE WE MAINTAIN THE ORDER OF THE UNIVERSE

A RATIONAL WORLD

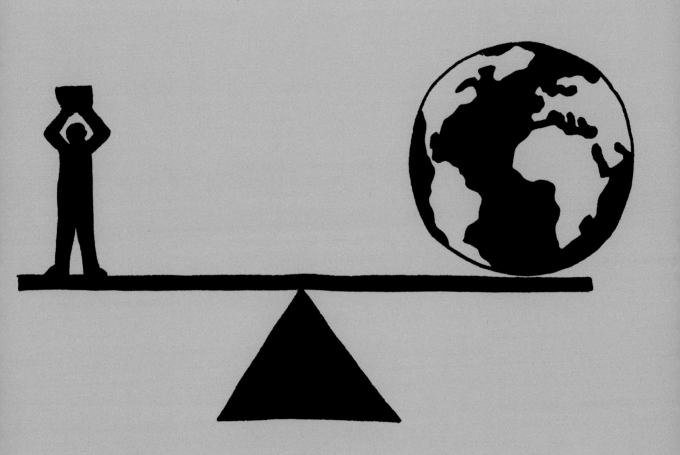

IN CONTEXT

KEY SOURCE
The Vedas

WHEN AND WHERE
1500–500 BCE

BEFORE
From prehistory Early beliefs regard events as unpredictable or at the whim of the gods.

1700 BCE Aryan races begin a migration into the Indian subcontinent.

AFTER
6th century BCE The authority of the Brahmin class to perform sacrifices is challenged by both Buddha and Mahavira, founder of the Jain movement.

6th century CE Devotional Hinduism, or bhakti, becomes popular; worshippers make their own offerings in order to develop a personal relationship with the gods, an idea very different from the establishing of order by Vedic sacrifice.

There is, strictly speaking, no single religion that can accurately be called "Hinduism"; this is a modern Western term for the different religions and spiritual philosophies that have originated within the Indian subcontinent. Nevertheless, there are some basic features of these religious ideas and practices that are shared by the majority of Hindus, and it is these ideas that are grouped together under the umbrella of Hinduism. In practice, individual Hindus are free to choose which deities they worship, whether they do so at home or at a temple, and how often they take part in religious activities. But they share a common social and religious background that sets Hinduism apart from other belief systems, especially the monotheistic faiths.

In the same way as other religions, however, Hinduism seeks to explain how human life fits into the universal context. Its rituals and practices aim to address three levels of relationship—person to the divine; person to person; and person to him or herself—and how all of these relate in turn to the universal order of all things.

The eternal cosmic order

Dharma, or "right way," is a key term for expressing what Hinduism is about. In its original form, *sanatana dharma*, it may be translated from Sanskrit as "the eternal order of things," truth, or reality. It expresses the idea that there is an underlying structure and meaning to the world; beneath the complexity and apparently random nature of events, there are some fundamental principles, and, underpinning these, a single, unchanging reality. These ideas are demonstrated in Hinduism in the hierarchy of gods and goddesses, each of whom expresses particular aspects of a single truth.

The idea of an eternal order also has implications both for the individual and for society. Religion is effectively a way of understanding the place of humanity in the world. If the world is capable of being understood, and if it has a definite hierarchy or structure, then, by following that order, a person can live in harmony with the rest of society and with the universe as a whole. A key feature of the forms of religion that came together as Hinduism was that, in following this

---

There is an **underlying, rational order** to the universe.

→

This sense of order is acknowledged when we **perform sacrifices to the gods**.

↓

Through sacrifice we maintain the order of the universe.

←

In the sacrifice, we **learn our place** in this order and **the right way to live**.

See also: Making sense of the world 20–23 ▪ Sacrifice and blood offerings 40–45 ▪ Man and the cosmos 48–49
▪ Beliefs for new societies 56–57 ▪ The ultimate reality 102–105

> Hinduism is not just a
> faith. It is the union of
> reason and intuition that
> cannot be defined but is
> only to be experienced.
> **Radhakrishnan, *The
> Bhagavad-Gita***

order, or dharma, a person may
be required to perform rituals and
make offerings to the gods (a form of
sacrifice) that are thought necessary
to maintain the sense of order.

Hindu ideas of time

Hindu thought sees time as cyclical,
with the universe already having
moved through three great cycles.
Each of these is said to have taken
millions of years; each coming
into being and then passing away.

Thinking of time as cyclical
has an important consequence for
religious thought. In the Western,
linear, concept of time it is possible
to think of everything as simply
the product of something else that
preceded it (the law of cause and
effect), and it is therefore natural to
wonder how the world began. This

By performing rituals in the
prescribed way, Hindus believe that
they are aligning themselves with
the rational ordering of the world and
becoming at one with it. The images
and actions are richly symbolic.

starting point is the only stage at
which linear theories of time require
some kind of input from outside the
world itself: something has to have
been responsible for setting the
great train of cause and effect in
motion at the beginning of time.

Conversely, in Hindu thought,
the ever-turning cycles of time
are contrasted with an eternal
and unchanging reality called
Brahman, which exists in and
through everything. Worldly time
runs in cycles, but Brahman is
timeless, the central force that keeps
the cycles moving; it is the eternal
reality that stands behind the
process of creation and destruction
that characterizes the world of
human experience.

If the great cycles of time are
utterly dependent upon a timeless
reality, then the right ordering of
this changing world depends on
awareness of that reality. This
logic gives rise to the idea that
one of the aims of religion is to
understand and maintain the
right ordering of the world.

Religious ritual and order

From perhaps as early as 1700 BCE,
and continuing over the next few
hundred years, there was a gradual
influx of Aryan people from Central
Asia into India. They brought
with them their pantheon of gods,
together with ideas that had
parallels with those of the Ancient
Greeks. The Aryans integrated
themselves into the Indus Valley
civilization of northern India, an
ancient society known to have had
its own religious traditions. There
is strong evidence to suggest ritual
bathing and worship of a great
mother goddess (p.100); other
artifacts found include cremation
urns and a seal depicting a horned,
cross-legged deity.

What took place was not a
sudden or overwhelming change,
but an intermingling of cultures.
In terms of religion, what emerged
was a tradition of sacrificial
worship and ritual that found
expression in the hymns of the first
great collection of Hindu sacred
literature, the Vedas. Within this »

> We concentrate our minds upon the most radiant light of the Sun god, who sustains the Earth, the Interspace and the Heavens.
> **Gayatri Mantra**
> **Rig-Veda**

new tradition, religious rituals and sacrifices were considered important, because they were thought to maintain the order of the cosmos. They also ensured that participants understood their place within that order and aligned themselves with it.

Sacrifice was the primary rite of the Vedic tradition. It was a symbolic reenactment of the creation of the world and invoked deities who represented either universal qualities, or different features of the one, true reality. It was through this worship that a human fulfilled the most important of human tasks: forging a link to the divine. The ritual sacrifice was believed not only to provide a connection to the invisible realm, but also to establish the right ordering of things. In exchange for the sacrifice, a human might obtain protection from evil forces and accrue worldly benefits—such as better crops, good weather, robust health, and increased happiness.

Sacrifice in this context simply meant making an offering to the gods, generally of food or drink.

Fire was an essential part of any sacrificial ritual; fire was thought to exist in both heaven and earth, and thus have a divine power that could reach the gods.

As the Vedic religion developed it became important that the sacrifices were performed by the right people (the Brahmin class) and in exactly the correct form. Details of the hymns to recite and actions to perform were carefully prescribed.

Sacrificial ground needed to be carefully prepared in a particular area as recommended by the ritualistic literature of the Vedas. The texts also specified the right wood needed to light the sacrificial fire, and the type of vessel required to hold the sacrificial offering (*huti*). Priests were expected to feed the sacrificial fire with offerings that might include ghee, cereal, fruit, or flowers, while chanting hymns from the Vedas.

The sacrifice also needed to be performed on an auspicious date. It might be an offering to a particular god or goddess, but especially favored were Agni, Varuna, and Indra. Agni is the god of fire; his most important role is to manifest as the fire that burns on the sacrificial altar, destroying any demons who may attempt to disrupt the sacrifice. Varuna, the god of the sky, water, and celestial ocean, is also the guardian of *rta*—the cosmic order. He is the most prominent god of the Rig-Veda (the ritual book of the Vedas), responsible for separating night and day. He is believed to have created the waters, to prevent the rivers and oceans from overflowing, and to sustain the universe. Indra, the god of thunder, rain, and war, is known for his indulgence in *soma*, a sacrificial drink (see below); securing his goodwill is considered essential—he is locked in an eternal struggle against the forces of chaos and nonexistence, and it is his efforts that separate and support heaven and earth.

Gods as aspects of order

As Hinduism developed, the Aryan gods of the Vedas were joined and in many cases superseded by others. Minor Vedic gods were also

The drink of the gods

The ritual drink *soma* appears in the Vedas and the sacred texts of Zoroastrianism, the ancient Persian religion, which, like Hinduism, has its roots in very early Aryan cultures. Produced by pressing the juice from certain plants, it had intoxicating, possibly stimulant and hallucinogenic properties. The Rig-Veda describes it as "King Soma," proclaiming: "We have drunk *soma* and become immortal: we have attained the light the Gods discovered." It was prepared by priests as an offering to the gods in order that its energizing properties might assist and inspire them, although it seems likely that the priests themselves also partook.

Fly agaric (*Amanita muscari*) or psilocybin mushrooms may have been the source of *soma*; both are common inducers of trance in shamanic rituals. Marijuana and ephedra have also been proposed, the latter for its highly stimulating effects, consistent with descriptions of the god Indra downing soma as a preparation for battle.

The dance of Shiva represents the cosmic cycles of creation and destruction, the balance between life and death. Shiva is the destroyer, but also the transformer.

elevated to much more prominent positions. Later Hindu literature contains a huge range of gods and goddesses, reflecting the blending of different traditions and different periods in the history of early Indian religion. From these gods there emerged a ruling triumvirate responsible for the existence, order, and destruction of the universe. These three gods—the Trimurti, or trinity—represent different aspects of reality: Brahma, the creator (not to be confused with Brahman); Vishnu, the protector and guardian of humanity; and Shiva, the destroyer, or, he who balances the forces of creation and destruction.

The god Shiva is often represented, in images and in sculpture, as Shiva Nataraja, the Lord of the Dance. Shiva's cosmic dance is shown as taking place within a circle of flames, which

You dwell in all beings; you are perfect, all pervading, all powerful and all seeing… You are the Life in all life, yet you are invisible to the human eye.
From a hymn to Vishnu

represents the ongoing process of birth and death. He has four arms: in his upper right hand he holds a drum, whose beat brings about creation, and in his upper left a destructive flame; his lower arms express a rhythmic balance between creation and destruction. His right foot is raised in the dance; his left treads on a demon, representing ignorance. This wild, exuberant figure symbolizes perfect balance in an ever-changing world. Given that time is cyclical, Shiva's destruction of the universe is seen as constructive, in that it paves the way for beneficial change.

The ordering of society
The classification of Indian society into four main groups has, since Vedic times, been based on the concept of dharma, extending the theory of the order and structure of the universe to include the correct ordering of human life and society.

Historically, it is probable that, with the invasion of the light-skinned Aryans, a contrast was established between them and the darker-skinned native inhabitants of India, with the latter being treated as inferior. This led to a social system of four main classes, or varnas, a word meaning "color."

However, in Hinduism, this historical explanation is overlaid by a mythological account of the origin of the class system. In the Rig Veda there is a hymn to the Divine Person (Purusha) in which the body of a primal human being is sacrificed and divided up to create the four main varnas or classes of people: Brahmin, Kshatriya, Vaishya, and Shudra. Brahmins are members of the priestly class, who are said to have been created from Purusha's mouth. Kshatriya is the military or administrative class, created from Purusha's arms, while »

According to Hindu tradition, the four varnas, or classes, were formed from the various body parts of Purusha, the primal man.

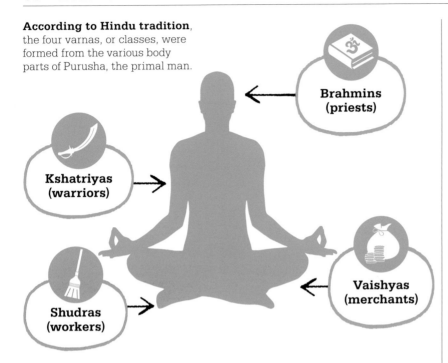

All living entities have different characteristics and duties that distinguish them from one another.
Bhavishya Purana

tradition to, literally, maintain the sense of order in the universe. By contrast, the caste system was discriminatory, emphasizing separation as being necessary in order to avoid "pollution": higher-caste people began to fear that they would be contaminated by contact with a low-status person. The caste system encouraged social fracturing, with rules forbidding people of different castes to mix together and especially to marry. This divisiveness was recognized in the Constitution of India, drawn up in 1948, which prohibited discrimination against lower castes, although popular prejudice has taken longer to eliminate.

Personal versus social
In the 6th century BCE, wandering teachers within India, such as Buddha and Mahavira, became critical of the formal and class-bound nature of Vedic worship. They welcomed followers from any class, and all were treated equally. These teachers argued for an emphasis on personal insight rather than inherited privilege. They also rejected the authority of the Vedas, and were therefore

Vaishyas are members of the merchant class, formed from Purusha's thighs. Shudra is the class of the common working people, hewn from Purusha's feet. Because they all come from the single human reality, Purusha, they are interdependent and all have an essential part to play in the ordering of society. Their roles reflect their dharma —their divine duty.

Members of the first three varnas are said to be twice-born in a sacred thread ritual, the *upanayana*, which marks the person's acceptance of responsibility as a Hindu. The ritual is generally performed when, or soon after, a child turns eight, and has the effect of establishing his or her social position. Below the four varnas are those who find themselves completely outside the class system; formerly called outcasts they are now generally referred to as Dalits, meaning "the oppressed."

Class distinctions
The four varnas are sometimes referred to as castes, but that is not strictly accurate. The Indian caste system is based on an equally ancient way of classifying people, broadly in terms of their occupation. There are a very large number of such classes, or *jati*, each with a corresponding social status. The two different approaches seem to have become entangled as Hindu society developed in the later Vedic period (from around 1000 BCE), and the crucial differences between them became blurred.

Under the varna system the different social classes are all essential to to the right ordering of the world; since everyone comes from a single primal human figure, Purusha, everyone depends upon one another. Only the Brahmins were portrayed as a superior class —understandably, given that in the Vedic literature they are the ones empowered and authorized by branded as unorthodox. But by around 500 BCE a definite shift in the way religion was viewed throughout Hindu society had taken place. Rather than being seen as a means of maintaining order, it now seemed to offer a way to escape the bondage of physical life by achieving a purely spiritual existence. Seeking liberation from, rather than alignment with, the established order became paramount. And in the centuries that followed, the Hindu tradition embraced the idea of personal devotion as a means of liberation, and worship became a matter more of personal engagement than simply the correct performance of sacrifice. Over time, personal forms of devotion and ritual developed, so much so that shrines became a common feature in people's homes, and a Brahmin was no longer required to enable acts of devotion to take place.

Religion and society

In the Vedic period, religion was focused primarily on the individual finding his or her place within the universe, and within society, and living in the way that had been

Not by birth is one an outcast; not by birth is one a Brahmin. By deed one becomes an outcast, by deed one becomes a Brahmin.
Buddha on the varnas

determined for that individual, according to the varnas; it had, therefore, both a personal and a social dimension, as well as an apparently rational system for prescribing how the personal and social interacted.

This early phase of Hinduism highlights an issue for all religion, namely whether it should be based mainly on the individual, or on society as a whole. Religions are embedded within society, and it is sometimes difficult to distinguish truly religious ideas from beliefs and attitudes that arise from the political or cultural milieu within which the religion developed. It is also the case that religious rules and traditions may be used by a ruling elite to maintain their own position.

Even posing the question of whether religion should focus on the individual or society is problematic, for it implies that a personal experience of religion is more valid than the social. ■

The concept of varna may need redefining in order to be workable in 21st-century India where newly defined roles and nontraditional careers challenge existing hierarchies.

The sacred literature of Hinduism

Hindu scriptures fall into two categories, distinguished by the names *sruti* and *smriti*. The term *sruti*, which means "that which is heard," is used to describe Vedic literature, which was heard by priests and scholars through the process of revelation, or of the realization of undoubted truth. This canonical knowledge was then passed down via the oral tradition from one generation of Brahmins to the next.

There are four collections of Vedic hymns, composed over a period of 1,000 years. The first, thought to date back to 1200 BCE, is the Rig-Veda. Associated with these, and also *sruti*, are the Brahmanas, which provide instructions about the performance of ritual; the Aranyakas, which outline discussions on meditation and ritual; and the Upanishads, which provide philosophical interpretations. Vedic *sruti* literature is the ultimate authority for Hindus.

The term *smriti*, which translates as "that which is remembered" is used to describe the remaining Hindu literature, notably the great epic poems, the *Mahabharata* and the *Ramayana*. While not having the same status as *sruti*, because they are not thought to be divinely inspired, these texts are nonetheless important because they are open to interpretation. This significant strand of Indian literature is still hugely influential and includes the Bhagavad-Gita, probably the most popular of all Hindu scriptures.

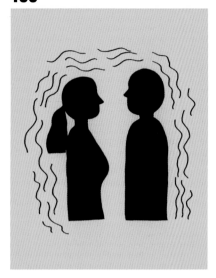

THE DIVINE HAS A FEMALE ASPECT

THE POWER OF THE GREAT GODDESS

IN CONTEXT

KEY TEXTS
The Vedas

WHEN AND WHERE
From 1700 BCE, India

BEFORE
3000 BCE Figurines dating to this time found in the Indus Valley suggest the worship of a fertility goddess.

AFTER
5th–3rd century BCE The Puranas, ancient Hindu texts, celebrate female power, and the goddesses described as consorts of the gods in the Vedas begin to gain their own followings.

300–700 CE Tantric rites use images of coupled male and female deities as a focus for meditation, and Shaktism becomes a fully fledged devotional branch of Hinduism.

c.800 CE Adi Shankara composes Saundaryalahari ("Waves of Beauty"), a hymn to Parvati and her sexual power.

While in many faiths the image of the divine has been mainly masculine, Hinduism has many goddesses, who represent creativity, fertility, or power. The general term for the feminine divine force is Shakti, which means "to be able." Shakti is personified in Maha Devi, the divine mother or "great goddess." She represents the active power of the divine, as well as its nurturing force, and in the Hindu school of Shaktism she is worshipped as the supreme deity. The great goddess takes on many different forms, each expressing particular qualities. In her aspect as consort to Shiva, for example, Shakti may appear as gentle, loving Parvati, but she is also Kali and Durga—terrible and threatening.

The coiled serpent

As well as being the creative power of the divine, Shakti represents the feminine element within the self. Hindus believe that our sexual energy and life force (kundalini) resides like a coiled serpent or

Lakshmi, goddess of good fortune, beauty, and fertility, is the consort of Lord Vishnu. She has four arms and hands, with which she dispenses material and spiritual gifts to devotees.

sleeping goddess at the base of the spine. Awareness and development of this force through yoga can be a form of spiritual release. Sometimes practiced physically, more often through meditation, these Tantric rituals are used to enhance the union between a person's male and female elements. ∎

See also: Physical and mental discipline 112–13 ∎ Devotion through puja 114–15 ∎ Buddhas and bodhisattvas 152–57 ∎ Shaktism 328

SIT UP CLOSE TO YOUR GURU
HIGHER LEVELS OF TEACHING

IN CONTEXT

KEY SOURCE
The Upanishads

WHEN AND WHERE
6th century BCE, India

BEFORE
From 1200 BCE The Vedas
provide texts and instructions
for rituals used exclusively
by the brahmins, or priests.

AFTER
6th century BCE In India,
traveling teachers, among
them Buddha and Mahavira,
attract their own disciples.

From 1st century BCE Six
distinct schools of Hindu
philosophy, known as the
Darshanas, develop.

800 CE Adi Shankara founds
four famous *mathas*, or
monastery schools, to teach
the ideas of the Upanishads.

1500 CE Sikhism takes its
name from the Sanskrit word
shishya, "student of the guru."

I s it realistic to offer the same religious teachings and truths to everyone? In Hinduism there are different levels at which the religion can be understood and followed. Its earliest texts, the Vedas, and the commentaries on them that followed, provided the texts, prayers, and instructions for the performance of sacrifices and other public acts of worship. Later, the epic, often action-packed stories of the gods, the *Ramayana* and the *Mahabharata* (p.111), were used for popular devotion. But by the 6th century BCE, another body of literature—the Upanishads —had developed, offering access for the initiated to a higher plane of spiritual knowledge.

Difficult concepts
The word "Upanishad" means "to sit up close," and it applies to teachings that are restricted to those who are accepted for religious study by a guru, or teacher. The Upanishads focus on abstract concepts concerning the nature of the self and of the universe.

In particular, the texts argue that there is a single universal reality, Brahman, which can be known only by thought and the analysis of experience. The Upanishads thus added a highly philosophical dimension to Indian religious discussion. The idea of sitting up close to your guru implies that there are levels of teaching which, by probing religious ideas for truths that are universal and rational, can give new depth to conventional beliefs. ■

On Earth, those who achieve greatness achieve it through concentration.
The Upanishads

See also: The ultimate reality 102–105 ▪ The self as constantly changing 148–51 ▪ The Protestant Reformation 230–37 ▪ The Darshanas 328

BRAHMAN IS MY SELF WITHIN THE HEART

THE ULTIMATE REALITY

IN CONTEXT

KEY SOURCE
The Upanishads

WHEN AND WHERE
6th century BCE, India

BEFORE
From 2000 BCE The idea of a soul that can be separated from the body is present in some early Indo-European beliefs, but describes a spirit that carries the essence of the individual rather than a soul at one with an ultimate reality.

AFTER
c.400 BCE Indian philosophy influences ancient Greek thinkers. Plato posits a supreme being from which all other living beings derive.

1st century Buddhist sage Nagasena rejects the notion of a fixed self, following Buddha's teaching that all things exist in a state of flux.

The Upanishads are a series of philosophical texts, the earliest of which had been composed by the 6th century BCE. They record the highest level of teachings, reserved for the finely trained, meditative minds of Hindu sages or gurus. Their central concern is the nature of the self; in effect they argue that to understand the self is to understand everything.

Western philosophy has traditionally taken two positions on the nature of the self. For the school known as dualist, the self is nonphysical and distinct from the body. Whether it is called the soul or the mind, it is the thinking and feeling aspect of what we are—the

See also: Animism in early societies 24–25 ▪ Man and the cosmos 48–49 ▪ Seeing with pure consciousness 116–21
▪ Man as a manifestation of God 188 ▪ Mystical experience in Christianity 238 ▪ Sufism and the mystic tradition 282–83

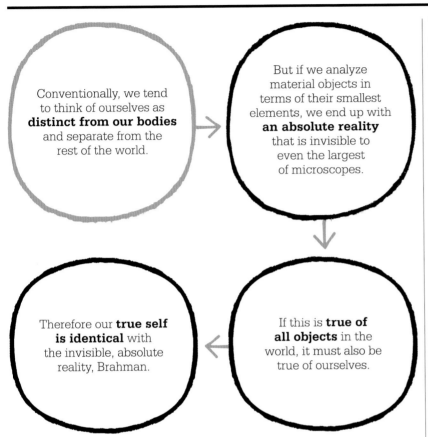

Conventionally, we tend to think of ourselves as **distinct from our bodies** and separate from the rest of the world.

But if we analyze material objects in terms of their smallest elements, we end up with **an absolute reality** that is invisible to even the largest of microscopes.

If this is **true of all objects** in the world, it must also be true of ourselves.

Therefore our **true self is identical** with the invisible, absolute reality, Brahman.

The sage then asks his son to divide one of those seeds, and describe what he sees inside that. The answer is "nothing." The sage then points out that the whole great fig tree is made of just such "nothingness." That is its essence, its soul, its reality. And, the dialogue concludes, "That is you, Svetaketu!"

The statement, "That is you!" (in Sanskrit, "*Tat tvam asi!*"), is probably the most famous in all Hindu philosophy. It rests on the idea that analysis of any apparently solid object will eventually arrive at an invisible essence, present everywhere, which is Brahman. This applies to everything, from a fig to the human self. Beyond the physical and mental aspects of the self, Hinduism says there is something greater, the atman, which can be nothing other than Brahman, the single, absolute reality. There is no distinction between us and this ultimate divine reality. »

"I" that experiences the world. It is this "I" that absorbs sensory data and makes sense of it. Materialists (or physicalists), on the other hand, argue that only physical things exist, therefore the self is no more than a way of describing the activity of the brain.

Within Hinduism, however, the Upanishads explored a view that differs from both of these Western approaches. In these texts, the self is described as having three parts: a material body; a more subtle body, which is made up of thoughts, feelings, and experiences; and a pure consciousness, called the atman. The atman, it is claimed, is identical with the absolute,

impersonal reality, Brahman. Therefore, although we may experience ourselves as separate, small, and vulnerable individuals, our true selves are actually at one with the fundamental reality of the universe.

The self as nothing

The Upanishads express the idea of atman by way of dialogues and images. One of the most famous is from the Chandogya Upanishad. It is a dialogue between the sage Uddalaka Aruni and his son, Svetaketu. The sage asks the boy to bring and cut open a fig. When his father asks him what he sees inside it, the son replies, "Seeds."

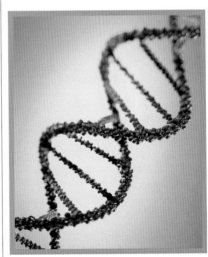

Microscopy has helped science to conclude that an entire human being is made from DNA—but does this include what we think of as our self?

An endless cycle of lives is what lies before us, unless we can be released from the suffering of reincarnation through the realization of the true nature of atman or Brahman.

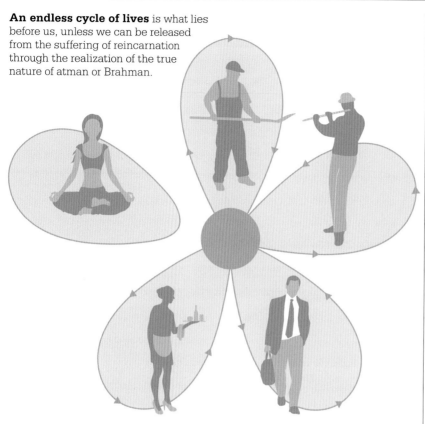

> All this is Brahman…
> He is my Self
> within the heart,
> smaller than
> a corn of rice…
> **Chandogya Upanishad
> 14th Khanda**

Understanding Brahman

The Upanishad dialogue about the fig seed is followed by a second, which attempts to give us some sense of what Brahman might be like. A bowl of water is brought and the son is asked to taste the liquid from different parts of the bowl. It tastes pure throughout. Salt is then dissolved in the water. Now, although the appearance remains the same, all of the water tastes of salt. In the same way, Brahman, the absolute reality, is unseen but present everywhere.

The Mundaka Upanishad uses a different image for Brahman. Just as thousands of sparks fly from a large fire and then fall back into it, so innumerable beings are created from Brahman, "the imperishable," or "Great One," which is described as unborn, breathless, mindless,
and pure—but bringing forth breath, mind, and all the senses. "Its heart is the whole world. Truly, this is the Inner Self of all."

In this understanding, the way we experience the world through the senses, viewing it as consisting of objects separate from ourselves, is not the absolute truth; there is a reality that underlies and sustains everything, which is invisible and within our innermost self.

Karma and reincarnation

In the earlier Vedic religion, it was believed that the act of offering sacrifices to the gods maintained the sense of order in the universe. The Upanishads internalized that process. They claimed that reality is to be found as an absolutely simple, still point, deep within the self. And that reality is universal,
not individual. Just as making a sacrifice in the correct way was thought to align the self with the universal order, so being aware of Brahman as the true self is to align yourself with reality itself.

Hindus believe that karma (actions) produce consequences —both good and bad—not just in the external world, but also for the person who performs them. Hinduism developed an idea of reincarnation in which the self takes on a succession of bodies over the course of many lifetimes. The form each life takes is determined by karma from the previous life. However, knowledge that "atman is Brahman" can release a person from the constant cycle of birth, death, and rebirth (which is known as samsara). Karma is generated by the actions of the physical body and the subtle mental body (such as an individual's thoughts and feelings), but the person who is aware of the atman, and therefore of Brahman, residing deep within the self, will transcend the level of the two bodies (physical and subtle mental) at which karma operates.

> When many candles
> are kindled from another,
> it is the same flame
> that burns in all candles;
> even so, the one Brahman
> appears to be many.
> **Sage Vasishtha**

Although Hindus hope that, by generating good karma, they will improve their prospects in future lives, there is always the threat that bad karma will lead to them being reborn into a lower caste, or as an animal. However, this is not as important as it first appears, because moving on to another life (good or bad) is not viewed as a final goal in Hinduism. Unlike in monotheistic religions, in which the prospect of life beyond death is a promise to be welcomed, in Hinduism the aim is to be released from the suffering that inevitably arises from living and dying in one life after another.

A conscious intuition

The arguments presented by the Chandogya Upanishad's stories about the fig seeds and the salt water are logical. In a sense, they are no more than scientific analysis of matter, but presented in the language of a prescientific age. Today, the equivalent would be to say that everything is comprised of subatomic particles, energy, and the fundamental forces.

However, the purpose and implication of the Upanishadic dialogues and modern science are quite different. In the Upanishads, reasoned argument is not an end in itself, but a means of leading a person to an intuition that goes beyond words. The logic of the argument for the identity of atman and Brahman represents no more than the starting point for understanding them. The aim of the Upanishads' teachings is to encourage students to internalize and meditate on the arguments until the reality that they suggest is directly experienced—in a way that goes beyond reason and language. This wordless awareness is said to produce a state of bliss (*ananda*).

It could be argued that a self formed by sense experience and reason alone would suffice for the purposes of a human life. This was challenged by the sages who produced the dialogues of the Upanishads. The Katha Upanishad uses a chariot as an analogy of the self. The senses are the chariot's horses and the mind is its driver. But riding in the chariot is the atman. The implication of this image is that, for someone whose whole awareness is limited to reason and sense experience, the onward rush of the chariot is without purpose, since it lacks a passenger who is making the journey. That is what the intuition of the atman restores.

Hinduism does not see gaining consciousness of the atman as easy. It can occur only after other possible identities have been examined and discarded as inadequate. It is not a fact to be learned, but an intuition that can gradually inform a person's conscious awareness. ∎

Death and beyond

If the self, or soul, is nonphysical and therefore separable from the physical body, the possibility of surviving death and living on in another form becomes logically possible. Most Western religions see each individual soul as being created at a particular point in time, but capable of living on indefinitely following the death of the body. Hindu thought sees the self as timeless, having no beginning, and identified with the single, undifferentiated reality. This self takes on physical form in a succession of lives, which is the idea of reincarnation. For Western monotheistic religions, the issue is whether the soul is genuinely separable from the body, and how, if separated, it might maintain its identity. For Hindus, the issue is to intuitively grasp that this self and this life are only a part of something much larger, and that the self is one with the fundamental reality of the universe.

> Concealed in the heart
> of all beings is the
> Atman, the Spirit,
> the Self; smaller than the
> smallest atom, greater
> than the vast spaces.
> **Katha Upanishad**

WE LEARN, WE LIVE, WE WITHDRAW, WE DETACH

THE FOUR STAGES OF LIFE

IN CONTEXT

KEY TEXT
The Dharma-shastras

WHEN AND WHERE
5th century BCE, India

BEFORE
From prehistory Many early belief systems have age-related rules and rites of passage.

From 1700 BCE The Vedic religion includes a tradition of ascetic discipline, but emphasizes social duty as the central goal for most people.

6th century BCE As ideas about reincarnation and liberation become more prominent in Hinduism; more people reject society and family life and choose the path of the ascetic.

AFTER
Today The majority of Hindus remain for most of their lives in the householder stage.

Implicit in all religions is the notion that there are aims in life, and correct ways of living that might secure these aims. Hinduism proposes that life has several main goals: *dharma* (right living); the linked concepts of *artha* (wealth) and *kama* (pleasure); and *moksha* (liberation). The pursuit of dharma—living as duty obliges —keeps a person on the righteous path. The search for wealth and pleasure leads people to learn valuable lessons, as well as producing children, supporting the family, and being in a position to give alms. The final goal, moksha, is a liberation from the concerns and things of the earthly world.

See also: ▪ Self-denial leads to spiritual liberation 68–71 ▪ A rational world 92–99 ▪ Selfless action 110–11 ▪ Finding the Middle Way 130–136 ▪ The purpose of monastic vows 145

The Four Stages of Life

We learn → In the first stage of life, students are expected to **study the Vedas** under instruction from a guru.

↓

We live → As a householder, a man is expected to **marry, have children, and work** to support family and others in society.

↓

We withdraw → With the birth of a grandchild, some may **retire from active work** and take time to reflect and advise.

↓

We detach → A few men may take the final step of becoming a **wandering ascetic**.

By the 6th century BCE two very different traditions in Indian religion existed. Most people in India followed the Vedic tradition, offering sacrifices to the gods and hoping for a life of wealth and pleasure, moderated by the moral and social principles encoded in dharma. However, others had become attracted to a different lifestyle—that of the wandering ascetic, committed to serious physical and mental discipline in order to achieve spiritual liberation, and shunning both wealth and pleasure. This ascetic tradition, known as *shramana* (a Sanskrit word that translates as something like "to work at austerity") was very influential in the development of both Buddhism and Jainism. The Dharma Sutras—sacred texts on the rules of correct behavior—suggested that a person who had studied dharma (virtue or right living) was essentially faced with three possible paths: the continued study of the Vedic texts as the principal goal in life; a life seeking wealth and pleasure; or the renunciation of everything in order to become an ascetic. The last choice was not an uncommon one in Hindu society at this time; the most famous example is that of Buddha, who abandoned his privileged life as Prince Siddhartha Gautama, leaving his wife and baby son in order to become a wandering teacher.

However, the position of the followers of the *shramana* tradition—that asceticism was more spiritually valuable than the seeking of *artha* (wealth) and *kama* (pleasure)—placed them in opposition to Vedic tradition. For around a thousand years, the Vedas had been used to teach that seeking material comfort and personal fulfillment were noble goals in life, if correctly pursued. So, was it necessary to choose between such radically different paths? Or might it be possible for a person to enjoy the benefits of all four traditional goals?

Having it all

In about the 5th century BCE, further commentaries on dharma known as shastras offered a new approach: instead of making one final choice, a person might work »

Of Brahmins, Kshatriyas and Vaishyas, as also the Shudras, O Arjuna, the duties are distributed according to the qualities born of their own natures.
The Bhagavad-Gita

> When one renounces all the desires which have arisen in the mind…and when he himself is content within his own self, then is he called a man of steadfast wisdom.
> **The Bhagavad-Gita**

toward different goals in succession, as they moved through four stages of life, or *ashramas*: student, house-holder, retiree, and renunciate, or ascetic. The correct aims in life, and correct behavior, would not only depend on the individual's varna, or social class (pp.92–99), but would also vary with the stage reached in life.

Not everyone is thought able to travel through these four stages. Women are (usually) excluded, as are Shudras (the laboring class) and those outside the class system (Dalits, or untouchables). Only men from the highest three varnas— Brahmins (priests), Kshatriyas (soldiers or protectors of the state), and Vaishyas (merchants and farmers)—undergo the rite, in which they are about eight years old, known as the sacred thread ceremony, where they are "twice born," and begin their journey through life.

Learning and living
The first stage of life is that of the *brahmacharya*, or student. The boy attends a *gurukula* (a school) where he studies Vedic literature with a guru, or teacher. He learns about dharma—right living—in an academic way, together with history, philosophy, law, literature, grammar, and rhetoric. Education traditionally continues until the age of around 25 or 30, and during this stage, as well as showing respect to parents and teachers, students are expected to abstain from sexual activity, sublimating all their energy into their learning.

At the end of his education, a Hindu man is expected to marry and have a family. This is the start of the *grihastha,* or householder, stage, during which every man is expected to be economically active, supporting not just his wife and children, but also elderly relatives. Traditional Indian households often include three or four generations who pool their income and use a single kitchen. This extended family tends to be organized on hierarchical lines, both for men and women. Householders are also expected to offer support to ascetics.

The householder upholds the duties of his dharma and his varna (class), but, unlike in the other three stages, part of his duty is the pursuit of *artha* (wealth) and *kama* (desire), including sexual pleasure and procreation. To describe this stage of life as one in which wealth and pleasure are the primary goals, however, may give a distorted view of its obligations, for it involves caring for the extended family and offering hospitality.

Withdrawal from the world
The third stage of life of is that of *vanaprastha*—retirement. This traditionally begins with the arrival of the first grandson. Originally, it involved becoming a "forest dweller," opting for a simple life of reflection into which a man could retire with his wife—although, at this stage, ceasing to have sex.

Today it is generally a matter of letting go of overall responsibility for business and financial matters, allowing the next generation to take over, but also having time to study and offer wise advice.

Most Hindus never get beyond the retirement stage to reach that of the ascetic; they are only allowed to enter the fourth stage of life once they have fulfilled all their obligations to their family. This is the point at which the individual sets aside all worldly concerns and ties, and devotes his life to the pursuit of final release (moksha).

A combined formula
The four stages of life combine with a person's class in a single concept that defines morality and lifestyle: *varnashrama-dharma*, literally the right ordering of life (dharma) according to one's class (varna) and stage in life (*ashrama*). As a formula for prescribing how to live correctly, it is very different to those of other religions, where one

A man measures fabric in his place of business. During the householder phase of life a man is expected to pursue wealth and provide for his family and for his extended family.

The various spiritual obligations of Hinduism could seem difficult to fulfill in one lifetime. However, by delineating four separate life phases, each with a different focus and with specific duties to perform for a limited period, the task seems more achievable.

set of moral commands applies equally to all. It is a moral system that recognizes flexibility and difference in people's circumstances. It also aims to prevent pride in those of the higher classes, who must undergo a disciplined education in order to develop self-detachment and prepare them, mentally, to relinquish their worldly gains and responsibilities in later life. It confers value on the labors of the householder, recognizing that, both economically and practically, those in the second stage of life support everybody else. And it gives dignity to the elderly, with the final letting go of practical and domestic responsibilities seen as a positive opportunity for spiritual growth.

In the modern world

Until very recent times, the extended family has been the dominant model throughout Hindu society, forming the background against which men lived out the four stages, with their moral and spiritual principles. In this traditional scenario, women do not feature in the first or last stages of a man's life, and marriage is considered to be a contract between families, rather than a matter of romantic attachment. If a new wife is to be introduced to an extended family home, it is clearly problematic if she is not well suited to the man in terms of dharma, varna, or his *ashrama*. This explains the origins of certain Hindu social attitudes and traditions—for example, the arranged marriage—but many of these now clash with the outlook of some Hindus brought up in a more individualized and secular society.

Hinduism is to a large degree more about practice than belief, and it is closely bound up with ideas about age and class. Western concepts of individual rights and equality do not sit easily alongside some of the early Hindu teachings, and with the Westernization of attitudes, greater social mobility in modern India, and the practice of Hinduism in communities globally, it remains to be seen whether the the four stages will remain a viable model for Hindu life. ■

Moral principles

Hinduism has five broad moral principles: *ahimsa* (not killing), *satya* (speaking the truth), *asteya* (not stealing), *brahmacharya* (sexual continence), and *aparigraha* (not being avaricious). The way each of these is practiced depends on the stage of life. For instance, celibacy will not be practiced by householders, whose duty it is to have children. These principles define external morality, but there is also a tradition of inner cultivation to practice during all stages of life, which involves the pursuit of five qualities: cleanliness, contentment, pure concentration, group study, and devotion to God. The five qualities reflect the progression from the early Vedic tradition, based on ritual, to a religion of personal spiritual development and devotion, which developed many centuries later.

IT MAY BE YOUR DUTY TO KILL
SELFLESS ACTION

IN CONTEXT

KEY SOURCE
The Bhagavad-Gita

WHEN AND WHERE
2nd century BCE, India

BEFORE
From 1700 BCE Dharma—the right way of living to preserve universal order—is a central feature of early Hindu thought.

6th century BCE Buddha upholds the concept of unselfish action, but teaches that all killing is wrong.

3rd century BCE The Indian emperor Asoka incorporates nonviolence and compassion toward all people into his rule.

AFTER
From 15th century Sikhism includes the duty to protect the weak and defend the faith.

19th–20th century Mahatma Gandhi develops the strategy of passive resistance as a nonviolent weapon against injustice.

The Bhagavad-Gita is an ancient Hindu scripture about virtue and duty. It tells of a dialogue between Krishna (an incarnation of the supreme god Vishnu) and the warrior-prince Arjuna. Arjuna is about to go into battle against another branch of his family in a dispute over who should rule the kingdom. As a member of the *kshatriya* class (the military or ruling elite), it is his duty is to fight. Yet he despairs of killing some of those on the other side—his relatives or those whom he respects as great teachers.

In the opening section of the Gita, Arjuna says that he would rather give up the struggle over the kingdom than be involved in the slaughter. Not only does the idea of killing members of his family and his teachers go against his deepest inclinations, but he also fears that it will have negative consequences, creating bad karma for all involved (in Hinduism, killing a relative is thought to lead to the downfall of a family and rebirth in hell).

Arjuna is caught between two apparently conflicting principles: should he do his duty as a member of the warrior class or avoid the disastrous karmic consequences of killing? Advice comes from his charioteer, who turns out to be none other than the god Krishna.

Krishna tells Arjuna that he should do his duty and fight. The act of killing would only create bad karma if it was done for the wrong reasons—out of hatred or greed, for example. The ideal is for the individual to do his or her duty, whatever it is and however much it goes against personal inclinations, but to do it with selfless motives. Not only will such action not cause harm, but it will be a step toward personal liberation.

Krishna argues that personal motives are what count when considering any type of action.

By fulfilling the obligations he is born with, a person never comes to grief.
Krishna

See also: Living in harmony 38 ▪ A rational world 92–99 ▪ Hinduism in the political age 124–25 ▪ Let kindness and compassion rule 146–47 ▪ Striving in the way of God 278 ▪ The Sikh code of conduct 296–301

Arjuna

I despair at the thought of going to war.

I do not wish to kill those I love and respect.

I grieve that my kindred and teachers will die.

But if I kill will I not have sinned?

Krishna reassures Arjuna that killing is the duty of a righteous warrior in a just war.

Krishna

You are a prince: it is your duty to fight.

Your feelings are immaterial; put them aside and do your duty.

The self is immortal and eternal, so it is wrong to think that anyone will die.

It is only by forgoing your duty to fight in a just war that you would sin.

He applauds the willingness to act dutifully out of selfless motives, setting aside any selfish preferences. Krishna then gives Arjuna a second reason for going into battle: the self is immortal and passes through a succession of incarnations, so no one is really killed. Only the body dies; the soul will live again in a different body.

A context of change

When the Gita was composed, there were two very different streams of religious thought in India. The older of the two, dating from the early Vedic period, promoted social order and duty as the basis of morality. However, it had been challenged by newer philosophies—particularly the Buddhist and Jain religions—in which *not killing* was the first precept and foundation of morality. This represented a departure from the Vedic class system and its traditional obligations. Arjuna's dilemma reflects that clash of moral priorities, and Krishna's advice is an attempt to maintain class obligations in the face of criticism from philosophies centered on the idea of karma and reincarnation. ▪

The epic poems

The teaching on selfless duty is just one of the themes to be found in the Bhagavad-Gita, a work noted for the beauty of its imagery and language. It is part of the *Mahabharata*, an epic poem that chronicles the rivalry between two branches of one family.

The other great Hindu epic is the *Ramayana*, which tells of the relationship between Prince Rama and his wife Sita, through her kidnap by the demon Ravana. Its narrative, has a wonderful, much-loved cast of characters.

These epics offer a positive view of the brahmins and Vedic sacrifices, and highlight the dire consequences of royal rivalry. They explore moral dilemmas and celebrate human qualities, presenting role models for Hindus to follow. Both epics were created over a long period, probably starting in the 4th or 5th century BCE.

Ravana, the vengeful demon king and villain of the Ramayana, is played by a dancer in a production of the Ramayana in Kerala, Southern India.

THE PRACTICE OF YOGA LEADS TO SPIRITUAL LIBERATION
PHYSICAL AND MENTAL DISCIPLINE

IN CONTEXT

KEY TEXT
The Yoga Sutras

WHEN AND WHERE
2nd century BCE, India

BEFORE
Before 1700 BCE An Indus Valley clay tablet showing a person sitting cross-legged suggests a yoga posture.

1000 BCE Indian Ayurvedic medicine analyzes the body and promotes exercise.

6th century BCE Daoism and Buddhism promote mental and physical discipline as aids to harmony and insight.

AFTER
12th century In Japan, Zen Buddhism refines the pursuit of mental stillness and focused thinking.

20th century In the West, yoga becomes popular in a secular context for its physical and mental health benefits.

The Sanskrit word yoga is used to describe a range of practices, both physical and mental, which are used to help achieve spiritual insight and escape the limitations of the physical body.

Ideas about yoga are found in the 6th century BCE in the early philosophical Hindu texts known as the Upanishads, and there is a section on yoga in the ancient Sanskrit scripture, the Bhagavad-Gita. The first systematic account of yoga is found in the Yoga Sutras. Some scholars attribute this text to the philosopher Patanjali, who lived in the 2nd century BCE. However, it is now generally agreed that it was written between the 2nd century CE and the 4th century CE by more than one author, and that it includes traditions and practices from earlier periods. The Yoga Sutras comprise a set of techniques to promote mental calmness and concentration, which are deemed necessary for gaining greater insight.

Physical postures and breath control techniques are used in yoga to still both body and mind. More advanced techniques can lead to the attainment of higher consciousness.

Although originally devised for those who had taken an ascetic path, yoga was later developed as a set of practices that could be used by everybody. The physical postures and techniques for breath control are not an end in themselves. They aim to calm the mind and make it singular in its focus—single-pointed. The mind can only become calm once the senses have been controlled. It is only then that inner freedom and insight may arise.

A path to release
According to the Yoga Sutras, yoga enables the practitioner to avoid mental afflictions, such as

See also: Aligning the self with the *dao* 66–67 ▪ Seeing with pure consciousness 116–21 ▪ Zen insights that go beyond words 160–63

Both **body and mind must be calm and focused** to be freed from earthly concerns.

⬇

Body and mind **influence one another**.

⬇

Thoughts and feelings can affect our **physical well-being**. ⬌ Posture and control can promote **mental alertness**.

⬇

Combining both mental and physical discipline with yoga will **help us escape our limitations**.

ignorance, ego-centered views, and extremes of emotion. It also offers freedom from the "three poisons" of greed, anger, and delusion (a goal that Buddhism shares).

The Yoga Sutras set out the practice of yoga in eight steps. The first two are preparatory and show the context in which yoga becomes effective. First is the practice of a morality of restraint, particularly of ahimsa (not taking life). The second focuses on personal observances, such as the study of philosophical works and contemplation of a god in order to gain inspiration. The next three steps aim to control the body and senses: adopting physical postures (asanas) to control the body, controlling breathing, and withdrawing attention from the senses. Finally, there are three mental steps: concentrating the mind on a single object, meditating

on that object, and arriving at a state of absorbed concentration. These steps are progressive, leading to the final release from a mundane awareness of self and world, with its mental afflictions, into a higher consciousness.

Today, yoga is widely practiced as a healthful physical regime that also promotes inner calm. But it is important to remember that in the context of Hindu religion, the term yoga encompasses disciplines and practices not only of posture, but of morality, meditation, knowledge, and devotion, and that taken together, their aim is to release the true self or consciousness (*purusha*) from the entanglements of matter (*prakriti*), thereby restoring it to its natural condition. So, while many in the West think of yoga as a form of physical exercise, for Hindus it is a path to ultimate freedom. ▪

A godless philosophy

Yoga does not require belief in any external deity, but is a natural process of clearing away the entanglements of physical experience, releasing the true self to realize its identity with the absolute. But this makes sense only in the context of the philosophy upon which it is based—Samkhya.

One of the oldest schools of Indian philosophy, Samkhya argues for an absolute dualism of *prakriti* (matter) and *purusha* (pure consciousness). Some philosophies contrast the physical with the mental, but Samkhya sees the mind as a refined form of matter. A person therefore comprises three elements—a physical body, a worldly self (with all its mental activity and sense experience), and a pure and eternal self, which is identified with the eternal *purusha*, and is free and beyond any limitations of time and space.

In Samkhya, rather than devoting the self to any god, the aim is to release the self to appreciate its pure spiritual nature, freed from the limitations of the physical, and the vehicle that is used to achieve this is yoga.

Yoga is the practice of quieting the mind.
Patanjali

WE SPEAK TO THE GODS THROUGH DAILY RITUALS
DEVOTION THROUGH PUJA

IN CONTEXT

KEY MOVEMENT
The development of bhakti

WHEN AND WHERE
6th century CE, India

BEFORE
From prehistory Making offerings before images of deities characterizes worship in many cultures.

From 1700 BCE In Vedic religion, as in other early civilizations, a priestly class performs religious rites on behalf of the people.

6th century BCE The Upanishads introduce more abstract concepts to Hindu religious thought.

From 2nd century BCE In Mahayana Buddhism, images of buddhas and bodhisattvas (enlightened beings) are used as devotional aids.

AFTER
15th century Sikh worship is based on devotional songs.

There has always been an element of ritual and worship in Hindu religion. In the earliest traditions prescribed by the sacred Vedic texts, it was vital that sacrifices made at the sacred fires be performed in exactly the right way, and solely by the brahmins or priestly class. However, in the early centuries CE, the approach to worship became less exclusive, and this evolved into the practice of bhakti (loving devotion). Temples were built housing images of the gods, which could be visited by worshippers, and gradually, alongside the priestly rituals connected with birth, coming of age, marriage, and death, there developed a tradition of making personal acts of worship, or puja, to the deities that was open to all, irrespective of class.

Honoring the gods

Puja involves making a simple offering—vegetarian food, incense, or flowers—before the image of a god or goddess. It can take place in a temple or in the home, and the people performing it often mark their foreheads with powder or paste in acknowledgment of the act of puja and the blessing of

A devotee performs puja by offering food to the image of a deity, as if enticing it to eat. Images such as this are believed to be filled with the deity's spiritual energy.

the deity that results from it. At the end of an act of puja, worshippers may receive any food that has been offered. The nature of the offering is less important than the intention behind the offering. Sometimes it is enough simply to go to a temple and look at the image of the deity.

See also: Sacrifice and blood offerings 40–45 ▪ Living the Way of the Gods 82–85 ▪ The Protestant Reformation 230–37 ▪ Devotion to the Sweet Lord 322

The Vedas said that the **rituals** performed by brahmins were important to **maintain the world order**.

But it is possible to **speak to the gods directly**, without recourse to a priest.

We speak to the gods through daily rituals.

Through **devotion and offerings**, we can develop **personal relationships** with the gods.

Divine love

In worship, the god or goddess (made visible in his or her image, or murti) is seen as a person with whom the worshipper can have a relationship. Through bhakti, the devotee develops an intense emotional bond with a chosen deity; the divine is then seen as dwelling within the heart of the devotee. Bhakti came to dominate Hinduism by the 12th century: temple worship involved singing and dancing, and the relationship between the devotee and his or her god or goddess was likened to a relationship between lovers.

Although practiced widely, many forms of bhakti were particularly focused on the god Vishnu (see below left), who is depicted in the great epics of the *Ramayana* and *Mahabharata* as coming down to earth to help humankind in the guise of one of his many avatars (embodiments of a god). The eighth avatar of Vishnu is Krishna, whose followers see bhakti as the highest path toward liberation. ▪

Through puja, people can both pay respects to the gods and ask favors of them. Hindu gods are frequently referred to according to the tasks they perform, such as "Ganesh, remover of obstacles." This enables Hindus to choose the goddess or god most appropriate to the help they need, and to ask them for it through puja. However, puja is not always connected with personal requests and thanksgiving. It may be performed by a large gathering of people at a festival, such as the Durga Puja. This annual, nine-day celebration of the goddess Durga, who embodies the female aspect of divine power, commemorates her slaying of Mahishasura, the terrible buffalo-demon. Devotees make offerings, say prayers, sing hymns, dance, fast, and feast in her honor.

Vishnu's nine forms of worship

In the *Ramayana*, Vishnu, in the form of Rama, describes nine modes of bhakti "guaranteed to reach and please me." "First is *satsang*, or association with love-intoxicated devotees. The second is to develop a taste for hearing my nectarlike stories. The third is service to the guru. Fourth is to sing my communal chorus. Japa or repetition of my Holy name and chanting my bhajans are the fifth expression. To follow scriptural injunctions always, to practice control of the senses, nobility of character, and selfless service, these are expressions of the sixth mode of bhakti. Seeing me manifested everywhere in this world and worshipping my saints more than myself is the seventh. To find no fault with anyone and to be contented with one's lot is the eighth. Unreserved surrender with total faith in my strength is the ninth and highest stage."

With hearts filled with love…all should satisfy me frequently with tears of love flowing from their eyes and with voices choked with feelings and with dancing, music, and singing.
The Devi-Gita

THE WORLD IS AN ILLUSION

SEEING WITH PURE CONSCIOUSNESS

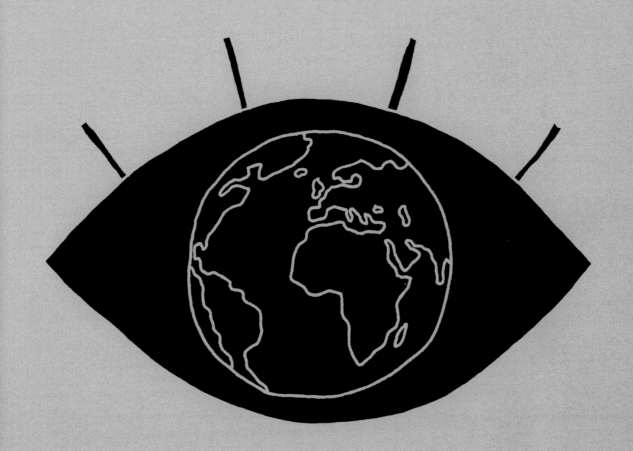

IN CONTEXT

KEY FIGURE
Adi Shankara

WHEN AND WHERE
788–820, India

BEFORE
6th century BCE The Upanishads describe Brahman as the ultimate reality.

4th century BCE The Greek philosopher Plato contrasts the objects of sense experience with reality itself; in some later Platonic thought, this ultimate reality becomes identified with a "transcendent One," or God.

2nd century CE Nagarjuna founds the Madhyamaka school of Buddhist philosophy, which is centered on the key idea of emptiness.

AFTER
13th century Soto Zen aims to go beyond awareness of the world of sense experience with the development of pure consciousness.

Through the work of the Indian philosopher Adi Shankara, a branch of Hindu philosophy known as Vedanta ("the end of the Vedas") developed in the 9th century. It sought to systematize and explain material found in the ancient scriptures of the Vedas, and to explore the nature of Brahman as discussed in the philosophical works, the Upanishads (the last section of the Vedas).

There are various branches of Vedanta, but the one established by Shankara is called Advaita (non-dualist) Vedanta. It states that there is only one reality, even if we may experience it in different ways. This non-dualist belief lies in contrast to later forms of Vedanta in which the deity assumes a personal role.

Shankara argued that human reason is limited to the objects of sense experience: that is, it is not possible to get outside or beyond the senses to see the world as it really is. Even within the world of experience it is possible to be mistaken, because all sensory knowledge is ambiguous. To use Shankara's example, a coil of rope may be mistaken for a snake, or vice versa. Further, a person may know it is possible to be fooled by what is seen, heard, or touched—but what if the whole enterprise of gathering information from the senses is itself a form of illusion?

An unknowable Brahman?

The Upanishads had taught that there is a single ultimate reality, Brahman, with which the innermost self, the atman, is identified. However, the problem is that Brahman is not an object of sense experience because it is not part of reality (as worldly objects are)—it is reality itself. Ordinary objects can be known because they are distinguished from one another by qualities that the senses can detect. Brahman, by contrast, because it has no physical attributes, cannot be grasped by rational interpretation of what is known through the senses.

So what should be made of the idea of a supreme being, or of the divinities used in religion? There appears to be a profound difference between what the Upanishads have to say in terms

---

Our **knowledge of the world** comes via the **senses**, so it is always liable to error.

We know Brahman—absolute reality— not through our senses but directly, as identical with the **atman, our inner self or soul**.

The world of our conventional knowledge is an illusion.

Absolute reality is not known through the senses.

See also: Higher levels of teaching 101 ▪ The personal quest for truth 144 ▪ The challenge of modernity 240–45 ▪ A faith open to all beliefs 321

> The problem for the Advaitin is to solve how from the pure Brahman the impure world of men and things came into existence.
> **T.M.P. Mahadevan**

> Brahman is real; the world is an illusory appearance; the so-called soul is Brahman itself, and no other.
> **Adi Shankara**

of philosophical argument and what is actually practiced in the Vedas, in terms of gods and goddesses that are addressed in worship. How, for example, can Brahman be both personal (knowable) and impersonal (unknowable) at the same time? How, if it is eternal and absolute, can it be described in any way?

Shankara's answer

Shankara attempts to answer these questions by making a distinction between *nirguna* Brahman (unqualified reality), known only through pure consciousness, and *saguna* Brahman (qualified reality), which is more like the traditional idea of a God who exists and acts in the world. Brahman remains the same reality, but can be known in different ways. One means of expressing this is to say that there

In Shankara's philosophy, human reason is limited to the information we gather with our senses; a different kind of knowledge, or understanding, is needed to grasp absolute reality.

is nothing in the world that is not Brahman—it is the basic reality; however, there is also nothing that is Brahman: there is no separable, knowable object that corresponds to the idea of Brahman. To explain this, Shankara offers the example of the sun shining down on a number of pots, all of which are filled with water: each pot offers its own particular reflection of the light of the sun, and yet there is still only

one sun. How then might Brahman be known? Shankara's answer lies in the identity of Brahman and the atman, the innermost self of pure consciousness. He states that Brahman cannot be known externally, via the senses, but can be known internally, because it is our innermost essence.

Consciousness and knowledge

Shankara proposes that there is a single reality, but two very different ways of understanding it. From the conventional and pragmatic standpoint, we have the world of sense experience, with all its variety. From an absolute standpoint, however, we need to recognize that the experienced world is unreal: it is an illusion. We can therefore only experience the ultimate reality, free from illusion, through an awareness that comes from pure consciousness.

It is possible that Shankara took this idea of the two levels of truth from Buddhism, in which a »

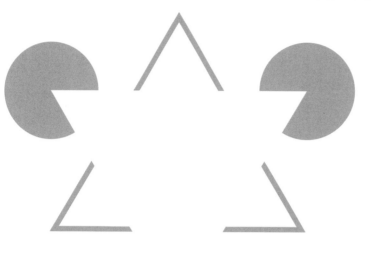

Shankara proposed that the world of the senses is an illusion and that we impose our ideas upon our environment, causing us, for example, to see things that may not be present.

This world is transitory. One who has taken birth in it is living as if in a dream.
Nirvana Upanishad

similar distinction was being made at this time between pragmatic and absolute truth. For both Hindu and Buddhist thought, this distinction represented a necessary step in bringing the fundamental philosophical ideas of religion together with actual practice. During the first millennium, religious practice had been moving increasingly toward devotion to various gods and goddesses (or, in the case of Buddhism, different bodhisattva images), each of which was regarded as reflecting a true aspect of reality. For both Hinduism and Buddhism, this was not an attempt to denigrate conventional religion, but to set it in a broader philosophical context.

Not quite an illusion

The most obvious way to describe Shankara's view of the world is that he regards it as an illusion (maya), although his claim is slightly more subtle than that. Shankara suggests there are two levels of reality, which are both false in some way: the apparent world (which we appear to see and touch around us), and the pragmatic world (which is a view of the world according to our own preconceived notions). While the apparent world is derived from our senses' interpretation, the pragmatic world is derived from our minds projecting outward, imposing our ideas upon our environment (such as organizing a spiky green shape into "a leaf"). However, both of these ideas of the world are incorrect since they are only our representations of the world. So we can say that the world of our experience is an illusion, but not that the world itself—beyond the knowledge given by the senses—is an illusion. The world of the senses is

maya (illusion). Shankara's philosophy is described as non-dualist because of this; there are not two different realities—the world and Brahman—but just one.

When a person becomes aware of the identity of atman (the true self) and Brahman (a single reality), there follows a recognition that the conventional self, as an object among other objects in the world, is partly an illusion. Enlightened awareness is a realization of what we have been all along—the atman of pure consciousness; and compared with this idea, the ever-changing and superficial physical body is relatively unreal.

The gods point the way

The distinction between *nirguna* and *saguna* Brahman (unqualified versus qualified reality), and the contrast between knowledge gained through sense experience, and understanding acquired through pure consciousness, are of fundamental importance—not just for an understanding of Hinduism, but for religion in general.

These distinctions suggest that there are two levels of religion. At a popular level there may be devotion to a chosen deity (as in the bhakti tradition), and the portrayal of gods and goddesses as having particular qualities or acting within the world. However, this devotion is no more than a preliminary step on the path toward knowledge and liberation. Liberation can only be achieved through the mental discipline required for a level of meditation that leads to insight. And that insight, for Shankara, is of a single reality; there is no separate world of the gods. This means that if there is only one reality that is knowable through inner consciousness, then no religious ceremonies are necessary; all a person needs to do is develop insight through the practice of meditation.

It is tempting to say that Shankara promotes philosophy rather than religion, but that would not be strictly true: the quest for an awareness of the unity of atman and Brahman requires disciplines of meditation that are more of a religious exercise than a philosophical questioning. The sort of self-control required for insight is not merely intellectual. Shankara's approach allows

The pure truth of Atman, which is buried under Maya […], can be reached by meditation, contemplation, and other spiritual disciplines such as a knower of Brahman may prescribe…
Adi Shankara

him to draw together two very different traditions into a single system: the religious ceremonies of the Vedas and the later commentaries on them; and the mental discipline of the ascetics, who saw themselves as beyond the stage of religious rituals.

Science and reality
Modern scientific theories are based on the premise that the universe is comprised of objects, structures, events, and sense experiences that are measurable and knowable. However, such theories—although considered by many to provide a reliable way to understand the world—often reflect only scientists' interpretation of the phenomena they examine and are always open to modification. The world of sense experience, for example, even when explored at the limits of scientific knowledge, is just an approximation of reality, measured through the tools available, as opposed to reality itself.

In addition, the scientific methods used in attempting to discover reality may actually interfere with and influence the nature of what is observed. For instance, the very act of observing and measuring an experiment at quantum level can significantly alter the outcome.

What science may perceive as truth or reality would, in Shankara's philosophy, still be considered an illusion, on the grounds that there are two completely different levels of truth, and that gods and scientific laws alike can only approximate to an ultimate reality beyond both reason and sense experience. Instead, pure consciousness can only be achieved by transcending illusion through meditation. ∎

Adi Shankara

Adi Shankara, the founder of the Advaita Vedanta tradition of Indian philosophy, was born in 788 into a Brahmin family in Kerala, and trained under a guru (teacher) from the age of seven. He later moved to Varanasi, where he gained his first followers, and then to Badrinatha, where, aged only 12, he is believed to have written a commentary on the *Brahma Sutras*.

Shankara became a guru and attracted many followers. He was also instrumental in a revival of Hinduism and establishing a number of monasteries. Shankara died at the age of 32. A number of works, mainly commentaries on the Upanishads, have been attributed to Shankara. His philosophy, which offered a systematic development of the Vedanta tradition in the Upanishads, remains a major contribution to Hindu doctrine.

Key works

8th century *The Brahma Sutra Bhaysa*
8th century *The Crest-Jewel of Discrimination*
8th century *A Thousand Teachings*

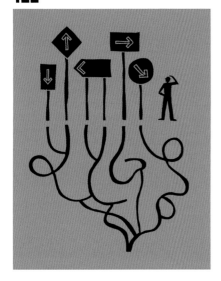

SO MANY FAITHS, SO MANY PATHS
GOD-CONSCIOUSNESS

IN CONTEXT

KEY FIGURE
Sri Ramakrishna

WHEN AND WHERE
19th century, India

BEFORE
From 3rd century BCE As Buddhism spreads, devotional images and practices diversify.

6th century The bhakti tradition in Hinduism accepts that the divine can be worshipped through any number of images.

15th century Guru Nanak, founder of Sikhism, opens his new religion to all who love one God, regardless of class and traditional faith distinctions.

AFTER
20th century Interfaith dialogue becomes common.

20th century A plethora of new religious movements offer a spiritual path open to all, irrespective of cultural and religious background.

Each **person on a spiritual quest** may worship a particular god or follow a particular path or religion.

But just as the different Hindu gods and goddesses all represent different aspects of Brahman, so **different religions** are all ways to **approach a single spiritual reality**.

It is better to allow each person to **follow their own religion** than try to convert them from one religion to another.

The idea that all religions lead to the same God was put forward by Sri Ramakrishna, a 19th-century mystic who practised bhakti (Hindu religious devotion) and followed the philosophy of Advaita Vedanta, as originally taught by Adi Shankara (p.121)—built around the notion of of a single underlying reality, Brahman, with which the self (atman) is identified. The starting point for Ramakrishna's thinking was the idea that, in meditation, a person comes to appreciate the divine within, and that, to whichever god or goddess they might be devoted, there is only one spiritual reality. Therefore, within Hinduism, each person is free to worship in his or her own way, while recognizing

See also: The ultimate reality 102–105 ▪ Class systems and faith 302–303 ▪ Cao Đài aims to unify all faiths 316 ▪ A faith open to all beliefs 321

We believe not only in universal toleration, but we accept all religions as true.
Swami Vivekananda

that ultimately there is only one "Holy Power" (Brahman). To Ramakrishna, this suggested that it might be possible to experience all religions in just this same, internal or personal way, and therefore all spiritual paths might eventually lead to the same goal.

An inner transformation

What Ramakrishna understood by this is illustrated by his claim that he became a Muslim for a short period. He immersed himself in the teachings of Islam and described the manner in which he performed Islamic prayers, so that, for a time, he felt he really possessed the Muslim faith, and did not even experience any desire to look at Hindu temple images.

The majority of Muslims would not consider this to be a valid experience of Islam, given that he did not engage with its cultural and social practices. However, for Ramakrishna, this entirely internal experience led him to conclude that any inner journey of self discovery will enable a person to identify with what Ramakrishna's disciple Vivekananda would later describe

as the "eternal ideal of the spiritual oneness of the whole universe." For Ramakrishna, if religion means a process of internal transformation, and if God represents the ultimate reality, it follows that, using whatever set of religious ideas are available, an individual can follow a path that is bound to converge with all others who are on a similar quest. Ramakrishna believed that an individual could encounter "the God within" through any religious tradition, and that this transcended any external, cultural, or doctrinal differences between religions. He therefore concluded that a truly religious person should think of all other religions as paths that all lead to the same truth. Rather than attempting to convert people from one religion to another, each person should be encouraged to follow his or her own religion, allowing a natural spiritual convergence to take place. ▪

An imam performs the Muslim call to prayer within the National Cathedral in Washington D.C. during an interfaith service attended by a joint Christian, Jewish, and Muslim congregation.

Sri Ramakrishna

Born Gadadhar Chatterjee into a poor brahmin family in Bengal in 1836, Ramakrishna became a priest in a temple dedicated to Kali just outside Calcutta, where he became well known as a charismatic figure. From an early age, he experienced religious trances, and saw the goddess Kali everywhere, as mother of the universe, even dancing before her image in an ecstatic state.

In 1866 a Hindu Sufi initiated Ramakrishna into Islam. He is said to have followed that faith for a few days, as well as possessing an image of Christ upon which he meditated.

His ideas were spread and given more systematic form by his disciple, Swami Vivekenanda (1836–1902), who emphasized that the Hindu religion was not a matter of trying to believe certain doctrines or philosophical propositions, but instead one of entering into an experience. Vivekananda presented these ideas to the World Parliament of Religions in 1893. He also established the Ramakrishna Movement to promote Sri Ramakrishna's work.

NONVIOLENCE IS THE WEAPON OF THE STRONG

HINDUISM IN THE POLITICAL AGE

IN CONTEXT

KEY FIGURE
Mahatma Gandhi

WHEN AND WHERE
1869–1948, India

BEFORE
From 6th century BCE
Ahimsa or nonviolence is the key ethical principle of the Jain and Buddhist religions.

3rd century BCE The Emperor Asoka converts to Buddhism and initiates social reforms inspired by nonviolence.

2nd century BCE The Hindu Bhagavad-Gita explores the dichotomy between ahimsa and the duty of the warrior class to fight in a just war.

AFTER
1964 The Baptist minister Martin Luther King preaches the use of nonviolent means to oppose racial inequality in the United States.

It was while working to oppose racial discrimination in South Africa that Gandhi coined the term satyagraha—"holding on to the truth." It was to become the key theme of his campaigns of nonviolent civil disobedience, both there and later in India.

Although raised a Hindu, Gandhi was deeply influenced by Jainism, with its emphasis on nonviolence and the welfare of all creatures. However, he was opposed to the idea that, in the face of social injustice, a person should simply retire into private spirituality and avoid confrontation. Hinduism had long been divided between those who thought that they should follow their social duty, as determined by their class and stage of life, and those who opted out of society in order to follow an ascetic path of personal religious discipline. Gandhi felt committed to seek political and social justice, while at the same time maintaining the fundamental ascetic value of

---

Inactivity and detachment allow social **injustice** to continue unchecked.

But **violence** only leads to retaliation and further violence, which is **self-defeating**.

Therefore **social and political change** is best achieved through **nonviolent protest** and a determination to stand by the **truth**, whatever the consequences.

> God is truth. The way to truth lies through nonviolence.
> **Mahatma Gandhi**

nonviolence. He also saw the self-destructiveness and futility of opposing violence with violence.

He believed that an individual could only genuinely seek the truth by discounting his or her social position and self-interest. He therefore argued that the way to oppose injustice was to have the courage and strength to hold on to the truth, whatever the personal consequences—and for him that included years spent in prison. He regarded noncooperation and civil disobedience as "weapons of truth" that an individual or society should not be afraid to deploy, provided that negotiation had failed. To accept the consequences of our actions is a sign of strength, if accompanied by the moral certainty of the truth.

Love all, hate no one

Gandhi emphasized that ahimsa (nonviolence) should be taken in its most positive sense: in other words, that it should mean the cultivation of love toward all, as opposed to simply abstinence from killing. This philosophy had further social and political consequences, since it must entail support for the oppressed. So, for example, Gandhi championed the cause of those who were outside the caste system and called "untouchables" since they were considered to be ritually impure. He regarded "untouchability" as a crime against humanity. It was later outlawed in India. He also argued strongly for religious freedom and against all forms of exploitation.

Unfortunately, the last year of Gandhi's life saw bloodshed and mass displacement as Muslim Pakistan was separated from Hindu India. However, his teachings, notably his legacy of nonviolent protest, spread globally, inspiring many of the world's leaders and political movements, including antiapartheid in South Africa and civil rights movements in the US, China, and elsewhere. ▪

A lone protestor defies tanks near Tiananmen Square in Beijing, in an image that became a global icon for the principle of passive resistance.

Mohandas Karamchand ("Mahatma") Gandhi

Born in 1869 in Porbandar, India, Mohandas Karamchand Gandhi (known as "Mahatma" or "great-souled") qualified as a lawyer in London. After a brief time back in India, he spent 21 years in South Africa giving legal support to the Indian community, during which time he launched a program of passive resistance against the compulsory registration and fingerprinting of Indians.

In 1914, he returned to India, where he opposed injustices imposed by the British rulers. During the 1920s, he initiated civil disobedience campaigns for which he was imprisoned for two years. He continued to promote similar campaigns, and suffered a further term in jail. He wanted to see an India free from British rule, in which all its religious groups could have a stake, and when independence was finally agreed in 1947, he opposed the partition of India because it conflicted with his vision of religious unity.

Gandhi was assassinated in Delhi in 1948 by a Hindu fanatic who accused him of being too sympathetic to the needs of the nation's Muslims.

Siddhartha Gautama
(later known as Buddha) is born in northeast India.

c.563 BCE

The **First Buddhist Council** is held in the year following Buddha's death.

5TH CENTURY BCE

Emperor Asoka of India converts to Buddhism and calls the **Third Buddhist Council**.

3RD CENTURY BCE

A collection of the teachings of Buddha, the **Pali Canon**, is written down in Sri Lanka and forms the basis of **Theravada Buddhism**.

1ST CENTURY BCE

5TH CENTURY BCE

Different **branches of Buddhism** evolve as the religion spreads across Asia.

4TH CENTURY BCE

The **Second Buddhist Council** is held, resulting in the first schism in Buddhism.

3RD CENTURY BCE

Buddhism spreads to Sri Lanka and Burma, and probably into Central Asia.

1ST CENTURY CE

Mahayana **Buddhism** emerges in India, with an emphasis on the bodhisattva ideal.

Buddhism is regarded by some as more of a philosophical system than a religion because it does not explicitly involve a god or gods. Its origins are also atypical: its founder, Siddhartha Gautama, the Buddha ("awakened one"), based his teachings not on any mystical vision or appearance, but on conclusions he reached after a long period of experience and thought—enlightenment, rather than revelation. Gautama neither affirmed nor denied the existence of deities, since they were irrelevant to his ideas, but some branches of Buddhism have since become more theistic, even if deities are not central to their practice.

The India in which Gautama grew up was dominated by the Brahmanic religions, and incorporated Hindu belief in the idea of samsara—a soul caught in an eternal circle of birth and rebirth. Buddhism proposed a radically different view of how the cycle could be broken. Instead of relying on Hindu religious practices, such as worship and ritual, Gautama advocated a change of lifestyle; instead of sacred texts giving divine guidance and authority, Buddhism offered its founder's teachings as a starting point for meditation.

Basic tenets

The doctrine of Buddhism was passed by word of mouth, at first to Gautama's immediate group of followers, and then through the teachers of the monastic order that he founded. It was not until the 1st century BCE, hundreds of years after his death, that Gautama's teachings first appeared in written form, in the *Tipitaka*. This was written in Pali, a Sri Lankan dialect, rather than Sanskrit, the language of the scholars. The so-called Pali Canon was followed by commentaries, such as the Mahayana Sutras, which interpreted Buddha's teaching.

What Buddhism lacked in theology, it made up for in its analysis of the reasons a soul might get caught up in samsara; it explored how one could achieve enlightenment and nirvana—the ultimate extinction of desire, aversion, and disillusionment. Gautama explained that the main obstacle to escape from the cycle of samsara was human suffering, caused by desires and attachments that can never be satisfied. He set

The **Mahayana Sutras** are composed.

1st–5th centuries ce

Vajrayana, or Tantric, Buddhism develops in India, from the Theravada tradition.

4th–5th centuries

Theravada Buddhism spreads from Sri Lanka into **Burma, Thailand, Laos, and Cambodia**.

11th–13th centuries

Zen Buddhism emerges in Japan from the Chinese tradition of meditation Buddhism.

12th–13th centuries

3rd century ce

Buddhism begins to flourish in **China**.

7th century

Mahayana Buddhism is adopted in **Tibet**, with an emphasis on imagery and ritual.

12th century

The **decline of Buddhism** accelerates as the Indian subcontinent is invaded by Muslims.

19th century

Western philosophers such as **Schopenhauer** begin taking an interest in Indian religions.

---

out "Four Noble Truths"—the central doctrine of Buddhism—to explain the nature of suffering and how it could be overcome: *dukkha* (the truth of suffering), *samudaya* (the truth of the origin of suffering), *nirodha* (the truth of the ending of suffering), and *magga* (the truth of the path to the ending of suffering). This last Noble Truth alludes to the Middle Way—the lifestyle advocated by the Buddha, which is simple in concept but hard to attain.

Spread and diversification
Buddhism spread rapidly from northern India southward across the subcontinent and northward into China. Different traditions of Buddhism began to emerge. The two main branches, Theravada and Mahayana, continue to the present day, much along regional lines.

Theravada, with its conservative and austere approach, remained closer to Buddha's original teachings, but became increasingly localized to southern India and especially Sri Lanka. Theravada was revitalized in the 12th century when trade took it into Burma, Thailand, Laos, and Cambodia.

Mahayana Buddhism had a more overtly religious following, offering its adherents temples and rituals, as well as rich symbolism and images of the Buddha. Like Theravada, Mahayana also dwindled in India, but it was enthusiastically adopted in Tibet, China, Vietnam, Korea, and Japan. A key element of Mahayana is the concept of religious leaders known as bodhisattvas, who have achieved enlightenment but remain on earth to show the way to others.

Later divisions within these two major traditions also occurred. These gave rise to such contrasting branches as Zen Buddhism, which aims to clear the mind in order to allow spontaneous enlightenment without ritual, scripture, or reasoning; and the various forms of Tibetan Buddhism that are characterized by colorful temples, images, and rituals.

Today, Buddhism is estimated to have more than 500 million adherents, and is considered to be the fourth largest religion in the world (after Christianity, Islam, and Hinduism). However, despite growing Western interest in it as both a religion and a philosophy, it has been in decline since the latter half of the 20th century, falling from its position as the largest single religion in the early 1950s. ■

FINDING
THE MIDDLE WAY
THE ENLIGHTENMENT OF BUDDHA

IN CONTEXT

KEY FIGURE
Siddhartha Gautama

WHEN AND WHERE
**6th century BCE,
northern India**

BEFORE
From 1700 BCE A multitude
of gods are ritually worshipped
in the Vedic religion of
northern India.

6th century BCE In China,
Daoism and Confucianism
present philosophies in
which personal spiritual
development is cultivated.

6th century BCE Mahavira
rejects his destiny as an
Indian prince and becomes an
extreme ascetic; his teachings
form the sacred texts of Jainism.

AFTER
1st century CE The first texts
containing Siddhartha
Gautama's teachings appear,
soon followed by the spread of
Buddhism into China.

I
n northern India, the 6th
century BCE was a time of
radical social and political
change. There was terrible
bloodshed as local rule by tribal
groups gave way to the rise of new
kingdoms. Cities were expanding,
drawing people away from the
simplicity of agricultural village life,
and trade was flourishing. At the
same time, people were starting to
ask fundamental questions about
life and the basis of religion.

On the one hand, there was the
established Vedic religion, based
on sacrifice and the authority of the
Vedic texts, to which few outside
the brahmin, or priestly class of
Indian society, had access. This was
a formal and conformist religion; it
required obedience to tradition and
maintained class differences. On
the other hand, many wandering
teachers were challenging formal
religion. Some of these withdrew
from society to practice asceticism
(the self-denial of material comforts),
opting for simplicity and deprivation
as a means of spiritual development.
They rejected both physical comfort
and social norms, and lived outside
the class system. Other wandering
teachers followed the Lokayata

Enlightenment came to Siddhartha
after meditation beneath the Bodhi Tree.
A descendant of the original tree was
planted in Bodh Gaya in 288 BCE and is
now a site of pilgrimage for Buddhists.

materialist philosophy, rejecting
conventional spiritual teachings in
favor of a life based on pleasure,
in the belief that there is nothing
beyond the physical world.

Siddhartha seeks answers
One wealthy man, Siddhartha
Gautama, decided, on reaching
adulthood, that his comfortable

Siddhartha Gautama

Born in 563 BCE into the ruling
family of the Shakya clan of
northeast India, Siddhartha
Gautama was expected to take
a prominent place in society.
Brought up in comfort and well
educated, he was married at 16
and had a son.

However, at the age of 29,
he became dissatisfied with his
life and left home, spending years
as a religious ascetic. Following
an experience he described as
enlightenment, he became a
wandering teacher and soon
attracted many followers, mainly
in the cities of the Ganges Plain.

Siddhartha set up communities
of monks and nuns, and also
gained a growing number of lay
followers. He also engaged in
discussions with princely rulers
and religious teachers of other
faiths. By the time he died, aged
80, Buddhism had become a
substantial religious movement.

Key work

29 BCE The Dhammapada, an
accessible summary of Buddha's
early teachings, forms part of
the Pali Canon (p.140).

See also: Aligning the self with the *dao* 66–67 ▪ Self-denial leads to spiritual liberation 68–71 ▪ Wisdom lies with the superior man 72–77 ▪ A rational world 92–99 ▪ A faith open to all beliefs 321

lifestyle was incompatible with his growing awareness of life's hardships and the certainty of death. In addition, material comforts offered no protection from these harsh realities of life. So he embarked on a religious quest to find the origin of suffering, and the answer to it.

For seven years he practiced severe asceticism, depriving himself of all but the minimum sustenance, but he found that this did not help him find the knowledge he sought. He therefore abandoned the ascetic life, while remaining determined to discover the cause of suffering. He is said to have gained enlightenment (becoming aware of the true nature of reality) during an all-night session of meditation, and this gave him an answer to the problems of suffering, aging, and death. From that point his followers were to refer to him as Buddha, an honorary title meaning one who is fully awake or the enlightened one.

The Middle Way

Buddha's teaching is known as the Middle Way. At the most obvious level, this suggests a middle way between the two types of existence that he rejected: the life of luxury, attempting to obtain protection from suffering with material comforts, and that of extreme austerity, denying himself almost everything in pursuit of spiritual growth. The approach or way he found involved a moderate amount of discipline in order to live an ethical life, free from indulgence in either sensual pleasures or self-mortification. But Buddha's Middle Way is also set between two other extremes: eternalism (where a person's spirit has purpose and

> However many **material comforts** I bring into my life, they **cannot protect me** from the pain of suffering.

> The total **denial of material comforts** and a life of asceticism **does not protect me** from suffering either.

> Each person needs to **find a balanced**, moderately disciplined lifestyle that takes account of their individual circumstances.

> **Find the Middle Way.**

lives forever) and nihilism (extreme skepticism in which the value or meaningfulness of everything in life is denied).

Eternalism and nihilism

The Vedic religion, particularly as it was developed in the texts known as the Upanishads (p.105), argued that the true self of every person is the atman, which is eternal and is reincarnated from life to life. The atman is linked to the physical body only temporarily, and is essentially independent of it.

Crucially, the Vedic religion identified this atman with Brahman, the fundamental divine reality that underlies everything. Ordinary things in the world (such as trees, animals, and rocks) are an illusion, known as maya; truth and

reality are to be found beyond these physical things. When Buddha rejected the eternal nature of the self, he was rejecting a key feature of Hindu thought and religion.

Buddha also rejected the other extreme—nihilism, which holds that ultimately nothing matters or has any value. Nihilism can be expressed in two ways, both of which were practiced during Buddha's lifetime. One way is the path of asceticism: purifying the body by the harshest austerity possible, and rejecting everything that the worldly consider to be of value. This was the path that Buddha had attempted and found wanting. The other way of living out nihilistic beliefs was that taken up in India by followers of the unorthodox Lokayata school of » philosophy: the wholehearted embrace of materialism. Their view was that if everything is simply a temporary arrangement of physical elements, there is no enduring soul that can be influenced by good or bad deeds during life. Furthermore, if there is no life after death, the best policy is to seek as much pleasure as possible in this life.

However, in rejecting these two extremes, Buddha did not simply opt for a Middle Way in the sense of a negotiated compromise; rather, his view was based on an insight that is key to understanding the whole of Buddhist teaching: the concept of interconnectedness.

Three marks of existence

Buddha pointed out that all things in life come about as a result of certain causes and conditions; when these cease, the elements that depend upon them will also cease. Nothing, therefore, has a permanent or independent existence. The Sanskrit term for such mutual dependence is *pratitya samutpada*, of which a literal translation might be things stepping up together. The phrase is sometimes translated as dependent origination, better to convey the idea that nothing originates in itself—everything is dependent upon prior causes. We live in a world in which everything is interconnected and nothing is the source of its own being.

This simple but profound observation leads to what are known as the three universal marks of existence. The first is *anicca*: that everything is impermanent and subject to change. We may wish it were not so, but it is.

The Buddha said that the quest for permanence and the certainty of things having a fixed essence leads people to have a general sense of dissatisfaction with life (dukkha), and this constitutes the second mark of existence. Dukkha is sometimes translated as suffering, but it means more than physical suffering or the inevitability of death—it points to existential frustration. Life does not necessarily provide us with what we want and, at the same time, it contains things, events, and other people that we don't want. Nothing in life gives us complete satisfaction; everything has its limitations.

The third mark of existence is anata: that, because everything is constantly changing, nothing has a fixed self or essence. Conventionally, we see things (such as trees) as separate from one another, and define them on that basis. In reality, however, because everything depends on those elements that bring it about (trees cannot grow without soil, water, and sunlight), nothing can be defined or permanently fixed in the way that our common sense and language supposes.

The idea of interconnectedness, as well as the three marks of existence implied within it, is a matter of observation rather than argument. It is not a statement of how the world should be, simply that this is how it is—and that attempts to deny it are the root cause of our daily frustration.

Buddha's subsequent teaching was shaped by the concept of interconnectedness. By relating dukkha, or dissatisfaction, to the process of change, the concept

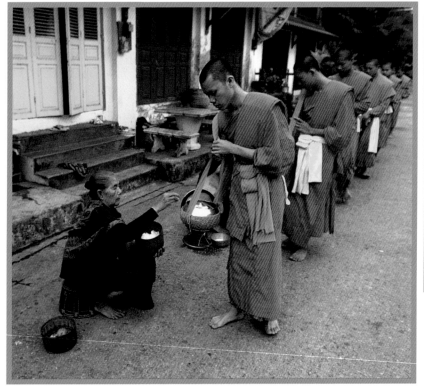

Buddhist monks do not cultivate hardship for its own sake; they are expected to eat moderately and depend on the gifts of lay people for their food— a practical example of interdependence.

suggests that there are ways or conditions under which it could be minimized. Buddha explained what these were in the teachings that became known as the Four Noble Truths and the Noble Eightfold Path (pp.136–43).

Applying the Middle Way to daily life

In many practical ways, the spirit of the Middle Way shapes Buddhist practice. For example, some branches of Buddhism emphasize the value of the monastic life, but vows are not taken for life, and many of those who spend either a few months or years as a monk or nun later return to family life (p.145). Similarly, in order not to cause unnecessary suffering, Buddhists aim to be vegetarian. But if it is difficult to obtain a vegetarian diet, or medical conditions suggest that a carnivorous diet is necessary, meat-eating is acceptable. Monks, who rely on gifts of food, are expected to eat whatever they are given. None of this is a matter of compromise; it is the recognition that everything depends on prevailing conditions.

When this exists, that comes to be; with the arising of this, that arises. When this does not exist, that does not come to be; with the cessation of this, that ceases.
Buddha

Just as a flower lives and then dies, Buddha's universal marks of existence hold that everything is impermanent and subject to change (*anicca*). Building upon this idea is anata: nothing has a fixed essence, because everything is in constant flux.

The Middle Way also has profound implications for our general understanding of religion, ethics, and philosophy. In practical terms, it argues that the reality of life, with its constant change and the inevitability of old age and death, cannot be permanently avoided either by material security or self-denial. Taken into a person's heart, this view can shape that person's values and ethics, and affect how they choose to live their life.

A flexible philosophy

In terms of religion, Buddhism's denial of the unchanging, eternal self as defined in the Hindu Upanishads was revolutionary. It suggested that life cannot be understood, or its suffering avoided, by conventional religious beliefs. Buddhism—if seen as a religion rather than an ethical philosophy—does not deny the existence of gods, or some form of an eternal soul, but regards them as an unnecessary distraction. When asked if the world was eternal, or whether an enlightened person lived on after death—questions that are often seen to be at the heart of religious belief—Buddha refused to answer. In terms of philosophy, Buddhism argues that knowledge starts from an analysis of experience, rather than abstract speculation. This meant that Buddhism was able to remain undogmatic, flexible, and open to new cultural ideas, while retaining its basic insight. The interconnectedness of all things, experienced in the balance between continuity and change, is the basis upon which Buddhist philosophy is built.

Buddhism's concepts also had psychological significance. By suggesting that the self was not simple and eternal, but complex and subject to change, it became possible for people to explore the self as a non-fixed entity. Moreover, Buddha's invitation to follow the Middle Way was open to all, making Buddhism, despite its lack of interest in a god or gods, an attractive proposition in a society bound by convention and ritual. ∎

THERE CAN BE AN END TO SUFFERING

ESCAPE FROM THE ETERNAL CYCLE

IN CONTEXT

KEY SOURCE
**Buddha's first sermon,
The Setting in Motion of
the Wheel of the Dhamma,
and subsequent teachings**

WHEN AND WHERE
6th century BCE, India

BEFORE
From prehistory Suffering
is often regarded as a
punishment from the gods.

From 700 BCE Hindus see
suffering as the inescapable
result of karma (actions in
past or present lives).

AFTER
3rd century BCE The
Mauryan emperor Asoka takes
practical and political steps
to minimize suffering by
promoting Buddhist values.

2nd century BCE Nagasena
argues that dissatisfaction
with life may be overcome by
recognizing the insubstantial,
changing nature of the self.

T he central aim of Buddha's
teaching—the dhamma—
is to overcome suffering.
Everything that does not contribute
to this aim is considered irrelevant.
The ideas of Buddhism are not to
be taken as ends in themselves, nor
are they the result of dispassionate
speculation about the nature of the
world. They are observations about
life and principles that are to be put
into practice.

The Noble Truths

The Buddhist dhamma starts with
four statements, known as the
"Four Noble Truths," which give

The Blessed One
[Buddha] is compassionate
and seeks our welfare;
he teaches the Dhamma
out of compassion.
Kinti Sutta

an overview of the human problem
of suffering and solutions for it.
The Truths, which are believed to
be the subject of the Buddha's first
sermon following his enlightenment
under the Bodhi Tree, revolve
around this issue.

The first of Buddha's Four
Noble Truths is dukkha, the truth
of suffering. This is the idea that
all life involves suffering, which lies
at the heart of Buddhist teachings,
and was the revelation that began
Siddhartha Gautama's long search
for truth. Human life, Buddha said,
is fragile and always vulnerable.
What is more, life is characterized
by suffering. The nature of this
suffering is very broad, meaning
not necessarily intense pain, but
also lesser, more widespread
feelings of dissatisfaction. It
may be the emotional suffering
caused by the death of a loved
one, an enduring sense that life
is somehow pointless or empty,
or simply a feeling of being stuck
in an unpleasant situation, such
as a traffic jam. Dukkha is the
feeling that arises in situations
that cause stress, discomfort, or
dissatisfaction. It makes us feel
that we want to be somewhere,
or even someone else.

Buddha thought that the search
for happiness leads people in the
wrong direction. Individuals crave
things—sensual pleasure, wealth,
power, material possessions—in
the hope that these things will
make them happy. But the falsity of
this thought lies behind *samudaya*,
the Second Noble Truth: that the
origin of suffering is craving.
Tanha, the Buddhist term for
this craving, indicates people's
attempts to hold on to what they
like, imagining that if only they
could have a certain thing and
keep it, all their problems would
be solved. *Tanha* can be translated
as "thirst," suggesting how natural
and essential this craving seems
to us. Buddha argued that even so,
this craving is counterproductive,
leading only to more suffering
and unhappiness.

According to Buddha, this
craving for things goes beyond
material objects and the wish
for power—it includes the need
to cling to particular views and

People are often moved to tears
at funerals and other sad events, but
Buddhists regard such suffering as
deriving from a mistaken wish to
hold on to something or someone.

See also: Aligning the self with the *dao* 66–67 ▪ A rational world 92–99 ▪ Physical and mental discipline 112–13 ▪ The enlightenment of Buddha 130–35 ▪ Sufism and the mystic tradition 282–83 ▪ Tenrikyo and the Joyous Life 310

ideas, rules, and observances, which is equally harmful. In this way, Buddhism takes a radically different view from the majority of religions, which tend to regard people's acceptance of doctrines and religious observances as essential to salvation. While Buddha did not say that such beliefs are harmful in themselves, he warned against clinging to them in the assumption that they will automatically help in the path to overcome suffering.

Finding nirvana

For Buddhists, everything arises from existing conditions. This means that something must cause suffering; and if that cause is removed, suffering will cease. The Second Noble Truth identifies craving as the cause—so Buddha said that if the craving were to stop, the suffering would cease. The Third Noble Truth, *nirodha* (the cessation of suffering and the causes of suffering), refers to the absence of craving. Putting an end to craving does not involve stopping life's normal activities —Buddha himself carried on teaching for 45 years after his enlightenment, and was subject to all the usual problems that afflict human beings. Rather, it refers to a state in which a person understands and deals with life, without the emotional need to crave for it to be other than it is.

With the Third Noble Truth comes a point of peace called, in Sanskrit, nirvana. This is a state beyond craving or desire for anything or anyone. It is not the same as extinction; Buddha was critical of those who tried to escape reality by craving annihilation.

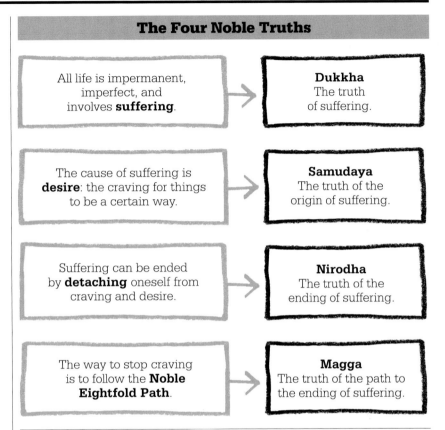

The Four Noble Truths

All life is impermanent, imperfect, and involves **suffering**. → **Dukkha** The truth of suffering.

The cause of suffering is **desire**: the craving for things to be a certain way. → **Samudaya** The truth of the origin of suffering.

Suffering can be ended by **detaching** oneself from craving and desire. → **Nirodha** The truth of the ending of suffering.

The way to stop craving is to follow the **Noble Eightfold Path**. → **Magga** The truth of the path to the ending of suffering.

Rather, the triple fires of greed, hatred, and illusion—three characteristics that perpetuate human suffering—are blown out like a candle. In other words, by letting go of destructive craving, the mind is liberated from suffering and unhappiness. This leads to a state of engaged happiness: a form of happiness that results from good moral conduct.

Unlike everything else, nirvana is not thought to be the result of cause and effect, but stands beyond or outside it. It is said to be permanent and unchanging: while everything in the world around us, and we ourselves, are temporary and have arisen because of certain conditions, nirvana is

an unconditioned, uncaused state and is therefore an absolute truth for Buddhists. This blissful state of being is accessible to us on earth and in our lifetimes. Unlike most religions, which encourage people to live a moral life in the present in order to attain happiness in a world beyond this one, Buddhism says that a true end to suffering is possible immediately, in this world.

Buddha himself attained a state of nirvana at the age of 35, and through his teachings sought to show others how to reach this enlightenment. The Fourth Noble Truth describes "the path that leads to the end of suffering." This is *magga*, the Middle Way, also known as the "Noble Eightfold Path." »

Material goods such as shoes may be advertised as must-have items, in an attempt to create a desire or craving in us. This desire, which can never be fully satisifed, leads to suffering.

The Noble Eightfold Path

The path to the cessation of suffering is set out as a path of eight steps. However, these need not be taken sequentially as they are eight principles, rather than actions, that allow Buddhists to overcome craving and achieve happiness. The Noble Eightfold Path deals with the three basic aspects of the Buddhist life: wisdom (in the first two steps), virtue (in the next three), and concentration (in the final three).

Wisdom, for Buddha, is made up of two directions in which to turn the mind: "right view" and "right intention." The first of these is important in order to be able to see and identify the cause and cure of suffering, as outlined in the Four Noble Truths. Without a willingness to explore that view, the rest of the path makes little sense. Right intention could equally be described as "right commitment"—it refers to our intention to follow the path,

because a mere understanding of the teaching (without also adopting an intention to act on it) is of no use.

Steps three, four, and five of the path offer practical moral guidelines. Buddhist morality is not about rules to be obeyed, but about creating conditions that facilitate the path toward enlightenment. Step three states that we must use "right speech": avoid telling lies, speaking harshly or cruelly, and listening to or spreading purposeless chatter and malicious gossip. Instead, we must cultivate the opposite: truthful, positive, kindly, and purposeful speech.

Step four says that we must take "right action" by following the five moral "precepts": not to destroy life, not to steal, not to misuse the senses, not to lie, and not to cloud the mind with intoxicants (the last is of particular importance for those who are engaging in the mental training that forms the final

The Pali Canon

In the 400 years after Buddha died, his teachings and the guidelines for monastic life were passed down orally using local languages, rather than Sanskrit, which was the language used in the Hindu scriptures. However, in the 1st century BCE, his teachings were written down in Sri Lanka using a language and script called Pali, which was closely related to the language that Buddha himself spoke. These

texts are collectively referred to as the Pali Canon, and they form the scriptures of the Theravada Buddhist tradition (p.330).

The Pali Canon is also known as the Tipitaka (in Pali) and the Tripitaka (in Sanskrit), meaning "three baskets." It is divided into three sections: the Vinaya Pitaka, which contains guidance on monastic life; the Sutta Pitaka, a collection of Buddha's sayings and accounts of events in his life; and the Abhidhamma Pitaka, a philosophical analysis of Buddha's teachings.

There are four kinds of clinging: clinging to sensual pleasures, clinging to views, clinging to rules and observances, and clinging to a doctrine of the self.
Sammaditthi Sutta

There is a Middle Way… which leads to peace, to direct knowledge, to enlightenment, to nirvana. And what is that Middle Way? It is just this Noble Eightfold Path…
Buddha

part of the path). The fifth step also supports an ethical approach, suggesting that we must pursue a "right livelihood." This is the requirement to earn a living in a way that does not go against Buddhist moral principles.

Cultivating right mind

The last three steps advise on how to carry out the right mental training for reaching nirvana. Step six says that "right effort" should be applied. This requires a person to be conscious of and set aside negative or harmful thoughts as they arise, replacing them with their positive equivalent. So, for example, at the beginning of the Dhammapada (the "Verses of the Dhamma"), the Buddha says that those who resent the actions of others, or brood upon injuries sustained in the past, will never become free of hate. Right effort encapsulates the conscious intention to break the cycle of resentment and negative response.

The seventh step tells us to pursue "right mindfulness." It is all too easy for our minds to become distracted, flitting from one thing

to another. An important step in mental discipline is to be fully aware of the present moment and to allow the mind to be quietly focused on just one thing. This is seen in meditation techniques such as "mindfulness of breathing" or "just sitting," which generally form the starting point for training in Buddhist meditation.

The final, eighth, step on the path encourages us to apply "right concentration." The practice of meditation is a crucial aspect of following the Buddhist dhamma. This step recognizes that control of the mind is central to being able to

overcome suffering, since what is being addressed is not physical pain or death itself, but the sense of existential angst that can accompany them. In insight meditation, a person may calmly and deliberately contemplate those things that most people try to avoid thinking about, such as death. In a meditation on *metta*, or love, positive thoughts are cultivated toward others, from people we love to those we naturally find most difficult. This exercise encourages benevolence and the development of a more positive set of mental qualities. »

The Noble Eightfold Path, or Middle Way, sets out the eight characteristics that we need to encourage in ourselves to bring an end to our suffering.

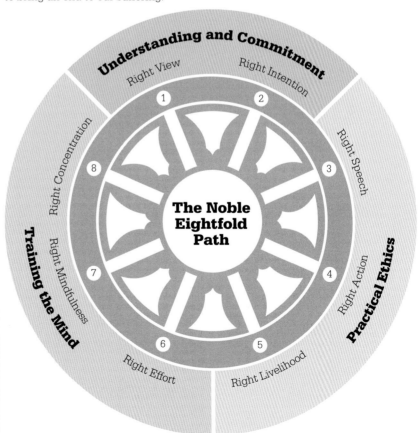

Understanding and Commitment
Right View
Right Intention
Right Speech
Practical Ethics
Right Action
Right Livelihood
Right Effort
Right Mindfulness
Training the Mind
Right Concentration

The Noble Eightfold Path

1 2 3 4 5 6 7 8

> If lust, anger, and delusion are given up, man aims neither at his own ruin, nor at the ruin of others…and he experiences no mental pain and grief. Thus is nirvana visible in this life.
> **Anguttara Nikaya**

The Noble Eightfold Path offers a program of self-development. However, Buddhism does not have a set of commands or doctrines to be accepted; instead, it suggests a way to live that will ease suffering. Different people will concentrate on different aspects of the path, depending on their circumstances. In addition, the path itself is not a straight route that begins at step one and ends at step eight. It is not considered necessary to deal with any one of the steps before moving on to another step. The three main aspects of understanding, morality, and meditation may be used to reinforce one another. Some steps, however, such as those that deal with ethical issues, may be important in setting up the conditions in our lives in which meditation can become truly effective.

The Wheel of Life

A key feature of Buddha's teaching is "interconnectedness" (pp.130–35): the idea that everything arises because of preexisting causes and conditions. The Buddhist path is therefore one that works always with context; it aims to create the conditions that allow angst and suffering to be replaced by contentment and happiness.

This means that if we look at the chain of causes and effects of events in our lives, we can look for the links that might be changed so that our lives can take a different course. If it were not possible to choose differently and alter the outcomes of situations, people's fates and their every action would be absolutely determined, with no escape from suffering. So, although Buddhism takes from Hinduism the idea of karma (that actions have consequences), it does not accept this in any rigid or mechanical sense. There is always an element of choice in our actions.

The Buddhist view of actions and consequences is presented in graphic form in the "Wheel of Life," a complex piece of iconography that depicts suffering and possible ways to overcome it. Everything within the wheel represents the world of samsara—a world of endless rebirth in which all beings are trapped as a consequence of their karmic actions. The wheel itself is held within the jaws of a fearsome demon, who represents death.

In the center of the wheel are three creatures—a cock, a snake, and a pig—that represent the three poisons: greed, hatred, and ignorance. Buddha saw these as the starting point or root of the unwholesome life and thus of human suffering. Surrounding them is a circle filled with human beings either descending or ascending, who pass by a series of realms depicted in the next circle. These realms are those of humans, animals, gods, *asuras* (warlike

The Buddha's teachings on the Four Noble Truths are compared to a physician diagnosing an illness and prescribing a treatment.

The doctor's prescription

The practical aim of Buddhism, much like that of a physician, is to eliminate suffering in the world. The faith's Four Noble Truths can be set out according to the stages involved in medical procedure: the diagnosis, its cause, the fact that suffering will be cured if its cause is removed, and the method of removing the cause.

Buddha described the human condition as being similar to a man who has been wounded by a poisoned arrow but refuses to have the arrow removed until he understands all the details of the arrow and who made it. The man's priority should be to have the arrow removed. Buddha discarded as irrelevant most of the questions posed by Western philosophy, such as speculation about why the world is as it is. Buddhism is therefore seen by some as a therapy rather than a religion: a health-giving regime to be followed, rather than a set of ideas to be believed.

> Finding themselves
> threatened by danger,
> people take refuge in spirits,
> shrines, and sacred trees,
> but these are not
> a true refuge.
> **Dhammapada**

beings constantly doing battle),
hungry ghosts, and hell (the lowest
of states). The implication is that
people can move from one realm
to another. It is from the human
realm that they may escape to a
happier state of existence through
the teachings of Buddha.

For those seeking to understand
the process by which Buddhists
can achieve this—by overcoming
suffering—it is the outermost wheel
that is the most important. The
twelve *nidanas*, or links, in the
outer wheel give graphic expression
to the interconnectedness that is
central to Buddhist teaching.
They feature people and buildings,
from a blind man (who represents
a starting point in total spiritual
ignorance) to a house with five
windows (representing the mind
and senses). There is a crucial
opportunity offered between the
seventh and eighth *nidanas*, which
show a man with an arrow in his
eye (representing feelings of pain)
and a woman offering a man a
drink (feelings leading to craving).
It is this link—between the pain or
pleasure that comes from contact
with the world and the resulting

craving—that is critical. If the link
holds, the process of re-becoming
(samsara) continues forever.
If it can be broken, there is the
possibility of escape from the
cycle of existence and suffering.

The breaking of the link signals
a return to the starting point of
Buddha's route to the end of
suffering: the ability to engage
with life without allowing that
experience to generate the craving
that arises from attachment and
disappointment. And to set up

The Buddhist Wheel of Life
represents the universe and the
endless cycle of death and rebirth,
within which humans are trapped
unless they follow the Middle Way.

the conditions to help break that
nidana link, people should follow
the Noble Eightfold Path. Through
taking action they may find
nirvana. According to Buddhism,
there is no god to save humanity,
so what people need to cultivate
is wisdom rather than faith. ■

TEST BUDDHA'S WORDS AS ONE WOULD THE QUALITY OF GOLD

THE PERSONAL QUEST FOR TRUTH

IN CONTEXT

KEY SOURCE
The Pali Canon

WHEN AND WHERE
6th century BCE,
northern India

BEFORE
From 1000 BCE Traditional
Hindu thought is based on
Vedic texts and the teachings
of the brahmin priests.

6th century BCE Jains and
Buddhists reject the Vedas
and brahmins as authorities.

AFTER
From 483 BCE For more than
four centuries after his death,
the teachings of Buddha are
passed on by word of mouth
among his followers.

29 BCE A written collection
of Buddha's teachings and
sayings is made at the Fourth
Buddhist Council in Sri Lanka.

12th century Zen Buddhists
reject the need for authoritative
scriptures of any sort.

In most religions, beliefs are based on authority, whether that of a particular leader, a priestly class, or sacred texts. People who accept these beliefs may seek to defend them rationally, while those who feel unable to assent to the beliefs of their culture may be branded as heretics.

Buddhism is different. It pays great respect to Buddha and other religious teachers, and some Buddhist traditions make much of the value of having a teacher with a particular lineage or tradition. However, the faith also values debate and discussion; teachers and intellectual convictions are seen as only a starting point. Buddha argued that people should not take any of his teachings on trust, but should test them out, both rationally and also in terms of personal experience.

Buddhist wisdom is therefore acquired in three stages: from teachers or by reading scriptures; from personal reflection and thought; and as a result of spiritual practice. The third stage generally involves

Accept as completely true
only that which is praised
by the wise and which
you test for yourself
and know to be good
for yourself and others.
Buddha

meditation, the search for truth and spiritual growth, and putting Buddhist teachings into practice.

Early followers of Buddha achieved enlightenment by seeking understanding of his teaching, not just by believing his word. Buddhism still argues that beliefs should be based on personal conviction and experience, rather than simply trusting external authority. ■

See also: Wisdom lies with the superior man 72–77 ▪ Buddhas and bodhisattvas 152–57 ▪ Man as a manifestation of God 188

RELIGIOUS DISCIPLINE IS NECESSARY
THE PURPOSE OF MONASTIC VOWS

IN CONTEXT

KEY SOURCE
Early Buddhist Councils

WHEN AND WHERE
From 5th century BCE, northern India

BEFORE
From prehistory Most religions combine spiritual development with awareness of a person's place in society or the religious group.

7th century BCE A new ascetic tradition of extreme self-denial arises in Hinduism.

c.550 BCE Buddha advocates a Middle Way between asceticism and hedonism.

AFTER
From 12th century CE In Japan, Pure Land Buddhism, and Nichiren Buddhism insist that faith in Amida Buddha and chanting, rather than following a particular lifestyle or discipline, are the way to gain enlightenment.

Throughout his life, Buddha had two kinds of followers: monks and householders. The monks were wandering preachers like Buddha at first, but later they settled in monastic communities. Here, they followed disciplines that aimed to benefit their own spiritual progress as well as the community. Householders too could achieve enlightenment, since they practiced Buddhism and helped the community of monks.

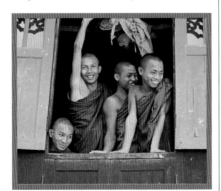

Young Buddhist monks accept monastic discipline for a short period. In their path toward greater personal and social awareness, they are required to follow some, but not all, monastic rules.

About a hundred years after Buddha died, debates began about how strictly the monastic rules should be obeyed. As Buddhism spread, it developed different traditions, some of which, particularly in China and Japan, placed less emphasis on monastic life. Nevertheless, monasticism remains an important feature of Buddhism, especially in Sri Lanka and Thailand, which follow the Theravada tradition (p.330).

In Buddhism, monastic vows are taken for a limited period, rather than for life. The vows are not an end in themselves, but aim to create conditions that assist Buddhist practice. They are not essential, but helpful, in following the Middle Way. However, individuals must not simply strive for personal enlightenment, because that would be self-defeating, implying a measure of selfishness incompatible with Buddhist teaching. Rather, they must attempt to develop universal compassion and good will, which have a social as well as a personal dimension. ■

See also: The four stages of life 106–109 ▪ The enlightenment of Buddha 130–35 ▪ Writing the Oral Law 182–83 ▪ Serving God on behalf of others 222–23

RENOUNCE KILLING AND GOOD WILL FOLLOW

LET KINDNESS AND COMPASSION RULE

IN CONTEXT

KEY EVENT
**The conversion
of Emperor Asoka**

WHEN AND WHERE
**3rd century BCE,
northern India**

BEFORE
From 2000 BCE The Vedic
religion, then Hinduism,
develop the doctrine of
ahimsa, or nonviolence,
but justify war in certain
circumstances.

6th century BCE Buddha
enjoins his followers to abstain
from killing; Mahavira founds
Jainism, which forbids the
taking of any life.

AFTER
17th century Sikhism
allows killing in defense of
the oppressed and the faith.

19th century Mohandas
Gandhi, raised as a Hindu,
adopts nonviolence as a
political strategy.

If people are killed, their
family, relatives, and
friends **will suffer**.

⬇

Therefore the **good leader
abstains from killing**
living beings and orders
others to do likewise.

⬇

He builds a **better society**
through cultivating an
attitude of loving-kindness
and fostering it in others.

⬇

**Renounce killing and
good will follow.**

Buddhism arose out of
Hinduism, a faith that had
always been ambivalent
about killing. On the one hand,
Hinduism promoted the principle
of ahimsa (not killing); on the other,
Hindu society required animal
sacrifice, allowed meat eating,
and regarded fighting in a just
war as an inescapable duty. Like
many other teachers of his day,
including Mahavira, founder
of the Jain religion, Buddha
emphasized the principle of not
killing, and it became the first of
the Five Precepts, principles that
form the ethical basis for those
following the Buddhist way of life.

Five rules for living

The Five Precepts forbid the taking
of life, stealing, sexual misconduct,
lying, and the consumption of
mind-dulling intoxicants such as
alcohol. Each of these precepts has
a positive counterpart, effectively
generating five rules relating to
things one should do. The first of
these is to treat all beings with
loving-kindness (*metta*); indeed,
one of the principal meditation
practices in Buddhism is the
cultivation of goodwill toward
everyone—treating friends,

If there is one practice that is sufficient to bring about buddhahood, it is the practice of great compassion.
Dalai Lama

strangers, and even those that one might find difficult with equal care and concern. The broad, positive approach evident in this first rule underpins the other four. Positive goodwill toward others supports the principles of generosity; nonexploitation (the third precept is generally taken to prohibit adultery, rape, and other forms of sexual exploitation); honesty; and the keeping of a clear head to ensure corrrect decisions and actions.

Although the principle of not killing was a key feature of Buddhism from its beginning, the first attempt to apply the principle to the whole of society was made by the Emperor Asoka in the 3rd century BCE. This is evident from the many edicts that he issued, 32 of which have been discovered carved on pillars or rock faces. As well as advocating the avoidance of killing, Asoka promoted support for the poor, the protection of servants, and the establishment of medical centers and veterinary services—all direct expressions of *metta*.

A peaceful ideal

Although there are rare cases of self-harm (as in the suicide of Buddhist monks, who have been known to set themselves on fire as an extreme form of political protest), in general Buddhism has never sought to impose its ideas upon society by force, nor has it ever become involved in war.

The principle of not killing suggests that, as an ideal, Buddhists should be vegetarian.

All life is sacred to Buddhist monks. They believe all living beings can exist peacefully side by side, even men and tigers—as demonstrated at the Tiger Temple in Kanchanaburi, Thailand.

However, Buddha's Middle Way (pp.130–135) indicates that self-denial must never be taken to life-threatening extremes, so Buddhists may eat meat and fish if it is deemed necessary for their health, or where there is a shortage of fruit and vegetables (as in the mountains of Tibet). Monks and nuns may eat meat and fish if it is offered to them and has not been killed for their benefit. ▪

The Emperor Asoka

Asoka was born in India in 304 BCE. He was the son of the Mauryan emperor Bindusara and came to the throne of the kingdom of Magadha in 268 BCE, having killed his brothers and other potential rivals in order to secure his position. He embarked on a brutal campaign of expansion, extending his rule to establish an empire that included all but the most southerly part of India.

After one particularly bloody battle, the sight of the dead and the grieving inspired him to pledge never to fight a battle again. He looked for answers in Buddhism and, on finding them, became a fervent convert. His conversion was marked by a dramatic change in attitude: he began to promote Buddhist principles throughout his empire, issuing edicts on moral matters, banning animal sacrifice, and increasing the provision of welfare. He sent missionaries to promote Buddhism abroad, but he also took a positive view of all religions, issuing only moral precepts that would be acceptable to all religious groups within his empire.

WE CANNOT SAY WHAT A PERSON IS

THE SELF AS CONSTANTLY CHANGING

IN CONTEXT

KEY FIGURE
Nagasena

WHEN AND WHERE
1st century CE, India

BEFORE
6th century BCE The Hindu Upanishads make a distinction between the physical body, the self made up of thoughts and experience, and an eternal self.

6th century BCE Buddha argues that everything is constantly changing and nothing has a fixed essence.

AFTER
12th century CE Teachers of Zen Buddhism distinguish between the small mind, or ego, and the Buddha-mind.

20th century Existentialist thinkers, like Buddhists, argue that individuals shape their lives through the decisions they make.

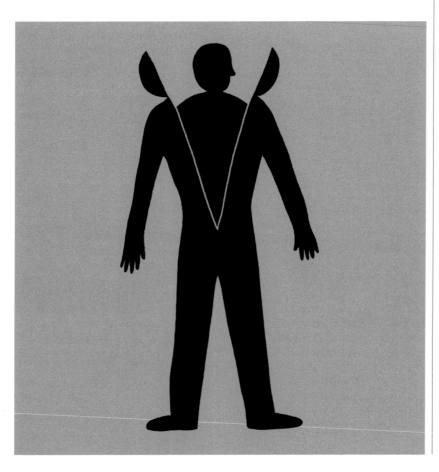

The idea that a human being comprises a physical body and a nonphysical self, or soul, is deeply ingrained in almost all religious traditions. It forms the basis of speculation about life after death—whether we survive in some form in heaven or hell, or are reincarnated as the nonphysical self takes on a new body. Belief in an immortal soul and in God seem the very essence of religion. Both, however, were rejected by Buddha, who believed we have no fixed self.

The idea that we do not have a permanent self, but are constantly changing, is absolutely central to Buddhist teaching, and sets Buddhism apart from most other

See also: Preparing for the afterlife 58–59 ▪ The ultimate reality 102–105 ▪ Seeing with pure consciousness 116–21 ▪ The enlightenment of Buddha 130–35 ▪ Immortality in Christianity 210–11

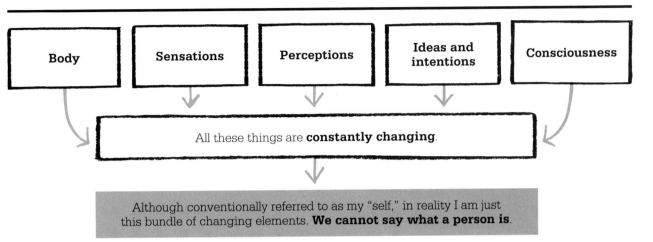

| Body | Sensations | Perceptions | Ideas and intentions | Consciousness |

All these things are **constantly changing**.

Although conventionally referred to as my "self," in reality I am just this bundle of changing elements. **We cannot say what a person is**.

belief systems and philosophies. It is implied by Buddha's teaching of the Middle Way (pp.130–35), and also reflects his teaching of the interconnectedness of all things. However, nowhere is the idea of the changing self better illustrated than in *The Questions of King Milinda*, written anonymously in the 1st century CE. This text describes the discussions between a Buddhist sage known as Nagasena, and King Milinda—the Indo-Greek ruler of northwestern India, c.150 BCE.

The monk Nagasena is often referred to as one of the Sixteen (or Eighteen) Arhats, beings who have realized a very high level of spiritual attainment.

Analyzing the self

Milinda starts by innocently asking whether the person he is greeting is indeed Nagasena, whereupon Nagasena launches straight into the discussion by stating that although the name Nagasena is conventionally used to refer to himself, there is actually nothing that corresponds to it. The word is a designation, a "mere name," because "no real person is here apprehended." In an absolute sense, Nagasena does not exist.

Bewildered, the King asks how that can be the case, since Nagasena is clearly standing there in front of him. To answer this, Nagasena uses an analogy. He observes that the King arrived in a chariot, so it is obvious that a chariot exists. But he then starts to analyze the various parts of the chariot: the axle, the wheels, and so on, and asks the King if any of these "are" the chariot—eliciting the answer that they are not.

So where is the chariot, Nagasena asks, if it is not the wheels, or the axle, and so on? Clearly, there is no chariot over and above the parts from which it is constructed. Chariot is a name applied to the collection of those parts when they are put together to make the vehicle. In the same way, Nagasena argues, there is no fixed or permanent self over and above the various parts of which we are made. Nagasena does not represent anything that Milinda could point to. »

I am known as Nagasena. But the word 'Nagasena' is only a designation or name in common use. There is no permanent individuality (no soul) involved in the matter.
Nagasena

We think of people as fixed objects. But Nagasena insists that the self is a process of ongoing change that can no more be pinned down than motion itself.

Like the chariot, "Nagasena" refers to a set of elements that exist in a state of mutual dependence.

Buddhists view the human being as made up of five interdependent *skandhas* (literally, heaps). These are: form (our physical body); sensations (information about the world that is constantly fed to us by our senses); perception (our awareness of the world through sensations); and mental formations or impulses (our ongoing flow of ideas, intentions, and thoughts about the things we perceive).

The fifth *skandha* is consciousness: the general sense we have of being alive—including an awareness of the information streaming in from our senses, and of our thoughts, ideas, and emotions.

The key feature of Nagasena's argument is that each of these *skandhas* is constantly changing. This is most obvious in the case of form, or the physical body, as we change from being a baby to an adult through the physical process of aging. But it is also true of the other four *skandhas*: they too are

in no way fixed. They reflect a constantly changing stream of experience and response as we engage with life. This means that not only is it impossible to point to Nagasena, it is also impossible to say whether anyone is the same person during the course of one lifetime. Nevertheless, we still have a sense of a person being the same over a lifetime, since each of us has a past and a future. Nagasena points out that it is absurd to say he remains the same over time, but likewise absurd to say he does not.

In fact, Nagasena insists that the questions themselves are wrong, because they presuppose a fixed self instead of one that is dependent upon the body. In a further example to illustrate the dependency of the self, Nagasena asks Milinda to consider milk, curds, butter, and ghee. These are not the same things, but the three later stages—curds, butter, and ghee—cannot be made unless milk first exists. That is to say that

A meeting of cultures

The meeting between King Milinda and Nagasena occurred in the context of a meeting of cultures. Buddhism had spread to northern India through the teachings of missionaries sent by the Emperor Asoka around 100 years earlier. Meanwhile, the influence of classical Greece was spreading eastward from the Mediterranean, and, when it reached northern India, it was adopted by local rulers (a process known as Hellenization).

Milinda—or Menander, as he is known in Greek—was one such king. He ruled a region known as the Indo-Greek Kingdom—in present-day northwestern India —in the 2nd century BCE, so we may assume that Nagasena lived in that area sometime between the 2nd and 1st century CE.

While evidence of Milinda exists in the form of coins and references by classical writers, we know very little about the philosopher-monk Nagasena. His

only appearance in literature is his dialogue with the King in *The Questions of King Milinda*, a widely respected text in Theravada Buddhism that was written in the 1st century CE. One legend about Nagasena states that while living in Pataliputra (modern-day Patna, India), he created the Emerald Buddha, a jade statue of Buddha clothed in gold, which is now in Wat Phra Kaew, Bangkok, Thailand.

butter only exists because milk exists; it depends on the existence of milk. In the same way, says Nagasena, "do the elements of being join one another in serial succession: one element perishes, another arises, succeeding each other as it were instantaneously."

A category mistake

In the 20th century, the British philosopher Gilbert Ryle attacked the idea that the material body is linked to a nonphysical mind. In doing so, he used an argument that is exactly parallel to Nagasena's. A visitor to the city of Oxford who has been shown various colleges, libraries, and so on, asks, "But where is the university?" Ryle claims that there is no university over and above its constituent parts.

Likewise, there is no mind that exists separately from the body. People who suppose that there is are making a category mistake—where things of one kind are presented as though they belong to another. It is wrong to treat the mind as though it is an object of substance, when mind refers to a collection of capacities and dispositions.

What we are today comes from our thoughts of yesterday, and our present thoughts build our life of tomorrow: our life is the creation of our mind.
Buddha

Which of these parts is the chariot? Nagasena would answer that none of them are. Likewise, whatever constitutes "me" cannot be pointed to, but nonetheless continues to affect things in the universe now and in the future.

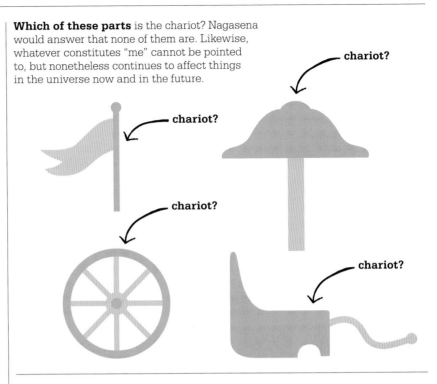

Toward the end of the 20th century, and into the 21st, most Western philosophers have argued for a materialist (or physicalist) view of the mind: that mind is simply a word that describes brain function. For modern science, there is no self over and above the body; the brain performs a complex processing of experience and response, which we think of as our mind, or self.

This differs from Nagasena only in the way that the sage applies a closer analysis of the way in which we experience ourselves as thinking, feeling, and responding beings. As he pointed out to King Milinda, even the fact that we do this does not mean that there is a separate thing called the self.

The other modern philosophy that unwittingly builds on this Buddhist idea is existentialism. It is often summed up in the phrase "existence precedes essence," meaning that we are born and exist before our lives have obtained any

sense of purpose. Existentialism suggests that we shape our lives by the choices we make, and should acknowledge our responsibility for doing so: we are what we choose to do—we do not have an internal real self or essence.

Absolute truth

This discussion of the self highlights an important feature of Buddhist teaching: the difference between conventional and absolute truth. In order to function normally, we have to assume a pragmatic or practical approach and refer to objects as though they have a recognizable, permanent, and independent existence.

It would be impossible to communicate if everything had to be described in terms of its constituent parts. Buddhism therefore accepts the need for such conventional truth, but constantly guards against mistaking it for absolute truth. ∎

ENLIGHTENMENT HAS MANY FACES

BUDDHAS AND BODHISATTVAS

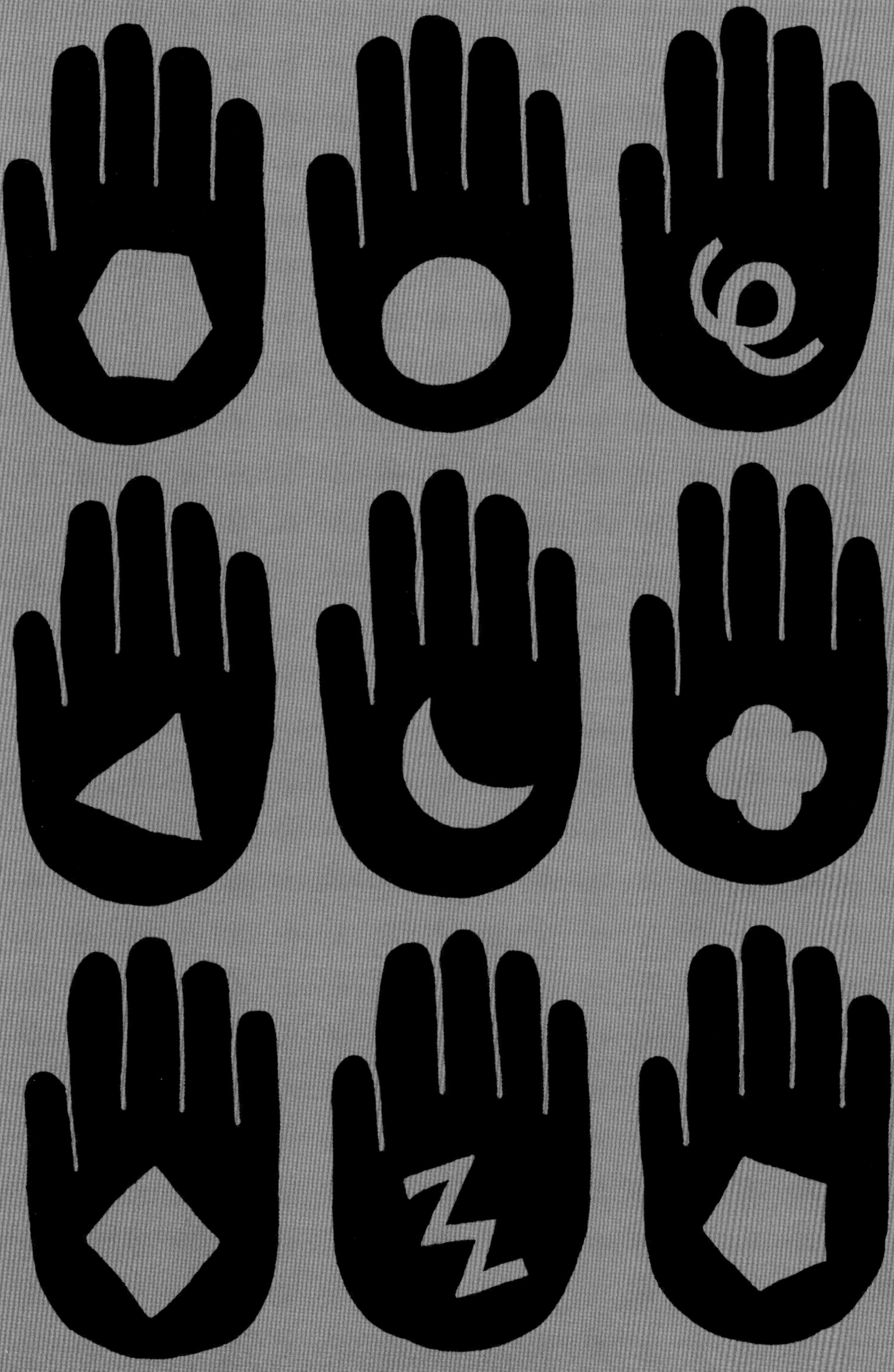

IN CONTEXT

KEY EVENT
The development of Mahayana Buddhism

WHEN AND WHERE
2nd–3rd centuries CE, India

BEFORE
From 1500 BCE The Hindu Vedas refer to many gods and goddesses, each depicting an aspect of nature and life.

From 2nd century BCE Devotional practices become influential in Hinduism.

AFTER
7th century CE Mahayana Buddhism, using elaborate images and ritual, is established in Tibet.

8th century CE Images of Buddhist teachers are used as a source of inspiration, as well as those of buddhas and bodhisattvas. A popular image is that of Padmasambhava, the Precious Guru, who introduced Tantric Buddhism into Tibet.

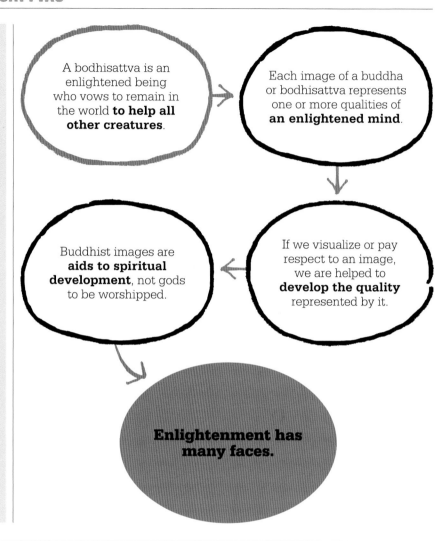

A bodhisattva is an enlightened being who vows to remain in the world **to help all other creatures**.

Each image of a buddha or bodhisattva represents one or more qualities of **an enlightened mind**.

Buddhist images are **aids to spiritual development**, not gods to be worshipped.

If we visualize or pay respect to an image, we are helped to **develop the quality** represented by it.

Enlightenment has many faces.

The teachings that Buddha encapsulated in his Four Noble Truths and Noble Eightfold Path (pp.136–43) were straightforward and rational. To follow them required mental training and analysis of experience, but did not entail metaphysical speculation (thinking about what does or does not exist), religious ritual, or—at least for the first few centuries—any use of images. However, a modern-day visitor to a Mahayana Buddhist temple in China or Tibet would see many elaborate images and forms of devotional worship.

Buddha figures—of different colors, male and female, some fearsome, others in calm meditation—appear to be the objects of devotion in a way that, to the external observer, appears not unlike devotion to the gods and goddesses of other religions. Since Buddhism still often claims to be rational, how did this imaginative transformation come about, and how is it justified?

The bodhisattva path
Given the general Indian belief in reincarnation, it was not long before people started to speculate about

Buddha's previous lives, and the actions and characteristics he must have displayed in those lives to move toward nirvana. These musings led to the compilation of Jataka tales or "birth stories," involving characters, sometimes human and sometimes animal, that depicted the Buddhist qualities of love, compassion, and wisdom deemed necessary for progress toward enlightenment. In turn, these stories led to the idea of the "bodhisattva": a being who is capable of enlightenment—or of buddhahood—but who chooses

See also: The ultimate reality 102–105 ▪ Physical and mental discipline 112–13 ▪ Seeing with pure consciousness 116–121 ▪ Zen insights that go beyond words 160–63 ▪ Man as a manifestation of God 188

There has arisen in me the will to win all-knowledge, with all beings for its object, that is to say, for the purpose of setting free the entire world of beings.
Sikshasamuccaya

to remain in the world, continuing to be reborn, in order to benefit all other beings. This idea brought about a remarkable change in the overall view of the Buddhist path. Instead of striving to become an arhat, or "worthy one" (the term used for those of Buddha's followers who have gained enlightenment), it was now possible for Buddhists to dedicate themselves to the more exalted path of becoming, in effect, apprentice buddhas—bodhisattvas who engage with the world out of universal compassion.

The great vehicle

Those who followed this new ideal called it Mahayana, or "great vehicle," in contrast to the earlier tradition, which they described as Hinayana ("small vehicle") and regarded as too narrow in scope. Practitioners of Mahayana believe that it represents a deeper teaching, which was implicit in the original Buddhist dhamma. Its scriptures—notably the Lotus Sutra—present an image of Buddha

preaching to beings in a vast universe made up of many world systems, of which this present world is a very small part. Followers of Mahayana argue that the earlier teaching was a necessarily limited version, and that their own was kept hidden for many centuries, awaiting the right conditions to allow it to be preached.

Mahayana Buddhism, although it developed in India, spread north and was established in China and then in Tibet. The earlier tradition still exists as Theravada ("tradition of the elders") Buddhism. It is found today mostly in Thailand, Sri Lanka, and Southeast Asia.

Two bodhisattvas

The earlier tradition, now known as Theravada, recognizes only two bodhisattvas: the incarnation of the historical figure of Buddha (who is also known as Sakyamuni Buddha or Gautama Buddha), and Maitreya, a bodhisattva who will arrive in the future to preach the truth of the dhamma. However, in Mahayana Buddhism, lay people, as well as the monastic community, are encouraged to reach nirvana and thereafter to become bodhisattvas. Once the possibility of a vast number of bodhisattvas was accepted, each dedicated to the task of universal enlightenment, the floodgates of Buddhist iconography were opened, because these beings could then be imaginatively depicted in order to provide inspiration to others.

Symbolism and images

Each bodhisattva vows to become a buddha ("enlightened being") and to lead others toward enlightenment. To do this, they

must cultivate six "perfections": generosity, morality, patience, energy, meditation, and wisdom. These qualities are shown in individual bodhisattva images. For example, the quality of wisdom is depicted through the image of Manjushri, a young man holding a lotus (representing the enlightened mind) and brandishing a flaming sword (representing the wisdom with which he cuts through the veil of ignorance).

The most widely venerated of images is that of Avalokiteshvara, the Bodhisattva of Compassion. His name is a Sanskrit word meaning "The Lord who looks down." He looks upon earthly beings as a good father would upon his children, offering them assistance and trying to liberate them from their faults and suffering through his unwavering compassion. »

This thangka, or silk wall hanging, depicts Tara, who vowed to become a female bodhisattva to show that the difference between male and female is unimportant, as these ideas are illusory.

May I be an unending treasury for those desperate and forlorn. May I manifest as what they require and wish to have near them.
Shantideva

Buddhists may offer incense or flowers before a buddha image as an act of devotion. This is not worship of a god but respect for an enlightened human being, imaginatively expressed.

Known to Tibetans as Chenrezig, Avalokiteshvara takes on a female form as Kuan Yin in China, and Kannon in Japan. Avalokiteshvara is most commonly depicted as having four arms: two are crossed over his heart, a third holds a lotus flower, and a fourth holds a rosary. The crossed arms symbolize the boddhisattva's compassionate outpouring from his heart to earthly beings. The lotus flower represents enlightenment and pure wisdom, while the rosary symbolizes his desire to liberate earthly beings from their endless cyclical existence. The 14th Dalai Lama (p.159) is traditionally thought of as an incarnation of this Bodhisattva of Compassion.

Not all Mahayana images are elaborate in appearance. Each of the *dhyana* or "meditation" buddhas such as Buddha Amitabha, for example, are depicted sitting cross-legged, wearing a very plain robe, their eyes closed in meditation.

However elaborate or not these images may be, and however far removed they may appear to be from the straightforward teaching of the historical Buddha, they are all taken to represent aspects of enlightenment. They are not gods to be worshipped, although it may be hard to remember this when observing Buddhists paying tribute to them in temples and shrines.

Focuses for meditation
Images of bodhisattvas and buddhas are regarded as aids to spiritual progress. In meditation, a person may become adept at visualizing his or her chosen image, being able to construct it imaginatively at will. So, the practitioner of meditation has an ongoing relationship with a particular image. It is often selected for that purpose, on the advice of a teacher, in order to address a particular quality—represented by the image of a bodhisattva or buddha—that the individual needs or wants to develop. The benefit of such a practice is generally only apparent over a period of time; it is not seen as an automatic process, but one

that requires sustained personal attention to the qualities and ideals that the image represents.

The impermanent mandala
The mandala is another Buddhist image created for the purpose of spiritual development, whether used for meditation or instruction. A mandala is a geometric pattern in which various shapes, letters, and images of buddhas and bodhisattvas are intricately interwoven in a complex image.

The patterns are carefully created out of colored sand, displayed at festivals, and then destroyed. Their destruction is important because it reinforces the idea that everything is temporary. To attempt to retain the images would encourage clinging and craving, which are counter to Buddhist teachings since they lead to frustration and suffering. It is only through letting go—embracing detachment—that the journey to enlightenment can begin.

Emptiness and buddhas
The Buddhist philosopher Nagarjuna (see facing page) argued that everything is empty

> If you want others to be happy, practice compassion. If you want to be happy, practice compassion.
> **The Dalai Lama**

of inherent existence. By this he meant that nothing in the world, including all living beings, has a self or, therefore, an underlying essence (or "inherent existence"). He maintained that this idea was implied by Buddha's original teaching about the concept of interconnectedness (pp.130–35),

which sees earthly items and beings as having no essence (or "own being") because they are all dependent on the prior existence of something else. Given that we ourselves have no independent, underlying essence, the aim of meditation is to see beyond our senses and the ideas we have gained from them, to look directly upon ultimate truth.

Given that the buddhas and bodhisattvas may be conjured up in meditation, this suggests that they are neither substantial (in other words, they do not have a physical embodiment), nor located somewhere else in the universe. Each of the images conjured up is not a representation of a person, but part of the ultimate truth about the person who sits in meditation. The vast array of buddha and bodhisattva images are merely temporary aids to assist a person in recognizing that every individual is a potential Buddha. ∎

Nagarjuna

Nagarjuna is considered the most important Buddhist philosopher after Buddha himself. He was born in the 2nd century CE to a brahmin (priestly) family, probably in southern India. An oracle predicted his early death at the age of eight, so when he was seven, his parents sent him to a monastery to study under the great Buddhist teacher Saraha. It is said that he avoided death by reciting a mantra without interruption on the eve and dawn of his eighth birthday. He then took monastic vows.

Nagarjuna is best known for the teaching of Buddha's Perfection of Wisdom sutras. According to legend, he rescued these from *nagas* (half-worldly spirits), gaining the name Nagarjuna (master of the *nagas*). He also wrote many sutras himself, and founded the Madhyamika (middle position) school of Buddhist philosophy.

Key works

c.200 CE *Fundamental Verses of the Middle Way; The Treatise on the Great Perfection of Wisdom*

There are three types of bodhisattva, who approach their task of helping others reach enlightenment in different ways.

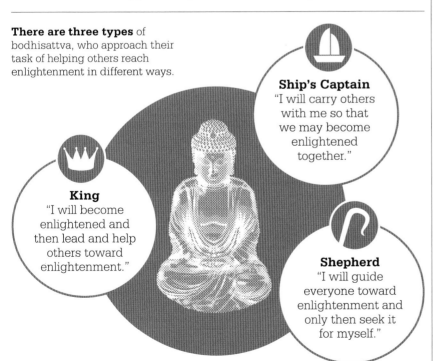

Ship's Captain "I will carry others with me so that we may become enlightened together."

King "I will become enlightened and then lead and help others toward enlightenment."

Shepherd "I will guide everyone toward enlightenment and only then seek it for myself."

ACT OUT YOUR BELIEFS
THE PERFORMANCE OF RITUAL AND REPETITION

Tibetan Buddhism uses **colorful and imaginative rituals**.

→ These aim to engage the Buddhist **emotionally and physically**, not just intellectually.

↓

Act out your beliefs.

← This allows the Buddhist to experience what it would feel like to **be enlightened**.

In most forms of Buddhism the rituals are simple (perhaps just making an offering before a Buddha image), while Tibetan Buddhism is colorful and dramatic. During worship, monks may chant repeated phrases (mantras), wear striking headdresses, blow horns, and use elaborate hand gestures (mudras)—often while holding small symbolic objects (*vajras*) and bells. Lay Buddhists may also chant, turn prayer wheels, and set out colorful prayer flags. At festivals, there may be dramatic performances and dancing, with huge images on cloth spread out or hung on temple walls, and the creation and destruction of intricate sand patterns, known as mandalas (p.156). How is all of this, which seems so different from the early simplicity of the Buddhist path, explained and justified?

For more than a thousand years, Buddhism and Hinduism coexisted in India and influenced one another. When Padmasambhava, revered as the founder of Tibetan Buddhism, took the religion to Tibet in the

See also: Symbolism made real 46–47 ▪ Living the Way of the Gods 82–85 ▪ Devotion through puja 114–15 ▪ Buddhas and bodhisattvas 152–57 ▪ Sufism and the mystic tradition 282–83 ▪ Devotion to the Sweet Lord 322

early 8th century, it was in a form influenced both by the general Mahayana tradition, which had already spread to China, and by the devotional tradition (bhakti) of Hinduism that had developed in India during the previous centuries. Bhakti involved a more personal and emotional engagement with worship, which was taken a step further in both Hinduism and Buddhism with the development of Tantra.

Tantra involves not just thinking about what will be achieved by spiritual practice, but also a process of acting out. For instance, rather than simply visualizing an image of a buddha, the practitioner imagines him or herself *as* that buddha. This process of emotional engagement involves the whole person, not just the intellect, encouraging him or her to feel what it would be like to be enlightened.

So, for example, the mudras that are made in Tantric worship are the same as those depicted on the images of buddhas and bodhisattvas. Each of the mudras expresses a particular quality: an open-handed gesture, palm turned outward, expresses generosity; the fearless mudra with the right hand raised as though giving a greeting, a blessing, or even a stop sign, is believed to induce a feeling of determination. By making these gestures, a Buddhist imitates the image of the buddha or bodhisattva, and thereby identifies with what it represents. Chanting, mudras, and other aspects of Tantric Buddhism aim to immerse the worshipper in a dramatic expression of what the path toward enlightenment is about, by not just explaining it, but making it feel real.

Personalized rituals

Tantric rituals are performed under the instruction of a teacher, or lama, who selects those that are likely to be of particular value to each individual. In other words, practitioners are given an individualized set of images to visualize, mantras to chant,

Buddhist monks perform a ritual at a northern Indian monastery. The bright clothing and headdresses are intended to engage believers emotionally.

and mudras to perform, depending on their personal inclinations and what they hope to achieve.

Although there are Tantric aspects to publicly accessible forms of Tibetan worship, many Tantric rituals are designed to be performed in private and their details are generally kept secret. But, whether performed in private or public, the feature common to all is that beliefs and values are acted out using esoteric texts and actions. ▪

The Dalai Lama is the 14th in line from Tsongkhapa, who founded the Gelugpa sect of Tibetan Buddhism in the 15th century.

Tibetan lamas

In Mahayana Buddhism, a bodhisattva is someone who remains on earth to help others, perhaps through many lifetimes (p.155). Tibetan Buddhism refines the idea to a *tulku*, or "reincarnate lama"—lama being the title given to a senior Buddhist teacher in Tibet. When a great lama dies, it is thought that another will be born to carry on his work. A search is made for the new lama, and the child candidate is expected to identify objects from his past life as a sign that he is indeed the reincarnation. There are hundreds of *tulku*: perhaps the best known is the Dalai Lama, considered the incarnate form of Avalokiteshvara, a bodhisattva of compassion and the patron deity of Tibet. While he is regarded as the bodhisattva's latest manifestation, he remains an ordinary human, albeit one with the extraordinary vocation of expressing Avalokiteshvara in today's world.

DISCOVER YOUR BUDDHA NATURE

ZEN INSIGHTS THAT GO BEYOND WORDS

IN CONTEXT

KEY EVENT
**The development
of Zen Buddhism**

WHEN AND WHERE
12th–13th century CE, Japan

BEFORE
6th century BCE The Buddha
teaches meditation leading
to insight and enlightenment.

6th century CE The Buddhist
monk Bodhidharma brings
meditation Buddhism (Ch'an)
to China, and is said to have
instigated martial arts training
at the Shaolin monastery.

AFTER
1950s–1960s Zen ideas
become popular in Western
counterculture, as seen in
the work of the Beat poets and
Robert Pirsig's *Zen and the
Art of Motorcycle Maintenance*.
Many Zen meditation groups
and California's first Zen
monastery are founded.

Zen and its Chinese
equivalent, Ch'an, simply
mean "meditation." As
a tradition of Buddhist practice,
it is generally regarded as having
been founded by an Indian monk,
Bodhidharma, who brought it to
China in 520 CE, and is credited
with the definition of Zen as "a
direct transmission of awakened
consciousness, outside tradition
and outside scriptures".

This definition highlights the
key features of Zen: it seeks to
allow enlightenment to happen
naturally, as a result of a clearing
of the mind, and does so without
the need for rational argument,
texts, or rituals. In other words,

See also: Aligning the self with the *dao* 66–67 ▪ Sufism and the mystic tradition 282–83 ▪ Life-energy cultivation in Falun Dafa 323

Using words—in prayer, or discussion—**creates clutter in our mind**.

↓

Thinking and reading silently just create more **words in our heads**.

↓

When we strive to find answers and insight, our **desire clouds the mind**.

↓

If we are to discover our Buddha nature, we must **empty our minds** of all these things.

↓

With an empty mind, **insight and understanding** will come to us without words.

Nishida Kitaro

The Japanese philosopher Nishida Kitaro (1870–1945) studied both Zen Buddhism and the history of Western philosophy, and tried to express Buddhist insights using Western philosophical terms. He taught at the University of Kyoto from 1910 to 1928, and founded what is known as the Kyoto School of Philosophy.

Nishida argued that pure experience took place before the split between subject and object, self and world—exactly the distinction made by Zen between the ego-based mind and the undifferentiated unity of the Buddha mind (see left). This he compared to the ideas of the German philosopher Immanuel Kant (1724–1804), who distinguished between a person's experience of things (phenomena) and the things themselves (noumena), the latter being unknowable. Nishida even introduced the idea of God as the basis of reality and our true self, and compared Zen with Heidegger, Aristotle, Bergson, and Hegel.

Key work

1911 *A Study of Good*

it creates the conditions in which a person's mental clutter, which detracts from clarity of the mind, can be replaced by direct insight.

Zen claims to continue a tradition that goes back to the earliest days of Buddhist teachings. There is a story that one day, surrounded by his disciples, the Buddha simply held up a flower, turning it in his hand without speaking. One of the disciples, Kasyapa, smiled; he had seen the point. That wordless insight, it is claimed, was passed down from teacher to disciple for 28 generations to Bodhidharma, who took it to China, from where it spread to Japan. So, rather than being a product of the development of the two main Buddhist branches, Theravada and Mahayana (p.330), Zen sees itself as having developed independently via a separate line of transmission.

Buddha mind

Central to Buddhism is the idea that existential unhappiness is caused by the illusion that each person has a fixed ego, which is separate from the rest of the world, yet which clings to it, trying to hold on to what changes.

Zen sees this as the small, superficial mind; one that people acquire at birth, then develop, influenced by those around them. However, it holds that people also »

Sitting and meditating is all that is required to achieve enlightenment in Soto Zen. The stilling of the mind dispels the illusion of self.

be repeated many times. It is said to happen almost as if by accident; it cannot be forced, because wanting to achieve satori is a form of grasping. Zen does not seek to define reality or the nature of satori.

Soto Zen was developed in Japan in the 13th century by the teacher Dogen, who had traveled in China and there encountered a meditation tradition called Ts'ong Tung. His form of meditation is very different from the Rinzai form. Instead of trying to trigger sudden insight, Soto Zen is based on sitting meditation (zazen) and a more gradual process of enlightenment.

Soto considered that religious traditions and rituals could be dispensed with: enlightenment could be achieved simply through the practice of zazen. This involves periods of sitting in an upright, cross-legged position, facing a blank wall, interspersed with reflective walking, known as *kinhin*. In meditation, the mind is cleared of its flow of ideas, so that the process of sitting is exactly what

have a Buddha mind, freed from egocentric, conceptual thinking. This is innate, but hidden by the clutter of the small mind. People gain nothing by discovering their Buddha mind, they simply recognize what they have had all along.

Zen teacher Dogen said that the true self is not the superficial ego that each person has now, but the original face he or she had before they were born and molded by experience. It is only when people develop their own faces that they see themselves as separate entities and become egocentric. Dogen is therefore suggesting that people should strive to recognize who they were before they were conditioned by life and experience.

Zen in Japan
There are two main forms of Zen: Rinzai and Soto. Rinzai Zen was established in Japan in the 12th century by Eisai, and reformed in the 18th century by Hakuin. This school introduced the Zen view that the world is an illusion and that reality is in fact a simple,

indivisible unity. Zen has no scriptures or formal teachings; it is an oral teaching, a tradition of meditation passed from teacher to pupil—hence the importance of practicing only under the guidance of an experienced teacher.

A key feature of Rinzai Zen, introduced by Hakuin, is the use of koans—unanswerable questions that shatter conventional thinking. Probably the best-known koan is Hakuin's, "What is the sound of one hand clapping?" Those who think they know the answer to a koan should think again, and let go of all preconceived notions. Rationally examining a koan, or a Zen dialogue (a *mondo*) is unlikely to yield great insight, since it is too easy to view it only within the parameters of personal discursive thought. A Zen teacher will try to guard against that happening.

As a result of Zen practice, a person may suddenly experience satori—insight or enlightenment. This is not a one-time or permanent state of enlightenment, but a momentary experience that may

If you understand the first word of Zen you will know the last word. The last word and the first word: they are not one word.
Mumon

> If you meet the Buddha on the road, kill him!
> **Zen koan**

enlightenment is about. A person does not sit in order to become enlightened; in the act of sitting that person is *already* enlightened. Stilling the mind and clearing away the illusion of a separate self is enlightenment.

Beyond words

In Zen meditation, something is seen but cannot be described. Careful attention to a piece of calligraphy or raking sand in a garden—both of which are features of Zen practice—can help to free the mind from the constant process of thinking, allowing a person to act in greater harmony with nature. That is why Zen finds expression in many artistic forms, from flower arranging to computer design.

Zen is about creating situations that bring insight, without trying to explain or express it rationally. To try to describe the goal of Zen is to have failed to understand it: Zen aims to set the mind free from content; it is not part of that content. Zen is not studied, it is practiced; and if satori or enlightenment is finally achieved, nothing new is known—all that is known is that it is not necessary to know anything. Deliberately full of paradoxes, Zen aims to gradually break down the normal processes of logical thought.

Attempting to explain something is to grasp at it, and that grasping is what the Buddha described as the cause of suffering. In a world where people seek to gain things, to claim knowledge and insight like personal possessions, Zen is the ultimate frustration. Collecting beautiful Zen artifacts could never result in understanding what lies behind their production. Zen is letting go.

In some ways, Zen returns to the earliest phase of Buddhism, before the buddha and bodhisattva images, devotional practices, and revered scriptures. Enlightenment is open to all: indeed, everyone is already enlightened, if only they could recognize it. Zen dispenses with almost everything related to religion and presents itself as a path of insight and understanding that is without religious trappngs.

It is also deliberately anarchic, its stories provocative, and its teachers notoriously challenging. Asked to summarize Buddhism, Bodhidharma is believed to have replied, "Vast emptiness; nothing holy"—not what was expected, but to the point. ∎

That wind, banner, and mind are not innately different is what this koan seeks to demonstrate. Externalization is a function of the ego-based mind, not of the undifferentiating Buddha mind.

> **Neither the wind nor the banner is moving. It is your minds that are moving.**

> **I say the banner is moving.**

> **I say the wind is moving, not the banner.**

The **era of the Patriarchs**: Abraham, his son Isaac, and grandson Jacob.

King David reigns over Israel as God's anointed one, or "messiah."

Millions of Jews die in two **revolts against Roman rule**, and are again driven out of Israel.

The **Talmud** is completed. It includes the Mishnah and the Gemara (commentaries on the Mishnah).

The Zohar, a key work in the kabbalah (the Jewish mystical movement), is compiled.

c.2000–1500 BCE   **c.1005–965 BCE**   **70 AND 135 CE**   **c.425 CE**   **1250**

c.1300 BCE   **EARLY 6TH CENTURY BCE**   **200 CE**   **900–1200**

Moses leads his people from captivity in Egypt to **Canaan, the Promised Land**, and receives the **Torah**.

Babylon conquers David's kingdom of Israel and in 586 BCE destroys the First Temple of Jerusalem.

A written version of **Jewish Oral Law**, the Mishnah, is compiled.

The **Golden Age of Jewish culture in Spain** expands; the philosopher Maimonides writes influential works.

O ne of the oldest surviving religions, Judaism evolved from the beliefs of the people of Canaan in the southern Levant region, more than 3,500 years ago, and is closely connected to the history of the Jewish people. The Hebrew Bible, the Tanakh, tells not only the story of God's creation of the world, but also the story of his special relationship with the Jews.

God's agreement, or covenant, with the Jewish people began with God's promise to Abraham that he would be the father of a great people. God told Abraham that his descendants must obey him and adopt the rite of circumcision as a sign of the covenant; in return, God would guide them, protect them, and give them the land of Israel. Abraham was rewarded for his

faith with a son, Isaac; he in turn had a son, Jacob, who, the Tanakh relates, was the father of the Twelve Tribes of Israel. Together Abraham, Isaac, and Jacob are known as the Patriarchs—the physical and spiritual ancestors of Judaism.

The Tanakh recounts how Jacob and his descendants were enslaved in Egypt, and then led to freedom by Moses at God's command in the Exodus. As part of Moses's covenant with God, he received the Torah (the Five Books of Moses) on Mount Sinai. Moses took his people back to the Land of Israel, where they settled once again. Later, God appointed David—the anointed one or "messiah"—as king, from which came the belief that a descendant of his, the Messiah, would come to bring in a new age for the Jewish people. David's son

Solomon built a permanent temple in Jerusalem, symbolizing the claim of the Jewish people on the Land of Israel. But twice the Jews were forced from their "Promised Land" and the temple destroyed: first by the Babylonians in the 6th century BCE, and again after they had returned and fallen under Roman rule, in the 1st century CE.

The Diaspora

As a result of foreign rule, the Jewish people became a widespread diaspora. Some Jews, later known as the Sephardim, settled in Spain, Portugal, North Africa, and the Middle East, but the majority, the Ashkenazim, formed communities in Central and Eastern Europe. Inevitably, the geographical separation led to differences in the way Judaism developed between

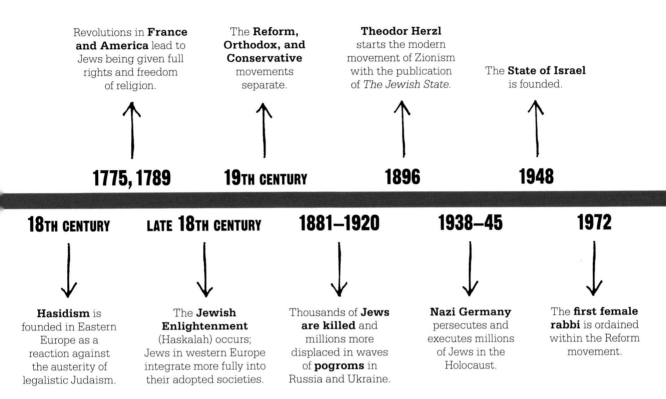

Revolutions in **France and America** lead to Jews being given full rights and freedom of religion.

The **Reform, Orthodox, and Conservative** movements separate.

Theodor Herzl starts the modern movement of Zionism with the publication of *The Jewish State*.

The **State of Israel** is founded.

1775, 1789

19TH CENTURY

1896

1948

18TH CENTURY

LATE 18TH CENTURY

1881–1920

1938–45

1972

Hasidism is founded in Eastern Europe as a reaction against the austerity of legalistic Judaism.

The **Jewish Enlightenment** (Haskalah) occurs; Jews in western Europe integrate more fully into their adopted societies.

Thousands of **Jews are killed** and millions more displaced in waves of **pogroms** in Russia and Ukraine.

Nazi Germany persecutes and executes millions of Jews in the Holocaust.

The **first female rabbi** is ordained within the Reform movement.

the groups, and various different religious traditions evolved. In Spain, a Golden Age of Jewish thinking flourished between the 10th and 12th centuries, which produced great philosophers such as Moses Maimonides. This was also the center, in the Middle Ages, of interest in the more mystical aspects of Judaism, known as kabbalah. In eastern Europe, a number of the more isolated small Jewish settlements, the shtetls, found that the scholarliness of their religion did little to promote strong community ties, and a more spiritual movement, Hasidism, emerged as a result. In the following centuries, there were further divisions in Judaism, largely over matters of interpretation of Jewish Law. Orthodox Judaism advocated a strict adherence to the

Torah, which was considered to be divine in origin, while Reform and Conservative Judaism took a less rigorous approach, regarding the Torah more as a set of guidelines rather than obligations. An issue that divided the different branches of Judaism in the 20th century was the status of women. In spite of the doctrine ruling that Jewish identity is passed down solely through the maternal line, women were not able to play an active part in religious ceremonies until recently.

Oppression and identity

Largely because of their position as displaced immigrants and their distinctive faith, Jews have been widely persecuted throughout their history. In many places, they have been isolated in ghettos, and suffered violent vilification and

attacks. From the 18th century on, countries such as the US and France granted them full rights, and there was a movement toward greater integration. However, this posed a question of identity. Were the Jewish people a religious, ethnic, cultural, or national group? Zionism, which arose in response, pressed for the formation of a Jewish state, and matters were brought to a head in the aftermath of the Holocaust with the formation of the State of Israel in 1948. Today, it is difficult to assess how many followers of Judaism there are, because many who identify themselves as Jewish are not actively religious. However, it is estimated that there are more than 13 million Jewish people in the world, the majority of them living in either North America or Israel. ∎

I WILL TAKE YOU AS MY PEOPLE, AND I WILL BE YOUR GOD

GOD'S COVENANT WITH ISRAEL

IN CONTEXT

KEY TEXT
The Torah

WHEN AND WHERE
c.1000–450 BCE,
the Middle East

BEFORE
c.1300 BCE Hittite royal treaties provide a model for the Torah's description of the covenant.

AFTER
200–500 CE The Mishnah and Talmud codify the oral law, or received body of rabbinic learning, and are used to offer further Biblical interpretation and guidance on the covenant.

1948 In the aftermath of World War II, the State of Israel is founded, allowing Jewish people to return to their historical homeland.

1990 US theologian Judith Plaskow urges Jews to reinterpret traditional texts that exclude women from the covenant.

God asked Abraham to **leave his home** and **family**, and go to another land.

If he did so, **God promised** to reward him; this promise became known as **the covenant**

This promise was that as long as Abraham and his descendants obeyed God, **God would protect his descendants** and give them the land of Canaan forever.

"I will take you as my people, and I will be your God."

The covenant, or contract, with God is the central concept of Judaism, and dates back to the beliefs of the Israelites, an ancient Middle Eastern people. In fact, Jews view themselves as bound to God by a series of covenants. The Abrahamic covenant was the first, specifically singling out the Israelites as God's chosen people, while the later Mosaic covenants (mediated by Moses) renewed this initial bond.

The Israelites, sometimes called Hebrews, were a people who occupied part of Canaan, roughly equivalent to modern Israel and Palestine, perhaps as early as the 15th century BCE. In around 1200 BCE, during a period when this part of the world was under Egyptian rule, an inscription was carved that contains the first mention of Israel as a people.

In the 6th century BCE, many of the Israelites were forced into exile in Babylonia. During this period of exile, much of the Hebrew, or Jewish, Bible was composed. It sets down the history of the Israelite people and the origin of their religious beliefs.

The first covenant

Like many peoples in the ancient Middle East, the Israelites were polytheists, but worshipped a national god, one whom they viewed as offering their people particular protection. Jews were later to deem their God's name too holy to pronounce and did not preserve its original vowels, so it became known only by its four consonants: YHWH (probably pronounced "Yahweh"). YHWH was also known by several other names, including El and Elohim, meaning God.

See also: Animism in early societies 24–25 ▪ Sacrifice and blood offerings 40–45 ▪ The burden of observance 50 ▪ A challenge to the covenant 198

According to the Book of Genesis, the first of the five books of the Torah (the first section of the Hebrew Bible), it was by God's decree that the Israelites first settled in Canaan. He called on a man, Abraham, born in the Mesopotamian city-state of Ur (in modern-day Iraq) and commanded him to travel to a place named Canaan, which was to become the Israelite homeland. The Torah recounts that in Canaan, God established a covenant with Abraham, which took a similar form to a type of royal grant that kings of the time handed out to loyal subordinates. It stipulated that, as a reward for Abraham's loyalty, God would grant him many descendants who would inherit the land. As a sign of this compact, Abraham and all the male members of his household were circumcised. To this day,

Abraham's loyalty was tested when God asked him to sacrifice his son Isaac. However, at the last moment, God sent an angel to stop Abraham, as shown in this 18th-century painting.

Jewish boys are circumcised on the eighth day after their birth as a sign that they are parties to this pledge.

Abraham had two sons, Ishmael and Isaac. God blessed Ishmael, promising that he would become the father of a great nation. But it was Isaac that God chose to inherit the covenant from his father, appearing to him directly. Isaac in turn handed down the covenant to his son Jacob, who in his turn received the name Israel from God and handed the covenant down to all his offspring.

Abraham, Isaac, and Jacob are known as Israel's patriarchs, because they represent the first three generations included in the covenant with God.

The covenant at Sinai

The Torah relates that when Canaan was struck by famine, Jacob and his sons migrated to Egypt, where their descendants were subsequently enslaved. Several generations later, when the Israelite population in Egypt had increased, God appointed Moses, an Israelite raised in the Egyptian court, to lead the people out of slavery and back to the land of Canaan. The Israelites' escape from Egypt (the Exodus) involved many miracles: God struck the Egyptians with plagues that included afflicting them with boils and turning the Nile to blood, and he split the Red Sea so that the Israelites could pass through. With these miracles, God demonstrated his power, and his loyalty to the covenant with the patriarchs.

After liberating the Israelites from Egypt, and before leading them into Canaan, God brought »

The Hebrew Bible

The Hebrew, or Jewish, Bible, the sacred scriptures of the Jewish people, is a collection of writings composed mostly in the Hebrew language and written over the course of the first millennium BCE. With some variations in sequence and content, these same scriptures make up the Old Testament of the Christian Bible.

Jewish tradition divides the Bible into three parts. The first, called the Torah or Pentateuch, describes God's creation of the world and his covenant with Israel, and outlines the commandments that were imposed on the Israelites. Tradition attributes the Torah to Moses, but modern scholars believe that it was written by many authors over several centuries.

The second part of the Bible, Prophets, includes a narrative of Israelite history. This runs from the people's entry into Canaan to the end of their kingdom, when their capital and temple are destroyed and their people exiled. It also contains the writings of the prophets.

The final part, called Writings, comprises a diverse collection of later literature.

them to a mountain called Sinai, or Horeb. Moses ascended the mountain to speak to God, and a new covenant was established between God and the entire people of Israel. The covenant at Sinai recalled God's salvation of Israel and promised the Israelites that they would be God's treasured possession if they observed the commandments that he had given to Moses on Mount Sinai.

According to the Torah, God spoke these commandments aloud from the top of Mount Sinai, which was covered by cloud and fire, while all the people of Israel listened from below. Tradition has it that these commandments were inscribed personally by God onto the two stone tablets that Moses brought down from the mountain, although the Torah is not consistently clear on this point. Moses broke the tablets in anger when he saw that the Israelites had built a false god, a golden calf, while he was on the summit. He returned to Mount Sinai to have a new set of stone tablets inscribed, and these were placed in a gilded chest called

> The whole land of Canaan… I will give as an everlasting possession to you and your descendants after you; and I will be their God.
> **Genesis 17:8**

the Ark of the Covenant. The ark was equipped with poles so that it could be carried by the Israelites as they continued to Canaan.

The commandments

The most famous commandments in the Sinai covenant are the Ten Commandments, or the Decalogue. The Decalogue comprises the most fundamental rules of Israel's covenant. It prohibits the worship of other gods or the depiction of God in physical form; it says that each week the Israelites must observe a sacred day of rest, the Sabbath; and it prohibits certain actions, such as murder and adultery.

In addition to the Decalogue, the Torah includes numerous laws that God is said to have conveyed to the Israelites indirectly through Moses, both at Sinai and on other occasions. These laws also form part of the covenant. According to a calculation in the Talmud (rabbinic interpretation of

When the Israelites fled Egypt during the Exodus, God protected them and supplied them with food, as shown here in *The Gathering of the Manna*, a 15th-century work.

Jewish law) there are a total of 613 commandments in the Torah. They address many aspects of the Israelites' life in Canaan. Some constitute what we would consider civil law, describing systems of government, regulating property disputes, and setting guidelines for dealing with cases of murder and theft, among other matters. Others relate to the construction of a sanctuary for worshipping God, and establish sacrificial rites to be performed by a hereditary priesthood. Still others direct the behavior of individual Israelites, instructing them on matters ranging from what they may eat, and whom they may marry, to the fair and charitable treatment of other people. Generally, the commandments aimed to establish a society that was just, by the standards of the day, and distinctive in its service of God.

The final book of the Torah, Deuteronomy, describes a third covenant between God and Israel, established in the land of Moab (in modern-day Jordan) before the Israelites entered Canaan. Deuteronomy tells that God commanded Moses to make this additional covenant with the people of Israel. It took the form of a final address from Moses, who was to die before he entered the promised land. Moses recalled God's salvation of Israel, relayed further commandments that God had given him at Sinai, and promised that God would bless the Israelites if they obeyed the commandments, and curse them if they disobeyed. The covenant at Moab reaffirmed the Israelites' loyalty to their God and his commandments.

The covenant in practice

In principle, traditional Jews consider the laws of the Torah eternally binding. However, the commandments have been subject to centuries of interpretation, and many are no longer applicable in practice. Certain laws pertaining to the rule of kings, for example, have not been applicable since the fall of the monarchy of Judah in the 6th century BCE, and the sacrificial rites have not been practiced by mainstream Jews since the Romans destroyed their temple in Jerusalem in 70 CE. In addition, many of the Torah's

The rituals of Judaism, such as the lighting of candles for Shabbat, the Sabbath or day of rest, serve to remind Jews of the bond created by their covenant with God.

laws deal with agriculture and are considered binding only in Israel. In the present day, Jews maintain a range of approaches to the commandments and their interpretations. Traditional Jews observe the Sabbath, the festivals, and dietary laws (such as avoiding certain meats and not mixing meat and dairy), as well as ››

Noah is not only an important figure in Judaism and Christianity, but also in Islam; his covenant with God forms part of the Qur'an.

The covenant with Noah

In addition to God's covenant with Israel, the Torah also tells of a covenant between God and all living beings. God made this covenant with Noah, whose family survived a primordial flood that wiped out most life on Earth. This covenant stipulated that God would never again destroy the world by flood. Like Israel's patriarchs after him, Noah was also promised many descendants who would fill the Earth. The sign of God's covenant with Noah was the rainbow, which would thereafter serve as a reminder of God's promise of safety. Later Jewish tradition understood the Noahide covenant to include seven commandments, which were incumbent on all humankind. These Noahide laws forbade idolatry, murder, blasphemy, theft, sexual immorality (such as incest), and consuming forbidden flesh, and required courts of justice to be set up.

The Israelites' loyalty to God was tested by 40 years of exile in the desert. This is commemorated in the festival of Sukkot, in which fragile booths are built to resemble their desert homes.

the promise of the land, although conditional, remains eternal: the Israelites might lose the land for a time due to their sins, but they need not lose hope of returning.

The "Chosen People"
The Torah offers little in terms of explanation as to why God chose the patriarchs and their descendants, yet it emphasizes that by virtue of their covenantal relationship with him, the Israelites are privileged above other nations. The authors of the Bible did not view the Israelites as inherently superior to other people—on the contrary, they often describe them as sinful and unworthy—but they clearly perceived Israel's status as special. As Jews came to believe that their god was the one God who ruled the whole world, their status as his chosen nation took on even greater significance.

Throughout history, Jews have struggled to understand why God chose them and what this choice implied about their place in the world. One ancient tradition suggests that, rather than God choosing Israel, Israel chose God. This tradition maintains that God offered the commandments to all the nations of the earth, but all except Israel rejected them, finding them too burdensome. In accordance with this view, the Israelites' status is not a result of choice on God's part, but a product of free will. At the same time, it seems to deny freedom of choice by holding individuals responsible for the decisions of their ancestors.

other rules. But for many modern Jews, the essential laws are those that pertain to the love of one's neighbor and the just treatment of other human beings. Progressive Jews often cite a dictum attributed to Rabbi Hillel the Elder on the Golden Rule: "That which is hateful to you, do not do to your neighbor. That is the whole Torah; the rest is the explanation."

If you will obey Me faithfully and keep My covenant, you shall be My treasured possession among all the peoples.
Exodus 19:5

The promise of the land
In his covenant with Abraham, God granted the land of Canaan to the patriarch's descendants as an inviolable gift. Yet it is stated elsewhere in the Bible that the Israelites' hold on the land is conditional on observance of the commandments. This conditionality is said to explain why the Israelites were eventually conquered by their enemies and exiled from their land. Parts of the Torah include exile among the curses that would befall the Israelites if they violated the covenants at Sinai and Moab; many modern scholars believe that these passages were written in response to these events.

At the same time, the Torah asserts that God never abandoned his covenant with the patriarchs. While in exile, the Israelites had the opportunity to repent, and God led them back to their land, thereby upholding his covenant with Abraham. In this way

> The meaning of Jewish history revolves around the faithfulness of Israel to the covenant.
> **Abraham Joshua Heschel, Polish-born US rabbi**

Some Jewish mystical traditions with origins in the Middle Ages suggest a different perspective, asserting that the souls of Jews were chosen at the time of creation and are qualitatively superior to those of non-Jews. However, prominent thinkers from the major modern denominations of Judaism (Modern Orthodox, Conservative, and Reform) emphatically reject any claims of essential difference between Jews and non-Jews. Modern Jewish thinkers tend to view the covenant instead as imposing a mission on Jews to live in accordance with God's will and thereby convey God's truth to the world. Some have suggested that Israel is not unique in having been chosen by God, and that other peoples may have been chosen to fulfill other missions. Some liberal Jews reject the idea of chosenness on the grounds that it presupposes superiority over other people and encourages ethnocentrism.

Joining the covenant

Traditional Judaism maintains that status in the covenant is transmitted from parent to child through the maternal line; so the child of a Jewish mother is automatically Jewish and bound by the commandments. This inherited status cannot be forfeited: a Jew who does not observe the commandments has violated the covenant, but he or she remains a Jew. On the other hand, it is possible for a non-Jew to become Jewish through conversion. Under rabbinic law, a convert to Judaism must accept the Jewish commandments and be immersed in a ritual bath (and if male, be circumcised), at which point he, or she, assumes all the rights and duties of a Jew.

Traditionally, conversion to Judaism involved a commitment to a strict regime of observance. Today, progressive Judaism places greater emphasis on individual autonomy in determining Jewish identity and its obligations. In both Reform Judaism in the US and Liberal Judaism in the UK, the children of Jewish fathers and non-Jewish mothers are accepted without formal conversion if they self-identify as Jewish.

In spite of varying beliefs and practices, the concept of the covenant remains central to all streams of Judaism. It represents and defines the individual Jew's purpose in the world, linking him or her to the Jewish people across the span of history, and to the Jewish God. ∎

How an individual joins the covenant depends on the faith, or otherwise, of his or her parents. Judaism does not actively seek converts, but accepts those who show commitment and sincerity.

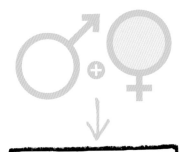

If your **mother is Jewish** and your father is not, then **you are Jewish**, and can never be not Jewish.

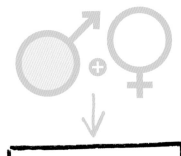

If only your **father is Jewish**, some modern denominations **will accept you** without conversion.

If neither of your parents is Jewish, **you may convert** to Judaism, following the correct rituals.

BESIDE ME THERE IS NO OTHER GOD

FROM MONOLATRY TO MONOTHEISM

IN CONTEXT

KEY SOURCE
Second Isaiah

WHEN AND WHERE
c.540 BCE, Babylon/Judea

BEFORE
1400–1200 BCE The prophet Zoroaster forms a new religion with one supreme god.

c.1000 BCE The "Song of the Sea," a poem in the Bible's Exodus, proclaims YHWH supreme over other gods.

c.622 BCE King Josiah of Judah abolishes worship of gods other than YHWH.

AFTER
c.20 BCE–40 CE Philo of Alexandria argues that biblical monotheism had anticipated later Greek philosophical conceptions of God.

7th century Islam is revealed to the Prophet Muhammad, and monotheism supplants polytheistic beliefs held among the tribes of Arabia.

YHWH is the **greatest god**; his power is supreme, universal, and eternal.

⬇

Because he is **omnipotent** he needs no subordinates.

⬇

No other being can **countermand** his wishes.

⬇

Even **events** that harm his people—the Israelites—are **orchestrated by him**.

⬇

Both the **evil and good** of the world are part of **his plan**.

⬇

There are no other gods but YHWH.

The earliest authors of the Jewish Bible seem to have acknowledged the existence of many gods, but insisted that the one whose name is rendered as YHWH was the greatest among them, and that the Israelites should worship only YHWH. It appears, then, that at some time during the biblical period, the Jewish people moved from this exclusive worship of one god among many (known as monolatry) to the belief that only one god existed (monotheism).

YHWH rules all nations
In addition to the views of the Bible's authors, archaeological evidence suggests that the early Israelites worshipped a variety of regional gods. The prophets of the god YHWH, whose writings comprise a large portion of the Bible, harshly rebuked the people for this practice. It is not clear whether the prophets were all true monotheists, but they did believe that YHWH was supremely powerful and ruled over all nations.

In 722 BCE, the Assyrians conquered the northern kingdom of Israel and exiled its people. Around 130 years later, the Babylonians

See also: Beliefs for new societies 56–57 ▪ The battle between good and evil 60–65 ▪ God's covenant with Israel 168–75 ▪ Defining the indefinable 184–85 ▪ The unity of divinity is necessary 280–81

The people of Israel were vanquished by the Assyrians during the 8th century BCE and led away to exile, as shown on this relief from the palace of Sennacherib at Nineveh.

conquered the southern lands of the Jewish people, known as the Kingdom of Judah. In the ancient Middle East, such conquests were usually interpreted as victories by the conquering people's god over that of the defeated people— so the supremacy of YHWH appeared to be challenged. Yet the prophets insisted that these events were all, in fact, YHWH's doing: he was using the other nations to punish the Israelites for violating their covenant with him (pp.168–75).

No God but YHWH

The Jews returned from exile in Babylon to their homeland in 538 BCE, under the decree of Cyrus the Great, emperor of Persia, where the Zoroastrian faith predominated.

Around this time, the earliest clear articulation of monotheism in the Bible emerged, in a collection of writings known as Second Isaiah. It emphasizes that YHWH created, and rules over, the world alone. Israel's restoration is a sign of YHWH's control over history, which is both transcendent and personal: he determines the actions of kings but also leads his people to salvation like a shepherd guiding his flock.

The problem of evil

Monotheism raises the problem of evil: namely, if there is only one God, who is just and merciful, as the Bible insists, then how can he preside over a world in which the righteous suffer? This is the theme of the biblical book of Job, which tells of a righteous man who questions how God could have allowed his terrible misfortune. God's response suggests that there is no answer: his rule over the world is beyond human understanding. ▪

Second Isaiah

The biblical Book of Isaiah claims to be the work of a prophet by that name who lived in the late 8th and early 7th centuries BCE. However, the latter portion of the book deals with the Jews' return from exile in Babylon in the 6th century BCE. Modern scholars refer to this section as Second Isaiah or Deutero-Isaiah and attribute it to one or more 6th-century writers.

Second Isaiah echoes the language and themes of the first part of the book, while also introducing new ideas and motifs, including explicit monotheism. Like earlier prophetic works, it interprets Israel's exile as punishment for the people's sins, but proclaims that the punishment has ended and it will be followed by everlasting glory when Israel finally embraces YHWH alone.

Many scholars believe that the final portion of the book was written later still and constitutes a Third Isaiah.

Before Me no God was formed, nor shall there be any after Me.
Isaiah 43:10

THE MESSIAH WILL REDEEM ISRAEL

THE PROMISE OF A NEW AGE

IN CONTEXT

KEY TEXTS
The Dead Sea Scrolls

WHEN AND WHERE
c.150 BCE–68 CE, Palestine

BEFORE
c.1005–965 BCE King David reigns over Israel as God's anointed one, or Messiah.

586 BCE The Babylonian conquest and exile of the Jews ends David's dynasty.

AFTER
1st century CE Jesus is proclaimed the Messiah.

2nd century CE Simeon Bar Kokhba is hailed as the Messiah.

20th century CE Menachem Mendel Schneerson, leader of a Hasidic sect, promotes Jewish observance as a way to bring the Messiah; he is himself hailed as the Messiah by his followers.

Throughout much of their recorded history, the people of Israel were ruled by kings. A ritual called anointing, in which oil was poured on the monarch's head, functioned much like a coronation and served to indicate God's election of the ruler, who was referred to as God's anointed one, or in Hebrew, Messiah. Originally, the term Messiah was used for any anointed leader, but over time it came to refer to a specific ruler who would arise in the future and rescue Israel from its enemies, ushering in a golden age—the Messianic Era. Jewish tradition offers much speculation as to the events that

See also: God's covenant with Israel 168–75 ▪ Faith and the state 189
▪ The origins of modern political Zionism 196–97

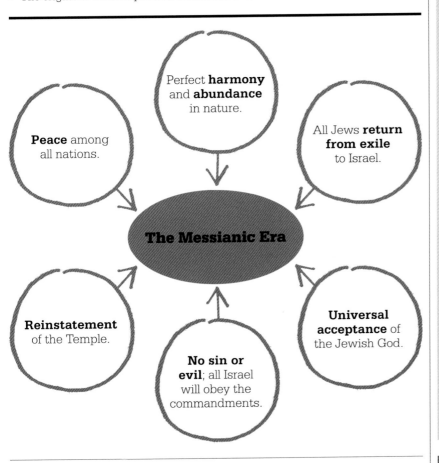

- Perfect **harmony** and **abundance** in nature.
- Peace among all nations.
- All Jews **return from exile** to Israel.
- **The Messianic Era**
- **Reinstatement** of the Temple.
- **No sin or evil**; all Israel will obey the commandments.
- **Universal acceptance** of the Jewish God.

Israelites and Jews

Abraham's son Isaac fathered two sons, Esau and Jacob; the Bible relates that God changed Jacob's name to Israel. The families of Jacob's 12 sons grew into the 12 tribes of Israel (Israelites), occupying an area roughly equivalent to the modern territory of Israel. In the late 10th century BCE, the Israelites were divided into two kingdoms—the southern tribes formed the Kingdom of Judah, while the northern tribes formed the Kingdom of Israel. These two kingdoms were subsequently conquered and broken up—Israel by the Assyrians in 722 BCE, and Judah by the Babylonians in 586 BCE. However, the people of Judah endured as a distinct group with a distinct religion. From this point, they were called "Jews" and their religion "Judaism", although they still thought of themselves as Israelites. Modern citizens of Israel are called Israelis.

would characterize the Messianic Era, but most agreed that it would be a period of brotherhood and glory on earth, when delicacies and miracles would be commonplace, swords would be beaten into plowshares, and the wolf would live with the lamb.

Some traditions speculated that the Messiah would be an earthly ruler (with a close connection to God), others that he would be a heavenly figure appointed in a time before creation itself. Similarly, a number of traditions envisioned the Messianic Era to be part of the normal course of history, while for others it was a miraculous time when God's spirit would reign on earth.

A Messiah from David's line

One of the first kings of the united monarchy of Israel and Judah was a man named David, who reigned from around 1005 to 965 BCE. According to the Bible, David was instrumental in uniting the people of Israel and defending them against the Philistines. The Bible relates that God loved David, referring to him as his son, and established an agreement, or covenant, with him, promising that his descendants would rule over Israel forever.

However, the Babylonians conquered Judah in 586 BCE, exiling most of its inhabitants and destroying the temple, and »

They will beat their swords into plowshares and their spears into pruning hooks. Nation will not take up sword against nation, nor will they train for war anymore.
Isaiah 2:4

David's dynasty came to an end. The fall of the kingdom might have suggested that God had broken his covenant with David. Yet the people of Judah continued to hold out the hope that, some time in the future, a descendant of David would once again rule over Israel as God's Messiah.

Foretold by prophets

Even before the fall of the monarchy, some of Israel's prophets predicted that a king descended from David would unite the two kingdoms and rescue them from their enemies. Although these prophecies were written in different periods and some referred to specific historical kings, later generations interpreted them as foretelling the advent of a future Messiah. After the Babylonian conquest, some prophets foretold that the people would eventually return to their homeland and rebuild their temple. A few envisioned that the nations of the world would one day recognize Israel's God and come to worship him in Jerusalem. These visions of a glorious future were not unconditional, however. The prophets believed that Israel's misfortunes were God's punishment for the sins of the people and its leaders and that future restoration would only be possible if Israel repented.

Foreign rule

The prophets' visions were partly realized when the Persian king Cyrus the Great defeated the Babylonians and allowed many Jews to return to their homeland and rebuild the Temple. Indeed, Cyrus is addressed in the Bible as the "Lord's Messiah". However, a lengthy period of domination by foreign powers, including the Greek and Roman Empires, followed the return of the Jews to the homeland. During this time, they turned again to biblical prophecies about the Messiah and an age of national restoration.

The Jews drew on prophetic traditions that envisioned a great battle between the forces of good and evil, in which God would emerge triumphant and sinners would be punished. Jewish apocalyptic works of this period, which include the Dead Sea Scrolls, offer elaborate descriptions of this battle and the accompanying

> My servant David will be king over them, and they will all have one shepherd. They will follow my laws and be careful to keep my decrees.
> **Ezekiel 37:24**

plagues and tribulations that would precede the advent of the Messiah: floods and earthquakes, the darkening of the sun and moon, and the falling of the stars from the sky. These events came to be known as the "birth pangs of the Messiah", since for all the agony that they would cause they were simply a precursor of the Messianic Era, when evil would be banished from earth, the rule of oppressive empires would be swept away, and people could live free of distraction and crime.

Biblical manuscripts make up almost half of the scrolls. Most are on parchment in Hebrew, Aramaic, Greek, or Nabatean.

The Dead Sea Scrolls

In 1947, a Bedouin goatherd discovered a cache of buried scrolls in a cave in Qumran, on the northwest shore of the Dead Sea. The scrolls are thought to be the writings of the Essenes—an ancient Jewish sect—that had been hidden when members of the sect fled the Romans during the Jewish revolt of 66–70 CE. The Essenes rejected the priesthood that was then in control of the Jerusalem temple and formed a community in the desert, where they awaited the end times, apparently believing that they alone would be redeemed in the Messianic Era, which would usher in a new, purer temple and priesthood. The scrolls include the earliest known manuscripts of nearly every book in the Hebrew Bible as well as a wealth of later Jewish literature, and they have contributed greatly to our understanding of Jewish thought in the period.

Some Jewish thinkers maintain that the return of the diaspora and the rebuilding of Jerusalem will be the two most important preludes to the coming of the Messiah.

Appearance of the Messiah

Every so often throughout history, an exceptional individual would appear whom some people thought might be the Messiah. One such person was Jesus of Nazareth, known to his followers as Christ, from the Greek word for Messiah. Jesus's followers, who became known as Christians, continued to believe that he was the Messiah after his execution by the Romans, but other Jews rejected this claim.

Another messianic claimant was Simeon Bar Kokhba, who led a revolt against the Romans in 132 CE. His revolt was a colossal failure, which effectively brought an end to Jewish life in Jerusalem and the surrounding area. Those Jews who were not killed were dispersed throughout the Roman Empire, and many were sold into slavery.

The failure of this, and other revolts against Roman rule and the loss, again, of the Jewish religious centre in Jerusalem brought new relevance to the prophecies from the Babylonian exile.

Resurrection and afterlife

The Messianic Era was originally envisioned by some traditions as a time of national restoration, when Israel would be redeemed and its oppressors would perish. Later, however, it was generally believed that it would also be a time of judgment for every person, living or dead, when the righteous would be rewarded and the wicked punished.

The Hebrew Bible says little about life after death. Most early biblical authors shared the ancient belief that the dead lived on in the underworld, but offered little detail on the subject. Many Jews came to believe that a person's ultimate fate depended on his or her conduct in life. Some said that the righteous lived on in Paradise while the wicked were condemned to a place of torment, called Gehenna. Others emphasized a final judgment in the Messianic Era, when the dead would be resurrected. Both ideas persisted in Jewish belief, and both the Messianic Era and the individual afterlife are commonly referred to as the "World to Come."

Jewish messianism today

Within Orthodox Judaism, the promise of messianic redemption remains a core belief. Many leaders state that if Jews, as a group, embrace God and obey his commandments, they can hasten the Messiah's arrival. Yet the idea of the Messiah has mostly flourished when Jews have been oppressed, and the relative freedom of Jews in much of the modern world has lessened the sense of urgency of the hope for national restoration. The Reform movement, in particular, rejected the ideas of a messianic king, a return to the Jewish homeland, and the rebuilding of the temple, although aspects of these beliefs have been reevaluated over the years. The one feature of messianism that remains central in all streams of Judaism is, however, the belief that humankind—and the Jewish people in particular—has the ability to bring about a better future through righteous action. ∎

King Messiah, the Son of Man, will arise in the future and will restore the kingship of David to its ancient condition.
Moses Maimonides

RELIGIOUS LAW CAN BE APPLIED TO DAILY LIFE

WRITING THE ORAL LAW

IN CONTEXT

KEY TEXT
The Talmud

WHEN AND WHERE
2nd–5th century CE, Palestine and Babylonia

BEFORE
140 BCE –70 CE The Pharisees espouse belief in an Oral Law.

2nd century CE Rebellions against Roman rule prompt the destruction of many of the Yeshivot (places for the study of the Torah); Rabbis write down the Oral Law.

AFTER
11th century CE Rabbi Solomon ben Isaac (Rashi) produces a commentary on the Talmud, which becomes standard in printed editions.

c.1170–80 The Jewish philosopher Maimonides composes the Mishneh Torah, a work describing and reviewing the laws mentioned in the Torah.

Each page of the Talmud holds the **text of the Mishnah**—a Hebrew account of the Oral Law

⬇

The text of the Mishnah is explained and discussed in the **surrounding Gemara**.

⬇

Texts of the Mishnah and Gemara are then **surrounded by other layers of text** and commentaries from a later period.

⬇

The text of the Talmud is a **discussion**.

⬇

Its arguments guide the reader to the **kernel of the truth**.

Jewish tradition maintains that God gave Moses a body of laws and teachings, which he passed on to the people of Israel (pp.168–75). Many of these are recorded in the first five books of the Hebrew Bible, the Torah, but some Jews also believe that Moses received additional teachings (transmitted verbally to the community's leaders, and then from generation to generation), which became known as the Oral Law. This Oral Law included additional details about, and interpretations of, the biblical laws.

From the 2nd century CE, Jewish rabbis (a word meaning "scholars" or "teachers") set out to record the Oral Law. The result was a large new body of literature. Many of the rabbis' writings are collected in a set of books called the Talmud which, for observant Jews, is the most important and authoritative religious text after the Bible itself.

Part of the reason the Oral Law is important is that the Bible's laws are frequently ambiguous. For example, the Bible prohibits working on the Sabbath, but it does not explain what kind of work is prohibited. The Talmud

See also: God's covenant with Israel 168–75 ▪ Progressive Judaism 190–95 ▪ The pathway to harmonious living 272–75

The primary purpose of the Talmud is to record the analysis of Jewish traditions by the best intellects of previous generations, and to challenge new students to find their own truths.

resolves this ambiguity by specifying 39 types of activity (including building, cooking, and writing) that are forbidden.

In addition to recording the laws given to Moses, the Talmud includes extensive discussions between rabbis over interpretation. These discussions are considered part of the Oral Law too, because the authority to interpret the laws was handed down through Moses.

Each page of the Talmud is designed to reflect this debate: the earliest writings, or Mishnah, setting out the law, are surrounded by the discussions, or Gemara, so the book can be read a series of conversations between rabbis.

Acceptance of the Talmud

The concept of an oral law has not been universally accepted among Jews. Prior to the writing of the Talmud, the doctrine of the Oral Law was promulgated by a Jewish sect called the Pharisees. However, two sects—the Karaites and the Sadducees—rejected this doctrine. The Karaites originated around the 8th century in Baghdad and (unlike the Sadducees) still exist today. Karaites have their own traditions for interpreting the Bible, but they do not believe that any teachings were given to Moses besides those in the biblical text. Nonetheless, other branches of Judaism accept the Talmud as a sacred text, and Orthodox Jews continue to trace its origins to the Oral Law given to Moses by God. Many modern Jews do not take this idea literally, but rather view the Talmud as part of a living tradition that preserves and interprets Jewish law for every generation and encourages theological debate. ▪

Versions of the Talmud

A collective work of thousands of rabbis over hundreds of years, the Talmud is organized into six orders that deal with different aspects of law and tradition, then into tractates and chapters. There are two versions of the Talmud: the Jerusalem Talmud, which was compiled in the 4th century CE in the Land of Israel, and the Babylonian Talmud, which was compiled c.500 CE in Babylonia (modern-day Iraq).

Although there are many similarities between the two versions, the Babylonian Talmud, which is more than 6,000 pages in extent, is generally considered to be more authoritative and is used more widely by students of Judaism. The Jerusalem Talmud was never completed due to the persecution of the Jews in Israel, and is thus far shorter and more cryptic than the Babylonian Talmud.

Moses received the Torah from Sinai and transmitted it to Joshua, Joshua to the elders, and the elders to the prophets, and the prophets transmitted it to the men of the Great Assembly.
Ethics of the Fathers

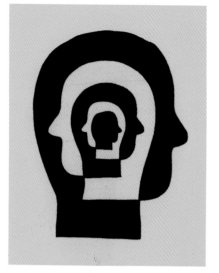

GOD IS INCORPOREAL, INDIVISIBLE, AND UNIQUE
DEFINING THE INDEFINABLE

IN CONTEXT

KEY THINKER
Moses Maimonides

WHEN AND WHERE
12th century, North Africa

BEFORE
30 BCE–50 CE The Jewish philosopher Philo describes the God of the Bible in Greek philosophical terms, as lacking Aristotelian attributes.

933 CE Rabbi Sa'adia Gaon's *Book of Beliefs and Opinions* proposes several arguments for God's unity.

AFTER
13th century The Zohar, a Jewish mystical text, propounds the idea that an infinite and unified Godhead became manifest in creation and in ten emanations.

c.1730 Rabbi Moshe Chaim Luzzatto's *The Way of God* states that God encompasses all perfections, but these exist in him as a single, essential attribute.

Since biblical times, belief in one God has been a central feature of Jewish religion. Yet the idea that God is one may be understood in a variety of ways: that is, God could be the greatest of many divine beings, or God could be a single being composed of several different elements. In the Middle Ages, a number of Jewish philosophers in the Muslim sphere of influence sought to demonstrate that the oneness of God, properly understood, excluded all of these other possibilities.

Moses Maimonides was a particularly influential philosopher of this school. He explained the

God has **no physical or mental attributes** that we can describe, as these cannot exist outside his oneness.

God is **all-powerful**, because there can be nothing over which he does not have control.

God has a **unity and nature** unlike anything that we can comprehend.

God is **infinite**, because we cannot imagine any limits to his presence and power.

God is **eternal**, because we cannot conceive of a time at which he did not exist.

See also: From monolatry to monotheism 176–77 ▪ Mysticism and the kabbalah 188 ▪ The unity of divinity is necessary 280–81

Jewish tenet of monotheism in terms of the classical Greek philosophical doctrine that God is "simple"—that is, not composed of parts or properties.

God's oneness, according to Maimonides, is different from the oneness of any other being: he is a single, unique, indivisible entity; he is also beyond human understanding and description, and therefore cannot be given specific attributes.

God cannot be categorized

God, Maimonides argued, is not "one of a species"—he is not a member of a group of beings that share certain characteristics. Three different men, for example, are each individuals, but they share the attribute of maleness and therefore belong to the category of males. God, on the other hand, has no attributes, and therefore cannot belong to a category of beings, divine or otherwise.

God's oneness also differs from that of a body, which is divisible. This means that God is not like

According to Maimonides, God existed before everything and is the creator of all things. His existence is independent of all other things but all other things need him in order to exist.

God is not two or more entities, but a single entity of a oneness even more single and unique than any single thing in creation.
Maimonides

a physical object, which can be broken into parts. But Maimonides went further, and argued that God is also intellectually indivisible: he cannot have any attributes (as defined by Aristotle), as he would then consist of both his essence and his attributes. If God were eternal, for example, there would effectively be two gods: God and God's eternity.

Maimonides' belief that God has no attributes is a product of a school of thought called negative theology, which maintains that it is inaccurate to characterize God in any affirmative way. Given the limits of human language, we may describe God as eternal, but in truth we can only affirm that God is not non-eternal: that is, his essence is beyond comprehension. Maimonides included the doctrine of God's oneness among his 13 essential principles of Jewish faith, which also include such concepts as God's antiquity and the belief that the Torah comes from the mouth of God. Many regard these principles as the fundamental elements of Jewish belief. ▪

Moses Maimonides

Moses Maimonides (also known as Rambam) was born in 1135 in Cordoba, Spain, into a Jewish family. His childhood was rich in cross-cultural influences: he was educated in both Hebrew and Arabic, and his father, a rabbinic judge, taught him Jewish law within the context of Islamic Spain. His family fled Spain when the Berber Almohad dynasty came to power in 1148, and lived nomadically for 10 years until they settled first in Fez (now in Morocco) and then in Cairo. Maimonides began training as a physician due to his family's financial problems; his skill led to a royal appointment within only a few years. He also worked as a rabbinic judge, but this was an activity for which he thought it wrong to accept any payment. He was recognized as head of the Jewish community of Cairo in 1191. After his death in 1204 his tomb became a place of Jewish pilgrimage.

Key works

1168 *Commentary on the Mishnah*
1168–78 *Mishneh Torah*
1190 *Guide for the Perplexed*

GOD AND HUMANKIND ARE IN COSMIC EXILE

MYSTICISM AND THE KABBALAH

The texts of Judaism include, along with the Hebrew Bible (p.171) and the Talmud (a compendium of rabbinic interpretations), a body of mystical knowledge known as kabbalah. Originally an oral tradition, it was collected in the Zohar ("Divine Splendor") in the late 13th century in Spain. The Zohar and its kabbalistic ideas took on a special significance for exiled Jews— in particular for the scholars of Safed in Palestine—after their expulsion from Iberia (present-day Spain, Portugal, and Andorra) in the 1490s. Among them was the

Jewish men at penitential prayers, the Selichot, in Jerusalem. According to kabbalah, observance of the commandments will help lead people from exile to redemption.

teacher Isaac Luria, whose interpretation of the Zohar gave a unique description of the creation that was applicable to the experience of Jews in exile. It provided an explanation of good and evil, and the way to redemption.

In Luria's interpretation, before the creation only God existed. In order to make space to create the world, he contracted or withdrew into himself (*tzimtzum*): a form of self-imposed exile for the sake of creation. A divine light streamed into the created space in the shape of 10 *sefirot*—emanations of the divine attributes of God. Adam Kadmon (meaning primordial man) formed vessels to contain the *sefirot*. But the vessels were too delicate to hold the divine light: the upper three were damaged, and the lower seven completely destroyed, scattering the divine light. This destruction of the vessels (known as *shevirat ha-kelim* or *shevirah*) upset the process of creation and divided the universe into those elements that assisted, and those that resisted, the creation: good and evil, and the upper and lower worlds.

This damage can be repaired, Luria explained, by detaching the holy sparks of divine light to which

See also: The promise of a new age 178–81 ▪ Man as a manifestation of God 188 ▪ Sufism and the mystic tradition 282–83

God contracted himself to **make a void** in which to **create the world** yet maintain his transcendence.

There then followed **10 emanations**, the *sefirot*, which together formed a **divine light** revealing God's purpose.

But the **vessels** containing the *sefirot* were not strong enough and **were destroyed** in a catastrophe, *shevirah*.

This is the **source of both good and evil**, and is embodied in the Fall of Adam.

The damage cannot be repaired until the **sparks of the divine light are reunited**, and until then…

…God and humankind are in cosmic exile.

Isaac Luria

Isaac ben Solomon Luria Ashkenazi was born in 1534 in Jerusalem. His German father died when Isaac was a child, so he moved with his mother to stay with her brother in Egypt. There he studied rabbinical literature and Jewish law with some of the foremost scholars of the day, including Rabbi Bezalel Ashkenazi, and traded as a merchant. He married aged 15, but continued his studies. Six years later he moved to an island on the Nile to study the Zohar and the early kabbalists, barely speaking to anyone, and then only in Hebrew. During this time, he said he had conversations with the long-dead prophet Elijah, who told him to move to Safed, a center of kabbalistic study in Ottoman-ruled Palestine.

Working with Moses Cordovero, Luria became known for his teaching of the kabbalah, and his disciples dubbed him HaARI, "the Lion," from the initials, in Hebrew, of "holy Rabbi Yitzhak." He died in Safed in 1572.

the forces of evil in the lower world are clinging, and restoring them to their source in the upper world: a process of *tikkun olam*—repairing the world. The responsibility for this rests on the Jewish people, who rescue a holy spark each time they obey a holy commandment, and pass one back to universal evil when they sin. Until all the divine sparks are reunited in the world of the good, there can be no redemption, and humanity will live in cosmic exile.

Although Luria did not leave a record of his interpretation of kabbalah, his esoteric teachings were preserved by his followers. After his death, his ideas spread quickly throughout Europe. Because of the rational, comprehensive nature of Lurianic kabbalah, kabbalistic study became a mainstay of Jewish thought, and in the 18th century it formed the basis for the Hasidic movement (p.188), which places particular emphasis on a mystical relationship with God. ▪

The Torah is concealed. It is only revealed to those who have reached the level of the righteous.
The Talmud, Hagigah

THE HOLY SPARK DWELLS IN EVERYONE

MAN AS A MANIFESTATION OF GOD

IN CONTEXT

KEY FIGURE
Israel ben Eliezer

WHEN AND WHERE
1740s, Ukraine

BEFORE
16th century Isaac Luria
and other teachers reawaken
interest in the mystical
elements of the kabbalah.

AFTER
19th century Hasidism
gains adherents in reaction
to the intellectualization and
secularization of Judaism.

1917 The Bolshevik Revolution
in Russia breaks up many
Hasidic communities.

1930s With the rise of Nazism,
Jews from Germany, Eastern
Europe, and Russia flee to the
US; all Hasidic communities in
Europe are destroyed during
World War II.

1948 The State of Israel is
founded. Many displaced
Hasidic Jews settle there.

Hasidic Judaism, founded by Israel ben Eliezer (known as Baal Shem Tov, or the Besht) in the 1740s, is characterized by enthusiasm and rituals of mass ecstasy, performed under the guidance of a spiritual leader, or *zaddik*. One of its main teachings is that the divine dwells within everyone. It is now one of the major branches of ultra-Orthodox Judaism.

The movement emerged from the Jewish communities of Central and Eastern Europe during the 18th century. These communities were often small and isolated, and their lifestyle was very different from that of urban Jews living elsewhere. Mainstream Jewish philosophy had, by then, become more intellectual, and theology more legalistic. This development was at odds with the needs of the inhabitants of small villages, or shtetls, especially in areas such as southern Poland.

To maintain cohesion in these communities, especially in the face of persecution by the Cossacks (East Slavic people), religious leaders traveled around from place to place.

They offered worshippers not only guidance, but also an opportunity to participate more actively in religious observances. Where rabbinical teaching had become detached from the people, charismatic leaders such as Baal Shem Tov explained that the Torah was not the exclusive realm of the rabbis. Spiritual learning was available to all: the holy sparks, or divine light—a manifestation of God—outlined in the mystical tradition of the Lurianic kabbalah could be found in everyone. ∎

Hasidic men dance at a wedding celebration. The distinctive clothing of Hasidic Jews, drawn from earlier styles of Eastern European dress, sets them apart from other branches of Judaism.

See also: Mysticism and the kabbalah 186–87 ∎ Mystical experience in Christianity 238 ∎ Sufism and the mystic tradition 282–83

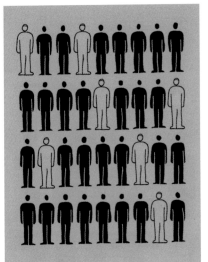

JUDAISM IS A RELIGION, NOT A NATIONALITY
FAITH AND THE STATE

IN CONTEXT

KEY FIGURE
Moses Mendelssohn

WHEN AND WHERE
Late 18th century, Germany

BEFORE
135 CE The Romans drive the Jews from the Land of Israel.

AFTER
1770s–1880 The Haskalah or Jewish Enlightenment: Jews, especially in western Europe, become increasingly integrated into their adopted societies.

1791 The emancipation of Jews in France during the French Revolution is followed by emancipation in Holland, and later in the countries conquered by Napoleon.

1896 Theodor Herzl publishes *The Jewish State* and starts the modern Zionist movement.

19th century Reform Judaism is inspired by the Haskalah.

1948 The State of Israel is founded.

Following in the wake of the Enlightenment in Europe, the Haskalah movement, or Jewish Enlightenment, was inspired largely by the work of the German Jewish philosopher Moses Mendelssohn. He believed that the persecution endured by the Jews was largely a result of their separateness from the societies in which they lived.

His criticism of the separation of Jews and Gentiles (non-Jews) also raised the issue of what it meant to be Jewish. In his opinion, Judaism was a religion that should be treated in the same way as any other in a tolerant, pluralistic society, and its followers should be allowed freedom of conscience as citizens of the country in which they lived; conversely, being a Jew did not imply belonging to a separate nation or people.

In his book *Jerusalem: or On Religious Power and Judaism* (1783), Mendelssohn argued not only for emancipation of the Jews, but also that they should "come out of the ghettos" and play a more active

The state has physical power and uses it when necessary; the power of religion is love and beneficence.
Moses Mendelssohn

part in secular cultural life. In particular, he promoted the idea of Jews learning the local language —as he had done—to help integrate themselves better into non-Jewish societies, and published his own translation of the Torah into German.

Although Mendelssohn was himself a practicing Orthodox Jew, his ideas and the Haskalah movement he inspired built the foundation for Reform Judaism in the 19th century. ∎

See also: God's covenant with Israel 168–75 ▪ Progressive Judaism 190–95 ▪ The origins of modern political Zionism 196–97

DRAW FROM THE PAST, LIVE IN THE PRESENT, WORK FOR THE FUTURE

PROGRESSIVE JUDAISM

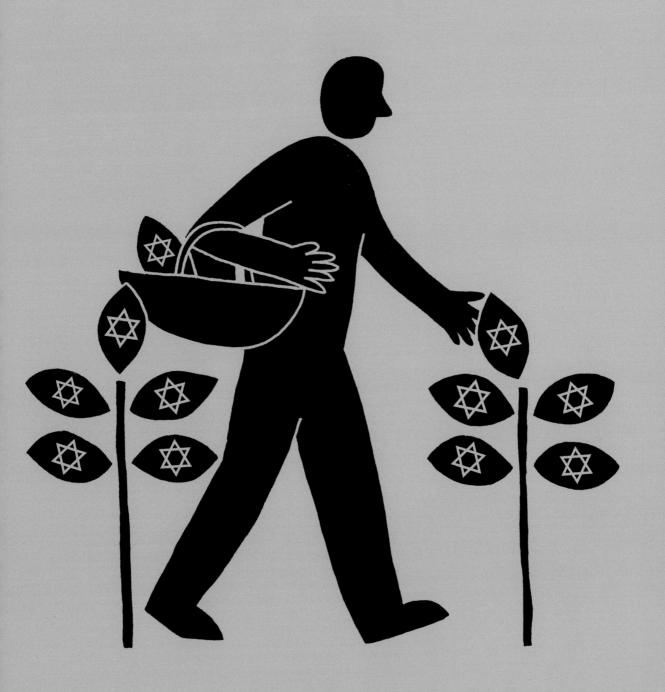

IN CONTEXT

KEY MOVEMENT
Progressive Judaism

WHEN AND WHERE
19th century,
Europe and US

BEFORE
19th century The German
Enlightment offers Jews the
possibility of secular education
and participation in society.

AFTER
1840 The West London
Synagogue is established.

1872 The Reform Academy
Hochschule für die Wissen-
schaft des Judentums is
established in Berlin.

1885 Reform Judaism
flourishes in the US. The
Pittsburgh Platform defines
the principles of Reform.

20th century Progressive
synagogues and communal
organizations are established
throughout the world.

J ewish emancipation in
Europe began in Germany in
the 18th century. Previously,
Jews had been restricted in where
they could live, and had been
barred from entering universities
and the professions, but the force
of European Enlightenment led to
them being given equal rights as
citizens. Yiddish-speaking Jews
learned German, became part of
the modern world, and began to
feel the freedom of individuality.
Many Jews started looking to
secular education—rather than
Jewish tradition—as a means
of achieving their potential.
Progressive Judaism, which
began with the Reform movement
in Germany, was a response
to these changes, to modernity,
and to the new freedoms.

The earliest and most visible
reforms emerged in Berlin and
Hamburg. They concerned the
synagogue service: the sermon
would be given in German, and
men and women would sit together
rather than being segregated. More
radically, the impact of modern
biblical scholarship led some Jews
to question the divine authority of
the biblical texts, and the traditions

> The Talmud speaks with
> the ideology of its own time,
> and for that time it was right.
> I speak for the higher ideology
> of my own time, and for
> this age I am right.
> **Extreme reformers in**
> **19th-century Germany**

that had kept them apart from
society. The authority of the classical
rabbis was now seen to be a
function of its time, and was
also called into question.

Some, faced with this new
insight and the opportunities
it gave rise to, abandoned their
Judaism in favor of secular
nationalism. Others sought instead
to modernize Judaism in the
light of historical, academic study
of the religion (*Wissenschaft des
Judentums*). The pace of change
was too rapid for some, and various

Abraham Geiger

Abraham Geiger was born in
Frankfurt-am-Main, Germany,
in 1810. He was educated in the
Jewish and German classics, and
studied Arabic for his dissertation,
"What Did Muhammad Take from
Judaism?". A passionate advocate
of *Wissenschaft des Judentums*,
the academic study of Judaism, he
set out to distill Judaism's eternal
spiritual and ethical core through
groundbreaking scholarship. He
sought to modernize Judaism
as a whole rather than to create
a separate movement, rejecting
practices if their historical reason
was no longer relevant. When he

was appointed as second rabbi
in Breslau, in 1838, Geiger found
his authority disputed by the
existing, traditionalist rabbi:
both were officially rabbis of the
whole community, but eventually
each served his own faction.
Geiger later presided as the
rabbi in Frankfurt and then in
Berlin, and also taught at the
new Reform Academy for two
years before his death in 1874.

Key works

1857 *The Original Text and*
Translations of the Bible

See also: The promise of a new age 178–81 ▪ The origins of modern political Zionism 196–97 ▪ The Protestant Reformation 230–37 ▪ The rise of Islamic revivalism 286–90 ▪ The compatibility of faith 291

groups seceded from the community, perhaps to be served by a more orthodox rabbi.

Questioning theology

Theological innovation led to liturgical reform and the publication of a new Reform prayer book in Hamburg in 1818. Scholars and rabbis, such as Abraham Geiger, now began to question key theological assumptions. Geiger recognized historical precedents for modifying Jewish tradition to adjust to new conditions, and suggested that some observances could be altered to be compatible with modern ways of living.

Some of Judaism's traditional theology was abandoned too. The German reformers no longer felt that they could pray for a messiah in the form of one person who would return the people to the Land of Israel to rebuild the Temple and restore the priestly sacrificial cult. Instead, they replaced the idea of the messiah with one of the messianic ideal—peace for every nation on earth—that every Jew

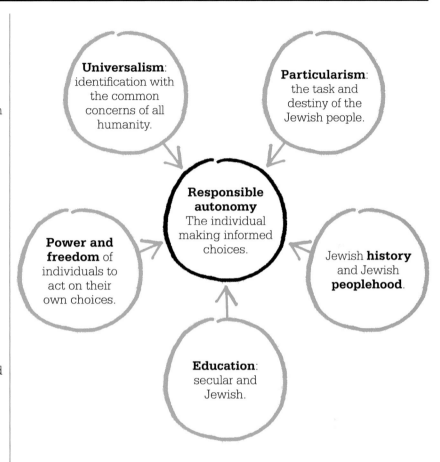

Universalism: identification with the common concerns of all humanity.

Particularism: the task and destiny of the Jewish people.

Responsible autonomy The individual making informed choices.

Power and freedom of individuals to act on their own choices.

Jewish **history** and Jewish **peoplehood**.

Education: secular and Jewish.

A minority is always compelled to think. That is the blessing of being in the minority.
Leo Baeck, progressive rabbi

would work to bring about. Even more daring was the new idea that the Jews were no longer in exile but could realize their Jewish destiny as citizens of a modern nation.

This dream was in some ways short-lived. For many there was no real social integration without conversion to Christianity, and the Holocaust of Nazi Germany and World War II made clear the limits of hope for an enlightened humanity.

Religious autonomy

There is a tension in progressive Judaism, as in other strands of the religion today, between being part of a nation and community (universalism), and having a unique destiny (particularism). What differs for progressive Jews is probably the modern focus on autonomy—their freedom to determine how they live their Jewish lives. Progressive Judaism teaches that responsible autonomy requires making choices based on ethics, Jewish education, and commitment to the Jewish people, with reverence for the past and a commitment to the future.

Jewish theologies continue to develop. Although monotheism remains a fundamental tenet » of the faith, progressive Judaism's theology extends the notion of a "commanding" God to the idea of an ongoing relationship with God, in which each Jew exercises his or her individual freedom. The mitzvot, or commandments, are expressions of this relationship.

The concept of monism

Another group of progressive thinkers believes God to be an inseparable part of the self, rather than an external divinity. Some have absorbed the views of Jewish mystics, who understand the entire creation as taking place within God, which means that everything *is* God. Monotheism, or the belief in one god, becomes monism, meaning that there is only oneness, and that this oneness *is* God. These theological transformations within progressive Judaism mean that the role of the individual and the commandments can no longer be seen as fixed. Along with the newly defined

relationship between individual, God, and the commandments, Jews in the progressive movement also came to review conventional interpretations of the Hebrew Bible. They now regard it as a composite text from different historical periods—a written record of a human encounter with the divine, rather than the recorded words of God, meaning that its authority is not straightforward. Since God's intentions were not fixed once in time, the revelation could be considered continuous.

In a similar way, progressive Judaism recognizes the impact of history and human authorship on the development of Jewish law, or Halachah, which is traditionally rooted in biblical commandments and the rulings of classical rabbis. Halachah has undergone transformation in both progressive and Orthodox communities. One progressive view sees Halachah as undergoing continual adaptation to respond to ethical and practical

problems in the contemporary Jewish world. This view takes account of modern scientific developments, such as stem cell research, and is strongly guided by contemporary ethics, tackling issues such as care at the end of life. Other progressives describe a post-Halachic Judaism, perhaps identifying more closely with the ancient Hebrew prophets and an ethically driven Prophetic Judaism.

Rituals and observances

Modern approaches to ritual practice also reflect the idea of Judaism's continuing evolution, stipulating that divine authority is not limited to the Torah. The Sabbath (Shabbat), for instance, is considered a day of rest and holiness distinct from the working week. Progressive Jews respect the Sabbath, and are still likely to begin it with lighting Shabbat candles on Friday evening, although not all will insist that this be done before sunset, if it occurs very early. They may also reject the traditional prohibition on driving a motor car to the synagogue on Shabbat.

Dietary laws

In matters of *kashrut* (dietary law), some progressive Jews might dismiss all the rules as antiquated, while others might avoid the meats that are forbidden in the Torah but not concern themselves with the later rabbinic prohibitions concerning the separation of meat and milk products and the utensils used in the preparation of each. Some might focus instead on the discipline of *kashrut* as a way of expressing consciousness of what they eat, perhaps extending this to eating organic, fair-trade products or food with low food miles. Others might view vegetarianism as a proper or suitable (from the

Orthodox Jews believe that the Torah was given by God to Moses at Mount Sinai. Progressive Jews, however, believe it was written by human beings under divine inspiration, and should be responded to accordingly.

Progressive communities mark the time when a girl becomes bat mitvah (a daughter of the commandment); traditional custom prohibited women from taking part in religious services.

meaning of the Hebrew word "*kashrut*") diet and therefore as a modern, progressive expression of the observance.

Liturgy for today

Historically, Jewish liturgy has tended to lengthen over the centuries as new prayers have been added. Progressive services retain the framework and core prayers, but remove some repetition; prayers, and their translations, reflect a reworking of concepts that do not accord with progressive beliefs, such as the resurrection of the dead, the restoration of the temple, and animal sacrifices. Many progressive liturgies avoid feudal and gendered language both for God and the community, referring, for example, to the Eternal instead of the Lord, ancestors instead of forefathers, and including the biblical matriarchs along with the patriarchs.

Novel liturgical compositions may sometimes be included, such as poetry or prayers of interfaith understanding, and a shorter weekly passage from the Torah read. In many congregations, services are conducted in Hebrew as well as the vernacular, and are often accompanied by music. Progressive Jews observe the Hebrew festival dates given in the Torah, as is the practice of all Jews in the Land of Israel. This is in contrast to Orthodox and Conservative Jews in the diaspora, who traditionally extend the duration of festivals by a day, as was the custom outside Israel before the Hebrew calendar was fixed in 358 CE.

Women and men in progressive communities generally enjoy full equality in communal leadership (including ordination as rabbis) and in ritual life, whether in the synagogue or home. Girls therefore celebrate their ritual adulthood at the age of 13 (becoming bat mitzvah) just as boys do (becoming bar mitzvah) by reading publicly from the Torah and even leading the congregation in prayer.

Progressive Judaism today

The core ideals of German Reform Judaism took root, and led to the growth of progressive Jewish communities in most countries in the world today. In the UK, Reform Judaism and Liberal Judaism emerged, and, with German Jewish immigration to the US, an American Reform movement came into being there. This gave rise to other progressive communities in the US, such as Reconstructionist Judaism, and Conservative Judaism, which is modern in its theology but traditional in its practices. Other progressive forms of Judaism are found worldwide, including in Israel, where the faith tends toward a more traditional expression of Judaism than in the diaspora.

A recent worldwide resurgence of interest in Jewish learning across the religious spectrum has led to an engagement with the study of classical texts in Hebrew for their spiritual, literary, and ethical value. Today's believers may draw from a wide range of Jewish and secular influences, and are therefore less likely to form a lifelong commitment to only one of the Jewish movements. ∎

The past has a vote, but not a veto.
Dr. Mordecai M. Kaplan, Progressive theologian

IF YOU WILL IT, IT IS NO DREAM

THE ORIGINS OF MODERN POLITICAL ZIONISM

IN CONTEXT

KEY FIGURE
Theodor Herzl

WHEN AND WHERE
1896, Austria-Hungary

BEFORE
586 BCE King Nebuchadnezzar of Babylon destroys the Temple in Jerusalem and drives the Jews into exile. From 538 BCE the Jews start to return to the Land of Israel, in accordance with a decree from Persian emperor Cyrus the Great.

70 CE The Romans destroy the second Temple; the Jews are exiled again.

635 The Islamic Caliphate conquers Palestine; in 1516 the Ottoman Empire takes control of the region.

AFTER
1882–1948 Jews from the diaspora immigrate to the Land of Israel in waves.

1948 The State of Israel is founded.

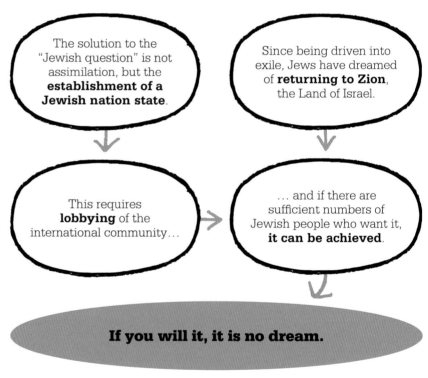

The solution to the "Jewish question" is not assimilation, but the **establishment of a Jewish nation state**.

Since being driven into exile, Jews have dreamed of **returning to Zion**, the Land of Israel.

This requires **lobbying** of the international community…

… and if there are sufficient numbers of Jewish people who want it, **it can be achieved**.

If you will it, it is no dream.

Ever since their expulsion from their homeland by the Babylonians and the Romans, many among the Jewish diaspora had dreamed of a return to Eretz Yisrael, the Land of Israel, also known as Zion after Mount Zion in Jerusalem. It was not until the late 19th century, however, that their hopes were consolidated into a political movement, Zionism, which aimed to establish a nation state in Palestine for the Jewish people.

During the Haskalah, or Jewish Enlightenment, Jewish thinkers inspired by Moses Mendelssohn (p.189) had urged Jews to assimilate themselves

See also: God's covenant with Israel 168–75 ▪ Faith and the state 189
▪ Ras Tafari is our Savior 314–15

I consider the Jewish
question neither a social
nor a religious one…
It is a national question.
Theodor Herzl

into the culture of their adopted
countries as a way to overcome the
persecution they had suffered. In
much of western Europe and the
US, emancipation had allowed
middle-class Jews, in particular,
to integrate into society.

One such Jew, the journalist
and writer Theodor Herzl, firmly
believed in Jewish assimilation,
until he experienced extreme
anti-Semitic feeling in France,
an ostensibly liberal country. He
came to realize that ghettoization
and anti-Semitism were inevitable:
Jews tended to gravitate to places
where they were not likely to be
persecuted, but once they had
immigrated in significant numbers
to these places, anti-Jewish feeling
arose, and persecution followed.
Similarly, even where Jews had
tried to blend in with the local
community and behave as loyal
citizens, they were still treated as
aliens and driven into isolation.
He concluded that the solution
to these problems lay not in
assimilation, but in the large-scale
separation of Jewish people into
one place. Anti-Semitism could not

be defeated or eradicated, but
could be avoided by establishing
a Jewish nation state.

A Jewish homeland

In Herzl's short book *The Jewish
State*, published in 1896, which
he described as a "proposal of
a modern solution for the Jewish
question," he set out the argument
for establishing a Jewish homeland.
The obvious choice for this was
the Land of Israel, then a part of
Ottoman-ruled Palestine. This
proposal marked the beginning
of modern Zionism as a political
movement, rather than a theological
aspiration. The following year,
1897, Herzl set up an international
conference, the First Zionist
Congress, at which it became clear
that the political will for a Jewish
state existed, and was achievable
if Jews in sufficent numbers were
to put pressure on the international
community for its foundation. A
phrase from Herzl's novel *Old New
Land* was adopted as the Zionist
movement's rallying cry: "If you
will it, it is no dream". ▪

Israel's flag, adopted in 1948, is
derived from a design produced for the
First Zionist Congress. It is inspired
by the tallit, or blue-bordered prayer
shawl, and the Star of David.

Theodor Herzl

Theodor Herzl was born in
1860 in Pest, part of modern-
day Budapest. He moved to
Vienna with his family when
he was 18. There he studied
law, and, in 1839, after a brief
legal career, he moved to
Paris. Here he worked as a
correspondent for the *Neue
Freie Presse* (New Free Press)
and as a theater writer.

After reporting on the
Dreyfus Affair of the 1890s,
in which a Jewish officer
was framed for treason by
the military, he concluded that
the establishment of a Jewish
homeland in Zion, the Land
of Israel, was essential. He
outlined his arguments in *The
Jewish State* and elaborated
on them in his novel, *Old New
Land*. Herzl worked tirelessly
to promote the ideals of
Zionism: he organized the first
congress of Zionism in Basel,
Switzerland, in 1897, and was
president of the World Zionist
Organization until his death
in 1904. In 1949 his remains
were moved from Vienna
and reburied in Jerusalem.

Key works

1896 *The Jewish State*
1902 *Old New Land*

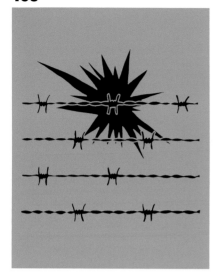

WHERE WAS GOD DURING THE HOLOCAUST?

A CHALLENGE TO THE COVENANT

IN CONTEXT

KEY MOVEMENT
Holocaust theology

WHEN AND WHERE
Mid-20th century, Europe

BEFORE
1516 The Republic of Venice establishes the ghetto, which becomes the model for ghettos created across Europe to isolate Jewish communities.

1850s Anti-Semitism in Europe takes on a more secular, racist stance.

1880s Beginning of a series of pogroms—violent anti-Jewish mob attacks—in Russia.

1930s Hitler becomes German Chancellor, and begins a campaign of harassment and genocide against Jews.

AFTER
1945 Jews are liberated from concentration camps at the end of World War II and resettled, many in the US and later in the newly formed State of Israel.

Ever since their expulsion from Israel by the Romans in 70 CE, the Jews have endured exile and persecution. However, the Holocaust, or Sho'ah (catastrophe)—the systematic genocide of around 6 million Jews, or two-thirds of the European Jewish population—was an event of unprecedented horror that tested the faith of the Jewish people in their covenant with God. This challenge raised an important question: was the Holocaust God's doing, or did he stand aside and allow it to happen? Jewish theology struggled to provide answers, and a number of Jews lost faith, believing God had abandoned his people.

The greatest test

Different groups of Jews offered a range of other interpretations of the Holocaust. Some saw it as being no different from the persecutions they had already suffered, except in scale. They defined it as an extreme example of suffering in the world, a test of faith, and a revelation calling for an affirmation of survival;

Never shall I forget those moments that murdered my God and my soul.
Elie Wiesel

others saw it as punishment for the sin of abandoning God and his laws, which God had responded to with his own temporary absence. A further group saw the Sho'ah as separate from God, an example of human free will and its fallibility, perhaps explained in kabbalistic terms as a stage of God's *tzimtzum*, or contraction, from the world.

A whole new field of Holocaust theology has since emerged, examining these various responses, and reappraising the covenant in the light of the Sho'ah. ∎

See also: God's covenant with Israel 168–75 ∎ Mysticism and the kabbalah 186–87 ∎ The origins of modern political Zionism 196–97

WOMEN CAN BE RABBIS
GENDER AND THE COVENANT

IN CONTEXT

KEY MOVEMENT
Feminism in Judaism

WHEN AND WHERE
**Late 20th century,
US and Europe**

BEFORE
19th century The Reform
movement emerges in
Judaism, and with it the
question of women taking
a fuller role in the covenant.

1893 The National Council
of Jewish Women is founded
after the World Parliament
of Religions in Chicago.

1912 The Women's Zionist
Organization of America,
Hadassah, is founded.

1922 The idea of ordaining
women rabbis is discussed at
the Central Conference of
American Rabbis, but no
agreement is reached.

1935 The first woman rabbi,
Regina Jonas, is ordained in
Berlin, Germany.

Paradoxically, while Jewish identity is traditionally transmitted matrilineally (p.175), women have been excluded from participation in the observance of Judaism for much of its history. Until the 19th century, the idea of women reading from the Torah to a congregation, for example, or leading prayer as a cantor was considered heretical; the notion of a female rabbi was unthinkable.

However, with the foundation of liberal Reform Judaism, and especially in the progressive Reconstructionist movement, the subject of women's role in the covenant became an issue of increasing importance. The first woman rabbi was ordained in the Reform movement in Germany in 1935. In the US, the UK, and elsewhere in Europe, real pressure for change came with the rise of feminism in the 1970s. The Reform movement in the US ordained its first woman rabbi in 1972, and three years later a female cantor. Following this lead, other branches of Judaism began to initiate reforms, allowing women to participate in rituals and as witnesses, and bringing in bat mitzvah ceremonies (the female equivalent of the bar mitzvah). Women were finally admitted into rabbinical schools in the 1980s. Today, only Orthodox Judaism still holds out against the ordination of women rabbis, but in all branches of the faith, women are taking an increasingly active, if not leading, role in the synagogue. ∎

The festival of Hanukkah is celebrated here by Barbara Aiello, the first female rabbi in Italy. Granting girls equal access to religious education has transformed their role in Judaism.

See also: God's covenant with Israel 168–75 ▪ Writing the Oral law 182–83 ▪ Progressive Judaism 190–95

Jesus is born in Roman Judea: he is believed by Christians to be the Son of God born to the Virgin Mary.

Jesus is crucified by Judea's Roman rulers. Christians believe that he rises again three days later and ascends to heaven.

The Roman emperor Constantine issues the Edict of Milan, allowing the **Christian faith to be freely practiced**.

Christianity becomes the **official religion of the Roman Empire**; converts include Augustine of Hippo.

c.4 BCE

c.30–36 CE

313 CE

380 CE

c.26 CE

CA. 44–68 CE

325 CE

1054

Jesus is baptized by John the Baptist and his ministry begins.

All but one of the apostles, John, are **martyred**.

The **Nicene Creed** is established at the Council of Nicea and later ratified as the universal creed of the Christian Church.

During the **Great Schism**, Christianity is divided into Western (Roman Catholic) and Eastern (Orthodox) branches.

Christianity takes its name from the Greek word *christós*, a translation of the Hebrew word for messiah, or anointed one. This title was given to Jesus by a Jewish sect who considered him to be the Messiah —the savior prophesied in the Tanakh, the Hebrew Bible—and the Son of God in human form. Christians believe that Jesus's arrival on earth heralded a New Covenant or New Testament with God that followed the Old Testament covenants between God and the Jewish people.

The main beliefs of Christianity are based on the life and teachings of Jesus as recorded by his followers in the 1st century CE in the Gospels (meaning "good news") and the Epistles (or letters) of the New Testament.

Christians give great significance to the story of Jesus's crucifixion, resurrection, and ascension to heaven. It is the central belief of Christianity that Jesus suffered, died, and was buried, before being resurrected from the dead—in order to grant salvation to those who believe in him—and that he then ascended to heaven to rule alongside God the Father.

Implicit in this belief is the acceptance that Jesus was, as the Son of God, God incarnate, both human and divine, and not merely a prophet. This led to the concept of the Trinity, that the one God exists in three distinct forms—the Father, the Son, and the Holy Spirit.

The life of Jesus also provides a framework for the rituals of Christian worship, the most important of which are known as

sacraments. Especially significant are the sacraments of baptism and the Eucharist—the taking of bread and wine, as Jesus instructed his followers at the Last Supper. Others include confirmation, holy orders (the ordination of ministers), confession, the anointing of the sick, and matrimony—although not all of these are accepted by every Christian denomination.

Persecution to adoption

From its beginnings in Roman Judea to its status as the religion with most adherents in the world today, Christianity has shaped the culture of much of Western civilization. The early Christians were persecuted by both Jewish authorities and the Roman Empire, and many were put to death. Nevertheless, the faith persisted

A series of religious wars, **the Crusades**, is launched by the Catholic Church to recapture Jerusalem from Muslim occupation.

A **rival papacy** to Rome is established in Avignon, France.

Martin Luther initiates the Protestant Reformation in Germany by publishing his 95 Theses, criticizing clerical abuses.

John Wesley founds the Methodist movement, and other Protestant Churches emerge in Europe.

1095–1291

1305

1517

17TH–18TH CENTURIES

1274

1478

1562–98

1925

Thomas Aquinas publishes *Summa Theologica*, which becomes the basis for official Catholic dogma.

The Spanish Inquisition, the most notorious of the inquisitions instituted to suppress heresy, is founded by King Ferdinand and Queen Isabella.

Catholics and Protestants wage war in France (known as the Wars of Religion).

The Scopes **Monkey Trial** pits evolutionary theory against Biblical Creation.

under the leadership of the early Church. Gradually, Christianity came to be tolerated by Roman leaders, and, after the Council of Nicea, where a universal Christian creed was agreed, it was eventually adopted as the official religion of the Roman Empire in 380 CE.

From then on, Christianity became a powerful force in the political and cultural life of Europe and the Middle East. Its influence spread rapidly and produced such thinkers as Augustine of Hippo, a convert to Christianity, who integrated Greek philosophical ideas into the doctrine. With the decline and fall of the Roman Empire, power in Europe moved to the popes, who were considered the natural successors of the apostles and the first bishops. In the 11th century, a split in the

Church over papal authority—the so-called Great Schism—divided Christianity into two distinct branches, the Western (Roman Catholic) Church and the Eastern (Orthodox) Church. Christianity also faced a challenge from the Islamic Empire from the 8th century on, and, through the 12th and 13th centuries, fought a series of Crusades to recapture Jerusalem from the Muslims.

Church power

The Catholic Church retained its influence in Europe, and its dogma dominated learning and culture throughout the Middle Ages. Philosophical and scientific ideas were often seen as heretical, and even the great Thomas Aquinas found his application of Aristotelian reasoning to Christian theology

initially condemned: only centuries after his death was it adopted as official Catholic dogma.

The Renaissance of the 14th and 15th centuries heralded a new challenge to the authority of the Church in the form of humanism and the beginnings of a scientific Golden Age. The revival of interest in classical learning prompted criticism of the Catholic Church, and the Protestant Reformation was triggered by publication of Martin Luther's 95 Theses in 1517. Protestantism began to flourish in northern Europe and paved the way for new Christian denominations. Of the roughly 2.2 billion Christians worldwide today (around a third of the world's population), more than half are Catholic, roughly one third are Protestant, and the remainder are Orthodox. ∎

JESUS IS THE BEGINNING OF THE END

JESUS'S MESSAGE TO THE WORLD

IN CONTEXT

KEY FIGURE
Jesus of Nazareth

WHEN AND WHERE
4 BCE–30 CE, Judea

BEFORE
c.700 BCE The Jewish prophet Isaiah foretells the coming rule of God.

6th century BCE During the exile of the Israelites in Babylon, the prophet Daniel has a vision of the end of oppressive earthly kingdoms.

c.450 BCE The arrival of the day of the Lord is a key theme for Jewish prophets.

AFTER
1st century CE The first Christians take Jesus's message throughout the Roman Empire.

20th century The kingdom of God becomes a major theme in Christian theology and ethics.

I n 63 BCE, the Roman general Pompey conquered Jerusalem, putting an end to a century of Judean self-rule and turning the region into a Roman client state. Rome was the last in a long line of invading forces, which stretched back over 500 years and included Babylon, Persia, Greece, Egypt, and Syria. This repeated loss of sovereignty had dented national pride and caused religious consternation, challenging the Jewish concept of themselves as God's chosen people.

Key Jewish religious texts from previous centuries (such as the prophetic work of Isaiah) had promised that a time would come

See also: The promise of a new age 178–81 ▪ Jesus's divine identity 208
▪ Entering into the faith 224–27 ▪ Awaiting the Day of Judgment 312–13

There is a **lack of justice and peace** in kingdoms ruled by humans.

God **promised to fulfill our hopes** for justice and peace **at the end of time**, in a kingdom He rules.

Jesus has taught and shown us how to experience the **forgiveness, peace, and justice** that God promised.

Jesus's ministry therefore marks the beginning of the kingdom of God: the **beginning of the end**.

Jesus of Nazareth

Jesus was born in Bethlehem, in the Roman province of Judea, in around 4 BCE, with the extraordinary claim that his mother Mary was a virgin. Little is known about Jesus's early life, but it is most likely that he was schooled in the Jewish scriptures and religion. It is believed that he may have shared his father's occupation as a carpenter, and lived and worked in Nazareth.

When Jesus was around 30 years old, he embarked upon a ministry of teaching and healing across the area where he lived. According to the Gospels, he drew huge crowds with his engaging stories, radical teaching, and astonishing miracles, but paid special attention to 12 followers, or disciples. However, his message about God's kingdom soon attracted the censure of the authorities. He was betrayed by Judas, one of his disciples, and arrested and condemned to death on fabricated charges. Three days after Jesus had been crucified, reports were made that his tomb had been found empty and that he had appeared to his disciples, resurrected from the dead.

when Israel's God would be the acknowledged ruler of the whole world. He would bring in a system of justice and peace for all through his appointed representative, known as the Messiah (meaning anointed one). This would be the climax of world history, so the prophecy said: the end of the old, existing era and the beginning of God's era. However, given the new Roman occupation, this kingdom of God seemed a distant dream.

Announcing a new world
In around the late 20s CE, a Jewish rabbi called Jesus began a brief, but extraordinary, ministry throughout Roman-occupied Israel. »

Preaching to his band of disciples, Jesus gave the core message of his ministry: the awaited arrival of God's kingdom had become a reality.

Jesus's core message was that God's long-awaited kingdom was now arriving. Some people who heard his message thought that he intended to raise an army to expel the Romans. However, his goal was not Israel's political independence, but the liberation of the entire world from all evil. According to a collection of Jesus's teachings, known as the Sermon on the Mount (found in the Gospel of St. Matthew in the New Testament), Jesus announced that God's kingdom now held sway over both heaven and earth, and that under this new rule the distorted values of human kingdoms would be overturned. God's kingdom, he said, belonged not to the greedy, the self-assured, and the warriors, but to the poor, the meek, and the peacemakers.

All are welcome

Jesus's message was manifested in his actions. Centuries earlier, the Jewish prophet Isaiah had said that when God's kingdom came, there would be wonderful miracles of healing: the blind would be able to see, and the deaf able to hear that

God was now king, and the lame would jump for joy. The biblical accounts of Jesus's ministry are full of stories of healings just like these. In addition, Jesus said there was no longer any barrier to entering God's kingdom. Until that time, the Jewish faith had viewed non-Jews as beyond salvation, along with those people who failed to adhere to God's laws (sinners), but Jesus said that even these groups would be welcomed into the kingdom. Jesus demonstrated the forgiveness of sinners by sharing meals—one of the most intimate and meaningful of Jewish activities—with social outcasts and religious renegades. The future was likened to a banquet prepared by God, to which people from all over the world would be invited.

But people were confused: wasn't the kingdom of God supposed to be the climax of world history? If so, why did the world not end with Jesus's announcement? The answer that Jesus gave them was that the kingdom would not arrive all at once, as most people had expected. In one of his many

Jesus's miracles, such as the healing of the blind, affirmed that, just as Jesus went among the poor and the outcast, so God invited everyone, regardless of status, into his kingdom.

parables (stories used to illustrate his message) he compared God's kingdom to the yeast in a batch of dough. In another, he described the kingdom as acting like seeds sown in the ground. Both yeast and seeds take time to produce results, growing almost imperceptibly, but are slowly and surely at work.

A new religion

Jesus invited those who heard him to allow God's kingdom and its values into their own lives without delay. He taught that the kingdom of God is both now, and not yet, here, that it has begun and continues to grow whenever people choose to live by the rule of God, embracing his values and experiencing healing and forgiveness. However, Jesus also acknowledged that there would be a future moment when, at the climactic end of the present world order, God's rule would triumph over all other kingdoms. When this day of judgment arrived, it would be too late to decide to be part of

Blessed are the poor in spirit, for theirs is the kingdom of heaven.
Jesus (Matthew 5:3)

How can the end have a beginning? Jesus said that the final replacement of our present world with the kingdom of God would be delayed, giving people time to secure themselves a place in that kingdom by believing in him.

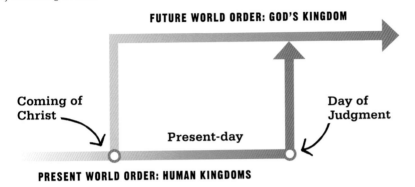

FUTURE WORLD ORDER: GOD'S KINGDOM

Coming of Christ

Day of Judgment

Present-day

PRESENT WORLD ORDER: HUMAN KINGDOMS

The time is fulfilled. God's kingdom is arriving! Turn around and believe the good news.
Jesus (Mark 1:15)

God's new world. This gave his message a note of urgency. People needed to make a decision now; far from being a distant dream, the end had already begun.

The idea that Jesus marked the beginning of the end led directly to the separation of Christianity from its Jewish roots. The early followers of Jesus claimed that they no longer had to wait to discover who God's Messiah would be, because Jesus was that Messiah—the one God had appointed to bring his kingdom to earth. However, Jesus's opponents refused to believe this and decided to silence him by killing him. When Jesus's followers did not give up their beliefs even after Jesus died, and in fact enlarged on them—by claiming that God had confounded Jesus's opponents by raising him from the dead—it became clear that their faith, led by a figure who could not be conquered by death, was something new and distinct within the catalog of religions.

From the earliest days, Christianity has been defined by the conviction that Jesus's ministry was the beginning of the end. One of the key prayers of Christianity,

the Lord's Prayer, taught by Jesus himself, asks that God's kingdom come on earth "as it is in heaven." In offering this prayer, Christians are asking for the earthly advent of God's kingdom now, even as they wait for it to arrive in fullness at the end of present world history.

God's kingdom today
Historically, the Christian church has sometimes understood the "kingdom of God" or "kingdom of heaven" as a purely spiritual realm that leaves the physical world unaffected. But in the early 20th century, New Testament scholars began to take a new interest in the Jewish context of Jesus's ministry, and since then Jesus's message about the kingdom of God has had an especially prominent place in Christian theology. By paying closer attention to the background of Jesus's original message, the political and economic implications of the arrival of God's kingdom have become clearer. Christians now believe that the kingdom occurs wherever present reality and its values are transformed by the rule of God, a belief that has inspired many Christians to

champion movements for social change; for example, Martin Luther King and the civil rights movement in the United States, Gustavo Gutiérrez and the liberation of the poor in South America, and Desmond Tutu and the end of apartheid in South Africa.

The end of all things
The idea that Jesus's ministry marked the beginning of the end is known in theology by the term inaugurated eschatology. Eschatology is a word that itself evolved from two Greek words meaning "last" and "study," and it refers to the study of the end of things, or the end of all things—the end of the world. To Christians, Jesus's message about God's kingdom gives Christianity an inaugurated eschatology: the end of all things was inaugurated (begun but not completed) by his message. The fact that the presence of God's kingdom today in the lives of Christians can still only be called the beginning of the end is a reminder that the Christian faith still looks toward a final, definitive action by God. ■

GOD HAS SENT US HIS SON

JESUS'S DIVINE IDENTITY

IN CONTEXT

KEY BELIEVERS
Early Christians

WHEN AND WHERE
1st century CE, communities around the Mediterranean

BEFORE
From c.500 BCE Jewish scriptures use the term son of God to describe God's earthly representative.

c.30 CE Jesus is arrested and accused of blasphemy by the Jewish authorities for claiming to be the son of God. He is sent for trial by the Roman governor Pontius Pilate on charges of sedition, and condemned to death.

AFTER
325 CE The Nicene Creed states that Jesus is the divine Son of God, using the phrase "of one substance with the Father."

451 CE The Chalcedonian Creed affirms Jesus as both fully God and fully human.

Many ancient kings and emperors claimed that they had been adopted by the gods, thereby giving themselves divine legitimacy to rule. On their deaths, some, such as Julius Caesar, were elevated to divine status—a process that was known as apotheosis—and worshipped.

In the Gospels, Jesus calls God his Father many times, in ways that are open to many interpretations, from the broadest—that God, as the creator, is the Father of all humankind—through the symbolic to the literal. The last of these was claimed by the first Christians as the truth. They pointed to the extraordinary miracles of Jesus's ministry decribed in the Gospels, and especially to his resurrection from the dead, as evidence of his unique place in God's plan.

God has become human

The early Christians also claimed that Jesus's divine status was unlike that of other rulers. Jesus was not adopted by God as a reward for his obedience; rather, Jesus had always been God's Son, even from before his birth, and so he shared God's divine nature throughout his human life.

This idea, known as the incarnation, became a central belief of Christianity. It is the opposite of apotheosis; in the incarnation, the eternally divine Son of God took on humanity in the person of Jesus. God had sent his divine Son into the world as a human in order to bring his kingdom from heaven to earth. ∎

You are the Christ, the Son of the living God.
Matthew 16:15

See also: Beliefs for new societies 56–57 ▪ The promise of a new age 178–81 ▪ A divine trinity 212–19 ▪ The Prophet and the origins of Islam 252–53

THE BLOOD OF THE MARTYRS IS THE SEED OF THE CHURCH
DYING FOR THE MESSAGE

IN CONTEXT

KEY DEVELOPMENT
Persecution of the early Christians

WHEN AND WHERE
c.64–313 CE, Roman Empire

BEFORE
c.30 CE Jesus is crucified, having told his followers to expect persecution in turn.

1st century CE In response to oppression by the Roman authorities in Jerusalem, Christianity becomes an underground movement, and Christians leave the city and spread out across the Empire.

AFTER
3rd century A breakaway Christian sect opposes readmitting to the Church those who had renounced their faith to avoid persecution.

16th century Catholic and Protestant factions in Europe persecute each other, each seeing their suffering as proof of their faithfulness.

O n 9 March 203 CE, two young mothers—a Roman noblewoman, Perpetua, and her slave Felicity—were led into the arena at Carthage with other Christians, where they were flogged, mauled by wild beasts, and finally executed. The story of these two female martyrs was recorded in *The Passion of Perpetua and Felicity*, in order to inspire other Christians to stay committed to their faith even when threatened with persecution and death.

Death brings life

The theologian Tertullian, writing in Carthage at that time, developed a Christian understanding of martyrdom, noting that "The blood of the Christians is the seed." The Roman emperors intended their waves of persecution to deter citizens from embracing a faith that put the authority of Jesus above that of the state. However, as Tertullian argued, far from being an obstacle to the growth of Christianity, persecution helped it to spread. The fact that Christians

The early martyrs went to their deaths willingly, believing that their example would seed Christianity's message into other hearts and minds.

were willing to be put to death rather than renounce their belief that Jesus was the world's divinely appointed and rightful ruler, both intrigued and attracted nonbelievers.

This understanding of martyrdom assisted the growth of Christianity throughout history, because it gave Christians the confidence that even the most violent opposition to their message was not a sign of failure, but rather the seed of success. ∎

See also: God's covenant with Israel 168–75 ▪ Faith and the state 189 ▪ The Protestant Reformation 230–37 ▪ The rise of Islamic revivalism 286–90

THE BODY MAY DIE BUT THE SOUL WILL LIVE ON

IMMORTALITY IN CHRISTIANITY

IN CONTEXT

KEY FIGURE
Origen

WHEN AND WHERE
3rd century CE, Egypt and Palestine

BEFORE
4th century BCE The Greek philosopher Plato popularizes Socratic teaching that death is the separation of the immortal soul from the mortal body.

c.30 CE At the time of Jesus's death, Jewish thought is divided: the Pharisees believe in an actual, bodily resurrection after death for God's faithful, while the Sadducee sect denies any form of afterlife.

AFTER
13th century Dante's *Divine Comedy* encapsulates the medieval view of the soul's journey after death.

1513 The Fifth Lateran Council of the Church declares the immortality of the soul to be orthodox Christian belief.

God **does not change**.

↓

God's relationship with humans therefore will not change.

↓

Human bodies die, so God's unchanging relationship cannot be with them.

↓

Humans must have **immortal souls**, so that their relationship with God can go on.

↓

The body may die but the soul will live on.

What happens when we die? Do we continue to exist in some form or does our entire being disintegrate like our bodies? Many thinkers in the ancient world considered these questions and the issues arising from them. Greek thought was influential in the Roman Empire, and Plato's ideas on these subjects gained widespread support in the centuries before Jesus's birth, death, and resurrection.

Plato's thinking was dualist. He believed there were two parts to human life: the physical body, which constantly changes and eventually dies; and the thinking soul, which exists eternally.

In the third century CE, the theologian Origen of Alexandria explained elements of the Christian message using terms from Greek philosophy. In particular, he developed Plato's thinking into a Christian understanding of the soul that would last for centuries.

Only souls matter

Like Plato, Origen believed that while human bodies are mortal and die, souls are immortal. For Origen, however, the immortality of the soul is a direct implication

See also: Physical and mental discipline 112–13 ▪ Man as a manifestation of God 188 ▪ The ultimate reward for the righteous 279

According to Origen, the soul is the part of us that returns to God after death. Artists found this hard to convey without giving the soul, and indeed God, a human appearance; this 16th-century panel shows St. Paul and the Trinity.

of God's unchanging nature. Since God cannot change, the relationship he has with humans cannot end once their bodies disintegrate. Therefore there must be a part of the human that does not die, and this is the soul. A typical Platonist, Origen thought the soul was far more important than the body, which was a distraction from a spiritual life.

Hell and heaven

Origen's teaching shaped the popular Christian understanding of salvation from that moment on. Unlike the Platonists, the writers of the Hebrew Bible had not separated the soul from the body. If there was going to be any life after death at all, then a person's body would need to be raised from the dead to go along with its soul. Jesus's bodily resurrection from the dead

showed that this was possible for those who believed in him. However, after Origen, less emphasis was placed on bodily resurrection, and much Christian teaching focused exclusively on the state of the soul before death and its fate after death. The souls of those who had rejected God were considered to be spiritually dead, and would live out their immortality in hell. However, the souls of those who had embraced Jesus's message would ascend to a state of perfection with God in heaven.

A modern perspective

Recent Christian thinkers have suggested that Origen relied too heavily on Platonism. A growing movement in Christian theology rejects dualism (the separation of body and soul), teaching instead that the life of the soul after death is possible only if God also resurrects a person's body. Another widespread belief today is that of conditional immortality: immortality is only given to those who have believed in Jesus, and not to everyone. ▪

…the soul, having a substance and life of its own, shall, after its departure from the world, be rewarded according to its deserts.
Origen

Origen

Origen was born to Christian parents in Alexandria, North Africa, in around 185 CE. When Origen was 17, his father was martyred, and Origen took up a life of disciplined study, becoming a respected thinker both inside and outside the Church. The bishop of Alexandria appointed him head of the catechetical school, instructing new Christian converts before their baptism. After a dispute with the bishop, Origen moved to Caesarea in Palestine, where his writings included an eight-volume defense of Christianity against one of its critics, the philosopher Celsus.

Around 250 CE, Origen was tortured by the Roman authorities in an attempt to make him renounce his faith. Origen refused, and was released. However, he died a few years later, in 254 CE, most likely as a result of injuries sustained while he was being persecuted for his faith.

Key works

c.220 *De Principiis (First Principles)*: the first systematic rendition of Christian theology
248 *On Prayer; On Martyrdom; Against Celsus*

GOD IS THREE AND GOD IS ONE

A DIVINE TRINITY

IN CONTEXT

KEY TEXT
The Nicene Creed

WHEN AND WHERE
4th century CE, Nicea and Constantinople

BEFORE
500 BCE Jewish daily prayer includes the Shema, affirming that God is one (monotheism).

1st century CE Christians worship Jesus and the Holy Spirit with the God of Israel.

c.200 CE Tertullian explains the Trinity as "three persons of one substance."

AFTER
c.400 CE St. Augustine's *The Trinity (De Trinitate)*, gives an analogy of the Trinity based on three elements of human life: mind, knowledge, and love.

20th century Trinitarian theology, starting with the doctrine of the Trinity, thrives with theologian Karl Barth.

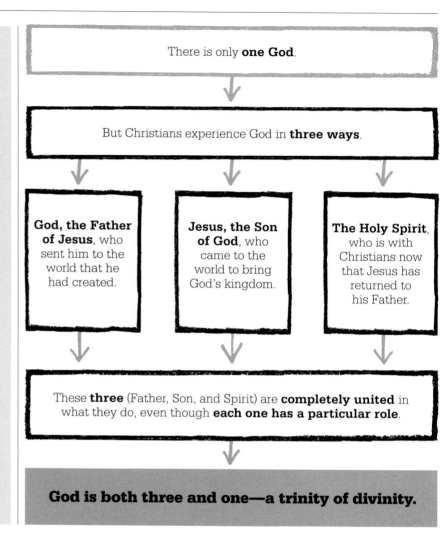

There is only **one God**.

But Christians experience God in **three ways**.

God, the Father of Jesus, who sent him to the world that he had created.

Jesus, the Son of God, who came to the world to bring God's kingdom.

The Holy Spirit, who is with Christians now that Jesus has returned to his Father.

These **three** (Father, Son, and Spirit) are **completely united** in what they do, even though **each one has a particular role**.

God is both three and one—a trinity of divinity.

I n a math test, it is safe to assume that 1 + 1 + 1 = 3, but not so in a theology exam. One of the most notorious conundrums of the Christian faith is that to describe God, 1 + 1 + 1 = 1, not 3. Some of the greatest Christian theologians have struggled to explain how God can be three distinct persons (Father, Son, and Holy Spirit) yet remain only one God. However, this idea, which is known as the doctrine of the Trinity, is a central plank in Christian theology, setting its understanding of God apart from other religions.

A standardized way of speaking about God, known as the doctrine of the Trinity, was settled upon by members of the early Church some 300 years after the death of Jesus. A range of ideas had emerged as the faith spread across the Roman Empire and beyond, so Church leaders articulated the doctrine as a response.

Rooted in Judaism

The roots of Christianity are in Judaism—the religion into which Jesus was born and of which he claimed to be the Messiah. Just as

Judaism is monotheistic, so is Christianity—Christians, like Jews, believe in just one God. But how could the first Christians claim to be monotheistic if they worshipped both Jesus as God and the God whom Jesus called Father? And how did this relate to the Spirit, whom Jesus said he would send, so that God's presence would remain with Christians? Since the Spirit was also worshipped as God, did this mean that Christians were tri-theists (believing in three gods) rather than monotheists?

The doctrine of the Trinity is an

See also: From monolatry to monotheism 176–77 ▪ Jesus's divine identity 208 ▪ The unity of divinity is necessary 280–81

The Trinity is portrayed as Son, Father, and dove—inspired by Jesus' baptism, when the Holy Spirit "descended on him like a dove"—in this 17th-century fresco.

attempt to answer these tricky questions, with the assertion that Christians worship one God in three persons.

What Jesus taught

As the Gospel writers recorded, Jesus referred to God as his Father throughout his ministry. The implication of this teaching was clear, Jesus was God's Son and he claimed the same divinity as God. He also spoke about his close relationship to the Spirit: "the Holy Spirit, whom the Father will send in my name, will teach you all things and will remind you of everything I have said to you" (John 14:26). Jesus again hinted at the shared divinity of the three persons of God in the Great Commission, a statement in which he commanded his followers to "make disciples of all nations, baptizing them in the name of the Father and of the Son and of the Holy Spirit" (Matthew 28:19). In accordance with these teachings, the early Christians worshipped Jesus. After all, he had made it possible for everyone who believed to be part of God's family (a status previously only accorded to the Jews), forgiving their past rebellion against God and assuring them that they would be included when God brought peace and justice to the world. Jesus had said and done things that only God could say and do: as he had implied during his life, Jesus was God.

Similar but not the same

The doctrine of the Trinity emerged in response to a series of other answers that the early Christians »

We believe in one God, the Father almighty…and in one Lord Jesus Christ, the only begotten Son of God…and in the Holy Spirit, the Lord and lifegiver…
Nicene Creed

The Nicene Creed

By the start of the 4th century CE, Christianity had spread across the Roman Empire. With such a wide appeal, it was increasingly difficult to establish a uniform understanding of the faith. The Emperor Constantine saw the problems these differences were causing, so he called a council of Church bishops from all over his empire to meet in Nicea in 325 CE. He encouraged the bishops to agree a statement of faith—in particular, to define the nature of the Trinity—that would be acceptable to all Christians. This creed would be recited in churches and would help steer Christians away from heretical beliefs, especially those of the Arians (see p.216). In 381 CE, Emperor Theodosius called another council, this time in Constantinople. The 325 CE creed was clarified and expanded, resulting in the Nicene Creed, which is still recited today in churches all over the world.

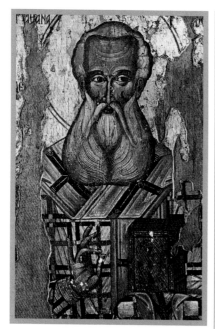

St. Athanasius of Alexandria is remembered for his staunch theological defense of Trinitarianism against the teachings of Arianism. He had a key role in drafting the Nicene Creed.

judged to be wrong, or heretical. One such idea was Arianism—the theology of Arius (c.250–336 CE), a Christian leader in Alexandria, Egypt—which emphasized monotheism so strongly that it denied the deity of the Son and, by implication, of the Spirit. For Arius, only the Father was truly God. Although the Son was to be honored for having the closest possible relationship with the Father, the Son was still only a representative of the Father's deity, and did not share that deity.

This tallied with some aspects of accepted Christian thinking: one of the essential characteristics of God was that he was uncreated— he had no beginning as well as no end to his life. The Arians therefore argued that since children have to be born, the Son of God could not possess all the essential characteristics of God, because, as a Son, he must have been born. An Arian dictum about the Son of God stated that "there was once when he was not": there must have been a time before the Son of God was born, when God existed without him. In their view, this logic proved that only the Father was truly God. One of the words used to describe the Son was *homoiousios*, which is a Greek term meaning "of similar substance." The Son was "of similar substance" to the Father, but not the same.

The Arians had preserved monotheism, but at the expense of the Son and the Spirit. This was potentially disastrous for the Christian faith, since the central claim of Christians was that through the life, death, and resurrection of Jesus—the Son of God—God himself had saved them. If the Son of God was not truly God, then how could they be sure that God really did want to forgive them their sins and receive them in his kingdom?

At the Council of Nicea in 325 CE, Arianism was condemned when its central tenet, that the Son was *homoiousios* with the Father, was rejected. Instead, Jesus was declared to be *homoousios*, which means "of the same substance." This distinction made all the difference—it was agreed that the Son utterly shares the Father's deity. Consequently, it was accepted that the Son had no beginning—God has always been a Father and a Son, together with the Holy Spirit.

Persons, not masks

A second answer deemed heretical to the question of the Trinity was given by a 3rd-century CE priest in Rome, Sabellius, and his followers. Unlike the Arians, the Sabellians affirmed that the Son and the Spirit were truly God. They solved the problem of whether God is one or three by maintaining that Father, Son, and Spirit are three modes of the one God's being. This idea is known as modalism.

Father, Son, and Spirit can be thought of as masks available to an actor in a play. There is only one actor, but he can play three parts, simply by wearing three different masks. At first, this might seem like a good way to describe how God is experienced: sometimes Christians encounter him as the Father, at other times as the Son, and still other times as the Spirit.

However, if Christians only ever encountered God's three masks, how could they be sure that they had met God himself? After all, people can wear masks in order to hide their true identity. What if God wore the masks to pretend to be something he is not? And so, instead of talking about masks or modes, Christian theologians began to use the Greek term *hypostases*, which was translated into Latin as *personae*, or persons. They posited that God is three hypostases of one *ousia* (Greek for essence/being—in Latin, *substantia*, or substance),

God is divided without division, if I may put it like that, and united in division. The Godhead is one in three and the three are one...
Gregory of Nazianzus

> Every act which extends from God to the creation… originates with the Father, proceeds through the Son, and is completed by the Holy Spirit.
> **Gregory of Nyssa**

so three persons of one substance. Such theological reasoning involved stretching the meaning of human terms in order to express the magnitude of God appropriately. Some of the theologians who achieved this most successfully were the Cappadocian Fathers: Basil of Caesarea, Gregory of Nazianzus, and Gregory of Nyssa (Basil's younger brother), who lived in the late 4th century CE. They explained the difference between *ousia* and hypostases (substance and persons) by giving an example: *ousia* is humanity as a general category, while each hypostasis is an individual human. Every person has their humanity in common with other people; but at the same time, each person has individual characteristics that make them who they are. Defining humanity accordingly would involve stating "we experience one common humanity in billions of persons," followed by listing every person who has ever lived, is living, and will live.

In this definition of the Trinity, the persons of the Trinity have their divinity in common, in the same way that people share their common humanity. There are just three persons of the one divine substance—Father, Son, and Spirit.

By using the language of hypostases or persons, Christian thinkers were able to avoid the problems of Sabellius and modalism. It was agreed that Father, Son, and Spirit were not three masks worn by a mysterious divine actor, just as there is no ideal human lurking somewhere behind all the humans who have ever lived. Instead, there are three persons (Father, Son, and Spirit) who, together, are God.

Understanding the Trinity

Why is it important to Christians that one God is worshipped in three persons, rather than as three separate gods? The easy answer is that if the Trinity was understood as three separate gods, Christians could not be certain that the God of the story of Jesus Christ had anything to do with the God who they believe created the world, or who is at work in the world today.

The idea of a Trinity safeguards the unity of God's relationship with the world. Traditionally, the Father is seen as the one who created the world, the Son is the one who came into the world to save it, and the Spirit is the one who transforms the world into the place God wants it to be. It is important that these are seen as one God working in three ways toward the same goal—to share God's love with the world—not »

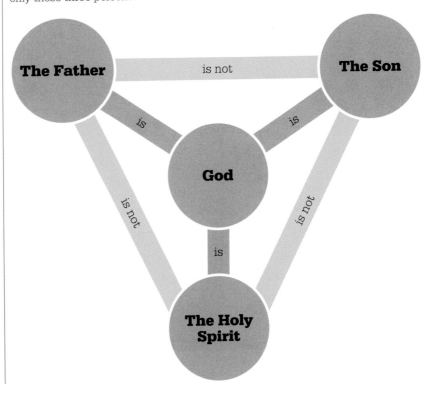

The Trinity comprises three distinct persons who are not interchangeable, yet share the same divine substance, and this divine substance is present in only these three persons.

Red rose petals fall inside the Pantheon, Rome, at the end of Pentecost Mass, commemorating the descent of the Holy Spirit onto the disciples on the day of Pentecost.

three times, as if telling the same story from three different, but complementary, perspectives. This repetition, maintains Barth, reflects what God's existence is really like—whatever God does, he does as Father, Spirit, and Son.

Defining principle

The doctrine of the Trinity is often considered one of the most obscure and complicated aspects of Christian theology. Nonetheless, Christians hold to the doctrine because they believe it reflects a vital characteristic of God. Just as in the debates with the Arians and Sabellians in the 4th century CE, the idea of the Trinity is essential to orthodox Christian faith. Groups, such as the Jehovah's Witnesses and the Unitarians, who hold conflicting views on this issue are generally not considered authentically Christian by the mainstream Church.

One interesting development in recent times has been the notion of the social Trinity, in which the cooperation of the three persons of

as three Gods pulling in three different directions. Augustine (p.221) explained that it is this love that binds the Trinity together.

Metaphors of the Trinity

Over the centuries, many people have tried to identify metaphors for the Trinity in order to explain how three can be one, and one three. For instance, St. Patrick—a 5th-century CE missionary who took Christianity to Ireland—used the image of a three-leaf shamrock. Others have used the analogy

of speech to explain the Trinity: the Father is the one who speaks, the Son is the word that is spoken, and the Spirit is the breath by which the word is spoken. By far the most influential Christian theologian of the 20th century was Karl Barth (1886–1968), a Swiss pastor and professor. He came up with a helpful guide for trinitarian thinking, which has been embraced by much contemporary theology. The doctrine of the Trinity means that whatever is said about the Christian God, has to be said

As Father, Son, and Spirit are three, they are three agents of what the one God does with creatures.
Robert Jenson

the Trinity is seen as a model for human community. Since God can only be God as long the relationships between Father, Son, and Spirit are maintained, so humans, made in God's image, can only be truly human as they maintain meaningful relationships with God and others.

The Trinity and the Spirit

The Spirit often seems like the forgotten person of the Trinity. Perhaps this is because the debates of the 4th century CE were primarily about the relationship between Jesus, Son of God, and God the Father, so the Spirit received only a brief mention in the creeds. It might also be because the Spirit seems the most difficult of the three persons to comprehend, a situation made more confusing by the use of the older English term Holy Ghost— from the word *gast*, meaning "spirit."

According to the Gospel of John, Jesus told his followers that he would send God's Spirit to be with them after he had left them and ascended into heaven. Because the Spirit was supposed to transform the lives of God's followers from the inside out, so that they would live the kind of holy lives that God wanted them to, the Spirit then became known as the Holy Spirit.

The name of Father, Son, and Spirit means that God is the one God in threefold repetition...
Karl Barth

While Christians of different denominations understand the Holy Spirit in different ways, the Pentecostal movement of the 20th century did much to raise the public profile of the Spirit. The movement was named after the day of Pentecost, when Jesus sent the Spirit to his disciples. On that day, the Spirit is said to have appeared as a flame above the heads of the disciples, who were filled with the Holy Spirit. This enabled them to preach in languages that had been previously unknown to them.

The idea of the Holy Spirit's transformative power is central to Pentecostal Christians. They believe that believers may be taken over by the Holy Spirit in the way in which the Spirit took hold of the disciples. This very intense, personal experience is called a baptism by the Holy Spirit, and worshippers actively seek this spiritual renewal over and above their normal Christian life.

Charismatic Christianity

Since the 1960s, the charismatic movement has introduced the Pentecostal enthusiasm for the Spirit into other denominations. The word charismatic comes from *charismata* (Greek for "gift of grace") and refers to the spiritual gifts which are evidence of the Spirit's activity among Christians, including gifts such as healing, prophesying, and speaking in tongues (or other languages).

The pronounced role of the Spirit in the Pentecostal and charismatic movements has prompted the Church to think through its understanding of all three persons of the Trinity, if it is not to inadvertently sideline one or more. The idea of the Trinity remains as vital now as ever, informing how Christians speak about the God they believe and worship. ∎

Gifts of the Holy Spirit

Many spiritual gifts are recognized in the Christian Church. For believers, these gifts are given by God to the Church to help it do the work of God's kingdom in the world. The gifts are for three main purposes: ministry, motivation, and manifestation.

Christians maintain that the Spirit enables some people to perform special roles within the Church. These ministry gifts include full-time callings to be a pastor or an evangelist. Motivational gifts are practical gifts that encourage the work of the church: these include prophecy, teaching, giving, leading, or showing mercy.

Sometimes, the Spirit's activity is seen in a special way, such as in tongues (speaking with unlearned words in order to praise God), healing, or other miracles. These gifts are called manifestations, which show the Spirit is at work.

The Bible says that the Spirit helps to produce good fruit in the lives of Christians: Christians grow into "love, joy, peace, patience, kindness, goodness, faithfulness, gentleness, and self-control" (Galatians 5:22–23).

GOD'S GRACE NEVER FAILS
AUGUSTINE AND FREE WILL

IN CONTEXT

KEY FIGURE
Augustine of Hippo

WHEN AND WHERE
**354–430 CE,
present-day Algeria**

BEFORE
From c.1000 BCE The Jews
understand themselves to
be chosen by God because
of his grace, not by virtue of
their inherent goodness.

c.30 CE Jesus teaches his
followers about grace: "You
didn't choose me. I chose you."

AFTER
418 CE Augustine's teaching
on grace is accepted by the
Church and Pelagius is
condemned as a heretic at
the Council of Carthage.

16th century Calvin develops
Augustine's thought in his
doctrine of predestination,
which becomes a central
element of the theology of
the Protestant Reformation.

D o we choose God, or does
God choose us? This
question has troubled
Christian thinkers since the
earliest days of the Church. At its
heart is the tricky philosophical
issue of free will, translated into
the context of the Christian faith.
It took the brilliant mind of the
theologian Augustine to come up
with a way of explaining how God's
choice relates to human choice.

The Pelagian controversy
Augustine was propelled into the
debate over free will in the early
5th century when Pelagius, a Celtic
monk, arrived in North Africa. The

Salvation is by **God's grace**,
not human capability.

The **human** will is **weak**.

God's grace **cannot fail**.

The **weak human** will
always **choose sin**
over God.

God gives grace to
people to **enable them**
to choose him.

Humans are thus **not
free to choose** God.

See also: God's covenant with Israel 168–69 ▪ Why prayer works 246–47 ▪ Striving in the way of God 278

In infant baptism, Christians believe that the stain of sin is washed away. Pelagius argued that because infants have not developed free will, they could not have sinned.

controversy was initially about the baptism of infants. Pelagius argued that there was no need for infants to be baptized to wash away the stain of sin, as was generally the belief of the time. He maintained that sin was a result of human free will, and since he believed infants had not developed free will, they could not have sinned. Moreover, if children chose to follow God's way as they developed free will while growing up, there would be no need for them to be baptized at all.

Augustine disagreed with nearly everything Pelagius said. He argued—based as much on experience as on logic—that it is impossible for humans to choose freely to follow God's way. From birth, the weak-willed human veers toward choosing what is wrong, an idea that became known as original sin. In order to choose God, Augustine believed that humans need God's help—which is precisely why baptism is so important. God chooses to give

humans his grace (his saving help), and because God is all-powerful, whatever he does must be effective. Those humans who receive God's grace are at liberty to make their own decision to choose God, rather than sin. Augustine maintained a careful balance: God's choice does not replace human choice, but rather makes it possible for humans to choose.

Predestination

Augustine's concept, which became known as the doctrine of predestination, was adopted by Protestant reformers, notably John Calvin. In some extreme statements of predestination, the idea that God's grace cannot fail was emphasized at the expense of human freedom, reducing human decisions to inconsequential acts, because God has already decided what will happen—the so-called paradox of free will, by which, many argue, that predestination robs humans of free will. Augustine's idea of grace is a valuable way of maintaining the balance between God's choice and that of humans. ▪

God extends his mercy to humankind not because they already know him, but in order that they may know him.
Augustine of Hippo

Augustine of Hippo

Aurelius Augustine was born in 354 CE in Thagaste, North Africa. He was brought up as a Christian by his devout mother, but renounced his faith during his youth and led a dissolute life for several years. After studying Greek philosophy in Carthage, he embraced Manichaeism, a Persian religion, but returned to Christianity after being impressed by the sermons of Bishop Ambrose in Milan and the example of the desert hermit Anthony (p.223).

Augustine was baptized on Easter Day in 387, and by 396 he had been appointed Bishop at Hippo. He preached and wrote prolifically about theological controversies until his death in 430. He is rightly regarded as one of the great Christian thinkers, and his teaching has continued to influence Christian thought throughout the Western world. Recognized as a saint by the Anglican and Catholic Church, he was awarded the highly honored title, Doctor of the Church, in the 13th century.

Key works

397–400 CE *Confessions*
413–427 CE *The City of God*

IN THE WORLD, BUT NOT OF THE WORLD

SERVING GOD ON BEHALF OF OTHERS

IN CONTEXT

KEY MOVEMENT
Monasticism

WHEN AND WHERE
**From 3rd century CE,
Mediterranean**

BEFORE
**2nd century BCE–1st
century CE** Within Judaism,
ascetic Essenes gather in
monastery-type communities
in order to live lives of purity
and abstinence.

AFTER
529 CE St. Benedict establishes
a monastic community in Italy;
in 817 his *Rule* becomes the
authorized set of precepts for
all monks in Western Europe.

11th century St. Francis and
St Clare found the Franciscan
order of monks, and the Order
of St. Clare for nuns.

16th century Monasteries
that are seen as too wealthy
and corrupt are closed during
the Protestant Reformation
in Europe.

Christians have to live
in **the world**.

↓

The world is full of
distractions from God.

↓

By **retreating** from the world,
monks and nuns can focus
on their **spiritual life**.

↓

Without distractions, they can
pray for and seek to better
the **world around them**.

↓

**Monasticism is about
being in the world,
but not of the world.**

Nowadays, monasteries
are sometimes thought
of as relics from a bygone
age. However, when they began
to flourish in the early medieval
period, after the collapse of the
Roman Empire in the 5th century,
they were at the forefront of
society. In a Europe that, culturally
speaking, was entering what
we now know as the Dark Ages,
monasteries became beacons of
learning and innovation. These
powerful institutions embodied
a central idea in Christianity:
that some people can be set apart
from the demands of conventional
living in order to focus on leading
a spiritual life that will be of benefit
to others as well as themselves. An
important aspect of monasticism
has always been praying for people
in the wider world.

From caves to cloisters
Monasticism has its roots in the
lives of the "fathers and mothers"
who lived in the Egyptian desert,
from the 3rd century CE. These early
monks and nuns had retreated from
the world in order to live simple
lives of devotion and prayer. They
took Jesus's words seriously—
"What good is it to gain the whole

See also: Self-denial leads to spiritual liberation 68–71 ▪ Higher levels of teaching 101 ▪ The purpose of monastic vows 145 ▪ Immortality in Christianity 210–211 ▪ The Protestant Reformation 230–37

In the 3rd century CE, one of the first desert hermits, St. Anthony, attracted thousands of followers, who settled in caves around him; this monastery was eventually built at the site in Egypt.

world but lose one's own soul?"—and so became ascetics, giving up worldly possessions and marriage to focus on their spiritual lives. The world was understood to be a place of many temptations, which could distract a person from the ways of God. As an antidote to the busyness of life, the ascetics sought quiet, contemplative prayer. It was said that, "Just as it is impossible to see your face in troubled water, so also the soul, unless it is clear of alien thoughts, is not able to pray to God in contemplation."

As monasticism spread out from the desert and into Europe, caves were superseded by specially designed buildings that became known as monasteries. Many were built around a cloister, an enclosed courtyard or garden used for meditation. Although monasteries had moved from the desert to more populated environments, the idea of retreating from the world in order to nurture spiritual life persisted.

A life for others

However, monasteries were not simply spiritual refuges from the outside world. At a time when most Christians were peasants, working long hours simply to survive, the monks and nuns worshiped and prayed on their behalf. Monastic groups such as the Benedictines (founded in the 6th century) and the Cistercians (12th century) offered hospitality and charity as well as prayer. Throughout the Middle Ages, monasteries remained centers of education. Monks and nuns copied and illuminated precious manuscripts, and passed on their knowledge. According to the monastic ideal, retreating from the world gave them the time and energy to serve the world in God's name. ▪

In the Eastern Christian church there is only one monastic order, which follows the instructions for monastic life written by St. Basil.

Eastern monasticism

While Western European monasticism is renowned for its great communal buildings, many Eastern monasteries follow an older tradition of monks and nuns living in relative isolation from each other, inspired by St. Anthony. Another extreme, early Eastern monastic tradition was practiced by the Stylites, such as St. Simeon, who lived on the top of pillars, fasting, praying, and preaching. Although Eastern monasteries have slightly different practices, they still embody the idea of separation from the world for the sake of a spiritual life, and for the benefit of others. One of the holiest places in Eastern monasticism is Mount Athos in Greece, the Holy Mountain, which has some of the oldest monastic buildings in the world. This isolated peninsula is completely autonomous and set apart from the world; women are not permitted access to the land.

THERE IS NO SALVATION OUTSIDE THE CHURCH

ENTERING INTO THE FAITH

IN CONTEXT

KEY MOVEMENT
**The Fourth Lateran
Council**

WHEN AND WHERE
1215 CE, Rome

BEFORE
1st century CE The first
Christian communities form.

313 CE The Roman Emperor
Constantine publishes the
Edict of Milan, allowing
Christians to worship freely.

1054 The Great Schism divides
the Roman Catholic and
Eastern Orthodox Churches.

AFTER
1545–63 The Council of Trent
reaffirms the seven sacraments
against Protestant calls for two.

20th–21st century The
ecumenical movement affirms
that all Christians, regardless
of denomination, are part of
one worldwide Church.

I s it possible to be a Christian
without also being a member
of the Church? Many people
today would answer "yes," pointing
out that Jesus did not provide his
disciples with instructions for
setting up a religious institution.
Some would contend that, in order
to be a Christian, it is sufficient to
have a personal belief in Jesus,
without even belonging to the
Church, in any of its denominations.

Despite this argument, being
a member of the Church has been
considered an essential element
of Christian faith for most of
its history. At first, in the years
following Jesus's death and
resurrection, Christians simply

See also: God's covenant with Israel 168–75 ▪ Faith and the state 189
▪ The central professions of faith 262–69 ▪ Awaiting the Day of Judgment 312–13

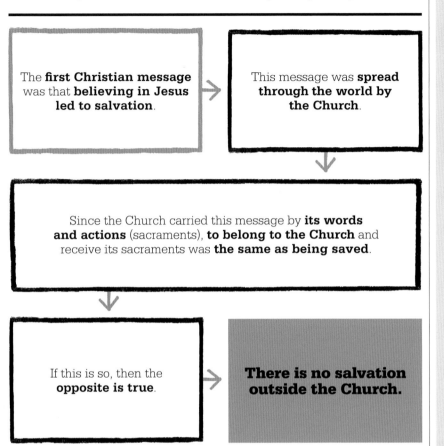

The **first Christian message** was that **believing in Jesus led to salvation**.

→

This message was **spread through the world by the Church**.

↓

Since the Church carried this message by **its words and actions** (sacraments), **to belong to the Church** and receive its sacraments was **the same as being saved**.

↓

If this is so, then the **opposite is true**.

→

There is no salvation outside the Church.

The Christian hell

Throughout Christian history, ideas of hell have symbolized the threat of exclusion from God's salvation. In Jesus's teaching, the word used for hell, Gehenna, referred to a real place outside the walls of Jerusalem, the Valley of the Son of Hinnom. It is thought that sacrificial burnings of children once occurred here, and the place was considered cursed. This gave rise to the popular image of hell as a place of permanent fire.

During the Middle Ages, the horrors of hell became a regular theme in religious art, reminding people of their need to stay within the Catholic Church if they wanted to escape the threat of eternal torment.

More recently, Christian thinkers have suggested that Jesus did not mean that there was an actual place called hell where those who failed to accept his message would be punished forever. Hell was just his name for an existence without God. Since God is understood to be the author of life, to be without his presence is simply nonexistence, or everlasting death.

adapted the religious gatherings at Jewish synagogues, from which many of the early believers were drawn. Like the Jews, Christians came together to pray and sing, share food, and read the Scriptures. For Christians, this meant the Hebrew Bible, which became known to them as the Old Testament, and a new collection of documents about Jesus and his significance, known as the New Testament.

As the Christian message spread into the non-Jewish world, Christian gatherings developed their own identity and were named *ecclesia*, from the Greek, meaning "called out." This referred to the idea that the group had been called out by God to share the message of Jesus with the world.

Mother Church
By the mid-3rd century CE, the theologian Cyprian had made it clear that belonging to the Church was a nonnegotiable element of Christian faith, not an optional extra. At this time many Christians were suffering intense persecution from the Roman authorities because of their faith; some had renounced their beliefs in order to save their lives. Church leaders were unsure what course they should take with such people. They questioned whether to »

readmit them to the Church if they truly repented, or whether to exclude them and let them form their own, separate communities. Cyprian was adamant that the Church should forgive them and allow them back, since in his understanding there could be only one true Church, and it was impossible for people to be saved outside it. He likened the Church to Noah's Ark in the Old Testament story of the flood, commenting that just as the only people who were saved were those on the Ark, so too the only people to be saved from God's judgment of evil were those in the Church.

By Cyprian's time, the Church had already developed a clearly defined structure. Deacons and priests led local congregations, while bishops and archbishops were responsible for slightly larger geographical areas. Partly due to the political and economic importance of Rome itself during this early period, the Bishop of Rome was increasingly seen as the leader of the whole Church, and by the 6th century was the only bishop called the pope (from a Greek word meaning "father").

Papal power increased during the medieval period. Although at first the Pope's preeminence was seen as a useful way to ensure the unity of the Church, by the start of the 11th century, Eastern Greek-speaking church leaders felt they were being unfairly dominated by the Western, Latin-speaking Pope. In 1054, in the Great Schism, the Church split into Eastern and Western branches, citing doctrinal differences as well as the issue of papal authority. However, the Pope in Rome still claimed to be leader of the worldwide Church, and at the

You cannot have God for your Father, if you do not have the Church for your mother.
Cyprian, *The Unity of the Church*

Fouth Lateran Council of Church leaders in 1215, Pope Innocent III reasserted his authority over the powerful bishops in the Eastern Church at Constantinople, Antioch, Alexandria, and Jerusalem.

In Western Europe, the Roman Catholic Church, presided over by the Pope, was seen as the only true family of faithful Christians until the end of the Middle Ages. The dominance of the Roman Catholic Church in medieval life added weight to the idea that it was impossible to be saved outside the Church.

Seven sacraments

While the Church had established massive political and economic influence during the medieval period, its main power was spiritual. It understood that one of its main functions was to bring visibility to the spiritual union between God and his people. Because the Christian relationship with God seemed intangible by nature, it was more convenient to assess Christian faith by the state of a person's relationship with the Church.

Within the Church, special rites were used to mark different stages of the Christian life. Known as

The seven sacraments of the Roman Catholic Church mark different stages of Christian life. Partaking in the sacraments shows membership of the Church; being part of the Church is, Catholics believe, necessary for salvation.

Confirmation

Baptism

Eucharist

Matrimony

Holy orders

Penance

Extreme unction

> There is one Universal Church of the faithful, outside of which there is absolutely no salvation.
> **Fourth Lateran Council**

sacraments, these rites were physical actions that had spiritual significance. Originally, the early Church celebrated only two sacraments—baptism and the Eucharist—tracing them back to the example and teaching of Jesus himself. However, during the Middle Ages, their number increased to a total of seven, all of which were offered with the authority of the Catholic Church. These were: baptism (the moment a person enters the Church and their sin is washed away); confirmation (the point at which a person receives the gift of God's Holy Spirit to help live a Christian life); the Eucharist (a regular celebration of the forgiveness achieved by the death and resurrection of Jesus); penance (the actions specified by a priest in order for a person to be reconciled with God after confessing sin); extreme unction, otherwise known as the last rites (anointing and giving comfort and the assurance of forgiveness to the dying); and holy orders (when a person decides to spend their life serving God within the Church). The last of the seven rites was marriage, which was considered a sacrament because the close relationship between a husband and wife was thought to mirror the close relationship between God and his people.

Receiving the sacraments was a clear indication that a person remained a member of the Catholic Church, and so could rely on being saved by God. Church legislation was therefore developed to guide both priests and lay people as to how the sacraments should be properly used. They were considered so important that the clergy were forbidden from making a profit from doing their duties. At the Fourth Lateran Council, it was decreed that all Christians should receive the Eucharist at least once a year at Easter, and should also confess their sins and do penance at least once annually. The prayers of a priest at the bedside of a sick person were considered so essential that doctors were required to call a priest to attend to the patient before they did their own work. These important regulations ensured that the Church offered the sacraments freely and regularly, and that Church members received what was offered.

Avoiding damnation

Like other Church councils before and after it, the Fourth Lateran Council made it clear that to reject the sacraments of the Catholic Church was to remove oneself from the Church and so also to lose the salvation offered on behalf of God. If the Church was to be seen as the mother of the faithful, then anyone who was not a child of the Church could not enjoy salvation.

Special condemnation was reserved for people who not only failed to receive the sacraments themselves, but also taught others to reject them. Since it was believed that the popes of the Roman Church had inherited and passed on true teaching from Peter, one of Jesus's closest disciples and considered the first pope, anyone who rejected the teaching of the pope was held to be rejecting the teaching of Jesus. Unrepentant heretics (believing in anything other than the teachings of the Catholic Church) faced the punishment of excommunication: they were removed from the Church and forbidden from receiving sacraments until they changed their minds. If they died before giving up their heresies, they could expect to miss out on God's salvation and to endure the horrors of hell.

At the end of the Middle Ages, the monopoly on salvation by the Catholic Church was challenged by the Protestant Reformation (p.230–37). No longer could a single Christian institution claim that there was no possibility of salvation outside itself. However, the idea that salvation is not possible outside the wider Christian Church has persisted among many Christian groups. ∎

St. Peter, close disciple of Jesus and martyred in Rome, is the source of papal prerogative. His authority is thought to be inherited by the popes, and so to reject their word is to reject Jesus.

THIS IS MY BODY, THIS IS MY BLOOD
THE MYSTERY OF THE EUCHARIST

IN CONTEXT

KEY FIGURE
Thomas Aquinas

WHEN AND WHERE
1225–74, Europe

BEFORE
From 300 BCE Jews add the drinking of a cup of wine that has been blessed to the eating of unleavened bread during the Passover meal.

1st century CE St. Paul writes with instructions for the early Christians as they regularly celebrate Jesus's last meal with his disciples.

1215 CE The Fourth Lateran Council defines the Eucharist as one of seven essential sacraments for the Catholic faithful.

AFTER
16th century The Protestant Reformers reject the concept of transubstantiation, generally favoring a more symbolic understanding of Jesus's words.

In the **sacrament** of the Eucharist, Christians experience the **real presence of Jesus**.

But the elements in the Eucharist are **bread and wine, not flesh and blood**.

Aristotle distinguishes between **substance** and **accidents** (the form or attributes of something).

The **accidents** of the bread and wine are clearly **unchanged**.

So it must be the substance that is **converted** from bread and wine **into the body and blood of Jesus**.

This is the mystery of the Eucharist.

efore his arrest and eventual crucifixion, Jesus shared a Passover meal of bread and wine with his disciples, saying, "This is my body" and "This is my blood." Since then, this ritual has been celebrated by Christians in an act of worship known variously as the Eucharist, Holy Communion, the Lord's Supper, and the Breaking of Bread. But over the centuries, the meaning and significance of his words have been the subject of huge controversy. In what sense does the bread and wine change into the body and blood of Jesus?

In the 13th century, the great medieval theologian Thomas Aquinas developed the theory of transubstantiation. He drew

See also: Beliefs for new societies 56–57 ▪ Entering into the faith 224–27 ▪ The Protestant Reformation 230–37

> The presence of Christ's true body and blood in this sacrament cannot be detected by sense, nor understanding, but by faith alone.
>
> **Thomas Aquinas**

on the recently rediscovered philosophy of Aristotle to clarify previous teaching about the Eucharist. Aquinas's teaching became the official doctrine of the Roman Catholic Church.

The purpose of Aquinas's teaching was to explain how the real presence of Jesus could be found in the elements of bread and wine. This was important because Christians believe that the Eucharist is a sacrament, a sacred act that is thought to embody a religious truth (p.226). If Jesus were not present when the bread and wine were shared, the sacrament would lose its meaning and significance.

When is bread not bread?

According to Aristotle, substance is the unique identity of an object or person—the "tableness" of a table, for example. Accidents are the attributes of the substance, and can change without its identity altering—a table might be wooden, and blue, but if it was metal and pink it would still be a table.

For Aquinas, this meant that it was possible for the substance or essence of an object or person (such as Jesus) to be found in the accidents or attributes of other objects (such as bread and wine). He said that it was also possible for one object to be converted into another object: so, as the priest prayed over the bread and the wine, the substance of bread and wine

Holy Communion is fundamental to the faith of nearly all Christians. Roman Catholic and Orthodox Christians believe in transubstantiation; others see it more as a symbolic act.

was converted into that of the body and blood of Jesus (hence the term transubstantiation—"to change from one substance to another"). However, the accidents or attributes of the bread and wine remained, so the real presence of Jesus in bread and wine was to be believed, but not physically seen. ▪

Thomas Aquinas

Thomas Aquinas is acclaimed as the greatest theologian in the medieval scholastic movement, which was characterized by a new method of contemplating the Christian faith in an academically rigorous way. Aquinas was born to a noble family in Roccasecca near Naples in 1225. While at the university in Naples, Aquinas joined the recently established Order of Preachers (later known as the Dominican Friars). He continued his studies in Paris and Cologne, subsequently becoming a highly regarded teacher in the Catholic Church. His major contribution to Christianity was his use of Greek philosophy, notably the work of Aristotle, to explain and defend Christian theology. Known as "Thomism," his system of theology became the standard within Catholic thinking for centuries. Aquinas died at the age of 49 in 1274, while he was traveling to the ecumenical Council of Lyon.

Key works

c.1260 *Summa contra Gentiles*
c.1265–74 *Summa Theologica* (Sum of Theology)

GOD'S WORD NEEDS
NO GO-BETWEENS
THE PROTESTANT REFORMATION

The Roman Catholic Church was a formidable institution in the late Middle Ages. From his palace in Rome, the Pope had power not only over Europe's religious life, but also over its politics and economics. The Church was a major landowner, and, through the feudal system, many peasants found themselves indebted to it for their homes and livelihoods, as well as for the care of their souls. At the other end of the spectrum, it was in the best interests of nobles and rulers to maintain good relations with the Church, obeying its laws, and paying tithes and taxes.

However, in the first decades of the 16th century, a spiritual and social revolution shifted power away from the Catholic Church, initiating a new chapter in the history of Christianity in Europe. This revolution, now known as the Protestant Reformation, was based on the idea that God could be known and worshipped directly, without the need for an authorized hierarchy of priests to act as intermediaries. The reformers placed the teachings and traditions of the Church under the authority of Scripture, and maintained that salvation could only come from personal faith rather than from following the Church's decrees.

Renaissance Europe

By the 16th century, Europe had begun to shake off the old ideas of medieval life. The horizons of the known world were expanding rapidly, with Spanish, Portuguese, and French explorers following in the wake of Columbus's voyage to the Americas in 1492. Transport and trade were flourishing as a result of advances in seafaring, including a new route around Africa to India.

In Europe, the feudal system was being abandoned in favor of new kingdoms and city-states controlled by rulers interested in improving the economic prosperity of their territories. Culturally, artists, philosophers, and scientists were rediscovering the classical learning of the past, in a loosely connected movement known as the Renaissance. In short, a new world was arriving and it seemed that the Church, with its ancient traditions and structures, was set to have a smaller role within it.

The Bible was written in the **common language** of the day (the Old Testament in Hebrew, the New Testament in Greek).

→

The first Christians were encouraged to **study the Scriptures** to make their own mind up about Christian faith.

→

Restricting the **Bible to Latin** during the Middle Ages meant that **most people could not make up their own minds** about what it said.

Translating the Bible into the vernacular meant that **everyone could read and hear** God's Word for themselves.

God's word needs no go-betweens.

See also: The power of the shaman 26–31 ▪ The personal quest for truth 144 ▪ St. Augustine and free will 220–21 ▪ Mystical experience in Christianity 238

Martin Luther preaches from the pulpit in this painting in the Church of St. Mary in Wittenberg. The presence of the crucified Christ is a symbol of a direct relationship with God.

Misunderstanding God

Church services in the Middle Ages were held in Latin, a language that most people did not understand. The authorized version of the Bible—a 4th-century translation from the original Hebrew and Greek by St. Jerome known as the Vulgate, meaning "commonly used" —was also written in Latin. As a result, most churchgoers relied upon their priests to explain the truths of Christianity to them. Priests held considerable power over their congregations and tended to advocate the traditions of the Catholic Church, rather than going back to the original texts.

Although this meant that there was a consistency to Catholic teaching across Europe, there were obvious dangers as well. For instance, how could people in the churches be certain that their priests were teaching them what the Bible really contained? How could they check the truth of what they heard?

Conflict with Rome

The Reformation began because a German monk, Martin Luther, believed that people were being deceived—sometimes unwittingly —by the priests and leaders of the Catholic Church of the day.

Luther was angered by the preaching of the Dominican Johann Tetzel, who had arrived in the villages near Wittenberg, Saxony, where Luther was a parish priest and university professor. Tetzel was essentially on a fundraising mission for the Church: in Rome, Pope Leo X was raising money to build a vast church, the Basilica of St. Peter; and, closer to home, the German Cardinal Albrecht needed to repay a loan taken out to defray the expenses of his position. Tetzel had been authorized to sell certificates, called indulgences, which claimed to release people from the threat of suffering for their sins in purgatory after their death. Indulgences had been available in the Catholic Church for many centuries, but Luther was appalled at Tetzel's blatant sales tactics, which frightened people with terrible images of how much their deceased loved ones were suffering in purgatory. "As soon as the coin in the coffer rings, the soul from »

A Christian is a perfectly free lord of all, subject to none. A Christian is a perfectly dutiful servant of all, subject to all.
Martin Luther

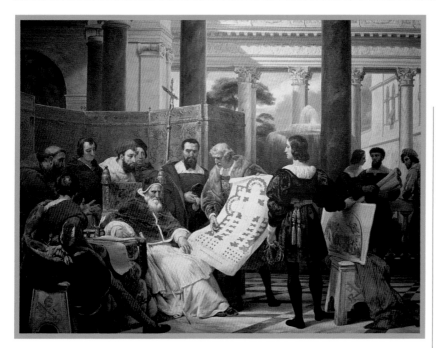

Pope Julius II is shown in this 19th-century painting in the process of instructing Bramante, Michelangelo, and Raphael to start work on the Vatican and St. Peter's Basilica.

purgatory springs," Tetzel warned, and many of Luther's parishioners duly paid for the indulgences in the hope of purchasing salvation.

Luther had become firmly convinced, from his studies of the Bible, and especially the Book of Romans in the New Testament, that salvation was a free gift from God to those who have faith, not something to be bought. He recorded his objections to the sale of indulgences in 95 theses, or statements, which he sent to his bishop, the Prince of Mainz, and reportedly pinned to the door of the church in Wittenberg. A copy of the theses found its way to a printer, and the publication became an overnight bestseller.

Far more was at stake than the collection of funds for a pope's building project and an archbishop's pocket: Luther's protest raised the issue of authority within the Catholic Church. In 1520, Pope Leo X responded by publishing a document explaining how Luther had misrepresented the teaching of the Church, and declaring him and his followers to be heretics. Luther was invited to retract his views, but he refused, and even burned his copy of the Pope's document.

Authority of the Scriptures

Luther's meaning was clear: even though the Pope may have been the leader of the Church, he was not the final authority when it came to matters of faith. The final authority was God's word itself, as recorded in the Bible, otherwise known as the Scriptures. Luther held that it was not necessary for Christians to rely upon the traditions and teachings of the Church to come to a true knowledge of God and salvation. Instead, Christians could bypass these human traditions, which were often inaccurate anyway, and discover truth directly from the Bible. This would later be expressed by the Latin phrase *sola Scriptura*, "Scripture alone": the Reformers were convinced that people do not need middle men to interpret the meaning of the

Scriptures for them. Anyone could read the Bible and come to a clear understanding of God's way of salvation, which, for Luther, did not involve indulgences, popes, or many of the other practices of the Catholic Church.

Luther's rejection of tradition in favor of returning to original biblical sources fell on fertile soil in the early 16th century. The Humanist movement (not to be confused with modern, secular humanism) was already seeking to recover the classical learning that had been forgotten during the Dark Ages. Christian Humanists such as Desiderius Erasmus (1466–1536) encouraged their students to study the original languages of the Bible (Hebrew for the Old Testament and Greek for the New) and the writings of the very first Christians, the Church Fathers. The Reformation encouraged everyone to join in by reading the Bible for themselves.

Those who preach indulgences are in error when they say that a person is absolved and saved from every penalty by the pope's indulgences.
Martin Luther

> Luther has been sent into the world by the genius of discord. Every corner of it has been disturbed by him. All admit that the corruptions of the Church required a drastic medicine.
> **Erasmus**

A revolution in print

While the direct engagement of people with the Scriptures was a central plank of the Reformation, there remained a large obstacle. Many people were illiterate, and even if they could read, the Bible was available only in Latin, and only to a select few, because every copy had to be written out by hand. Earlier attempts to translate the Bible into the vernacular had been resisted strongly by the Catholic Church. As far back as 1382, John Wycliffe had translated the Bible into English, but it was not available to all.

By Luther's day, however, the printing press, which had been invented by Johannes Gutenberg in nearby Mainz in 1440, had revolutionized the publishing process. Luther harnessed this new technology: he set out to translate the Bible into the German language as it was spoken by ordinary people, publishing the New Testament in 1522 and the whole Bible in 1534. The combination of Luther's colloquial language and the relative cheapness of the printed Bible meant that Christians across Germany could soon read the Scriptures for themselves. Before long, both French and English translations were printed, and these fueled the spread of Reformation ideas throughout Europe. Alongside Bibles, the printing presses of Europe churned out hundreds of pamphlets and books written by the Reformers, which were eagerly consumed by people thirsty for new ideas.

Protest and schism

At first, Luther and his followers simply wanted to bring about reform within the Catholic Church, hence their name, Reformers. However, in a series of church meetings known as "diets" (similar to sessions of a parliament), it became clear that the Catholic Church would not accept the demands of the Reformers, which included independence from the Pope, services in the local language rather than Latin, and marriage for the clergy. Hopes for reform of the Catholic Church were finally dashed at the Diet of Speyer in 1529.

Luther's followers submitted a "Letter of Protestation," refusing to submit to the authority of the Church. From then on, they took on the new name of Protestants, which expressed their rejection of Catholic authority in favor of their newfound confidence in interpreting the Bible themselves.

Political support

The Protestant movement was backed by a number of German princes who took advantage of Luther's religious revolt to secure the political independence of their states. They began suppressing the Catholic faith and Church influence within their territories, adopting the motto, *Cuius regio eius et religio* ("Whoever is the »

Martin Luther

Martin Luther was born in Germany, in 1483. He gave up law school in order to become a monk, after nearly being hit by a lightning bolt in a thunderstorm. By 1508 he was teaching theology at the University of Wittenberg, where he was also a priest. Luther's studies led him to his key insight, which would develop into the doctrine of justification by faith: God declares Christians to be righteous in his sight simply on account of their faith in Him, and not because of anything good they might do (or, in the case of indulgences, might buy). Luther's challenge to the pope's authority made him a wanted man, but he refused to recant. He spent the rest of his life preaching and writing, and by the time he died in 1546, the Lutheran Church was well established.

Key works

1520 *Appeal to the German Ruling Class,* calling for reform of the church.
1534 the *Luther Bible* (translation of Old and New Testaments).

ruler, his must be the religion"). In other words, they demanded the right to impose the Church of their choice upon their people.

Once established, the Protestant principle changed both the religious and the political landscape of Europe forever. It gave other rulers the grounds they needed to remove their kingdoms from the control of the Pope. The English Reformation, for example, began when King Henry VIII, a one-time opponent of the reformers, sought to curb the Pope's authority in order to divorce his wife, Catherine of Aragon, and marry Anne Boleyn.

Protestantism gave rise to a number of new branches of the Church, known as denominations. While the Catholic Church had been the only Church in Europe for centuries, a whole host of denominations emerged following the Protestant Reformation. While Protestants were agreed that the authority of the Roman Catholic Church was to be rejected, they could not agree on a unified alternative system of thought. Disputes between some Protestant movements were at times as fierce as those between the Catholics and Protestants.

Protestant proliferation

Three main Protestant strands arose from these turbulent times: Lutherans, who followed the ideas of Martin Luther; Presbyterians, who were influenced by the work of John Calvin (see opposite); and Anglicans, moderate Protestants based in England who kept hold of many aspects of Catholicism the other movements rejected.

… Scripture, gathering together the impressions of Deity, which, till then, lay confused in our minds, dissipates the darkness, and shows us the true God clearly.
John Calvin

The Counter-Reformation

In a sense, the Catholics had been right about controlling the means of communication with their flock: without the regulation of papal authority, the Church was no longer united in its thinking. To try to stem discontent over corruption and worldly attitudes, and reclaim lost souls from the Protestants, the Catholic Church launched a Counter-Reformation. In 1545, Catholic leaders met in the Italian city of Trent, aiming to reestablish the superiority of the Catholic Church against the rising tide of Protestantism. By the end of the Council of Trent, which spanned 18 years to 1563, traditional Catholic doctrines had been reaffirmed, but reforms were also introduced addressing the unacceptable practices of the clergy that had sparked the Reformation.

An *Index of Forbidden Books* was published, naming 583 heretical texts, including most translations of the Bible and the works of Erasmus, Luther, and Calvin (the *Index* was enforced until 1966). A church building

The Reformation depended upon the widespread dissemination of the Christian scriptures. The Bible was translated into the vernacular, printed in the presses, and distributed.

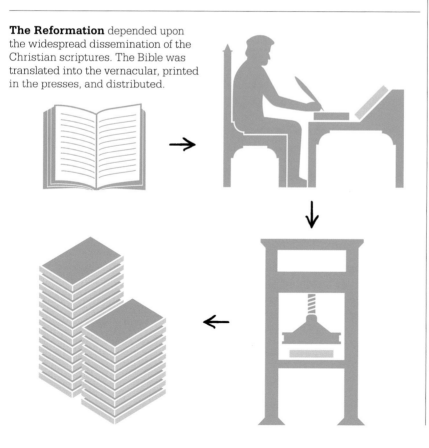

Churches built in northern Europe for Protestant congregations, such as this Lutheran church in Vik, Iceland, are often plain in design, eschewing any embellishment or decoration.

program was started, with the intention of constructing great new churches with space for thousands of worshippers, and acoustics designed—for the first time—for vernacular sermons. Ignatius Loyola, a former soldier and the son of a Spanish nobleman, was charged with setting up the Society of Jesus, an order of missionaries also known as the Jesuits, who were willing to go anywhere without regard to their own safety, to spread Catholicism. The Church also used a process known as the Inquisition to reassert its authority, prosecuting people accused of heresy and using often brutal methods to extract the truth from the accused.

Exit from the Dark Ages

The Counter-Reformation was partly successful in Italy, Spain, and France, but changes made to the Catholic structures elsewhere were minimal, and certainly not enough to entice the Protestants back to the fold. From then on, Europe was host to a marketplace of different churches, each vying for the hearts and minds of Christians. While Catholicism could claim a long and illustrious heritage, the idea of Protestantism seemed to match the spirit of the age. One of the mottos of the Reformation was *post tenebras lux*, "after darkness, light." After the so-called Dark Ages, the Protestant spirit sought to shed the skin of medieval Catholicism and embrace a new world of ideas. It was especially confident that reading and hearing the Bible in a language that could be clearly understood would lead to a relationship with God that was uncluttered by priests, popes, and indulgences. ∎

John Calvin

Born in northern France in 1509, John Calvin came into contact with Christian Humanism while at the University of Bourges, where he devoted himself to theological study. During this period, he experienced a religious conversion that caused him to break with the Roman Catholic Church and join the growing Protestant movement. Forced to flee France, Calvin became a minister in Geneva, Switzerland, from 1536 to 1538, then Strassburg (now Strasbourg) until 1541, before returning to Geneva, where he remained until his death in 1564.

Calvin stressed humanity's sinfulness and inability to know God without the study of Scripture; he emphasized God's sovereignty, which meant God could freely give the gift of salvation to whoever he chose. Followers of Calvin, known as Calvinists, established churches around the world that became known as presbyterian, from the Greek for "elder."

Key works

1536 *Institutes of the Christian Religion* (first Latin edition)

GOD IS HIDDEN IN THE HEART

MYSTICAL EXPERIENCE IN CHRISTIANITY

From the earliest days of Christianity, Christians believed that Jesus had made it possible for them to have a direct relationship with God. However, some Christians struggled with worship in churches, finding it too ritualistic. A quest for an intensely personal experience of God emerged in the later Middle Ages, as a reaction to formalized worship. It became known as Christian mysticism. Rather than following the usual pattern of reciting authorized prayers, mystics advocated silent contemplation of God. This often led to overwhelming experiences of God's love. Mysticism has been embraced by many Christians because it requires neither priests nor prayer books to guide the believer, only a personal communion with God.

The interior journey
One of the classic works on mystical experience was written by Teresa of Avila (1515–1582), a Spanish Carmelite nun. In *The Interior Castle*, Teresa narrates the journey of the Christian soul through six rooms in a castle until it reaches the seventh, innermost room, where God dwells. Each room represents a more intimate level of prayer until the soul achieves the goal of perfect union with God's life, which Teresa described as "spiritual marriage." ∎

In a male-dominated Church, some of the most renowned mystics were women, such as Teresa of Avila (left), Catherine of Siena (1347–1380), and Julian of Norwich (c.1342–1416).

See also: Self-denial leads to spiritual liberation 68–71 ▪ Man as a manifestation of God 188 ▪ Sufism and the mystic tradition 282–83

THE BODY NEEDS SAVING AS WELL AS THE SOUL
SOCIAL HOLINESS AND EVANGELICALISM

IN CONTEXT

KEY FIGURE
John Wesley

WHEN AND WHERE
18th century, UK

BEFORE
1st century CE Jesus preaches to open-air gatherings, which anyone may attend. He reportedly urges his followers to feed the hungry, clothe the naked, and care for the sick.

Late 17th century
The Pietist movement in Continental Europe stresses practical Christian living.

AFTER
19th century In the US, the Wesleyan and Free Methodists are active in the anti-slavery abolitionist movement.

1865 William Booth, a Methodist minister, founds the Salvation Army with the mission of saving bodies as well as souls.

The Industrial Revolution posed a new challenge for Christianity. While a select few enjoyed unprecedented wealth, thousands of people in towns and cities endured perilous working conditions and suffered ill health and extreme poverty. In Britain, brothers John and Charles Wesley, both Anglican priests, responded to the needs of a changing society with a message of social holiness. John Wesley described social holiness as a faith that was not just private and internal, but publicly engaged with the social issues of the day.

The Christian message
In May 1738 the Wesleys were deeply moved by reading the works of Martin Luther and came to a new understanding of the necessity of faith for salvation. The experience had a profound effect on their ministry and caused them to join a growing number of evangelicals who took the Christian message out of churches, preaching in marketplaces, fields, and homes. Evangelicals fervently believed

By salvation I mean not barely deliverance from hell or going to heaven, but a present deliverance from sin.
John Wesley

that experience of Christianity could transform individuals and society. They were at the forefront of important movements, such as the abolition of the slave trade, the trade union movement, and the provision of free education for working-class children. The Wesleys' followers became known as Methodists, after the methodical, practical way in which they applied their faith to meet the needs of others. ■

See also: Living in harmony 38 ▪ Let kindness and compassion rule 146–47 ▪ The Sikh code of conduct 296–301

SCIENTIFIC ADVANCES DO NOT DISPROVE THE BIBLE

THE CHALLENGE OF MODERNITY

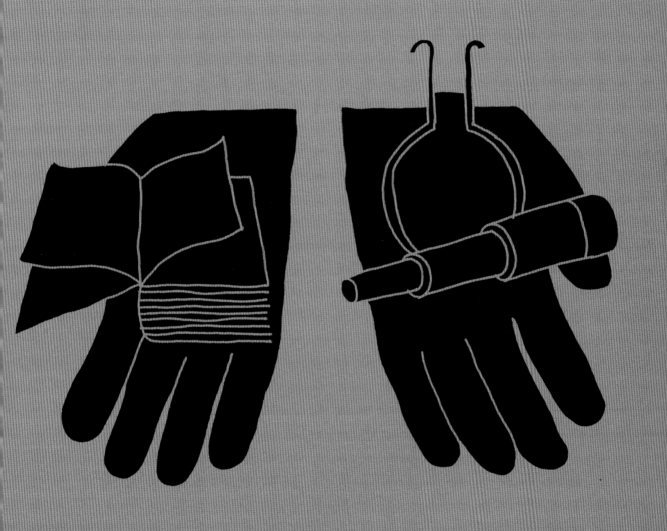

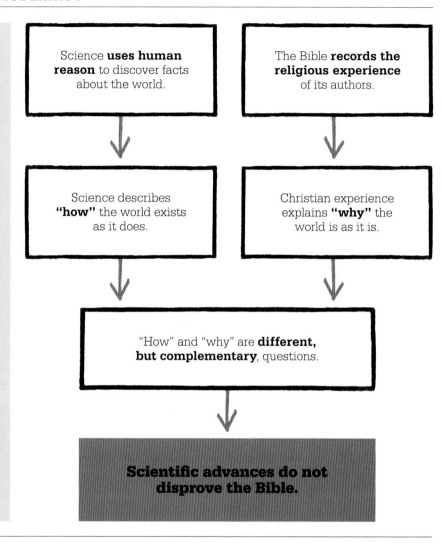

Science **uses human
reason** to discover facts
about the world.

The Bible **records the
religious experience**
of its authors.

Science describes
"how" the world exists
as it does.

Christian experience
explains **"why"** the
world is as it is.

"How" and "why" are **different,
but complementary**, questions.

**Scientific advances do not
disprove the Bible.**

T he idea that the earth
revolves around the sun,
rather than the other
way around, is today accepted
as fact. However, in the early
17th century, this theory, which
had been published by the Polish
astronomer Copernicus in 1543,
was in direct opposition to the
teachings of the Catholic Church
and sparked a controversy that
embroiled the finest natural
scientists of the day. Most notably,
Galileo Galilei, a mathematician in
Florence, was condemned as a
heretic for supporting the theory.

The positions of the Church and
of Galileo differed because of
the different ways in which they
arrived at truth. According to the
Church, truth was revealed by God,
and was supported by passages in
the Bible that suggested the earth
was at the center of the universe.
Science, on the other hand, used
experimental observations—
Galileo was a pioneer of using the
telescope in astronomy—to build
theories about the workings of the
world. Until well into the medieval
period, these two methods had
existed happily side by side.

In the 13th century, for instance,
the medieval theologian Thomas
Aquinas (p.229) had encouraged
the systematic exploration of the
natural world. He took it for granted
that a deeper understanding of
creation would lead to a better
knowledge of the creator.

This mutual respect was
conceivable as long as the results of
scientific reasoning coincided with
the concept of "divine revelation"
(truth communicated by God to
humans through Scripture) but not
when the two thought systems
reached different conclusions.

See also: The Protestant Reformation 230–37 ▪ The compatibilty of faith 291 ▪ Jewish Science 333 ▪ The Church of Christ (Scientist) 337

While both Catholic and Protestant denominations of the Church insisted that their faith in divine revelation was well placed, it seemed obvious to many that the results of experiment and reason were far more reliable. Difficult questions were soon being asked that would shake the foundations of Christian belief across the modern Western world, and by the end of the 18th century the Church was in danger of losing popular support as people increasingly doubted the rationality and relevance of the Christian faith. In response, Christian thinkers needed to articulate, in a radically new way, how religion and science, faith and reason, could coexist.

From facts to feelings

This new era of Christianity was heralded by the German theologian Friedrich Schleiermacher (see right). While working as a hospital chaplain in Berlin, he had come into contact with Romanticism,

a cultural movement that had been born out of a reaction against what was perceived as the soulless rationalism of the Enlightenment. The Romantics emphasized the importance of feelings and emotions in human life at a time when ideas and objects in the world were being valued purely for their scientific credibilty and usefulness. Schleiermacher realized that as long as Christian belief was assessed according to the same criteria and at the same level as scientific knowledge, it would be considered unreasonable. Instead of trying to prove the truth of Christianity as though it were a scientific theory (as many of his predecessors had), he translated it into the realm of feelings, as championed by the Romantics. **»**

Romanticism valued emotion above reason and the senses above the intellect. The movement found expression in the art, literature, and philosophy of the early 19th century.

Friedrich Schleiermacher

Friedrich Schleiermacher was born in 1768 in Breslau (then Prussian Silesia), the son of a reformed clergyman. He was educated by the Moravian Brethren, a strict Pietist sect, before moving to the more liberal University of Halle to study theology and philosophy (focusing in particular on the work of Kant). When he moved to Berlin in 1796, he was introduced to key members of the Romantic movement. Schleiermacher became a professor of theology at Berlin University in 1810. When he died in 1834, his radical reinterpretation of doctrine had given rise to a completely new form of theology known as theological liberalism, which would be a dominant intellectual force in Europe and the United States for a century.

Key works

1799 *On Religion: Speeches to its Cultured Despisers*, Schleiermacher's most radical work on theology.
1821–22 *The Christian Faith*, Schleiermacher's major work of systematic theology.

Friedrich Schleiermacher identified true religion with a specific type of feeling. It was distinct from knowledge or activity and was an end in itself. Knowledge, action, and feeling were different but related realms.

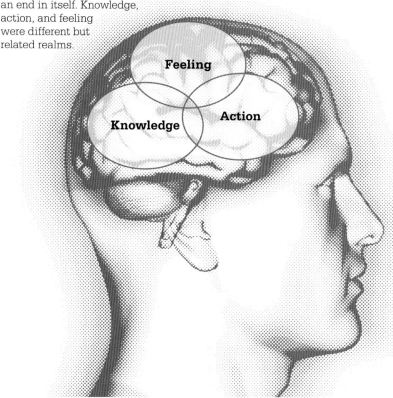

He emphasized that science and faith were not in competition: they should be seen as complementary because they both focused on different aspects of human life.

Redefining religion

Schleiermacher's most significant idea was his redefinition of the nature of religion. In his first important book on the subject, *Religion: Speeches to its Cultured Despisers* (1799), he discussed three realms of human life: knowledge, action, and feeling. Although he recognized that these three realms are necessarily related to each other, he was convinced that they ought not to be confused: according to him, knowledge belongs to science, action belongs to ethics,

and feeling belongs to religion. Schleiermacher believed that the problem facing Christianity was that it had often focused too heavily on knowledge and action, and too little on feeling. In doing this, Christianity had opened itself up to attack by the rationalism of the modern world. On the one hand, scientific reason disputed some of Christianity's fundamental beliefs, such as the miracles and resurrection of Jesus. On the other hand, the philosophy of Kant and others saw morality as based on universal principles, rather than on the contents of the Bible. The challenge to Christianity posed by science and philosophy did not, however, disturb Schleiermacher; on the contrary, it presented an

opportunity to recover what he considered to be at the very heart of the Christian religion, which was simply, "a sense and taste for the infinite." In his book *The Christian Faith* (1821–22), Schleiermacher systematically reinterpreted Christian theology as a description of Christian experience. For example, according to him, a statement such as "God exists" does not make any claim about the actual existence of God; instead, it describes a person's feeling that he or she is dependent upon something that is beyond him or herself.

A record of experience

In the mid-19th century, a number of scholars, primarily based in Germany, were using a form of analysis known as historical criticism to look at biblical texts. They studied the Bible's original sources from the Middle East to reinterpret its content within a historical context. By focusing on the ways in which the Bible had been composed and compiled as a set of human documents, this analysis appeared to strip the sacred text of its supernatural

The self-identical essence of piety is this: the consciousness of being absolutely dependent, or, which is the same thing, of being in relation with God.
Friedrich Schleiermacher

origins (the belief that it was of divine authorship). The result was that, for many people, the Bible could no longer be referred to as the inspired word of God.

Friedrich Schleiermacher's view, however, helped to rescue the Bible from what some perceived to be irrelevance. He claimed that since religion relates fundamentally to experience, the Bible is supremely important as a record of religious experience. It can therefore be used as the ultimate guide to Christian experience, as believers compare their own feelings of dependence on God with those described within the sacred text.

This approach to the Bible became known as the liberal view, as opposed to the more conservative view, which insisted —in the face of this historical criticism—that the Bible contained facts about God, and not just facts about human experience. Tension between these two views has shaped Protestantism ever since.

Unintended consequences

Schleiermacher developed his idea of religious experience in order to protect Christianity from being

> Christian doctrines are accounts of the Christian religious affections set forth in speech.
> **Friedrich Schleiermacher**

relegated to history while science moved forward to shape the future of the world. By assigning religion and science to different spheres of human life (religion to feeling, and science to knowledge), he was successful in establishing a means by which they could coexist.

However, while many Christians embraced Schleiermacher's thesis as a solution to the friction between science and religion, others were dissatisfied with what they saw as the relegation of Christian faith to the sphere of feelings. They also identified an unintended consequence: Christianity could no longer claim to have an authoritative voice in the public sphere if it was associated most strongly with an individual's feelings, since feelings are always personal. This seemed to be at odds with the original message of Christianity, which concerned the arrival of God's kingdom in the whole world (not just in private religious experience) and indicated an important societal role.

Taking a stand

In the 20th century, the liberal movement was strongly criticized by a new generation of scholars, including the eminent Swiss theologian Karl Barth. He was particularly appalled that his liberal theology teachers had failed to take a principled stand against the rise of Nazism in Germany in the 1930s, and claimed that this was because Schleiermacher's theology had been allowed to become far too influential within the Church. He maintained that a private Christian experience could be too easily indifferent to the needs of the world outside.

Barth argued that for Christianity to be successful in opposing some of the obvious

Clergymen carry a symbol of peace, indicating their opposition to nuclear arms. Critics of theological liberalism argued that an emphasis on personal feelings encouraged indifference to important issues in the world.

misuses of science and knowledge —such as genocide, the arms race, and nuclear armament—in the modern world, Christian theology would need to be based on more than private feelings.

Today, Christian thinkers still face the challenge of explaining to peple how they can trust what the Bible says about God, when what it says about the world is often disputed by scientific reasoning. Many Christians would answer with a modified form of Schleiermacher's argument. The Bible talks about the same reality as that described by science, history, politics, and other social sciences. However, it simply answers different questions: not, "how did this come to be?" but "why did this come to be?" Science and faith—the "how?" and the "why?"—do not disprove each other, but complement each other. They help Christians to reach a more complete understanding of the universe that Galileo observed through his telescope. ∎

WE CAN INFLUENCE GOD
WHY PRAYER WORKS

IN CONTEXT

KEY MOVEMENTS
**Process theology
and open theism**

WHEN AND WHERE
**Late 20th century,
US and Europe**

BEFORE
From prehistory Many
primal belief systems use
prayer and ritual to seek
the favor of supernatural
forces or beings.

First millennium BCE
The Bible tells that God
answered Moses's prayer
to change his mind about
destroying the Israelites after
they worship the golden calf.

AFTER
1960s The Liberation
Theology movement in
South America emphasizes
social and economic justice,
maintaining that God
responds especially to the
prayers of the poor and
oppressed in society.

F from the earliest times,
Jewish and Christian
theologians have
wrestled with complex issues
surrounding the nature of God
and the relationship of God to
humankind. To some he is a
vengeful God, who not only
stands in judgment at the end of
time, but also chooses whether or
not to respond to those who pray.
To others, he is perceived as an
all-knowing presence who has
decided the course of world history
and has reasons for all events, so
that every detail of the future is
mapped out in advance. In this
latter representation, God is
immune to appeals from humans
for help because he has absolute
prior knowledge of the outcome
of every situation.

The relevance of prayer
How the relationship between
God and the things that happen is
understood has deep implications
for the role of Christian prayer.
If God already knows the past,
present, and future, then prayer—

God knows everything that exists.

The **future** hasn't happened yet, so it **doesn't exist**.

Therefore, the future is still **open to change**.

We can **influence** what the future becomes **by our prayers and actions** today.

See also: The battle between good and evil 60–65 ▪ Divining the future 79 ▪ Devotion through puja 114–15 ▪ Jesus's message to the world 204–207 ▪ Augustine and free will 220–21

God…is so related to the world that there is between him and that world a "give-and-take"… He is influenced by what happens.
W. Pittenger

Theologians of hope

The rejection of traditional theological concepts such as God's foreknowledge (his awareness of future events), immutability (his unchanging nature), and impassibility (his freedom from emotion and independence from other beings) was not confined to any one school of theology during the 20th century. The ideas have been labeled in various ways, including process theology, the openness of God, and open theism. In the later 20th century, a group of theologians emerged who have been loosely termed the "theologians of hope." These include, in Germany, Jürgen Moltmann and Wolfhart Pannenberg, and in the US, Robert Jenson. One of their principal arguments was that because the future does not yet exist—even for God—the essential characteristic of Christianity is hope.

communicating with God by offering verbal praise or requests, through thoughts and meditations, or in the form of deliberate acts of worship—seems irrelevant. Merely telling God what he already knows would carry no hope of changing what will happen. However, if the future is not already determined by God and is truly open, then prayer becomes an essential part of shaping that future.

Inside the mind of God
Although Christian theology has traditionally regarded God as omniscient, possessing a complete knowledge of all things past, present, and future, in the 20th century some theologians began to reject the idea of his foreknowledge (knowledge of the future). If God knows what will happen, then the future must already be set in stone, which, they argued, would remove true freedom and spontaneity from history. This would also raise questions about God's essential goodness, and whether he is complicit in evil if

he has prior knowledge of it, but takes no preventive action—as may be evident, for example, in his knowledge, even before the creation, that humans would bring suffering and wickedness into the world.

The future is open
The classic Christian view of God's foreknowledge depends upon the belief that God exists outside of time, so that what is in the future for human beings (and hence is nonexistent and unknowable) is in the past for God (and therefore both exists and is knowable). However, this view owes more to ancient Greek philosophy than genuine Christian thinking. The Bible describes a God who actively accompanies his people through time, not simply watching them from a distant position outside of time. Moreover, Christians believe that the coming of Jesus as a human being should be understood as the clearest indication that God is not outside of time or the reality of human life

on earth, since he lived a human life, with all its limitations. Consequently, if the future does not yet exist for either humans or God, then it can be truly open. Seen from this perspective, God is not a distant observer but an active participant in the historical process, a presence who listens to the prayers and appeals of people, responding to their needs and walking beside them in their journey through life. ▪

The misuse of weapons of war, such as nuclear bombs, indicates the human capacity for evil—in the future as well as the past. Does God know about this and choose to do nothing?

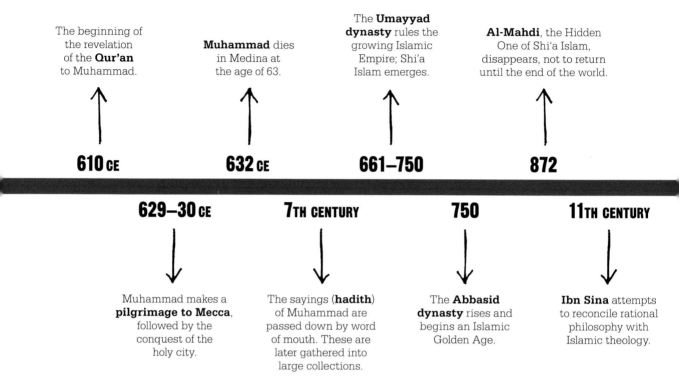

The beginning of the revelation of the **Qur'an** to Muhammad.

Muhammad dies in Medina at the age of 63.

The **Umayyad dynasty** rules the growing Islamic Empire; Shi'a Islam emerges.

Al-Mahdi, the Hidden One of Shi'a Islam, disappears, not to return until the end of the world.

610 CE

632 CE

661–750

872

629–30 CE

7TH CENTURY

750

11TH CENTURY

Muhammad makes a **pilgrimage to Mecca**, followed by the conquest of the holy city.

The sayings (**hadith**) of Muhammad are passed down by word of mouth. These are later gathered into large collections.

The **Abbasid dynasty** rises and begins an Islamic Golden Age.

Ibn Sina attempts to reconcile rational philosophy with Islamic theology.

Founded in the 7th century, Islam is nevertheless regarded by its followers as an ancient faith—one that has always existed as God's intended religion. Along with Judaism and Christianity, it is an Abrahamic religion, tracing its roots back to Ibrahim (Abraham), the first of a line of prophets sent to reveal the faith—a line that also includes Musa (Moses) and Isa (Jesus). Muslims believe the last in this line is the Prophet Muhammad, who received the revelations contained in the Qur'an and established Islam as it is known today.

Islam is a strongly monotheistic religion, emphasizing the oneness of an incomparable God, Allah (Arabic for "*the* God"), and people's duty to serve him. Islam teaches that human life is a gift from God,

and the way a person lives their life will be assessed on the Day of Judgment. The central professions of the faith are summed up in the Five Pillars of Islam. Religious life revolves round the mosque, which, as well as being a center of worship and teaching, acts as a focus for the social life of the community.

The last prophet
The revelation to Muhammad is considered the final and complete revelation from God. Memorized by Muhammad's immediate followers, it was written in the form of the Qur'an—Islam's holy scripture and the ultimate and unquestionable word of God. Beyond the Qur'an, there also exist sayings attributed to Muhammad, collectively known as the hadith. The scriptures have inspired a rich tradition of scholarly

interpretation. From the judgments of theologians on the holy books and an examination of the life of the Prophet Muhammad, has emerged a system of religious law and moral codes known as shari'a, which informs the civil law of many Islamic countries.

From its origins, Islam has been entwined with civil and political life. Muhammad himself was as much a political as a religious leader and thinker. Because of his preaching of monotheism, he and his followers were forced to flee Mecca (an event known to Muslims as the Hijra, commemorated annually) for Medina, where he established the first Islamic city-state, with himself as spiritual, political, and military leader. He then led his people back to Mecca, conquering the city and establishing the beginnings of an

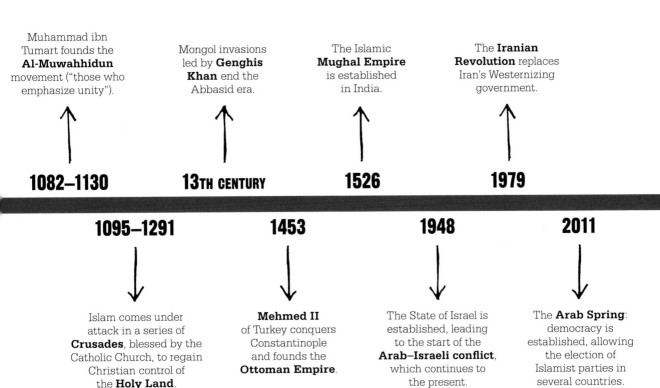

Muhammad ibn Tumart founds the **Al-Muwahhidun** movement ("those who emphasize unity").

Mongol invasions led by **Genghis Khan** end the Abbasid era.

The Islamic **Mughal Empire** is established in India.

The **Iranian Revolution** replaces Iran's Westernizing government.

1082–1130 **13TH CENTURY** **1526** **1979**

1095–1291 **1453** **1948** **2011**

Islam comes under attack in a series of **Crusades**, blessed by the Catholic Church, to regain Christian control of the **Holy Land**.

Mehmed II of Turkey conquers Constantinople and founds the **Ottoman Empire**.

The State of Israel is established, leading to the start of the **Arab–Israeli conflict**, which continues to the present.

The **Arab Spring**: democracy is established, allowing the election of Islamist parties in several countries.

empire to unite the disparate tribes of Arabia. Within a century of his death in 632, the Islamic Empire had expanded across northern Africa and into Asia. Despite disputes over who should succeed Muhammad, which led to the division between Sunni and Shi'a Islam, the Islamic Caliphate—the Muslim political and religious state ruled by a caliph—wielded great political unity and power.

The Islamic Golden Age
Soon, the Islamic Empire extended over a wider area than Christian Europe. However, in contrast to Christianity, which saw scientific thought to be a threat to its dogma, Islam saw no incompatibility between its theology and the disciplines of philosophy and science. Cities such as Baghdad

and Damascus became centers of scientific inquiry and learning. Islamic writing and poetry also flourished, along with decorative arts, including calligraphy.

The Islamic Empire eventually fragmented, but Islam remains one of the largest of all religions, practiced by some 25 percent of the world population. About three-quarters of adherents are Sunni, and 10 to 20 percent, Shi'a. Around 50 countries have a Muslim majority: of these, a handful, including Saudi Arabia, Afghanistan, Pakistan, and Iran are considered Islamic states, based on religious law; a large number of other countries, mainly in the Middle East, have Islam as their official state religion; others still have secular governments, but predominantly Islamic

populations. Indonesia is the country with the largest number of Muslims, followed by Pakistan, India, and Bangladesh.

Approximately 25 percent of Muslims live in the Middle East and North Africa, and there are now Muslim communities in almost every other country in the world.

Islam has come into conflict, both ideologically and politically, with the Christian world since the Crusades, and following colonial domination by the West. Recent tensions have given rise to a radical interpretation of jihad (struggle) by some fundamentalist Muslims as a religious duty to defend their faith through conflict. However, Islam is essentially a peaceable religion, and most Muslims identify more closely with the compassionate principles of their faith. ■

MUHAMMAD IS GOD'S FINAL MESSENGER

THE PROPHET AND THE ORIGINS OF ISLAM

IN CONTEXT

KEY FIGURE
Muhammad

WHEN AND WHERE
570–632 CE, Arabia

BEFORE
c.2000–1500 BCE In the Hebrew Bible, God makes a covenant with the patriarch Abraham; Islam will recognize this figure (in Arabic, Ibrahim) as one of the first prophets.

c.14th–13th century BCE In Jewish, Christian, and Muslim tradition, Moses, leading the Israelites, receives commandments from God on Mount Sinai.

1st century CE Jesus, later recognized by Muslims as a prophet, foretells the coming of a final prophet or messenger of God.

AFTER
19th century In India, Mirza Ghulam Ahmad claims to be a prophet bringing a new message that will reform Islam.

God **revealed** His Word to Moses and Jesus.

⬇

Humanity **misinterpreted and corrupted** the message of the revelations.

⬇

God now **transmits His Word** directly to Muhammad.

⬇

The pure **message of Islam** is His final message to humanity.

⬇

Muhammad is God's final messenger.

According to Islamic tradition, in around 582 CE a Christian hermit, Bahira, was living in the Syrian desert when, one day, a boy passing by with a camel train caught his attention. After talking with him, Bahira concluded that the sign of prophecy was upon the boy. He was destined for greatness, Bahira foretold, and should be cared for well.

The young boy was Muhammad ibn 'Abdallah, who became the prophet of Islam and, according to Muslims, God's final messenger. This implies, of course, that there were messengers sent by God (in Arabic, Allah) before Muhammad; these include notable figures such as Musa (Moses) and Isa (Jesus). To Musa, God revealed the Tawrat, or Torah, to guide the Jews. To Isa, God gave the Injil, a lost scripture with a name that translates as Gospel, although it did not resemble in its form the four canonical Gospels of Christianity.

Muslims consider Jews and Christians to be People of the Book, because, like Muslims, they are also monotheists with a holy scripture that was revealed to them by God. Muslims honor, in some ways, the revelations God gave to messengers

See also: God's covenant with Israel 168–75 ▪ Jesus's message to the world 204–207 ▪ The origins of Ahmaddiya 284–85

> Muhammad is…the Messenger of God and the Seal of the Prophets.
> **Surah 33:40**

before Muhammad, but they also believe that these revelations became corrupt. Jews introduced elements to the Torah that did not come directly from God. Likewise, Jesus's followers mishandled his message and distorted the Gospels, misrepresenting God's original intentions. Therefore, Islam teaches that the Jewish and Christian scriptures in their current form are no longer God's pure revelations, but corrupted by human error.

God's word uncorrupted

In order to overcome this corruption, God sent down his undefiled word one final time, in the form of the Qur'an, through Muhammad—his final messenger. Thus, Islam is not seen by Muslims as a new religion with a new holy book. Instead, Islam is considered the original, pure, and unique revelation of God. It supersedes those revelations that were given to Moses and Jesus and mishandled by their followers.

Now in Saudi Arabia, Mecca is the holiest city of the Islamic faith since it is the birthplace of Muhammad. This is the Grand Mosque, the heart of the city.

Moreover, it marks an end to further revelation. Muhammad is the Seal (last) of the Prophets: he marks a close in God's revelation and is the last of God's special messengers.

By the early 7th century, Muhammad claimed the authority of a prophet, whose mission was to preach the worship of the one, true God. Many Jews, Christians, and polytheists in his native Mecca believed his message. This fledgling community of Muslims was persecuted for its beliefs, and so Muhammad left Mecca for nearby Medina, where the Muslim community expanded.

Given Muhammad's eminent status in Islam, Muslims have always looked to his life and words as a model for Islamic living. Many of the things he said and did are recorded in the Sunna, which comprises authoritative collections of Muhammad's sayings (*hadith*) and actions (*sunna*). These serve as examples to Muslims seeking guidance on how to live their lives. ▪

Muhammad ibn 'Abdallah

Born near Mecca around 570, Muhammad ibn 'Abdallah was raised by his uncle, Abu Talib. The young Muhammad accompanied his uncle on many of his journeys as a camel-train merchant, meeting travelers from a wide variety of cultures and religions. He gained a reputation for being wise and trustworthy.

When in his early 20s, Muhammad was employed by a wealthy widow, Khadija, to manage her business. She, too, was a camel-train merchant. Khadija later proposed to him and they were married. After her death, Muhammad remarried and is said to have had 13 wives or concubines.

Muhammad would often retreat from business and family life to a cave in the desert, where he would meditate. In 610, during a moonless night of meditation, the angel Jibrail (Gabriel) appeared in a bright light to Muhammad, offering to him the first of many revelations that would eventually make up the Qur'an, Islam's holy book. Muhammad's career as a prophet lasted for 22 years. He died in 632 in Medina.

THE QUR'AN WAS SENT DOWN FROM HEAVEN

GOD REVEALS HIS WORD AND HIS WILL

According to the Islamic faith, God has revealed his will to humankind through nature, history, and, most importantly, his word. Nature, or God's creation, is a sign pointing to God's existence. In history, the rise and fall of empires are signs of God's sovereignty over humankind. But of greatest significance is that God's will is revealed through his word and conveyed by his messengers.

In Islam, God's ultimate word and will are contained in the Qur'an, the book that was revealed to the Prophet Muhammad, chosen by God as His final messenger (pp.252–53). Within it are *ayat*—verses, or signs, that reveal to the world what God desires and commands. Another name for the Qur'an is *al-Tanzil*, the Downsent. For Muslims, the Qur'an is God's literal word that has been sent down to humankind from heaven.

The recitation
According to Islamic tradition, Muhammad spent many days meditating in a cave on Mount Hira overlooking Mecca. One night the angel Jibrail (the Arabic name

Recite! In the name of your Lord who created, created man from a blood clot. Recite!
Sura 96:1–5

for Gabriel) appeared to him in the cave, summoning Muhammad to prophethood and demanding that he "Recite!" (p.253). What followed was the first revelation of the Qur'an. The whole of the Qur'an was revealed to Muhammad at intervals over a prolonged period of time so that he could gradually recite it (the Arabic word *qur'an* means recitation) to others. The revelations, many of which Muhammad was to receive in a trancelike state, began in 610 CE and continued over the next 22 years. At first, Muhammad memorized the revelations and

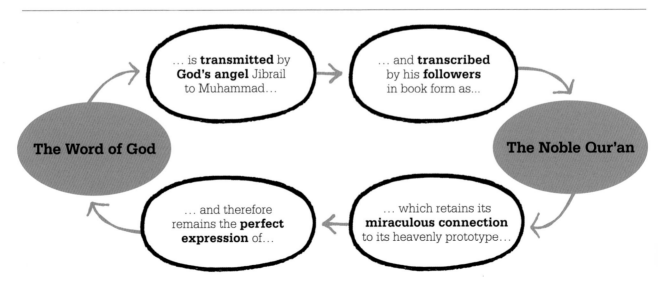

... is **transmitted** by **God's angel** Jibrail to Muhammad...

... and **transcribed** by his **followers** in book form as...

The Word of God

The Noble Qur'an

... and therefore remains the **perfect expression** of...

... which retains its **miraculous connection** to its heavenly prototype...

See also: God's covenant with Israel 168–75 ▪ The Prophet and the origins of Islam 252–53 ▪ The central professions of faith 262–69 ▪ The pathway to harmonious living 272–75

The angel Jibrail appears to Muhammad and delivers the first revelation. Here, in accordance with Islamic tradition, a faceless figure represents the Prophet.

speaking, by length. The longer chapters are found at the beginning of the Qur'an, with shorter chapters arranged toward the end. As a whole, the chapters cover a wide range of topics, providing guidance on worship, politics, marriage and family life, care for the disadvantaged, and even matters of hygiene, community affairs, and economics.

In an attempt to classify and date the chapters of the Qur'an, modern scholars have created a system for identifying them. In this method of classification, revelations that appear to have been given to Muhammad early in his prophetic career, when he resided in Mecca, are known as the Meccan chapters. The earliest of these Meccan revelations are often very rhythmic and full of imagery. Many begin with oaths. »

[It is] a Qur'an which we have divided [into parts], in order that you might recite it to the people at intervals. And we have sent it down progressively.
Sura 17:106

passed them on orally. His followers memorized them in turn, but the revelations were eventually written down, sometimes by Muhammad's secretaries, at other times by his followers. Portions of the Qur'an have been found written on pieces of animal bone, leather, stones, palm leaves, and parchment.

A standardized version of the Qur'an in book form was compiled in the mid-7th century, soon after Muhammad's death. Muslims believe that this compilation, and the ordering of the 114 chapters and 6,000 verses that resulted, were divinely inspired.

Many sections of the Qur'an contain material that matches, or at least corresponds closely to, portions of the Hebrew Bible and Christian New Testament. However, according to the Muslim view, these holy books are corrupted (pp.252–53): the Qur'an is therefore believed to function both as a corrective to, and a progression beyond, previous revelations.

The ordering of the suras

The chapters (suras) and verses that make up the Qur'an are not arranged chronologically or according to topic but, broadly

For example, chapter 95 of the Qur'an is introduced with, "By the fig and the olive and by Mount Sinai and by this city of security!"

Later Meccan chapters are more serene and contain frequent illustrations of the truth of God's message drawn from nature and history. They are more formal than other chapters and often discuss matters of doctrine. God is frequently referred to in these chapters as the Merciful.

Revelations accorded to Muhammad when he was living in the city of Medina are classified by scholars as the Medinan chapters. These chapters are quite different from the Meccan ones because, by this time, Muhammad was no longer leading a fledgling group of followers, but had become the head of a large, independent community of Muslims.

As a result, the Medinan chapters are characterized less by themes of doctrine and the proofs of God's signs. Instead, more time is spent in discussion of legal and social matters and how such rulings should be applied in order to regulate life within the growing Muslim community.

For example, in chapter 24 of the Qur'an, Muslims are told to bring four witnesses in order to corroborate an accusation of adultery. This was an important safeguard for women in a society in which even the sight of an unrelated man and woman together might be considered

> This Qur'an is not such as could ever be produced by other than God.
> **Sura 10:37**

cause for suspicion. The testimony of those who do not provide the necessary witnesses should be rejected and such persons dealt with harshly according to this Medinan chapter of the Qur'an.

Rote and recitation

Western scholarship has added numbers to the chapters and verses of the Qur'an for ease of reference. For Muslims, however, chapters are referred to by specific, distinguishing words that appear within each chapter. For example, the Qur'an's second and longest chapter is known as The Cow. This chapter is named after a story it contains about a heifer that is reluctantly sacrificed by the Israelites. In the account, the flesh of the sacrificed animal is used to bring a slain man to life again in order to identify his murderer.

Muslims also rarely refer to individual verses by number, instead preferring to quote the beginning of a passage under discussion. This form of referencing of course requires not only great familiarity with the text of the Qu'ran but also considerable memorization skills. Nonetheless, many Muslims memorize large

The Qur'an is not arranged in any narrative or chronological order. Opened at any point, it will offer reassurance of God's will to the reader through suras (chapters) that often take their name from a story, theme, or truth that they contain.

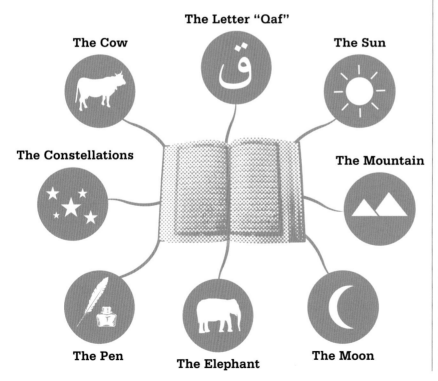

The Cow

The Letter "Qaf"

The Sun

The Constellations

The Mountain

The Pen

The Elephant

The Moon

Reading, learning, and reciting portions of the Qur'an are central to Islamic education, and remain an everyday activity for Muslims thoughout their adult lives.

portions of the Qur'an, and some are even able to commit the entire book to memory.

To learn the entire Qur'an by heart brings great prestige and blessing, and a Muslim who has achieved this is known as a hafiz or a guardian of the Qur'an. A hafiz keeps God's holy book alive, and is often called *shaykh*, a mark of great respect. Such Muslims often become reciters of the Qur'an, a role that is undertaken during daily prayers and other important rituals and ceremonies. This skill is so highly prized that auditoriums are often filled to capacity for recitation contests.

The Qur'an has a preeminent place both in Islam and within God's plan for the world. It is considered the divine miracle brought by the Prophet Muhammad —the only miracle, in fact, as Muhammad himself did not perform them. Muslims believe that the Qur'an is based on a heavenly prototype, a book written in Arabic and existing with God in heaven.

This means that, even though the Qur'an was given to Muhammad in the form of oral recitations and only later written down, the physical book itself is regarded as sacred.

Respect for the Qur'an

The Muslim belief that the Islamic holy scripture exists in heaven makes the handling of its earthly representations a matter of great care and delicacy, and there are several guidelines regarding how Muslims should treat their sacred book. The Qur'an, and the Arabic text in particular, should never be left on the floor or in any unclean place. When displayed among a pile of books, it should always be positioned on top; and when placed on a bookshelf, it should rest on the highest shelf, with nothing else beside or above it.

In addition, before handling the Qur'an, Muslims should make certain that they are ritually clean by washing themselves, just as they would before worshipping God. The Qur'an should also be carried with care, and for this »

The Qur'an and the Bible

Readers of the Qur'an and both the Hebrew Bible and the Christian Bible will find many characters and stories in common. The words of the Qur'an appear to assume some familiarity with Jewish and Christian texts, while offering some gentle correctives in certain details. In the Qur'an, for example, Adam and Hawwa (Eve) are forgiven by God before being sent from paradise, because they begged for His mercy, rather than cast out and cursed as in the Bible. Jesus (as prophet, rather than divine figure) appears several times, but nowhere near as often as his mother Mary, spoken of in the Qur'an with a special fondness. In a miracle unreported in the Bible, the infant Jesus speaks up from the crib to defend his mother's honor when ill-wishers accuse her of fornication.

...recite the Qur'an in slow, measured rhythmic tones.
Sura 73:4

Printed and bound copies of the Qur'an are checked meticulously for accuracy before being distributed—here by a 600-strong team of readers at the King Fahd printworks in Saudi Arabia.

reason it is frequently carried in a bag to avoid damage. If it should accidentally fall, then it is honored, sometimes with a kiss, and returned to safety. Some Muslims will make a charitable donation in cases where they have handled the Qur'an carelessly.

The sacred respect shown towards the Qur'an is maintained for old and worn-out copies as well, which may not be thrown away, but instead should be disposed of through a respectful burial. This can be done in any appropriate place for a burial, including at sea. Some Muslims will also allow a disposal by fire.

Stipulations for the disposal of the sacred text are also meant to apply to any paper, jewelry, decoration, or other material on which verses of the Qur'an have been written. For this reason, some Muslim-majority regions provide special disposal bins so that such material can be collected and disposed of properly.

Many of these rules of respect apply not only to the written text of the Qur'an, but also to its oral recitation. Since the Qur'an is perceived as God's literal word, it is thought to come alive when it is recited. As a result, many Muslims cover their heads when it is read aloud and sometimes even during their personal study of the Qur'an.

The role of language

The belief that the heavenly prototype of the Qur'an is written in Arabic makes Qur'anic Arabic not only the sacred language of Islam, but the language of God as well. For Muslims there is therefore a very real sense that the Qur'an loses its status as divine revelation when it is translated into other languages. Due to this belief, translations of the Qur'an are frequently accompanied by the Arabic text, and even then these texts are considered mere interpretations or translations of the meaning of the original Arabic. They are in no way substitutes or equivalents of the Arabic Qur'an.

Since Qur'anic Arabic is considered a divine language, other aspects of Muslim life and thought are further shaped around the language. For example, Muslims throughout the world memorize the Qur'an and their prayers in Arabic, regardless of whether or not they understand the language.

Perhaps most importantly, the text of the Arabic Qur'an, since it is holy, shares certain characteristics with God, its author. Thus, it is perfect, eternal, uncreated, and unchangeable. Known as *i'jaz al-Qur'an* (the miraculousness or inimitability of the Qur'an), this doctrine means that the language, literary style, and ideas revealed in the Qur'an are irreproducible and cannot be matched by any human

endeavor. Everything about it, from the grammatical constructions of the Qur'an's Arabic, to the sound of it when it is read and chanted, and the prophecies it foretells, is considered miraculous and matchless. According to Muslims, any attempt to equal or surpass the Qur'an will surely fail.

Another aspect of the Qur'an's miraculous nature is its unique repetition of basic themes. Opening the Qur'an at any section will often yield a treatment of the book's essential message. This formulaic, and almost abbreviated, style is challenging for non-Muslims, or those familiar with the narrative structure of other holy scriptures. For Muslims, however, this style is a mysterious testament to the Qur'an's unparalleled beauty.

The Qur'an is not only the most sacred book of Islam, but is also considered by Muslims, and even many non-Muslims, as the crowning achievement of Arabic literature. As such, the Qur'an is studied for its poetic prose as much as it is read for its divine guidance. But the respect,

Falsehood cannot come to it from any direction, it is preserved by God Who said: "Verily, We, it is We who have sent down the Qur'an and surely, We will guard it from corruption.
Sura 15:9

>
> …a guidance for the people and clear proofs of guidance and the criterion [of right and wrong].
> **Sura 2:185**

appreciation, and matchlessness accorded to the Qur'an are not limited by Muslims to its message or its recitation. Even the Arabic script within the holy book has significant visual value and plays a central role in Islamic art.

The art of Islam
Motivated by a desire to avoid idolatry in all its forms, Muslim tradition forbade representational illustration within the Qur'an.

However, abstract images, such as patterns, were permitted, and the Arabic script itself developed into an elevated art form: beautiful Arabic calligraphy was used to write out the Qur'an, often in spectacular colored inks and precious gold leaf.

As a result of the prohibition on portraying animals or human figures, artists also developed the Islamic arabesque style. This is a form of artistic decoration that consists of rhythmic lines, elaborate scrolling and interlacing foliage, and repeated geometric motifs. These artworks—which appear on mosaics, in the Qur'an, and inside mosques—also have an important spiritual message: the endlessly intertwining shapes and patterns, in which there appears to be no beginning or end, are intended to prompt reflection on the infinity of Allah. ∎

Islam does not allow representation in religious imagery; instead, beautiful calligraphy and patterning are used. The geometric designs reflect the order and harmony that Allah brings.

The transcribers of the Qur'an

In order to safeguard the integrity of the Qur'an, Zayd ibn Thabit, one of the Prophet's close companions, formed a group of scribes responsible for writing down revelations as they came to Muhammad. Eventually, Zayd and his scholars produced a full-length manuscript of the Qur'an, which was cross-checked with those who had memorized the revelations to ensure that there were no errors. The finished manuscript was presented to Hafsah, one of Muhammad's wives.

Since Arabic is written without vowels, a correct reading and pronunciation of the text depends upon the reader's familiarity with the language. When discrepancies cropped up, the dialect of the Quraysh, Muhammad's tribe, was given precedence. Even so, variations of the written Qur'anic text arose. Consequently, Uthman ibn Affan, one of Muhammad's companions, oversaw the production of an authorized version in the mid-7th century. The book of the Qur'an as it is known today is largely a result of this compilation.

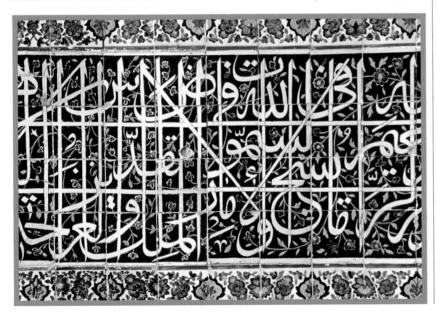

THE FIVE PILLARS OF ISLAM

THE CENTRAL PROFESSIONS OF FAITH

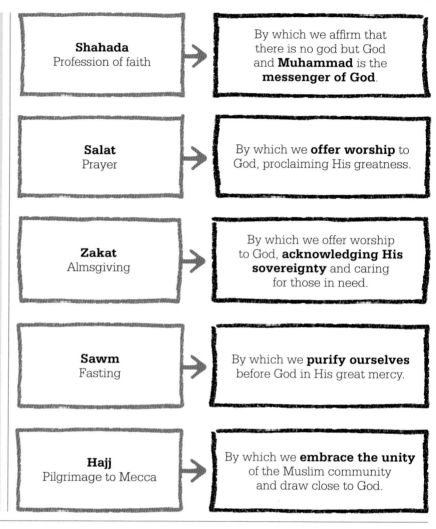

Shahada
Profession of faith

→ By which we affirm that there is no god but God and **Muhammad** is the **messenger of God**.

Salat
Prayer

→ By which we **offer worship** to God, proclaiming His greatness.

Zakat
Almsgiving

→ By which we offer worship to God, **acknowledging His sovereignty** and caring for those in need.

Sawm
Fasting

→ By which we **purify ourselves** before God in His great mercy.

Hajj
Pilgrimage to Mecca

→ By which we **embrace the unity** of the Muslim community and draw close to God.

According to a tradition narrated by Abdallah ibn 'Umar ibn al-Khattab, one of Muhammad's companions, the Prophet summarized Islam by saying that the religion is based on five principles: "To testify that there is no god but God and Muhammad is God's messenger; to offer the prayers dutifully and perfectly; to pay the obligatory alms; to perform the pilgrimage to Mecca; and to observe the fast during the month of Ramadan."

Known as *'ibadat* (acts of worship) to Muslims, and often referred to as the pillars of Islam,

these five practices lie at the core of the faith, and all branches of Islam accept and perform them.

The profession of faith

While not summarizing the whole of Islam as a religion, the pillars serve as a kind of outline of minimal obligations for Muslims to abide by. Their simplicity and straightforwardness are intentional, for Muslims are intended to follow God unencumbered by the heavy burden of religious stipulations. As the Qur'an confirms, "[God] has not laid upon you in religion any hardship." With this in mind,

the first pillar, and central creed of Islam, is a simple acknowledgment of the distinctiveness of the one, true God and the unique place of his messenger, Muhammad. This profession of faith, known as the shahada (witness), is the only means by which a person may become a Muslim. The shahada is whispered in a Muslim's ear at birth and at death. It is also offered as a testimony throughout the day when Muslims are called to prayer. Although succinct, the shahada is made up of two significant parts. In the first part, Muslims bear witness to the absolute oneness

See also: The burden of observance 50 ▪ Self-denial leads to spiritual liberation 68–71 ▪ From monolatry to monotheism 176–77 ▪ Writing the Oral Law 182–83 ▪ The emergence of Shi'a Islam 270–71

Each Muslim baby has the shahada, the profession of faith, whispered in his or her ear at birth; an earlier Arabic tradition still practiced by many is to dab honey on the baby's lips.

of God. This affirms one of the core beliefs of Islam (*tawhid*, or God's unity), but it also functions as a reminder that polytheism (belief in more than one god) and the worship of any being or thing alongside, or in association with, God is the ultimate sin in Islam.

The second part of the shahada recalls that Muhammad is not just God's prophet, but his special messenger, surpassing other prophets before him. He is also honored as the final prophet.

Commitment to prayer

The second pillar of Islam is *salat* (prayer). While Muslims may offer informal, personal prayers or requests to God as they wish, the main prayers of Islam are prescribed, quite formal and regulated, and are a designated opportunity to worship God.

Muslims are summoned to prayer five times every day: at dawn, noon, midafternoon, dusk,

There is no god but God and Muhammad is the messenger of God.
The shahada

and evening. In earlier times, and in some cases even today, a prayer leader, or muezzin, would ascend a minaret, a tall tower outside the mosque, and call local Muslims to prayer by chanting the shahada and urging them to come to the mosque. Today, muezzins often chant into a microphone, which projects the summons into the community via loudspeakers. Sometimes a prerecorded call may be played. Often, Muslims gather for prayers at a mosque, but when this is not possible, prayers can be performed alone or in groups in any location.

Prayers are preceded by purification, an act so important that Muhammad is thought to have said it was "half the faith." For the five prayers, Muslims begin by washing their hands, mouth, and nostrils with water. They wash their entire face and clean their forearms, also passing a wet hand over their heads, and cleaning their feet and ankles. The number of times each body part is cleansed varies in different schools of Islam. Having ritually cleansed themselves, Muslims »

Abdallah ibn 'Umar

Abdallah ibn 'Umar ibn al-Khattab was the oldest son of 'Umar I, the second leader of the Muslim community after Muhammad's death. He was born in the early 7th century and converted to Islam along with his father. As a close companion of Muhammad, Ibn Umar stood by the Prophet's side in several battles and was esteemed for his nobility and selflessness.

Most importantly, Ibn 'Umar is known as one of the most trustworthy authorities on the early history of Islam. Given his close relationship with Muhammad and other important figures in early Islam, he had extensive knowledge of the period. He also served as a credible source for many Hadith (sayings) of Muhammad. When he was approximately 84 years old, Ibn 'Umar made a pilgrimage to Mecca and died there in 693.

stand facing the direction of Mecca, the holiest city of Islam, and recite their prayers. In mosques, this direction is marked by a decorated niche known as a mihrab. Outside mosques, Muslims may find the exact direction of Mecca using specially marked compasses and even web-based applications. Those praying outside the mosque will usually perform their prayers on a special prayer mat, signifying that the act of prayer is performed in a clean place.

Prayer is begun with the declaration, "God is most great." Then Muslims recite a set of fixed prayers that include, among other passages, the opening chapter of the Qur'an: "In the name of God, the Most Gracious, the Most Merciful. All praises and thanks be to God, the Lord of the Universe, the Most Gracious, the Most Merciful, the Ruler on the Day of Judgment. You do we worship and You we ask for help. Guide us along the Straight Path, the way of those on whom You have bestowed Your grace, not of those who earned Your anger or who are lost." The profession of faith is then repeated

and an offering of peace to others is offered with the words: "May the peace, mercy, and blessings of God be upon you." These prayers are offered in Arabic and worshippers accompany them with prostrations and bows, together with raising and lowering their hands.

To non-Muslim observers, the Islamic prayer rituals may appear complex and overly regulated. For Muslims, however, participating in the habits of ritual purification and prescribed prayer allows them to worship God freely, unencumbered by the burden of their own agendas. As they join in unison with other Muslims to pray, they are also reminded of God's greatness, knowing that fellow believers all over the world are worshipping God in the same way.

The importance of charity

The third pillar of Islam is zakat (almsgiving). A central concern in the Qur'an is the treatment of the poor, marginalized, and disadvantaged. Consequently, Muslims are enjoined to care for the social and economic well-being of their communities, not simply

God is most great. I testify that there is no god but God. I testify that Muhammad is the messenger of God. Hurry to prayer. Hurry to success. God is most great.
Call to prayer

through acts of charity, which are encouraged, but also by paying an alms tax. All adult Muslims who are able to do so offer a percentage, not just of their monetary income, but of their entire assets for this tax. This percentage is traditionally set at 2.5 percent, a figure arrived at by scholarly agreement, and drawn from references in the Sunna, for instance "one-quarter of one-tenth" of silver. In some cases, the offering may be up to 20 percent of farming or industrial assets.

Often, almsgiving is voluntary, but in some countries it has been regulated by governments. In such cases, stamps made specifically for sending alms are distributed. Otherwise, offerings can be placed in distribution boxes in mosques and at other locations.

Not only is the giving of alms considered an act of worship to God, but it is also thought to be something that is owed. If what

The call to prayer is made from the top of the mosque's minaret or tower by a chosen individual known as a muezzin, who may also indicate the prayer schedule to be followed.

> Righteous are those who…give the zakat.
> **Sura 2:177**

Muslims receive comes to them from God's sovereign blessing, then it is only right for them to give to those who have received less. With this in mind, almsgiving is not considered an act of charity for Muslims, but a duty they perform on behalf of those who require and deserve assistance. According to the Qur'an, worthy recipients of alms are the poor, orphans, and widows, as well as causes that aim to eliminate slavery, to help those who are in debt, and to spread Islam.

Observance of Ramadan

The fourth pillar of Islam is *sawm* (fasting), and in particular, the fast of Ramadan. This is the name for the ninth month in the Islamic lunar calendar. The penultimate night of this monthlong fast commemorates the time when Muhammad received the first revelation of the Qur'an from the angel Jibrail. Pious Muslims may pray for the entire evening, hoping that their prayers will be answered. In general during Ramadan, all Muslims who are physically able abstain from food, drink, and sexual relations during daylight hours. Instead, they use this time for purifying themselves by reflecting upon their spiritual

The direction of Mecca from any location is determined using the Great Circle method—in other words, the shortest route (over one of the Poles if necessary). Calculating this was a preoccupation of Muslim scientists during the Golden Age of Islamic scholarship, from the 8th to the 13th centuries.

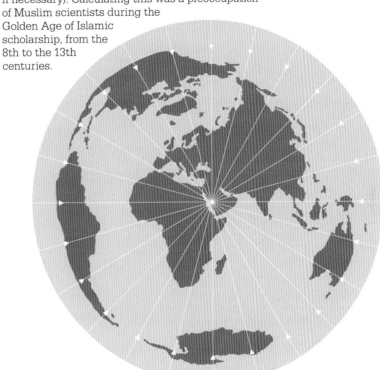

condition, considering any wrong committed, remembering God's great mercy, and contemplating the needs of their communities.

Each morning before daybreak, families gather for a small meal that must sustain them throughout the day. In the evening, after dark, families visit one another and take part in a larger meal that often includes special foods, such as dates, which Muhammad is believed to have eaten in order to break his fast.

Many Muslims go to their local mosque for evening prayer during Ramadan and recite a special

The direction of Mecca, or Qibla, is commonly shown in public buildings in the Muslim world for purposes of prayer.

prayer said only during the month of fasting. Likewise, some Muslims use Ramadan for acts of piety, such as reciting the entire Qur'an.

Ramadan ends with a special feast, known as 'Id al-Fitr, which breaks the month of fasting. The feast is obligatory and is an »

The *hilal* or crescent moon that appears after the new moon announces the beginning and the end of the fasting month of Ramadan, although this period may also be calculated.

Muhammad's guidance, it was cleansed of these shrines and restored as a symbol of worship of the one God, Allah.

Before arriving at the Kaaba, Muslim pilgrims must purify themselves. To do so, men wear seamless white robes and cut their hair, and some even shave their heads. Similarly, some women wear white robes, but many others choose to wear simple clothing that is traditional to their country of origin. In this state of purity, both men and women refrain from sexual activity, and from wearing jewelry or perfume. They also refrain from bathing, arguing, or anything that might taint their purity. In essence, everyone in their white robes represents not only purity, but unity and equality as well. On the one hand, the hajj is meant to be free of hierarchy and disunity, placing emphasis on total devotion to God and Muslims' special worship

enormously joyous occasion. Families visit one another to share in special meals and to exchange gifts and sweets. Businesses often close for part of the celebrations, which can sometimes continue for several days.

Pilgrimage to Mecca

The fifth pillar of Islam is hajj: making a pilgrimage to the holy city of Mecca in Saudi Arabia, which begins after the month of Ramadan. Every adult Muslim who is physically able, and has the financial means to make the trip, should perform the pilgrimage at least once in his or her lifetime. To do so, Muslims travel by whatever means possible to Mecca. Many Muslim travel agencies even offer special hajj packages to groups and individuals to help ensure a memorable and problem-free experience. As pilgrims near the city, they often shout, "I am here, oh Lord, I am here!" The main focus of the pilgrimage is the Kaaba, the cube-shaped structure sitting at the center of Mecca's Grand Mosque. According to tradition, the Kaaba was originally

built by Ibrahim (Arabic for Abraham) and his son Ismail (Arabic for Ishmael) in order to house a black stone given to Ibrahim by the angel Jibrail (Gabriel). The stone was meant to symbolize God's covenant with Ismail. In pre-Islamic times, the Kaaba was also a pilgrimage site for followers of polytheistic religions. At that time, the Kaaba was filled with shrines to various tribal gods. But under

…eat and drink until the white thread of dawn appears to you distinct from the black thread, then complete your fast until the nightfall.
Sura 2:187

Whoever performs hajj for the sake of pleasing God… shall return from it as free from sin as the day on which his mother gave birth to him.
Hadith Sahih Bukhari 26:596

> I am here, oh Lord,
> I am here!

**Pilgrim's prayer upon
reaching Mecca**

Permissible pilgrimage

Only Muslims may enter the holy city of Mecca and, in the very conservative form of Sunni Islam that is practiced in Saudi Arabia, the Kaaba is the only permissible destination for pilgrimage. Under this orthodox form of Islam, known as Wahhabism, veneration of historical sites, graves, and buildings associated with Islamic history is strongly discouraged, because it might lead to worship of things other than God—the sin of idolatry, or shirk. Since there is no concept of a sacred site or shrine, therefore, many old buildings in Mecca have been demolished to make way for new development, giving the city an almost entirely modern appearance. Not all forms of Islam follow this interpretation of shirk—Sufism, for example, holds the tombs of its saints and scholars in deep reverence.

during the pilgrimage. On the other hand, the great variety shown in female pilgrims' clothing reflects the diverse character of the global Muslim community coming together in spiritual unison at the Grand Mosque.

Rites of Mecca

Once pilgrims enter the Grand Mosque they perform the *tawaf*, walking around the Kaaba in an conterclockwise direction seven times. They will try to get as close as they can to the structure, and, if possible, will kiss or touch the black stone exposed in one of the Kaaba's corners. During the following seven days, pilgrims pray in the Grand Mosque and take part in other ceremonies. For example, pilgrims drink water drawn from the Zamzam well inside the mosque. According to Muslim tradition, this well was miraculously created by God in order to sustain Ismail as a baby when he was stranded in the desert with his mother, Hajar (Arabic for Hagar). Some pilgrims run between two hills, Safa and Marwa, to commemorate Hajar's search for water. They may also travel beyond Mecca, to Mina and Mount Arafat, where they pray to

God, asking for forgiveness for the sins of the entire Muslim community. From here, pilgrims return to Mecca, to the Grand Mosque, where they circle the Kaaba again in a farewell *tawaf*.

The pilgrimage ends with a feast commemorating Ibrahim and his obedience to God. Even Muslims who have not made the pilgrimage celebrate this feast, which lasts for three days. Much food is eaten, with the leftovers distributed to the poor and needy.

Those who have made the journey to Mecca honor the faithfulness shown by Ibrahim by symbolically stoning the devil: they throw stones at three pillars representing evil. Finally, many pilgrims end their pilgrimage by visiting the city of Medina and the mosque in which the Prophet Muhammad is buried.

Lightening the burden

The five pillars of Islam may be seen to be representative of the faith as a whole, and to reflect the light burden that God places on his followers. However, although they show the simplicity of Islam, any number of practical difficulties may be encountered in attempting to follow the necessary stipulations.

What if the direction of prayer cannot be established? What if a Muslim is unable to fast on one of the days of Ramadan? God offers a simple solution to such obstacles: "And to God belong the east and the west, so wherever you turn there is the face of God. Surely God is All-Sufficient for his creatures' needs, All-Knowing."

The essential point for Muslims is to turn toward God in worship in the best way that they know how, until such a point in time when they may worship him just as their fellow believers. ∎

The Kaaba in Mecca is a square, stone building that predates Islam by many centuries. The Grand Mosque was built around it.

THE IMAM IS GOD'S CHOSEN LEADER

THE EMERGENCE OF SHI'A ISLAM

IN CONTEXT

KEY FIGURE
'Ali ibn Abi Talib

WHEN AND WHERE
c.632–661, Arabia

BEFORE
From 1500 BCE The Hebrew Bible identifies Abraham and his successors as having been chosen by God to lead the Israelites.

1st century CE After his death, Jesus is known as Jesus Christ, the Messiah or anointed one. His mother Mary becomes a major devotional figure.

c.610 CE In Islam, Muhammad is chosen by God to receive the revelation of the Qur'an.

AFTER
c.1500 The Persian Safavid dynasty converts from Sunni to Shi'a Islam, and Iran develops as the major bastion of Shi'ism, while Arabia remains mainly Sunni.

When the Prophet Muhammad, founder of Islam, died in 632, he had established Islamic authority over the entire Arabian peninsula through a campaign of warfare and conquest. However, Muhammad had no sons who survived him, and on his death the Muslim community was divided over who was to succeed him as their leader.

Muhammad was considered to have a divine right to rule, but this prerogative ended with him. The majority of Muslims believed that the small group known as the Companions of the Prophet were best suited to leadership, since they were the people most closely guided by Muhammad and they were also the compilers of the Qur'an. One of Muhammad's

Who should **succeed the Prophet Muhammad?**

Many followers believe that **electing a leader** is in accordance with the Sunna—the teachings and sayings of Muhammad.

The Shi'a 'Ali party believe that God has indicated **a line of rightful succession** within the Family of the Prophet.

Sunni Islam is therefore headed by a **leader chosen by consensus**.

Shi'a Islam is therefore headed by an **imam who is chosen by God**.

See also: God reveals his word and his will 262–69 ▪ Striving in the way of God 278 ▪ The origins of Ahmaddiya 284–85

The first imam, 'Ali ibn Abi Talib, and his sons were members of the Household of the Prophet, so were seen to have divine knowledge, here depicted as shining down from heaven.

son-in-law and cousin 'Ali ibn Abi Talib, because Muhammad had publicly honored 'Ali's ability to lead the community. Shi'a Muslims take their name from 'Ali, whom they see as the Prophet's rightful heir—they are known as the Shi'a 'Ali (Party of 'Ali).

'Ali was eventually appointed to lead the whole Muslim community in 656, after the death of Uthman, but when 'Ali died, Muslims were again divided; Shi'as supported 'Ali's son as successor, while Sunnis supported the election of Muawiyah I, a powerful governor of Syria. To this day, Shi'as remain a minority group within the Muslim community, dedicated to 'Ali and his successors. These descendants of Muhammad, known as imams, have absolute religious authority— their knowledge is considered to be divine and infallible. The largest branch of Shi'a Islam, whose imam is currently absent (see right), is led by proxy figures, or *marjas*—for example, Iran's Ayatollah Khomeini.

Since the dispute concerns the issue of leadership, Shi'a Islam is considered a movement within Islam, not a separate belief system. However, it does have its own emphases. To the Five Pillars of Islam Shi'as add another five: making offerings for the benefit of the community, commanding good, forbidding evil (all beliefs shared by many non-Shi'as), plus two unique to Shi'a Islam—loving the Household of the Prophet, and turning away from those who do not. ▪

closest companions, Abu Bakr, was adopted as his successor. Abu Bakr was to be succeeded in turn by two more of the Companions, Umar and Uthman, as caliph, or ruler, of the Islamic territories. These caliphs were recognized as wise leaders and the best of Muslims. Their followers believed that choosing a leader by community consensus best accorded with the ideas in the Sunna, Muhammad's teachings and sayings. These early caliphs were therefore appointed or elected, and the supporters of Abu Bakr and his two successors became known as Sunni Muslims.

An alternative choice
A minority group of believers disagreed with Abu Bakr's original appointment; they believed that the rightful leader should have been a close relative of Muhammad, and, in particular, a member of a special group known in the Qur'an as the Household (family) of the Prophet. This group claimed that Muhammad had suggested a successor: his

God intends only to remove from you the impurity [of sin], Oh People of the [Prophet's] Household, and to purify you with purification.
Sura 33:33

GOD GUIDES US WITH SHARI'A

THE PATHWAY TO HARMONIOUS LIVING

IN CONTEXT

KEY FIGURE
Abu 'Abdallah Muhammad ibn Idris al-Shafi'i

WHEN AND WHERE
767–820 CE, Arabia

BEFORE
1500 BCE The Torah records the Ten Commandments: religious and ethical laws given to Moses by God.

7th century CE The Prophet Muhammad receives the revelation of the Qur'an; his sayings and actions are passed down by his followers.

AFTER
c.14th century Ibn Taymiyyah, an Islamic scholar, issues a fatwa against the Mongols for not basing their laws on shari'a.

1997 The European Council for Fatwa and Research is founded to assist European Muslims in interpreting shari'a.

I n Islamic thought, to submit oneself to God's guidance (*islam* means submission) is the mark of a true Muslim. To help followers navigate life in ways that are pleasing to him, God has offered a pathway known as shari'a, meaning literally "the road to the watering hole." In the context of Arabia's deserts, a road to water is a great treasure and, similarly, shari'a is the pathway, by God's law, to harmonious living. It is a system of ethics and a science of law (*fiqh*) that is meant to govern humankind and guide everything people do.

This system required sources to refer to, and, early on, Muslims relied on Muhammad's revelations (the

See also: Living in harmony 38 ▪ Wisdom lies with the superior man 72–77 ▪ The personal quest for truth 144 ▪ Writing the Oral Law 182–83 ▪ God reveals his word and his will 254–61

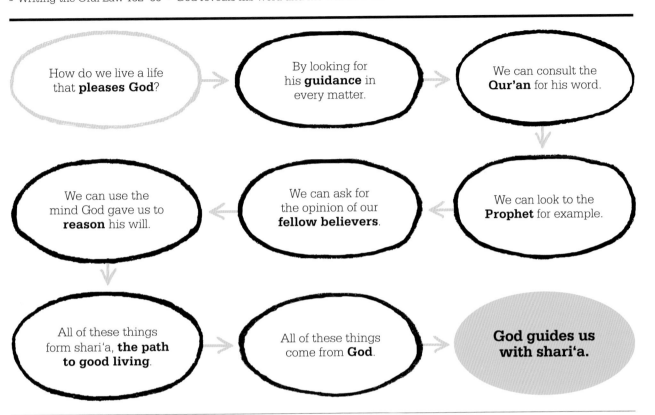

How do we live a life that **pleases God**?

By looking for his **guidance** in every matter.

We can consult the **Qur'an** for his word.

We can use the mind God gave us to **reason** his will.

We can ask for the opinion of our **fellow believers**.

We can look to the **Prophet** for example.

All of these things form shari'a, **the path to good living**.

All of these things come from **God**.

God guides us with shari'a.

Qur'an) and his example (Sunna) for direction. With his death, however, this guidance ceased. As it was, the question of how to apply existing revelations to everyday life, across the various cultures of the growing Muslim community, was a delicate matter. Despite the emergence of Islamic judges who could rule on public and private concerns, there was a call for more uniform and clearly defined shari'a.

Defining Islamic law

Scholars keen to standardize Islamic jurisprudence emerged in many Muslim communities, leading to disagreement over how to apply the law. Should its scope be restricted to the teachings of the Qur'an and the Sunna, or could jurists incorporate their own analysis and reason?

By the 8th century, Muslims differed widely on the application of shari'a. Scholar Abu 'Abdallah Muhammad ibn Idris al-Shafi'i, seen by many as the father of Islamic jurisprudence, came to the fore to offer unifying thought on the legal concerns of the day. According to al-Shafi'i, there were four sources of law: the Qur'an, the Sunna, the consensus of the community (*ijma*), and analogical reasoning (*qiyas*).

Believed to be the literal word of God, the Qur'an is the primary source for Islamic principles and values. In many passages, it directly addresses matters such as murder, exploitation of the poor, usury, theft, and adultery, clearly condemning them. In other instances, the Qur'an works to curb certain behavior over time. For example, early ›

"The road to the watering hole"— the literal translation of shari'a— is a concept that has considerable resonance for believers who came from an unforgiving desert climate.

revelations on alcohol suggest that while some good may be found in it, it may also have a connection to sin (2:219). Later revelations prohibit Muslims from praying while drinking (4:43), and the latest plainly condemn the use of alcohol (5:93). The Qur'an also guides Muslims in personal and community affairs. For instance, while it does not expressly prohibit slavery, it does offer guidance on how to treat slaves. Marriage concerns such as polygamy, dowry, and inheritance rights for women are also governed.

Stipulations such as these are explicit in the Qur'an and offer clear guidance. However, while the Qur'an treats other matters of morality and civic duty in a similar fashion, much of its treatment of legal concerns tends to be generic. In these cases, the example of Muhammad given in the Sunna supplements the Qur'anic material. While the Sunna cannot replace the Qur'an's authority, the belief that Muhammad was inspired by God led to the acceptance of his example as authoritative. Al-Shafi'i refined the use of the Sunna in legal matters by restricting the use of the term Sunna to Muhammad. Doing so eliminated any confusion with local customs, and added greater authority to the traditions of the Prophet. However, collections of Muhmmad's sayings, actions, and what he prohibited and allowed grew in number, requiring the application of a strict process of validation. As a result of this, legitimate traditions of Muhammad —that is, those with a proper chain of authority and not contradicting the Qur'an—can be brought to bear on legal matters.

Legal interpretation

Even with al-Shafi'i's definitions, situations could arise that are not specifically addressed in either the Qur'an or Sunna. With Muhammad no longer alive to offer guidance on such legal matters, the role of interpretation became crucial. Al-Shafi'i therefore sought to give authority to legal interpretations reached by consensus among the Muslim community. Early on, this was a practical way for solving problems on which the Qur'an and the Sunna were silent; majority opinion would help in reaching decisions. Over time, however, "the community" came to be defined in legal terms as a collective body of legal scholars and religious authorities whose decisions would be made on

> There has come to you from God a light and a clear book by which God guides those who pursue his pleasure to the ways of peace...
> **Sura 5:15–16**

behalf of wider Muslim society. There remained some situations where no authoritative text existed, and when consensus could not be reached. Initially, jurists used their own judgment to arbitrate new legal concerns. This was known as *ijtihad*, or striving intellectually, and incorporated a judge's personal opinion or reasoning. Al-Shafi'i restricted the role of personal reasoning in *ijtihad* to the use of deductive reasoning to find analogous situations in the Qur'an or Sunna from which new legal rulings could be derived. For example, the Qur'an prohibits making a sale or a purchase during the call to Friday prayers: Muslims are instead urged to cease trading so that they may gather for worship (62:9–10). What about other contracts that might be made during the call to prayer? Should a marriage, for example, be arranged during this time? The Qur'an is silent on the matter, but analogical

Muslim scholars and religious leaders are relied upon to interpret original sources where guidance on certain matters is not explicit.

Analogical reasoning can be used to determine acceptable behavior. The Qur'an makes no mention of drugs, but does forbid alcohol. So we can infer that other intoxicants are forbidden too.

reasoning can be used to derive a legal opinion. If the aim of the Qur'an is to discourage actions preventing Muslims from worship, then, likewise, restriction on business can be applied to other contracts, actions, or services such as a marriage. Instead of scholars merely offering a personal opinion on matters such as these, al-Shafi'i helped to ground creative thinking in the authoritative sources of Islam, the Qur'an and the Sunna.

Schools of law

Although al-Shafi'i's summation of the four sources of law—the Qur'an, the Sunna, community consensus, and analogical reasoning—did much to unify shari'a, different schools of law use these sources in different ways. From the 13th century, four schools have predominated in Sunni Islam, the largest branch of the faith. Each school is named for the individual who framed its main concerns: Shafi'i, Hanbali, Hanafi, and Maliki. The Shafi'i and Hanbali schools rely on evidence from the sources in interpreting law, while the Hanafi and Maliki encourage analagous reasoning as well.

Further schools of law developed in Shi'a Islam. Given the key role of the imam for Shi'a Muslims, these schools emphasize the traditions of 'Ali and the imams. Muhammad's cousin 'Ali is seen by Shi'as as the first imam—a point on which Sunnis and Shi'as disagree. Shi'as often favor the rulings of the imam, their supreme leader and highest authority on law, over analogical reasoning and community consensus.

The schools of law remain in Muslim society today. In regions where Muslims are predominant, scholars rule on legal matters in courts of law and issue fatwas (rulings). In turn, judges enforce and uphold the law. Muslims facing more mundane questions as to the best way to live a Muslim life may also ask for authoritative advice. In non-Muslim societies, local scholars offer guidance to their communities and, in a modern twist, Muslims can also consult web-based helplines run by international centers devoted to Islamic law. While there is still debate about how best to derive legal rulings, shari'a remains for many a straight path to the best life God can give to his followers. ∎

Abu 'Abdallah Muhammad ibn Idris al-Shafi'i

Much legend has grown up around the life of al-Shafi'i. As a result, the details of his early years remain uncertain, but according to the oldest surviving accounts he was born in Gaza in 767. When he was young, his family moved to Mecca, where he studied Hadith (the words and deeds of Muhammad) and law. He is said to have memorized the Qur'an by the age of 10. He then moved to Medina, studying law under Malik ibn Anas, founder of the Maliki School of Islamic law. He taught in Baghdad, finally settling in Egypt. Through his work as a teacher and scholar, he became known as the father of Islamic jurisprudence, helping to shape Islamic legal thought. He died in 820 and was buried in al-Fustat (Cairo).

Key works

9th century *Treatise on the Foundations of Islamic Jurisprudence; The Exemplar*

My community will never agree on an error.
Hadith of Muhammad

WE CAN THINK ABOUT GOD, BUT WE CANNOT COMPREHEND HIM
THEOLOGICAL SPECULATION IN ISLAM

IN CONTEXT

KEY FIGURE
Abu al-Hasan al-Ash'ari

WHEN AND WHERE
10th century, Arabia

BEFORE
c.990 CE Syrian philosopher Abu al-'Ala al-Ma'arri uses rationalism to reject religious dogma, denouncing its claims as "impossible."

AFTER
11th century Ibn Sina (known in the West as Avicenna) attempts to reconcile rational philosophy with Islamic theology.

11th century Al-Ghazali writes *The Inconsistency of the Philosophers* on the use of philosophy in Islamic theology.

12th century Ibn Rushd (known in the West as Averroes) publishes a response to al-Ghazali's work: *The Inconsistency of the "Inconsistency."*

We are told that **all bounty is in the hand of God**.

We do not know how, or in what sense, this is true.

Questioning it would **lead to innovation**, which is forbidden.

We must just **believe and accept it**.

We can think about God, but we cannot comprehend him.

Islam teaches that God is transcendent, or beyond human comprehension. While this does not prevent Muslims from thinking about God, and reflecting on aspects of who he is and what he does, they must never do so in the expectation of being able to understand his nature or his actions. This was the conclusion reached by Abu al-Hasan al-Ash'ari in the 10th century, when Islam entered a controversy stirred up by philosophical speculation about the nature of God.

In the 8th century, caliphs (civil and religious heads of the Muslim state) of the Abbasid dynasty

See also: Defining the indefinable 184–85 ▪ The pathway to harmonious living 272–75 ▪ The unity of divinity is necessary 280–81

> God…is unlike whatever occurs to the mind or is pictured in the imagination…
> **'Ali al-Ash'ari**

had encouraged the development of scholarship and the arts in the Islamic world, and Arabic translations of works by Greek philosophers, such as Aristotle, became available to Muslim theologians. Some of these scholars applied the new Greek ways of thinking to the content of the Qur'an. They formed a group called the Mu'tazilites, which became a prominent force in Islamic theology in the 9th century.

Radical thinkers

The Mu'tazilites were inspired by the idea that Greek philosophical methods could be used to resolve apparent contradictions in the Qur'an. The Qur'an stresses the unity of God—he is indivisible, and so cannot have any kind of body, made up of parts, as humans have. Yet there are passages in the Qur'an that specifically refer, for example, to God's hands and eyes. To take descriptions such as these literally would lead to anthropomorphism (attributing human characteristics to God) and might be seen as comparing God with the beings he created,

which was the greatest sin. The Mu'tazilites proposed that such references are metaphorical. So, for example, a reference to God's hand could be interpreted as indicating his power. They then applied Greek logic to other theological issues, such as free will, predestination, and determining the nature of the Qur'an itself—whether it had existed eternally, or had been created by God at some point.

Before long, however, the wide-ranging speculation of the Mu'tazilites began to attract censure and turn public opinion against them. Theological and philosophical speculation about God is permissible and indeed important to Islamic thought, but seeking answers to questions not specifically addressed by the Qur'an or Muhammad is, according to Islam, not only unnecessary, but also a sin—*bid'ah*, the sin of innovation.

One Mu'tazilite thinker, al-Ash'ari, refused to reduce the Qur'an's descriptions of God to metaphors, but he also refused to anthropomorphize God. Instead,

he asserted that God might be described as having hands without Muslims knowing how this might be possible. Al-Ash'ari and his group of fellow-thinkers, known as the Ash'arites, left the words of the Qur'an intact, but also kept theological thinking about God pure, by refraining from speaking about him in human terms, since God is beyond comprehension. ▪

Islamic scholars are free to think about God and reflect on aspects of who he is and what he does, but they must never expect to understand his nature or his actions.

Abu al-Hasan al-Ash'ari

Abu al-Hasan al-Ash'ari was born in around 873 CE in Basra, in present-day Iraq. He is credited with much of the development of *kalam* (the science of discourse on divine topics), and taught many of Islam's greatest scholars. Through his thinking and the work of his pupils, Ash'arite theology became the dominant school of theology for orthodox Muslims. He remained a

Mu'tazilite theologian until the age of 40, when he abandoned much of Mu'tazilite thought. Some say this followed a theological dispute with his teacher, others that he realized there were contradictions between Islam and Mu'tazilite theology. He died in 935.

Key works

9th–10th century *Theological Opinions of the Muslims*; *The Clarification of the Bases of the Religion*

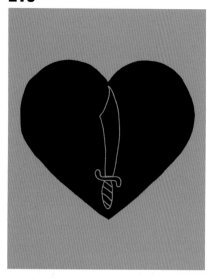

JIHAD IS OUR RELIGIOUS DUTY
STRIVING IN THE WAY OF GOD

IN CONTEXT

KEY FIGURE
Shams al-A'imma al-Sarakhsi

WHEN AND WHERE
11th century, Persia

BEFORE
7th century CE Muhammad's armies conquer and unite much of Arabia under the banner of Islam.

8th century Islamic expansion continues into Spain in the west and Persia in the east.

8th century Legal scholar Abu Hanifa argues that Islam only permits defensive war.

AFTER
12th century Ibn Rushd (Averroes), an Islamic philosopher, divides jihad into four types: jihad by the heart, by the tongue, by the hand, and by the sword.

1964 Egyptian author Sayyid Qutb argues for jihad as the mission to make Islam dominant in all the world.

Despite the guidance given by the Qur'an, Muhammad, and shari'a, maintaining a focus on God and a disciplined life remains a challenge for Muslims. Disobedience is always a temptation and evil is a constant presence. Muslims, therefore, must constantly strive to stay close to God and struggle against evil. This striving or struggling is known as jihad.

For most Muslims, jihad is used in two different ways. The "greater jihad" is the most common. This is the constant struggle against personal sin, involving repentance and seeking God's mercy, avoiding temptation, and pursuing justice for others. The "lesser jihad", although less common for Muslims, is the more widely known. It involves the legitimate use of force, sometimes militarily, against those who do evil.

In the 11th century, one of Islam's most noted legal scholars, Shams al-A'imma al-Sarakhsi, discussed lesser jihad as a four-stage process. He argued that in the first stage, jihad toward others should be peaceful and passive. In the second

Even the youngest students learn the importance of striving to be a good Muslim by upholding the faith, seeking God's mercy, avoiding temptation, and pursuing justice for others.

stage, Islam should be defended with peaceful argument. The third stage allowed for followers to defend the Muslim community against injustice. In the fourth stage, Muslims are called on to engage in armed conflict, within specific legal and Qu'ranic guidelines, when the Islamic faith is under threat. ∎

See also: Augustine and free will 220–21 ▪ The pathway to harmonious living 272–75 ▪ The rise of Islamic revivalism 286–90

THE WORLD IS ONE STAGE OF THE JOURNEY TO GOD
THE ULTIMATE REWARD FOR THE RIGHTEOUS

According to the Qur'an, the end of the world will be accompanied by the Day of Judgment, when the fate of every person will be determined by the scales of justice. Those whose good deeds on earth outweigh their bad deeds will proceed to *jannah* (paradise), depicted in Islam as a luxurious garden; while those whose bad deeds outweigh their good deeds will be relegated to the fiery torments of *jahannam*, or hell.

This idea of divine judgment is set against the Qur'an's pervasive descriptions of God's mercy and forgiveness. Indeed, Muslims are distinguished clearly from non-Muslims as those who hope for God's mercy. They also hope for a meeting with God (the Day of Judgment is often referred to as this in the Qur'an), when they will receive his clemency.

Hope and paradise
The Muslim scholar Abu Hamid Muhammad al-Ghazali focused on the relationship between the Muslim concepts of hope and

paradise in a treatise entitled *The Book of Fear and Hope*. He argued that those who truly fear God will run toward him, longing for his mercy. Al-Ghazali likens the desire for a meeting with God to a farmer who sows seed in tilled ground, faithfully waters the seed, weeds the ground regularly, and rightly hopes for a harvest. Similarly, the Muslim who believes in God, obeys his commands, and pursues morality can expect both compassion from God and the rewards of paradise. ∎

And nothing but the reins of hope will lead to the vicinity of the Merciful and the joy of the Gardens.
Al-Ghazali

See also: Preparing for the afterlife 58–59 ▪ The promise of a new age 178–81 ▪ Jesus's message to the world 204–207

GOD IS UNEQUALED
THE UNITY OF DIVINITY IS NECESSARY

IN CONTEXT

KEY FIGURE
Muhammad ibn Tumart

WHEN AND WHERE
1082–1130, North Africa

BEFORE
c.800–950 CE Aristotle's works are translated into Arabic.

10th century Muslim scholar al-Farabi discusses the First Cause (God).

1027 Persian philosopher Ibn Sina (known in the West as Avicenna) argues that reason requires God's existence.

AFTER
c.1238 Ibn 'Arabi, a prominent Sufi teacher, reflects on the "Oneness of Being."

1982 The Palestinian thinker Ismail al-Faruqi writes *Tawhid: Its Implications for Thought and Life*.

1990 Ozay Mehmet argues that *tawhid* is the basis for Muslim religious and secular identity.

I slam is a monotheistic religion and one of its central tenets is *tawhid* (literally "oneness") —the doctrine of divine unity. According to Muslim thought, there is only one God, and he is single in nature; he is not a trinity, as Christians believe. The notion of *tawhid* features widely in the Qur'an and forms the first part of Islam's central creed, the shahada: "There is no god but God." Conversely, the doctrine of divine unity also forms the basis for the greatest sin in Islam, and one that is unforgivable:

Reason tells us that things in the world (including humans) are changing, impermanent, and were **created by something** that preceded them.

→

However, **at the beginning** of all events and beings, there must be something that was **not itself caused by any other thing**.

↓

The unique creator did not "begin" and will not end— **God has existed and will exist forever**.

←

This is God, the **unique creator.**

↓

The absolute creator is **the only being** that is unchanging, eternal, and the First Cause of everything.

→

God is one being, that has **no partners or equals**.

See also: Defining the indefinable 184–85 ▪ A divine trinity 212–19 ▪ The central professions of faith 262–69 ▪ Theological speculation in Islam 276–77

shirk, which is the violation of *tawhid*. Literally meaning "to share," the sin of shirk is committed when a partner is attributed to God. This is because it suggests either a belief in many gods, or a belief that God is less than perfect and therefore requires a partner.

A creed of unity

Throughout the history of Islam, Muslims have reflected on the notion of divine unity. In the 12th century, this gave rise to a movement whose followers were known as Al-Muwahhidun ("those who emphasize unity"), or the Almohads. Founded by Muhammad ibn Tumart, this movement was based on its conception of divine unity, which came to be expressed in the Almohad *'aqida*, or creed.

The Almohad creed combined elements of *kalam*—theological speculation on God's nature—with direct interpretation of the Qur'an and the Sunna (the sayings and actions of Muhammad). One of its most significant characteristics is that it was meant to appeal not

High in the Atlas Mountains of Morocco, the Tin mal Mosque became the spiritual center of the Almohad creed in the 12th century.

just to scholars, but to a wide audience that would be able to test its assertions against their own logic and personal experience.

Cause and effect

The Almohad creed begins with certain sayings of Muhammad that suggest the notion of divine unity was, to him, the most significant part of Islam. The creed then offers the unique assertion, largely derived from Aristotelian philosophy: that reason and logic—rather than faith—demand the truth of God's existence. As a result, those with reason can deduce whether or not God exists.

The Almohad creed uses deductive reasoning to argue for God's unity, building each of its assertions on the one before it. It argues that everything has a maker —something has caused each thing in the world to be made (whether that was a human making a tool, or an acorn growing into a tree). Humans themselves are creations of extraordinary complexity. And if everything in the world was made by something, there must be a being at the beginning of that chain of cause and effect that was not brought about by something before it— the initial cause of everything else. This being is God—who is unique and absolute (without a beginning or an end). If we acknowledge his absolute existence, then we must also acknowledge that no other god can share his power, and therefore, God alone is one and unequaled. ▪

Muhammad ibn Tumart

Muhammad ibn Tumart was a Berber born in the Atlas Mountains of modern-day Morocco in around 1082. He traveled to the East to study Islamic theology and, growing in religious fervor, he formed a movement based on a desire to reform Islam along the lines of his vision of the oneness of God.

Ibn Tumart returned to Morocco around 1118; here his movement grew in strength and numbers. In 1121, he proclaimed himself the Mahdi (Guided One, or redeemer) who would restore purity to Islam. He died in around 1130, before his followers came to reign over large portions of northwestern Africa and parts of Spain.

Ibn Tumart's movement receded in the 13th century. None of his texts survive, although writings about him and his followers (including those of the Almohad creed) are preserved in *Le livre de Mohammed ibn Toumert* (The Life of Muhammad ibn Tumart).

It is by the necessity of reason that the existence of God, Praise to Him, is known.
Almohad 'aqida

ARAB, WATER POT, AND ANGELS ARE ALL OURSELVES

SUFISM AND THE MYSTIC TRADITION

IN CONTEXT

KEY FIGURE
Jalal al-Din Rumi

WHEN AND WHERE
13th century, Persia

BEFORE
8th century An early Sufi poet, Rabi'a al-'Adawiyya, from Basra, Iraq, fuses asceticism and devotion in her development of Sufism.

10th century Persian master al-Hallaj declares in a trance "I am the Truth"; his words are interpreted as a claim to be God, for which he is executed.

AFTER
13th century Some Sufi practices, such as reciting God's names, are incorporated into Jewish worship.

19th century Emir 'Abd al-Qadir, a Sufi scholar, leads the struggle against the French invasion of Algeria.

21st century More than a hundred Sufi orders exist.

If shari'a law is, for Muslims, an exterior pathway leading to the true worship of God, then Sufi mysticism is an interior path helping its practitioners not only to follow God, but to be closer to him. In the early stages of Islam's development, simple obedience to the will of God was not a strict enough doctrine for some Muslims. In response to the growing indulgence of the ruling

Revered for his asceticism and kindness, Sufi saint Nizamuddin Awlia's tomb is visited by thousands of Muslims and non-Muslims each day, where they light incense and pray.

Muslim elite as they gained in power, disenchanted Muslims wished to return to what they felt was the purity and simplicity of Islam during the time of Prophet Muhammad. They pursued an ascetic lifestyle by removing themselves from the material world and seeking a direct, personal experience of God. Some Sufi Muslims even declared that God was within them.

As Sufism developed, groups, or orders, were founded, in which religious masters taught the doctrine to students. At the heart of many of these orders lay the belief that the self must be renounced in order to fully abide in God. Accordingly, Jalal al-Din Rumi, a 13th-century Sufi master, wrote of an impoverished Arab and his greedy wife who live in the desert. The woman urges her husband to offer their filled water pot to God, hoping they might receive something in return. Although reluctant, the husband succumbs to his wife's urgings and offers the pot—and, in return, it is filled with gold. This treasure is, however, of little use to them in the desert and therefore acts as a reminder that the pursuit of wealth and self-interest detracts from the correct focus on

See also: The performance of ritual and repetition 158–59 ▪ Zen insights that go beyond words 160–63 ▪ Mystical experience in Christianity 238

God **cannot fill a vessel** that is **already filled**.

↓ ↓ ↓

We must **empty our lives** of material concerns.

We must **cleanse our minds** of selfish distractions.

We must **free our hearts** of earthly desires.

↓ ↓ ↓

We must let ourselves be filled by **nothing but God.**

↓

Thus we will **find God within ourselves**.

God. In the same parable, Rumi recounts the heavenly angels' jealousy of Adam. They, too, forsake their focus on God. The parable, for Rumi, describes humanity in general and the temptation to pursue the self. For Sufis, an individual's focus should be the denial of the self in the pursuit of an experience of God.

Renouncing the worldy

In Sufism, achieving a personal experience of God involves moving through successive stages of renunciation, purification, and insight. As a result, not only are Sufis ascetic—breaking ties to the material world through poverty, fasting, silence, or celibacy—but they also place great emphasis on devotional love of God, often through religious experiences or psychological states. This is often achieved through the repetition of God's names (for example,

God the merciful, God the great) or meditative breathing exercises. Becoming absorbed in these exercises helps the Sufi practitioner to forget worldly attachments and focus more fully on God.

Rumi placed particular emphasis on using both music and dance to pursue a direct experience of God's presence. The Whirling Dervishes, the Sufi order founded by his followers, use singing or chanting and bodily movements to enter ecstatic states to experience union with God. Their rhythmic spinning dance is said to symbolize the solar system, which they mimic by turning in circles around their leader.

In the view of many Muslims, some Sufis pressed the boundaries of Islamic orthodoxy, and Sufism was suppressed from the 17th century onward. However, orders are still found worldwide, attracting both Muslims and non-Muslims. ▪

Jalal al-Din Muhammad Rumi

Jalal al-Din Muhammad Rumi was born in 1207 in Balkh (in modern-day Afghanistan). His family claimed descent from Abu Bakr, the Prophet Muhammad's companion and successor. After traveling with his father throughout Persia and Arabia, he settled in Konya (in modern-day central Turkey).

In Konya, Rumi met the Sufi master Shams-i Tabrizi (of Tabriz). At the time, Rumi was a professor of Islamic sciences, but the Sufi master had such a deep impact upon him that he abandoned his studies in order to devote himself to mysticism. His followers founded the Mawlawi order of Sufis, known to many as the Whirling Dervishes.

Though known for his philosophy and scholarship, Rumi is best remembered for his mystic poetry. He died in Konya in 1273.

Key works

1258–1273 *Spiritual Couplets*
13th century *The Works of Shams of Tabriz*
13th century *What is Within is Within*

THE LATTER DAYS HAVE BROUGHT FORTH A NEW PROPHET
THE ORIGINS OF AHMADIYYA

IN CONTEXT

KEY FIGURE
Mirza Ghulam Ahmad

WHEN AND WHERE
Late 19th century, India

BEFORE
632 The Prophet Muhammad, the final prophet of Islam, dies in Medina.

872 The Mahdi, the Hidden One of Shi'a Islam, disappears, supposedly not to return until the end of the world.

19th century The anti-British Indian independence movement grows in strength, with some militant elements.

AFTER
1908 Hakim Noor-ud-Din assumes Ahmadiyya leadership.

1973 Ahmadiyya splits into Qadiani and Lahori groups.

1983 A Qadiani Ahmadiyya conference attracts 200,000 participants; the following year, restrictions are placed on the group in Pakistan.

There can be **no prophet after Muhammad**.

But Islam's followers have **lost the pure message** from God that he brought.

A **new message** is needed to steer Muslims back to the **pure path of the faith**.

Mirza Ghulam Ahmad, as renewer and minor prophet, **brings that message**.

In 1882, Mirza Ghulam Ahmad declared himself to be a minor prophet, or divinely appointed reformer, of Islam. He had come, so he claimed, to rejuvenate Islam and to return it to its pure foundations. The movement that formed around him came to be called Ahmadiyya.

In orthodox Muslim thinking, the Prophet Muhammad is the final prophet of Islam, and anyone else claiming the status of prophet should therefore be denounced. But Ghulam Ahmad did not claim to bring a new revelation beyond the Qur'an. Rather, he simply offered a new interpretation, with the aim of bringing the Muslim community back to its roots. As such he was comparable with other, minor prophets who did not bring the law, but restored it: Aaron, for example, who is thought by Muslims to have been sent by God to revitalize the message given to Musa (Moses).

Ghulam Ahmad had previously developed some unorthodox teachings. Part of his message was that Isa (Jesus) did not die on the cross, nor was he—as Muslims traditionally believed—saved from death on the cross by being raised up to heaven by God. Ghulam Ahmad claimed that Jesus merely

See also: The Prophet and the origins of Islam 252–53 ▪ The emergence of Shi'a Islam 270–71 ▪ Striving in the way of God 278 ▪ The rise of Islamic revivalism 286–90

The Qadiani belief in Ghulam Ahmad's prophethood continues to incite strong feeling in orthodox Islam, even leading to occasional public protests against the movement.

swooned, subsequently recovered, and went to Afghanistan and Kashmir in search of the lost tribes of Israel. Ghulam Ahmad also challenged Islamic thinking concerning jihad, claiming that the only acceptable form was a spiritual jihad designed to peacefully spread the message of Islam. This was a particularly significant idea in the context of 19th-century India, where anti-British unrest was growing.

Controversial claims

Ahmad's claims evolved as his followers grew in number, and he declared himself not just to be Islam's prophetic reformer, but its redeemer —a messianic figure known to Muslims as the Mahdi—and the spiritual successor of Jesus. For many Muslims, these claims went too far and challenged the place of Muhammad and the revelation

given to him. For these reasons, Ghulam Ahmad and his followers were rejected by many Muslims.

Even within his own movement, Ghulam Ahmad's assertions caused controversy. After his death in 1908, the Ahmadiyyas split into two factions: Qadiani Ahmadiyyas, who maintained Ghulam Ahmad's teachings, and a new branch known as Lahori Ahmadiyya. The Lahori branch accepted Ghulam Ahmad as a renewer of the Islam faith, but this was as far

as they were willing to go. They, too, rejected his claim that he was a minor prophet.

In Pakistan in 1973, Qadiani Ahmadiyyas were legally declared non-Muslims, and, in 1984, an ordinance was drafted allowing for punishment of any Qadiani who claimed to be a Muslim, used Islamic terminology, or referred to his or her faith as Islam. The Qadiani Ahmadiyyas have since moved their international headquarters from the Indian subcontinent to London. ▪

Mirza Ghulam Ahmad

Mirza Ghulam Ahmad was born in 1835 in Qadian, a village near Lahore in India. His twin sister died shortly after their birth. In a society where the majority was illiterate, Ghulam Ahmad studied Arabic and Persian, and learned aspects of medicine from his father, a physician. As a young man, he took a position with the government, while continuing his religious studies.

He announced his divine mission in 1882, and in 1888 he asked his followers to formally pledge allegiance to him. Some 40 did so, and in 1889 he published

a set of rules to guide all who joined his movement. Ghulam Ahmad traveled widely across northern India, spreading his message and debating with Islamic leaders. He died in 1908, leaving the leadership of the Ahmadiyya movement to a companion, who eventually passed it to Ahmad's eldest son.

Key works

1880–84 *The Arguments of the Ahmadiyya*
1891 *Victory of Islam*
1898 *The Star of Guidance*

ISLAM MUST SHED THE INFLUENCE OF THE WEST

THE RISE OF ISLAMIC REVIVALISM

IN CONTEXT

KEY FIGURE
Sayyid Qutb

WHEN AND WHERE
20th century, Egypt

BEFORE
1839–97 Activist and writer Jamal al-Din al-Afghani criticizes the colonial presence in Islamic countries.

1849–1905 Egyptian scholar, jurist, and reformer Muhammad 'Abduh decries Western influence.

1882 British forces occupy Egypt. The British presence and influence grow with time.

AFTER
1903–79 Abul A'la Mawdudi, a revivalist thinker, becomes one of the most widely read Muslim writers.

1951 Ayman al-Zawahiri, a friend of Sayyid Qutb, plays a major role in the militant group al-Qaeda.

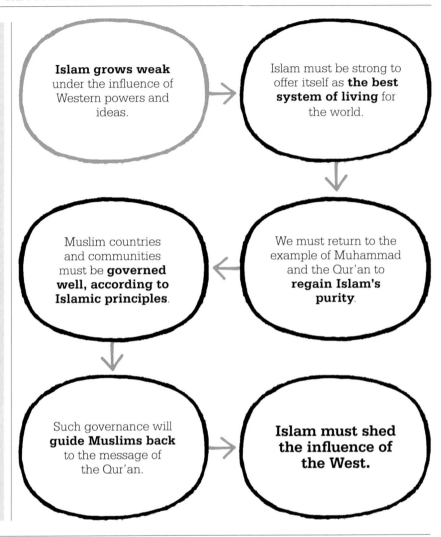

Islam grows weak under the influence of Western powers and ideas.

Islam must be strong to offer itself as **the best system of living** for the world.

We must return to the example of Muhammad and the Qur'an to **regain Islam's purity**.

Muslim countries and communities must be **governed well, according to Islamic principles**.

Such governance will **guide Muslims back** to the message of the Qur'an.

Islam must shed the influence of the West.

By the end of the 18th century, the world's great Muslim powers were in decline. The Ottoman and Mughal empires had lost political influence, and Western powers were colonizing the predominantly Muslim areas of northern Africa and parts of Asia—French North Africa, British India and the Middle East, and Dutch Indonesia. Some Muslims welcomed the changes and modernizations that came with the Western presence. For others, however, the influence of the West forced them to consider the place

that science and technology, Western politics and economics, and even fashion had in their lives. Some wished simply to protect Islam against the secularization that came with modernization; others were more militant and anti-Western, seeking to overthrow imperialist governments; others still were prepared to accept a degree of Western influence, but sought clear dictinctions between what was Islamic and un-Islamic.

Out of this context emerged a number of very influential Islamic thinkers and reformers. Although

each had their own contexts and emphases, they were all aware of the weakness of the global Islamic community at the time, and felt that Muslims straying from Islam under Western influence were responsible. As a result, they sought to revive the role of Islam as the dominant influence in their societies.

Many Muslim revivalists felt that the best way forward was to restore Islam by not only shedding the influence of the West, but by emphasizing the superiority of Islam as well. To do this, they argued for the central role of jihad

See also: God reveals his word and his will 254–61 ▪ The pathway to harmonious living 272–75 ▪ Striving in the way of God 278

Egyptian workers are searched by British soldiers during the Suez Crisis in 1956. Religious insensitivity and poor treatment by the British troops fed Islamic revivalism.

(p.278) in religious and political life. Taken in this sense, jihad became a revolutionary struggle against un-Islamic forces, eliminating perceived evil in pursuit of what revivalists believed was justice and righteousness. Likewise, the revivalists thought that immoral governments should be replaced by Islamic systems established according to divine principles. In many Muslim revivalists' minds, a government based upon the Qur'an and Islam would provide the perfect social system, and the best way to achieve it was by a jihad that expressed itself through militant action, resistance, and revolution.

Egyptian activism
Sayyid Qutb, a Muslim activist in 20th-century Egypt, became one of the most influential revivalist thinkers. From Qutb's perspective, Egypt had grown increasingly weak and corrupt under British colonial rule. Having become disillusioned by his experience of the West and its cultural influence, Qutb sought to lead fellow Muslims out from under foreign control and back to Islam. He wrote extensively on the Qur'an and its interpretation, as well as matters of religion and the state, and joined the Muslim Brotherhood, a group formed in Egypt in the 1920s, which aimed to use the Islamic faith as a means of "ordering the life of the Muslim family, individual, community…and state."

Ages of ignorance
Qutb's interpretation of jihad was consistent with the perception of Islam as a religion that provides the perfect model for living. He believed that Muslims had an obligation to establish their moral standards on earth so that everyone could benefit from them. Jihad, then, became a continual struggle against unbelief and injustice, or what Qutb called *jahiliyya*. This term was traditionally used to describe the age of ignorance —the period before the revelation of the Qur'an—but it was applied by Qutb to everything he considered »

I went to the West and saw Islam, but no Muslims; I got back to the East and saw Muslims, but not Islam.
Muhammad 'Abduh

Sayyid Qutb

Born in 1906 in Qaha, a farming town just north of Cairo, Sayyid Qutb attended a local school, where he memorized the Qu'ran by the age of 10. He went on to a British-style education in Cairo and began work as a teacher. At first enamored with Western culture, he developed an interest in English literature and studied educational administration in the US.

However, his experience of what he considered the irreligious culture of the US, along with his view of British policies during World War II, soured his vision of the West. Back in Egypt, he joined the Muslim Brotherhood, began writing on Islamic topics, and advocated an Islamic ideology in place of Western influences.

In 1954, Qutb was arrested along with other Muslim Brotherhood members for conspiring to assassinate Egypt's president, Gamal Abdel Nasser. After serving a 10-year sentence, he was released, only to write his most controversial work, *Milestones*, in which he called for a re-creation of the Muslim world based on Qur'anic principles. In so doing, he rejected forms of government that were not truly Islamic. He was arrested and sentenced to death for plotting to overthrow the Egyptian state. In August 1966, he was executed and buried in an unmarked grave.

Key Works

1949 *Social Justice in Islam*
1954 *In the Shade of the Qur'an*
1964 *Milestones*

> We…believed once in English liberalism and English sympathy; but we believe no longer, for facts are stronger than words. Your liberalness we see plainly is only for yourselves…
> **Sayyid Qutb**

alien to Islam. For him, *jahiliyya* was not just a period of time, but a state of being that was repeated every time a society strayed from the path of Islam.

Islamic governance

Qutb applied the concept of *jahiliyya* to governments that he did not consider properly Islamic.

He strongly opposed any system of government in which people were in "servitude to others," considering this to be a violation of God's sovereignty. This included communist nations (because of their state-imposed atheism) as well as polytheist nations such as India, and Christian and Jewish states. Qutb also argued that many Muslim countries lived in a state of *jahiliyya* because they accepted alien—and in particular Western—ideas and tried to incorporate them into their governments, laws, and cultures. For Qutb, the only effective way to rid society of *jahiliyya* was by implementing an Islamic way of life with its superior strategies and beliefs for governing humanity.

Renewed jihad

This line of thinking about *jahiliyya* led Qutb and his followers to advocate the implementation of jihad. Understood this way, jihad might be necessary for each new generation of Muslims, at least as long as foreign, un-Islamic forces

> …Islam possesses or is capable of solving our basic problems…without doubt it will be more capable than any other system we may seek to borrow or imitate, to work in our nation.
> **Sayyid Qutb**

exerted their influence. This meant that Muslim scholars who interpreted the Qur'an in such ways as to suggest that its discussions of jihad were no longer applicable in the modern world were misled. Qutb argued that jihad was meant to be enforced in his day in the same way it was when the Qur'an was revealed; this might not mean eliminating every non-Muslim from power, but it did mean shedding the influence the West had upon the world. Muslims should do what was necessary to ensure that a pure Islam as a system of governance could flourish uninhibited by un-Islamic pressures. In this way, Qutb helped to shape not only how future Islamic revivalists would see the world but how the people in the West would come to perceive Islam in the late 20th century. ■

Supporters of Mohamed Morsi, a prominent member of the Muslim Brotherhood, celebrate his election as President of Egypt in 2012. The Muslim Brotherhood remains a major force in Egyptian social and political life.

ISLAM CAN BE A MODERN RELIGION
THE COMPATIBILITY OF FAITH

IN CONTEXT

KEY FIGURE
Tariq Ramadan

WHEN AND WHERE
1960s, Switzerland

BEFORE
711 CE Muslims begin raids
on the Iberian Peninsula.

827 Muslims begin conquest
of Sicily and establish an
Emirate in 965.

15th century Islamic
Ottoman Empire expands
in the Balkans.

AFTER
1960s Large-scale Muslim
emigration begins from
Turkey and northern Africa
to Europe.

1979 The Iranian Revolution
leads to the overthrow of Iran's
Westernizing government.

2008 Rowan Williams, the
Archbishop of Canterbury,
states that the adoption of
aspects of shari'a law is
inevitable in the UK.

One of the most significant
questions faced by
Muslims today is how
to relate Islamic faith to secular,
modern life. This question becomes
more pressing when people from
Muslim countries move to the
West, bringing with them not just
their religion, but their religion as
practiced in a specific cultural
context. As a result, many Muslims
face a disconnection between what
is Islamic and what is modern,
secular, or Western.

The idea developed by Tariq
Ramadan—an Islamic scholar,
whose family went into exile from
Egypt to Switzerland because of
his father's membership of the
Muslim Brotherhood (p.289)—is that
it is possible to be at once a Muslim
and an American or a European:
religion and national culture are
separate concepts, and it is the
duty of a Muslim not only to respect
the laws of the host country' but to
"contribute, wherever they are, to
promoting good and equity within
and through human brotherhood."
Ramadan encourages Muslims to

Tariq Ramadan advises European
governments on Muslim relations;
he is a prominent communicator
and advocate of Muslim integration.

take the traditional sources referred
to by Islamic scholars—the Qur'an
and Sunna—and to interpret them
in the context of their own cultural
background, taking responsibility
for their faith in the environment
they inhabit. Ramadan's goal is to
help Muslims contextualize many
modern issues facing Islam, so that
they are able to become Western
Muslims whose culture and religion
are compatible. ∎

See also: Faith and the state 189 ▪ Progressive Judaism 190–95
▪ The central professions of faith 262–69

Guru Nanak founds Sikhism in the Punjab region of India during a time of tension between Hindus and the Muslim Mughal Empire.

Claiming guidance from God and the angel Moroni, **Joseph Smith, Jr.** translates the Book of Mormon and founds the Church of Jesus Christ of Latter-day Saints, US.

Mirza Husayn 'Ali Nuri proclaims himself a messenger of God, adopts the title Baha'u'llah, and founds the Baha'i Faith in Persia.

Western trade in the Pacific region leads to the rise of the so-called **cargo cults** in Melanesia and New Guinea.

1499   **1830**   **1863**   **1885**

18TH–19TH CENTURY   **19TH CENTURY**   **1880s**   **1926**

Creole religions evolve within communities of African slaves in the Caribbean.

A number of new religions emerge in Japan, including **Tenrikyo, Oomoto, and Kurozumikyo.**

The Watch Tower Tract Society, part of the Bible Student Movement in the US, lays the foundations for what becomes known as the Jehovah's Witnesses.

After a revelation from the **Supreme Being**, Ngô Van Chiêu founds the **Cao Đài** religion in Vietnam.

Most of the world's major religions evolved out of the ancient civilizations, with their foundations in the folk traditions that preceded them. The Abrahamic religions (Islam, Judaism, and Christianity), for example, trace themselves back to the stories of Noah and the Flood, long before any Middle Eastern civilizations, and, similarly, the various branches of Hinduism are based on beliefs that predate Indian civilization.

As philosophical and scientific thinking became increasingly sophisticated over the millennia, these faiths faced a choice: to adapt with the times and embrace change, or denounce anything new as heretical. Breakaway sects emerged, and—driven by events such as the Industrial Revolution

in Europe, and the exploration and colonization of new lands—gave rise to a number of new religious movements fueled by reluctance to compromise in the face of change.

New faiths

It is often difficult to determine whether a breakaway group is a branch of an older religion, or a completely new faith. Mormons and Jehovah's Witnesses, for example, both believe in the divinity of Jesus, but many of their other beliefs separate them from mainstream Christianity. Similarly, Tenrikyo and other new Japanese religious movements bear many similarities to both Buddhism and Shinto, and both the Hare Krishna and Transcendental Meditation movements are obviously derived from Hinduism.

Their status as new religions depends greatly on how much they are accepted or rejected by the parent religions.

In some cases, syncretic religions—amalgams of two very different faiths—have evolved, especially among displaced or oppressed people. For example, while Africans taken to the Caribbean as slaves were forced to adopt their masters' Christianity, they used it as a framework for practicing the religions of their homelands, resulting in creole faiths, such as Santeria (also known as Regla de Ocha or Lukumí), Candomblé, Orisha-Shango, and Vodun (or Voodoo), depending on the tribe they had come from. In the 20th century, a Jamaican religion, the Rastafari movement, grew out of the Black

The **Rastafari** movement begins in Jamaica, after Ras Tafari becomes Emperor Haile Selassie I of Ethiopia.

Based on **L. Ron Hubbard's** theories of *Dianetics*, Scientology is developed as a religion in the US.

Maharishi Mahesh **Yogi** founds the Transcendental Meditation movement, using traditional Hindu meditation techniques.

A.C. Bhaktivedanta Swami Prabhupada takes the Hindu tradition of chanting to the US, where he founds ISKCON, the Hare Krishna movement.

1930   **1952**   **1957**   **1965**

1950s   **1954**   **1961**   **1992**

One of a number of neopagan religions, **Wicca** is founded in Britain after the repeal of the Witchcraft Act.

Sun Myung Moon establishes the Unification Church in Korea.

The "non-creedal, non-doctrinal" **Unitarian Universalist Association** is founded in the US.

In China, **Li Hongzhi** combines meditative qigong practices with Daoist and Buddhist ideas in **Falun Dafa**, also called Falun Gong.

Consciousness movement, building a mythology around the Emperor Haile Selassie of Ethiopia, a country that Rastafarians consider to be Judah. Western influence in the Pacific region also led to new varieties of traditional folk religions, known as the cargo cults.

Many other new religions have emerged as specific to a particular location. Sikhism, for example, is associated with the Punjab region of Pakistan and India; the religion was founded as a reaction to the hostility between Hindus and Muslims in the area, and was based on a peaceful, democratic social foundation. The Church of Jesus Christ of Latter-day Saints in its Book of Mormon provided a specifically US addition to the Christian Bible, with a mythology of saints and angels among the indigenous American people. Other modern religions have been established with the aim of uniting all faiths, or at least recognizing the validity of other beliefs and embracing them in their own faith: these, which include Baha'i, Cao Đài, and Unitarian Universalism, have arisen in various areas of the world where a variety of major faiths have historically coexisted.

Search for the spiritual

A quest for mystical enlightenment produced the Hasidic movement in Judaism, and Sufism in Islam, and some Christian denominations have become more charismatic in recent years. Others in the West have drifted away from religious tradition: some to the past and neopagan religions such as Wicca; others to movements from the East such as ISKCON, Transcendental Meditation, and Falun Gong; while others, notably Scientology and some modern Japanese religions, have grown out of loosely science-based beliefs. Many of these new religions were founded by a charismatic leader or prophet who claimed divine revelation, and have been dismissed as cults designed for the glorification of their leaders. Some such faiths have declined in popularity, but others have gained a strong following and an eventual acceptance as new religious movements in their own right. Before dismissing them, it is as well to remember that Christianity was initially considered a cult by the Romans and Jews, and that Muhammad was driven out of Mecca with his small group of followers for his heretical beliefs. ■

WE MUST LIVE AS SAINT-SOLDIERS

THE SIKH CODE OF CONDUCT

IN CONTEXT

KEY FIGURE
Guru Nanak

WHEN AND WHERE
15th–16th century, India

BEFORE
6th century BCE Jainism and Buddhism reject the Hindu concept of a just war, arguing for absolute nonviolence.

7th century CE The Qur'an contains verses that suggest war in the defense of the faith and the faithful is righteous.

AFTER
1699 The Sikh Khalsa order sets out the conditions and principles justifying conflict.

18th century Sikh armies engage in war with the Mughal and Afghan empires.

1799 The Sikh kingdom of Punjab is established.

1947 The partition of India and Pakistan splits Punjab and sparks religious tension.

The Sikh religion was founded by Guru Nanak, a devoutly spiritual man who became disillusioned with the Hinduism that had surrounded him when he was growing up in a village near Lahore (in modern Pakistan) in the 15th century. Islam had also influenced this area since the 10th century, and its importance grew as the Mughal empire in India expanded.

Guru Nanak viewed the Hindu emphasis on ritual, pilgrimage, and reverence for prophets and holy men as a hindrance to what he considered most important—our relationship with God. Although he used many different names for God, he recognized him as one omnipresent, transcendent divinity, similar to the concept of Brahman in Hinduism. Following a revelation from God when he was around 30 years old, Nanak devoted his life to preaching the path to salvation. He argued that the way in which believers conduct their lives is an integral part of achieving unity with God and finding salvation. After accepting the title of guru, or teacher, from his followers, he went on to become

the first of a succession of 10 Sikh gurus, whose teachings are collected in the Sikh holy book, the Adi Granth. This book came to be considered as the 11th and final guru of Sikhism, and is known as the Guru Granth Sahib (p.303). Nanak's followers became known as Sikhs, from the Sanskrit word for learner or disciple, guided in their way of life by God and the gurus.

Finding God in a good life

Like Hindus, Sikhs believe in the cycle of death and rebirth. However, they take a different view of the purpose of human life. For the Sikh, the aim is not to attain a place in paradise, since there is no final destination of heaven or hell. Instead, Sikhism teaches that being born human is a God-given opportunity to take the path to salvation, which follows five stages, from sinning to achieving freedom from the cycle of death and rebirth. The five stages are: wrongdoing; devotion to God; spiritual union with God; attainment of eternal bliss; and freedom from rebirth.

To make the most of this opportunity, Sikhs follow a strict code of conduct and conventions,

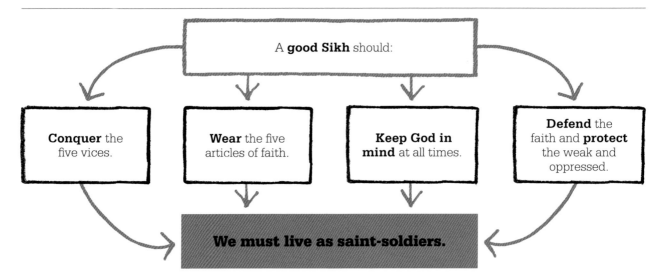

A **good Sikh** should:

Conquer the five vices.

Wear the five articles of faith.

Keep God in mind at all times.

Defend the faith and **protect** the weak and oppressed.

We must live as saint-soldiers.

See also: Living in harmony 38 ▪ The battle between good and evil 60–65 ▪ Selfless action 110–11 ▪ Physical and mental discipline 112–13 ▪ Striving in the way of God 278 ▪ Class systems and faith 302–303

The Khalsa belongs to God, and Victory belongs to Him.
Traditional Sikh greeting

The Khalsa order was founded in response to persecution of Sikhs under the Mughal empire, when Guru Gobind Singh called for Sikhs willing to lay down their lives in defense of the faith.

which was formally laid down by the 10th guru, Guru Gobind Singh, when he created the order of the Khalsa, the community of all Sikhs baptized into the faith, in 1699.

Virtue and courage
The idea of social justice lies at the heart of the Khalsa order (the name means "the pure" or "the free"). Members are encouraged not only to share with others, but also to protect the poor, the weak, and the oppressed. This was a crucial part of Guru Nanak's original philosophy, and it was reinforced during the period of the Ten Gurus, when Sikhs were persecuted both by their Muslim rulers and by Hindus, who regarded the Sikh faith as heretical. Guru Gobind Singh's intention in forming the Khalsa was to establish an order of Sikhs that embodied the twofold virtues of bhakti (spirituality, or devotion) and shakti (powerfulness). He envisioned an ideal of the *sant-*

sipahi, or saint-soldier, who first and foremost led the life of a saint in his devotion to God, but would act as a warrior to defend his faith or prevent injustice, if necessary.

The Khalsa would protect the weak, and dedicate themselves to a virtuous lifestyle of chastity and temperance, ridding themselves of the five vices—lust (*kaam*), anger (*krodh*), greed (*lobh*), emotional attachment (*moh*), and egotism (*ahankar*)—and keeping God in mind at all times. Guru Gobind Singh codified a lifestyle that was appropriate to all Sikhs when he established the Khalsa order: not only did he prohibit rituals, pilgrimages, and superstitious practices, but he also outlined the virtues necessary to a life devoted to God, such as honesty, simplicity, monogamy, and avoidance of alcohol and drugs.

The Khalsa were not asked to renounce the world in their devotion to God, in fact quite the

opposite: they were asked to play an active part in it by commitment to family and community, and by demonstrating a social conscience, which is considered one of the highest of all the Sikh virtues.

Guru Gobind Singh stressed that a Sikh should act like a warrior only out of necessity in leading a saintly life: he should be a soldierlike saint rather than a saintlike soldier, and all Sikhs should act on the principle of "fear not, frighten not." Singh likened the courage needed to behave in this way to that of the lion, and suggested that Sikhs being baptized in the Khalsa order should adopt the surname Singh ("lion") or Kaur ("lioness").

Five articles of faith
After they are baptized in the Khalsa order, Sikhs are expected to wear the five articles of faith, commonly known as the "five Ks", as an outward expression of »

their status as saint-soldiers. Each of these—*kesh* (uncut hair), *kangha* (comb), *kara* (bracelet), *kachera* (undergarment), and *kirpan* (sword) —has a deep symbolic meaning, as well as distinctively identifying the wearer as a Sikh.

Hair is considered by Sikhs to be a gift from God, and *kesh* (the practice of leaving the hair and beard uncut) is seen, in part, as the avoidance of vanity. However, it is also a symbolic representation of the ideal of leading a life in a way that God intended, without interference, and in harmony with his will, and as such is an important outward sign of the Khalsa code of conduct.

Sikhs are expected to keep their hair clean and well-groomed, combing it twice daily with the *kanga*, a special comb that is also used to hold it in place under a turban. This regular grooming is a constant reminder of the Sikh's duty to lead a virtuous life devoted to God, which is why the *kanga* is also considered one of the five articles of faith.

The most easily identifiable aspect of a male Sikh, his turban, is not actually one of the five articles of faith. Nevertheless, it has become an essential item of Sikh clothing and has helped to give its wearers a strong sense of identity and social cohesion. The turban was adopted at the suggestion of Guru Gobind Singh, who pointed out that all the gurus had worn a turban, and that doing likewise would help the wearer to concentrate on following their example. The primary purpose of the turban, however, is to pull back and protect the uncut hair of male Sikhs.

Proofs against temptation
Just as important as the positive virtues is the avoidance of vice. The steel bracelet known as the *kara* is a symbol of the vows taken by a Sikh during baptism to refrain from the five vices. Because it is worn on the wrist it is often visible to the wearer, and therefore acts as a frequent reminder to consider carefully whether his or her actions will lead to evil or wrongdoing. The Jain faith uses a very similar device, in the form of its emblem of the raised palm (p.70): a reminder to stop and consider the intention behind

> God approves not the distinction of high caste and low caste. None has he made higher than others.
> **Sri Guru Granth Sahib**

any action. Similarly, the *kachera*, a cotton undergarment—worn by both men and women—that resembles loose-fitting shorts, ostensibly acts as a warning to control sexual passion and desire, but is also a symbolic reminder that Sikhs should strive to overcome desires of all kinds and lead a faithful life in a broader sense.

Defending the faith
The soldierly aspect of Sikhism is encapsulated in the *kirpan*, the ceremonial sword, which symbolizes courage and dignity. It encourages its wearer to be constantly determined to defend the Sikh faith and its moral values, and protect the downtrodden from tyranny.

Sikhism has at various times been associated with nationalist political movements in the Punjab, where it originated. The region has often suffered from religious conflicts, which Sikhs have

The Sikh turban is an important symbol of faith and dignity. By keeping the hair well groomed, it distinguishes the Sikh man's appearance from the matted locks worn by Hindu ascetics.

inevitably been drawn into. There was even a short-lived Sikh Empire formed in 1799 but dissolved by the British in 1849. After the formation of the Akali, a Sikh reform movement, in the 1920s, and the Akali Dal political party in 1966, there were calls for an autonomous Sikh state in the Punjab, where violent incidents between Sikhs and Hindus, along with tensions between Muslim Pakistan and Hindu India, have continued into modern times. Outside the Punjab, however, the Sikh diaspora has generally integrated into society.

An updated code of conduct for contemporary Sikhism is offered in the *Sikh Rehat Maryada*, published in 1950, which gives guidance on personal and public life, including ceremonies and worship. However, as Guru Nanak originally preached, devotion to God and a socially responsible lifestyle are more important in Sikhism than rituals and reverence. This is reflected in the institution of the gurdwara, which, as well as being a temple for worship, is also the hub of the Sikh community. Sikh worship is generally not prescribed by the gurus, other than the early morning prayer, which uses the Mul Mantra composed by Guru Nanak as a meditation on God's Name. This can be practiced anywhere, not just in the gurdwara, and because there is no priesthood in Sikhism, this, alongside readings and hymns from the Guru Granth Sahib, can, in the spirit of Sikh egalitarianism, be performed by anyone. ◼

Guru Nanak

The founder of the Sikh religion, Guru Nanak, was born in 1469 into a Hindu family in Talwandi, in the Punjab region of India (now known as Nankana Sahib, Pakistan). Tension was running high between the Hindus and Muslims there as the Mughal Empire spread south into the Indian subcontinent. As a young man, Nanak worked as an accountant, but was always fascinated by spiritual matters. According to Sikh tradition, after receiving a revelation, in which God gave him a cup of nectar and told him of his vocation to spread the message of his Name, Nanak embarked on a 25-year mission, traveling and preaching with his companion, the Muslim minstrel Bhai Mardana. In five long trips, he visited the major cities and religious centers of India and Arabia, where he set up *dharamshalas*, centers of worship. He was given the title guru, or teacher, by his followers. After his final journey, to Baghdad and Mecca, he returned to Punjab, where he remained until his death in 1539.

The "five Ks" of the Sikh religion here surround the Sikh symbol of crossed swords. The sword or *kirpan* is one of the "Ks," or articles of faith. The others are uncut hair and beard, comb, bracelet, and cotton shorts.

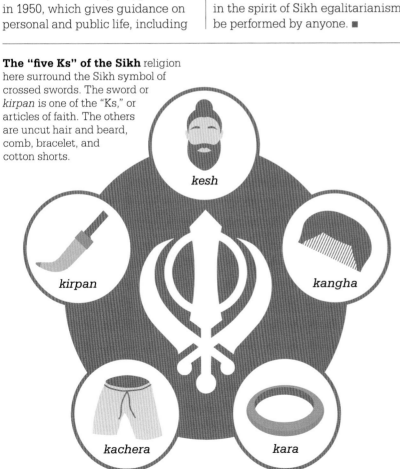

ALL MAY ENTER OUR GATEWAY TO GOD

CLASS SYSTEMS AND FAITH

IN CONTEXT

KEY FIGURE
Guru Nanak

WHEN AND WHERE
From 15th century, India

BEFORE
From 1700 BCE The Vedic scriptures divide society into four varnas, or classes, with brahmins (priests) at the top; this rigid social hierarchy pervades Indian society to the present day.

AFTER
c.1870 Indian sage Sri Ramakrishna advocates religious tolerance, stating that all religions may lead to God via a heightened state of consciousness.

1936 Indian philosopher and political leader Mahatma Gandhi propagates the notion of *sarvadharma samabhava*, the equality of all religions, and speaks out against the Indian caste system.

Sikhism is one of the most egalitarian of all religions, quite free of division or discrimination by race, class, or sex. All are welcome in gurdwaras (Sikh temples) regardless of faith; there are no priests—decisions are made by the community—and both men and women may read from the Sikh holy book. This inclusiveness can be traced to Sikhism's origins, when Guru Nanak (p.301) received a revelation from God, and announced: "There is no Hindu or Muslim, so whose path shall I follow? I shall follow the path of God."

Disillusioned about the existing religions of India at that time, and by the social divisiveness he saw in all religions, Guru Nanak considered that, from the divine perspective, religious labels—such as Hindu or Muslim—were irrelevant. In their place, Guru Nanak offered an alternative, all-embracing faith based on devotion to God rather than the observance of ritual and reverence for individual holy men.

A legacy of equality

Guru Nanak's teachings were consolidated by subsequent Sikh gurus, and when the 10th guru, Guru Gobind Singh, established the Khalsa order, into which most Sikhs are initiated (p.299), he made the order open to everyone. Controversially, for the time, he denounced the caste system and gender discrimination. He also abolished the priesthood in Sikhism, which he felt had become corrupt and self-serving—guilty of the very vices the faith seeks to overcome. Instead, he appointed custodians of the holy book, the Guru Granth Sahib, at each temple, while also permitting all Sikhs, male or female, to read from it in worship at the gurdwara or at home.

Both Sikhs and non-Sikh visitors are welcome to join in communal meals at Sikh temples. Everyone, whatever their race, class, or sex, sits on the floor to eat, to emphasize the equality of all.

See also: God-consciousness 122–23 ▪ Gender and the covenant 199 ▪ The Sikh code of conduct 296–301 ▪ Cao Đài aims to unify all faiths 316

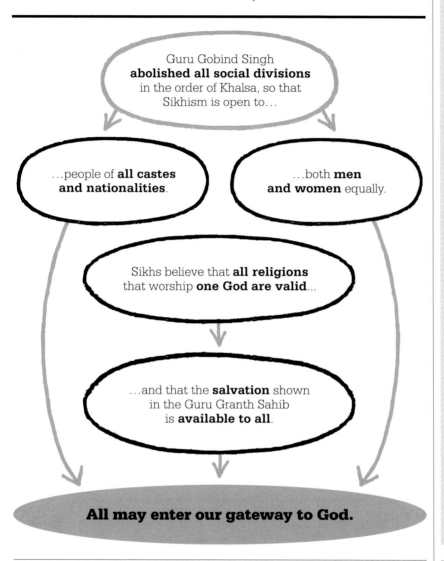

Guru Gobind Singh **abolished all social divisions** in the order of Khalsa, so that Sikhism is open to…

…people of **all castes and nationalities**.

…both **men and women** equally.

Sikhs believe that **all religions** that worship **one God are valid**…

…and that the **salvation** shown in the Guru Granth Sahib is **available to all**.

All may enter our gateway to God.

The Guru Granth Sahib

The central religious text of Sikhism is a collection of hymns and verses compiled and written by the succession of 10 Sikh gurus, the leaders of the faith, who lived between 1469 and 1708. This collection consists of some 1,430 pages, or *angs*, of their teachings. The first version of the book, known as the Adi Granth, was compiled by the fifth guru, Guru Arjan Dev, from the sayings and writings of his predecessors, and was added to by subsequent gurus. Guru Gobind Singh, the 10th guru, completed the text and nominated it, rather than another human leader, as his successor, calling it "the embodiment of the gurus," and giving it the title Guru Granth Sahib. Unlike its predecessors, this "11th guru" is available for all to consult, and a copy takes a place of pride in every gurdwara, or Sikh temple. Originally written in a specially devised script, Gurmukhi, in a mixture of dialects collectively known as Sant Bhasha, it has since been translated into several modern languages.

Sikhs do not need to perform any particular rituals or undertake pilgrimages, but they are expected to show their devotion to God in their everyday lives. It is not even a requirement to worship at the gurdwara. These temples serve as social centers and exemplify the notion of community spirit that is such an important component of Sikhism. For Sikhs, anyone who believes in and worships one God follows the same path as Sikhism, and their faith deserves respect. Sikhs regard an individual's religion to be largely the result of the culture in which he or she was brought up: Hindus, Muslims, Christians, and Sikhs have a common inspiration, but the particular form this takes is determined by society. For this reason, Sikhs do not attempt to convert people of other faiths. ▪

All beings and creatures are His; He belongs to all.
Guru Granth Sahib

MESSAGES TO AND FROM HOME
THE AFRICAN ROOTS OF SANTERIA

IN CONTEXT

KEY BELIEVERS
Displaced Yoruba people from western Africa

WHEN AND WHERE
From 16th century, Cuba

BEFORE
From prehistory African tribal mythologies incorporate strong links to the land and to the ancestors.

9th–6th centuries BCE The people of the kingdom of Judah maintain their faith while in exile in Assyria, Babylon, and Egypt.

15th–19th centuries European colonial conquests are accompanied by forcible conversions to Christianity.

AFTER
19th century The slave trade is abolished; Creole religions are practiced more openly in the Caribbean and Brazil.

1970s Santeria becomes established in the US.

Santeria is a religion that combines traditional western African religion with Catholicism. This blended, or syncretic, religion developed in Cuba between the 16th and 18th centuries. During this period, huge numbers of people from western Africa were enslaved and taken to work on the Caribbean plantations that were established following the Spanish colonization of the islands. The Yoruba people of present-day Nigeria and Benin formed the majority of those taken to the Cuban sugar plantations. These slaves came from the well-established Oyo Empire, which had a sophisticated religious tradition. This was outlawed by the Spanish.

Slaves taken from western Africa to the Caribbean

↓

...took their religion with them and **incorporated it into the Christianity** of their owners, initially to conceal its nature from them.

↓

However, they **retained the elements of communication** with their gods, spirits, and ancestors in Africa through trances and possession.

↓

In this way, believers continued to **transmit messages to and from home**.

See also: The power of the shaman 26–31 ▪ The spirits of the dead live on 36–37 ▪ Living the Way of the Gods 82–85 ▪ Ras Tafari is our Savior 314–15

A Santeria altar often blends imagery from both Catholicism and western African beliefs, with particular saints identified with particular African deities, or orishas.

However, the Yoruba slaves soon learned to conceal the worship of their African gods by appearing to practice Catholicism. Unaware of this, the Spanish slave-owners dismissed the religious practices of their slaves as merely a simplistic form of Christian worship, and sarcastically dubbed it Santeria, the "way of the saints" (a term now viewed as pejorative by some).

The Rule of Osha

The Yoruba religion, known as Regla de Ocha or "Rule of Osha" (Regla Lucumí, in the Yoruba language), already had similarities to Catholicism. The Yoruba believe in one God, Olorun (or Olodumare), the source of all spiritual energy—analogous to Catholic worship of the one God. They also believe in a lesser pantheon of spirits known as orishas, each with an area of responsibility—akin to Catholic reverence of the saints. So, while ostensibly praying to a Catholic

saint, the Yoruba slaves would communicate with an orisha with similar characteristics. This hybrid religion allowed the Yoruba to maintain contact with their culture and a link with their homeland, and, they believed, to communicate with their ancestors through the spirits.

Hybrid elements of the religion include the adoption of numerous Spanish words and the addition of images of Catholic saints alongside the traditional portrayals of orishas, and in some cases, the retention of the traditional framework of a Catholic service. Rituals are presided over by a priest or *santeros*. Hymns are replaced with drumming and chanting, with the aim of inducing a trance state. While in a trance, the believer may become possessed by spirits conveying messages from their ancestral home. The drums convey messages to the orisha.

Although there is a strong element of the supernatural and magic in Santeria, and some ceremonies call for ritual sacrifice (usually of a chicken), believers are insistent that black magic is not involved. They maintain that their beliefs are distinct from other syncretic religions of the Caribbean, such as Haitian voodoo.

The relationship between Santeria and Catholicism still exists today, although the need for secrecy no longer remains. Adherents of Santeria are often baptized in the Catholic faith and practice separate ceremonies for the saints and orishas. ▪

Hybrid religions

Santeria is just one of many Creole religions—hybrids of African and European faiths—that had their origins in slavery. Yoruba (the dominant culture of the area plundered by slave traders in western Africa) figures largely in many Creole religions: Candomblé in Brazil, Santeria in Cuba, and Orisha-Shango in Trinidad and Tobago. However, other African peoples, including the Igbo from Nigeria, added their cultures to the mix, in religions such as Umbanda and Obeah. Perhaps the best-known African-European faith emerged in Haiti, where French, rather than Spanish, Catholicism was incorporated into African *vodun* beliefs as voodoo. This also made its way into the southern United States. The religions of the African diaspora gained some political significance after the abolition of slavery, especially as Pan-African and black civil rights movements grew in the 20th century, giving rise to another hybrid religion in Jamaica: the Rastafari movement (pp.314–15).

I humble myself before the mysteries of Eshu-Elegba. You are the messenger of Olodumare and Orisha and the Ancestors.
Prayer to the orisha Eshu

ASK YOURSELF: "WHAT WOULD JESUS DO?"

FOLLOWING THE EXAMPLE OF CHRIST

IN CONTEXT

KEY FIGURES
Joseph Smith, Jr.,
Brigham Young

WHEN AND WHERE
1830, US

BEFORE
1790–mid-19th century The Second Great Awakening, a Protestant revival movement in the United States, leads to the formation of several Adventist churches, based on belief in the imminent Second Coming of Christ.

AFTER
Late 19th century In the US, the Bible Student Movement advocates a return to the earliest teachings of the Christian Church. This movement will become the Jehovah's Witnesses.

1926 Following what is claimed to be a new phase of revelations from God, the Cao Đài religion is founded, with Jesus as one of its saints.

After the **ascension** of Jesus and the **martyrdom** of the apostles…

…the original Church **turned away from the Gospel** in the Great Apostasy.

In a series of revelations, **priesthood authority** was **restored** to Joseph Smith, Jr. and his successors, the Latter-day Saints…

…who take as **their model Jesus** himself, rather than the dogma of any existing church.

Ask yourself: "What would Jesus do?"

In reaction to the rationalism of the Enlightenment that spread from Europe to the American colonies in the 18th century, a Christian revival occurred in the United States at the beginning of the 19th century. Many breakaway Christian groups were formed at this time. They rejected the traditions of the established church and incorporated charismatic elements of the faith—"gifts of the spirit," such as prophecy and visions. There was also a move to restore Christianity to the principles of the New Testament.

It was against this background that Joseph Smith, Jr. had the first of a series of visions, in which God

Mormonism is the pure doctrine of Jesus Christ, of which I myself am not ashamed.
Joseph Smith

and Jesus Christ came to tell him that he had been chosen to restore the true Church. How the Church of Christ would differ from the other restorationist groups was explained when Smith said an angel had guided him to find and translate a text, the Book of Mormon, which described how God had led his followers to the New World. He was told of the Great Apostasy that followed the ascension of Christ and the martyrdom of the Apostles,

when the original Christian Church became corrupted and diluted. God conferred on Smith the authority to reestablish the Christian Church.

Modern-day prophets
Smith, and his successors, are considered by their followers to be modern-day prophets, seers, and revelators, who received guidance from God in the form of revelations from Jesus Christ. Church members believe that, rather than following the doctrine of any existing Church, they are living as Christ has taught them, as "latter-day saints"—a term adopted by Smith when he established the Church of Jesus Christ of Latter-day Saints, although the movement is more commonly called Mormonism. In addition to taking their lead from revelations, Latter-day Saints believe they should follow Jesus's example. The most important consideration for them is, "What would Jesus do?"

After Joseph Smith's death, the movement divided into several branches, with the majority following Brigham Young (1801–1877), who set

A Mormon family prays together in their living room during their family home evening. These evenings are a Mormon tradition intended to reinforce and solidify family ties.

up a Mormon community in Utah. They hold to a strict moral code, The Word of Wisdom, avoiding alcohol, tobacco, coffee, tea, and extramarital sexual activity. Marriage is among the rituals they believe necessary for salvation, as are baptism and confirmation. Early Mormons practiced polygamy, but this was renounced by the mainstream movement in 1890. ▪

Joseph Smith, Jr.

The son of tenant farmers, Joseph Smith, Jr. was born in 1805 in Vermont, but in 1820 moved with his family to western New York, a center of the Protestant revival movement known as the Second Great Awakening. Confused as to which of the numerous denominations he should follow, he prayed for guidance and had a vision in which God the Father and Jesus appeared to tell him all the Churches had "turned aside from the gospel." He later said he had been visited by the angel Moroni, who told him of scriptures inscribed on golden plates, written

by ancient inhabitants of America. With divine guidance, Smith supposedly located and translated the scriptures, the Book of Mormon, and published it in 1830, the year that he also founded his Church.

Persecuted for his heretical beliefs, he moved around frequently, establishing Latter-day Saint communities in Ohio and Missouri before finally settling in Nauvoo, Illinois. He was arrested for inciting a riot in Carthage, Illinois, in 1844, but was killed by an angry mob before he could stand trial.

WE SHALL KNOW HIM THROUGH HIS MESSENGERS
THE REVELATION OF BAHA'I

IN CONTEXT

KEY FIGURE
Baha'u'llah (Mirza Husayn-'Ali Nuri)

WHEN AND WHERE
From 1863, Persia

BEFORE
7th century Muhammad is hailed as God's final prophet, bearing the message of Islam. After his death, leadership disputes cause a split between Shi'a and Sunni Muslims.

1501 Shah Ismail I establishes the Safavid dynasty, ruling over a united Persia whose state religion is Shi'a Islam.

1844 Siyyid 'Ali Muhammad Shirazi claims he is the Mahdi, the redeemer predicted in Shi'a Islam. He adopts the title Bab (Gate), and founds a new religion to succeed Islam.

AFTER
1921 In Lahore (modern Pakistan), Mirza Ghulam Ahmad claims to bring a new message from God for Islam.

Different religions have been established in various places and at various times in history.

These religions were **founded by divine messengers** such as Moses, Buddha, Jesus, and Muhammad.

Each of these divine messengers **revealed God** in a way that suited the time and place…

…and **prophesied messengers** yet to come.

…but will be followed by other divine messengers in a **continuing and progressive revelation**.

Baha'u'llah is the most recent of these messengers, revealing **religious truth for modern society**…

We shall know him through his messengers.

See also: The promise of a new age 178–81 ▪ The Prophet and the origins of Islam 252–53 ▪ The emergence of Shi'a Islam 270–71 ▪ Cao Đài aims to unify all faiths 316 ▪ A faith open to all beliefs 321

In Shi'a Islam, most followers believe that the Mahdi, the descendant of Muhammad who will come to restore the religion of God, is Muhammad al-Mahdi, the Twelfth Imam, who lived on earth until 941. His return to bring peace and justice to the world is a cornerstone of the branch of Shi'a known as the Twelvers (p.271). This belief was especially prevalent in 19th-century Persia, where Shi'a Islam had for centuries been the state religion. It was here, in 1844, that Siyyid 'Ali Muhammad Shirazi (1819–50) declared that he was the Bab (Gate), and had come to establish a faith in readiness for the coming of "He whom God shall make manifest."

The Islamic authorities persecuted his followers, known as Babis, for their beliefs. Among them was Mirza Husayn 'Ali Nuri, who came to believe he was the one whose coming had been predicted by the Bab. He adopted the title Baha'u'llah (Glory of God) in 1863, proclaiming that he was a messenger of God, the latest in a line of such messengers including Moses, Buddha, Jesus, and Muhammad. Throughout history, he explained, religions have been established by these messengers, with each one in turn bringing the religious truth in a manner that was well-suited to the time and place. Each messenger has also prophesied the coming of another messenger, in a progressive revelation, a continual unfolding of the message of God.

The nature of the message

In his writings, Baha'u'llah explains that God has two reasons for sending these prophets to the world: "The first is to liberate the children of men from the darkness of ignorance, and guide them to the light of true understanding. The second is to ensure the peace and tranquillity of mankind, and provide all the means by which they can be established."

Baha'u'llah's own mission, as the messenger prophesied by previous prophets, was to bring a message that was relevant to the modern world, one of worldwide

> All peoples and nations are of one family, the children of one Father, and should be to one another as brothers and sisters
> **Baha'u'llah**

peace, unity, and justice. Central to his message was the concept of unity of religion, acceptance of the validity of all the world's major religions, and respect for their prophets as messengers of God. With this teaching he hoped to avoid what had before now become a source of religious conflict, while promoting the unity of humankind and rejecting inequality, prejudice, and oppression. ▪

Baha'u'llah

The founder of the Baha'i faith was born Mirza Husayn 'Ali Nuri in Tehran, Persia, in 1817, but is better known by his adopted title of Baha'u'llah ("Glory of God"). He was brought up as a Muslim, but became one of the first followers of the Bab, Siyyid 'Ali Muhammad Shirazi. In the 1850s, he came to believe that he was the fulfillment of the Bab's prophecies. He was imprisoned for his heretical beliefs, then banished to Baghdad and later to Constantinople (modern Istanbul), where, in 1863, he declared himself as Baha'u'llah, God's latest messenger on earth.

Most of the Babis believed his claims, and, as his followers, became known as Baha'is. In 1868, Baha'u'llah again fell foul of the Ottoman authorities, and was sent to a penal colony in 'Akka, in Palestine. He was gradually permitted greater freedom, but nevertheless remained a prisoner in 'Akka until his death in 1892.

Followers of the Baha'i faith consider it more respectful to depict Baha'u'llah not with an image, but with a stylized version of his name in Arabic calligraphy, as shown left.

BRUSH AWAY THE DUST OF SIN
TENRIKYO AND THE JOYOUS LIFE

IN CONTEXT

KEY FIGURE
Nakayama Miki

WHEN AND WHERE
From 1838, Japan

BEFORE
6th century Buddhism spreads to Japan, bringing with it ideas of reincarnation derived from Hinduism.

8th century In response to increasing Buddhist influence, traditional Japanese beliefs in gods and spirits are codified in the Kojiki and the Nihon Shoki, the first texts of Shinto.

AFTER
Late 19th century Tenrikyo believers attach themselves to a Buddhist sect to avoid persecution, but Tenrikyo is forcibly incorporated into the official state religion of Shinto.

1945 After World War II, State Shinto is disestablished and Tenrikyo is classified as a separate religion.

enrikyo is one of the so-called Japanese New Religions that appeared in the 19th century and were regarded as sects of Shinto. Tenrikyo was founded by a peasant woman, Nakayama Miki, following revelations to her from Tenri-O-no-Mikoto, God the Parent, during a Buddhist exorcism ritual in 1838. She recorded the substance of these revelations in the Ofudesaki ("Tip of the Writing Brush"), Tenrikyo's sacred text, and became known to her followers as Oyasama ("the Parent") or the Shrine of God.

Tenrikyo followers believe in a single, benevolent God, who wishes humans to find happiness in their lives on earth. A major part of Tenrikyo practice is to follow the Joyous Life, avoiding what are seen as negative tendencies. What other religions consider as sins, Tenrikyo describes as mental dust that needs to be swept away by *hinokishin*—the performing of acts of kindness and charity. Believers identify eight mental dusts that need to be swept away

> Throughout the world, God is the broom for the sweeping of the innermost heart.
> **The Ofudesaki**

in order to follow the joyous life successfully: *oshii* (miserliness), *huoshii* (covetousness), *nikui* (hatred), *kawai* (self-love), *urami* (grudge-bearing), *haradachi* (anger), *yoku* (greed), and *koman* (arrogance). *Hinokishin* is also practiced to give thanks to Tenri-O-no-Mikoto for allowing believers to borrow their bodies in a cycle of reincarnation based on the notion of *kashimono-karimono* ("a thing lent, a thing borrowed"). ∎

See also: Living the Way of the Gods 82–85 ▪ Escape from the eternal cycle 136–43 ▪ Let kindness and compassion rule 146–47

THESE GIFTS MUST BE MEANT FOR US

CARGO CULTS OF THE PACIFIC ISLANDS

IN CONTEXT

KEY BELIEVERS
Pacific islanders

WHEN AND WHERE
Late 19th century, Pacific

BEFORE
Precolonial times Tribes
in Melanesia, Micronesia, and
New Guinea hold a variety
of beliefs involving ancestral
spirits as well as deities.

1790s The first Christian
missionaries arrive in the
Pacific islands.

AFTER
1945 The term cargo cult
is coined in the colonial news
magazine *Pacific Islands
Monthly*, and is popularized
by anthropologist Lucy Mair.

1950s Some Tanna islanders
in Vanuatu start to worship
Prince Philip, husband of
Britain's Queen Elizabeth II,
believing him to be John
Frum's brother, who "married
a powerful lady overseas."

Western trade and colonialism during the 19th century brought modern goods in abundance to the islands of the Pacific and, despite the work of Christian missionaries, this had an unexpected impact on indigenous belief systems. Islanders came to believe that this material wealth, the cargo of the Western traders, was of supernatural origin, and had been sent to them as a gift from their ancestral spirits, but had been seized by the white men.

Followers of the John Frum cult figure "drill" with model weapons to attract well-stocked military vessels. Some say the name "John Frum" was originally "John From" America.

They developed the idea of a golden age to come, when—by propitiating their ancestors and deities with religious rites—the cargo would be restored to them, and the Westerners would be driven out of their lands.

These cults sprang up in parts of Melanesia and New Guinea, and proliferated in the 1930s as air transport increased. Their spread accelerated during World War II, when the islands were used as bases by American and Japanese forces, bringing in large quantities of equipment and supplies. The cult figure John Frum, revered on the island of Tanna in Vanuatu, is often depicted as an American serviceman. As well as developing special religious ceremonies that frequently mimicked military drills, with flags and uniforms, cult followers built wharves, landing strips, and sometimes even life-size models of aircraft to attract the bringers of goods.

Cargo cults persist in some remote areas of the Pacific, but have been largely superseded as Western influence has spread. ■

See also: Making sense of the world 20–23 ▪ Social holiness and evangelicalism 239 ▪ The African roots of Santeria 304–305

THE END OF THE WORLD IS NIGH

AWAITING THE DAY OF JUDGMENT

The Jehovah's Witnesses emerged from the Bible Student movement in the United States in the 1870s. They see their faith as a return to the original concepts of 1st-century Christianity, and refer to this early interpretation of the Bible as "the Truth." The group believes that all other religions, and all forms of present-day government, are controlled by Satan, and face complete destruction in the battle at Armageddon with Satan, when only true Christians—Jehovah's Witnesses—will be spared.

According to the movement, the present world era is nearing its end, having entered its "last days" in October 1914. This was first thought to be the beginning of the battle at Armageddon, but is now accepted as the time when God, known as Jehovah, entrusted the

In 1914, Jesus Christ began his **rule of God's heaven** and **expelled Satan** to earth…

…where he has **corrupted** the world and **fights** the true believers, **Jehovah's Witnesses**.

God will establish his **kingdom on earth** after destroying the world ruled by **Satan**.

The world is now in its **last days** before the battle at Armageddon.

The end of the world is nigh.

See also: The battle between good and evil 60–65 ▪ The end of the world as we know it 86–87 ▪ Jesus's message to the world 204–207 ▪ A divine trinity 212–19 ▪ Entering into the faith 224–27 ▪ The ultimate reward for the righteous 279

Judgment Day is near, according to Jehovah's Witnesses, who believe that those not of their faith can soon expect a reckoning, as depicted here in John Martin's *The Great Day of His Wrath*.

rule of the Kingdom of Heaven to Jesus Christ, who then expelled Satan to earth. During this final phase, Jesus, aided by a "faithful and discreet slave" in the Governing Body of Jehovah's Witnesses, will maintain his invisible rule over earth. For Jehovah's Witnesses there is no literal second coming; rather, Jesus will at some unknown point begin the battle against Satan, after which God will extend the Kingdom of Heaven, creating an earthly paradise under Christ's Millennial Reign. They believe Christ to be God's representative ruler and not part of a Trinity. Similarly, the Holy Spirit is not part of the deity, but manifests in forces such as gravity.

During the thousand-year reign of Christ on earth—a prolonged judgment day—the dead will be resurrected and judged by Jesus, facing a final test when Satan is released into the world. Only true believers, a select 144,000 Jehovah's Witnesses, will remain when Jesus passes the rule of the Kingdom back to God.

Because of their dismissal of other faiths (even other Christian denominations) as corrupted by Satan, Jehovah's Witnesses have been rejected by most other religions. Public opinion has been adversely affected by their insistent door-to-door evangelizing and the selling of their publications *The Watchtower* and *Awake!*—which nevertheless command high circulation figures worldwide. But their rejection of "corrupt" government has had surprising results. Many Jehovah's Witnesses who would not fight for the Nazis ended up in concentration camps. Elsewhere, their refusal to engage in the wars of secular governments helped to bring about changes to the laws of conscientious objection, and their refusal to compromise their beliefs has led to many court cases and influenced civil rights legislation in several countries. ▪

Joseph Franklin Rutherford

Born in rural Missouri in 1869, Joseph Rutherford came from a poor farming family and was raised as a Baptist, but became disillusioned with religion after he left home. He studied law and had a successful legal career in Missouri and New York. His interest in religion was renewed in the 1890s by the work of Charles Taze Russell, founder of the Bible Student movement, and he became actively involved with the Watch Tower Society, becoming its second president in 1917, after Russell's death. Dramatic changes were made to the organization under his leadership, and the doctrines of present-day Jehovah's Witnesses were established. He remained president of the Society, increasing its membership by introducing door-to-door evangelizing, among other things, until his death from cancer in 1942.

The Lord declares he has entrusted his people with the privilege and obligation of telling his message.
The Watchtower

THE LION OF JUDAH HAS ARISEN

RAS TAFARI IS OUR SAVIOR

IN CONTEXT

KEY FIGURE
Haile Selassie

WHEN AND WHERE
From 1930s, Jamaica

BEFORE
18th–19th century Creole, or syncretic, religions arise among slave communities, fusing African beliefs with the Christian faith that slaves are forced to adopt by their masters.

1920s Written in Anguilla, the Holy Piby identifies Ethiopians as God's chosen people, and Marcus Garvey as a prophet; it becomes an influential Rastafari text.

AFTER
Mid-20th century In the US, the Nation of Islam movement proclaims W. Fard Muhammad to be the messiah predicted by both Judaism and Islam. While fighting for African–American and black Muslim rights, the movement becomes heavily politicized.

The black peoples of Africa have been **exploited for centuries** by "Babylon," the white men…

↓

…but it was prophesied that a **savior** from the family of Judah would come to "Zion" (Africa) to **free them from oppression**.

↓

The savior appeared in the form of **Ras Tafari**, God's chosen king on earth…

↓

…who became **Emperor Haile Selassie I of Ethiopia**, the Holy Land for Rastafarians.

↓

The Lion of Judah has arisen.

Unlike the Creole religions that developed among the black slaves in the Caribbean (pp.304–305), Rastafari has little to do with traditional African religions. Instead, the movement is largely based on the Christian Bible. It nevertheless emphasizes its binding links to Africa.

Rastafari (followers dislike the term Rastafarianism, and indeed all "isms") is as much a political or social movement as a religious faith. It emerged during a period of increasing awareness of the "African-ness" of the black population of the New World. Pan-Africanism—the movement to unite and inspire people of African descent—was also on the rise. This movement had begun in the 19th century, but gained momentum in the 1920s and 1930s, particularly through the work of the political activist Marcus Garvey (1887–1940). He was especially influential in his native Jamaica, which at that time was still under British rule.

Garvey's denunciation of oppression and exploitation chimed with many Jamaicans, especially as large numbers lived in poverty. The vast majority of

See also: Jesus's message to the world 204–207 ▪ Social holiness and evangelicalism 239 ▪ The African roots of Santeria 304–305 ▪ The Nation of Islam 339

Jamaicans were descended from African slaves, and had been forced to adopt the British slave-owners' mainly Protestant Christianity, while their own African-based religious beliefs and traditions had been largely quashed. What evolved was therefore a uniquely black Jamaican interpretation of

The Rastafari flag with its imperial lion is waved behind Damian "Jr. Gong" Marley, son of reggae legend Bob Marley.

the Christian scriptures, rather than a synthesis of African and Christian beliefs.

A savior in Zion
Inspired by black nationalism and Pan-Africanism, some Jamaicans claimed that much of the Bible had been changed by white men as part of their ongoing oppression of Africa and Africans. They interpreted the Old Testament's Zion as Africa, and believed that a savior would come to rescue African peoples from oppression by "Babylon"—the corrupt Europeans. The savior was prophesied to come to Zion from the family of Judah. When Ras Tafari came to the throne of Ethiopia with the dynastic title "His Imperial Majesty Haile Selassie I, Conquering Lion of the Tribe of Judah, Elect of God and King of the Kings of Ethiopia," the prophesy was seen as fulfilled, and the Rastafari movement was born. Most Rastafarians

believe Haile Selassie to be the second coming of Jesus, an incarnation of their God, Jah, but some see him as simply God's earthly representative and ruler.

Rastafari spread in the post-World War II years as Caribbean migrants left to seek work in Britain and America. Jamaican culture and music, especially reggae, became very popular in those countries in the 1960s and 1970s, and Rastafari gained a considerable following in its wake. ▪

Many discouraging hours will arise before the rainbow of accomplished goals will appear on the horizon.
Haile Selassie

Haile Selassie

Born Tafari Makonnen, inheriting the title "Ras" (analagous to Duke) as the son of Ethiopian nobility, Haile Selassie became Regent of Ethiopia in 1916. He replaced the heir to the throne, Iyasu, whose links with Islam and general misconduct precluded his becoming head of state. On the death of the Empress Zewditu in 1930, Tafari, a devout member of the Ethiopian Orthodox Church, was crowned Emperor, and took the regnal name of Haile Selassie, "Might of the Trinity." He spent some years in exile in England following Mussolini's invasion of

Ethiopia, returning in 1941 after the British liberation. Although respected around the world, he became increasingly unpopular in his home country, and in 1974 was deposed and imprisoned by members of the armed forces calling themselves the Derg (Committee). Many members of his family and government were imprisoned or executed, and, in August of the following year, it was announced that the ex-Emperor had died of respiratory failure, although there was some controversy around the causes of his death.

ALL RELIGIONS ARE EQUAL
CAO ĐÀI AIMS TO UNIFY ALL FAITHS

IN CONTEXT

KEY FIGURE
Ngô Van Chiêu

WHEN AND WHERE
From 1926, Vietnam

BEFORE
6th century BCE In China, Confucius teaches a philosophy of morality, respect, sincerity, and justice.

3rd century BCE Buddhism, founded in India by Siddhartha Gautama, spreads to China.

1st century CE Jesus, revered as a saint in Cao Đài, promises to return to earth to complete God's purpose for humankind.

6th century Muhammad receives the Qur'an, and says it is a renewal of the message given to Moses and Jesus.

AFTER
1975 The Communist regime in Vietnam proscribes Cao Đài.

1997 Cao Đài is granted formal recognition by the Vietnamese authorities.

I n 1920, a Vietnamese civil servant, Ngô Van Chiêu, stated that during a seance he was contacted by the Supreme Being, who informed him that the time had come to unite all the world's religions into one. Referring to himself as Cao Đài (Supreme Palace or Altar), God explained that in the past, his message had been revealed through prophets in two periods of revelation and salvation, which had given rise to all the world's major religions. He had now chosen, in a third period, to reveal his truth via seance ceremonies. Ngô Van Chiêu, along with others who had received similar revelations, founded the Đài Đao Tam Ky Pho Đo ("Religion of the Third Great Period of Revelation and Salvation"), commonly known as Cao Đài.

Combining elements of several religions, especially Buddhist and Confucian philosophy, Cao Đài reveres the prophets of all the major world faiths, along with more surprising figures such as Joan of Arc, Shakespeare, Victor Hugo, and Sun Yat-sen. In unifying the world's faiths and removing the religious differences that lead to aggression, Cao Đài hopes to achieve world peace. Despite this ambition, the movement became associated in the mid-20th century with the Vietnamese nationalist movement, and was involved in political and military resistance to French colonialism and, later, Communism. ∎

Because of the very multiplicity of religions, humanity does not always live in harmony. That is why I decided to unite all…into one.
God's message to Ngô van Chiêu

See also: God-consciousness 122–23 ∎ Jesus's message to the world 204–207 ∎ The origins of Ahmadiyya 284–85 ∎ The revelation of Baha'i 308–309

WE HAVE FORGOTTEN OUR TRUE NATURE
CLEARING THE MIND WITH SCIENTOLOGY

IN CONTEXT

KEY FIGURE
L. Ron Hubbard

WHEN AND WHERE
From 1952, US

BEFORE
1950 L. Ron Hubbard sets up the Hubbard Dianetic Research Foundation and publishes an article on Dianetics in the sci-fi magazine *Astounding Science Fiction*, followed by his book *Dianetics: The Modern Science of Mental Health*.

AFTER
1982 A Religious Technology Center is established to oversee Scientology technology; some members see this as against original Scientology principles and form a breakaway group, which they call the Free Zone.

1993 Scientology is formally recognized as a religion in the US.

Scientology as a religious philosophy evolved from the work done by science-fiction author L. Ron Hubbard in the 1930s and 1940s on Dianetics. This was a self-help system based on elements of psychotherapy with an emphasis on dealing with past traumatic experiences to achieve spiritual rehabilitation. This process of counseling, known as auditing, is at the heart of Scientology.

Followers of Scientology believe that man's true spiritual nature is embodied in an eternal spirit known as the Thetan, which has been reborn continually in human form, and has consequently lost its true nature of spiritual purity. By undergoing one-to-one auditing, using an E-meter (an instrument for detecting electric current, designed by Hubbard), practitioners can free their unconscious minds of images of trauma, known as engrams, and return to the state of Clear—their true spiritual identity. Progressing through various levels of auditing, they eventually reach the level of

Scientology headquarters in Berlin, Germany, displays the eight-pointed cross, representing the eight dynamics of existence that are defined in the movement's theology.

Operating Thetan, and rediscover their original potential. Hubbard was keen to secure celebrity endorsement for Scientology, and this, along with the high cost of one-to-one auditing sessions and study materials, led to accusations that it was a moneymaking cult. After protracted court cases in the US and elsewhere, Scientology now has tax-exempt status as a religion in some parts of the world, but is still not recognized in many countries. ∎

See also: The ultimate reality 102–105 ▪ Escape from the eternal cycle 136–43 ▪ Purging sin in the Unification Church 318

FIND A SINLESS WORLD THROUGH MARRIAGE

PURGING SIN IN THE UNIFICATION CHURCH

IN CONTEXT

KEY FIGURE
Sun Myung Moon

WHEN AND WHERE
From 1954, South Korea

BEFORE
1st century St. Paul affirms that all humankind inherits sin from the Fall, and also that marriage is a sacred state.

From 2nd century The early Christian Fathers formulate the doctrine of original sin, but dispute whether Adam or Eve was more responsible for it.

4th century St. Jerome uses the example of Jesus to argue that celibacy is the preferred state for a truly holy life.

7th century The notion that Mary, mother of Jesus, was herself conceived free from original sin gains ground.

16th century Martin Luther reasserts that all humans are born sinful, with the exception of Mary, mother of Jesus.

The Holy Spirit Association for the Unification of World Christianity, commonly known as the Unification Church, or more pejoratively as the Moonies, was founded by Sun Myung Moon in Seoul, South Korea, in 1954. His family had converted from Confucianism to Christianity when he was ten years old, and, as a teenager, Moon had a vision of Jesus asking him to complete his mission of redemption.

To do this, Moon established the Unification Church, which he saw as a Christian denomination based on the Bible and on his own book the *Divine Principle*, but offering a radically different interpretation of the Christian story of the Fall that led to original sin: Moon believed that Eve's spiritual relationship with Satan before her sexual one with Adam led to all of her progeny being born with defective, sinful natures, and, crucially, that Jesus came to rectify this, but was crucified before he had the opportunity to marry—and therefore he only achieved a partial redemption.

Wedding Blessing ceremonies, often with hundreds of couples participating, are not legal marriages, but are believed to free the couple's offspring from original sin.

Children born without sin

The path to complete redemption for humankind, Moon maintained, would begin with his own marriage to Hak Ja Han in 1960, and be followed by the mass weddings and rededications that became characteristic of the Unification Church and are its core ceremonies. Children of these marriages, in which premarital and extramarital sex are prohibited, would then be born without fallen natures, thus heralding the advent of a sinless world. ∎

See also: The battle between good and evil 60–65 ▪ Wisdom lies with the superior man 72–77 ▪ Augustine and free will 220–21

SPIRITS REST BETWEEN LIVES IN SUMMERLAND
WICCA AND THE OTHERWORLD

IN CONTEXT

KEY FIGURE
Gerald Gardner

WHERE AND WHEN
From 1950s, UK

BEFORE
Pre-Christian era Celtic and Norse mythologies include the idea of otherworlds such as Asgard, where the Norse heaven Valhalla is situated.

19th century Spiritualists and Theosophists coin the name Summerland to describe an astral plane where virtuous souls rest in bliss.

1920s Anthropologist Margaret Murray publishes work on the Christian persecution of witches in history, identifying witchcraft as a pagan religion separate from black magic cults.

AFTER
1970s In the US, feminist politics is incorporated into Wicca by practitioners of Dianic Witchcraft.

Probably the best known of the 20th-century neopagan (new pagan) religions, Wicca originated in England, and was popularized by a retired civil servant, Gerald Gardner, in the 1950s. Although he referred to the religion as witchcraft, and its adherents as the Wica, the version he founded and its various subsequent branches or traditions are today known as Wicca.

Wiccan beliefs are centered on the principles of masculine and feminine, as embodied in the complementary Horned God and Moon Goddess, and the existence of an otherworld known as Summerland where souls spend the afterlife. Many branches of Wicca also believe in reincarnation, and see Summerland as a resting place for souls between lives, where they can examine their previous life and prepare for the next. These souls are sometimes contacted by Wiccans in magic ceremonies similar to those of spiritualism, involving mediums or ouija boards, but this practice is not universal.

Although Wiccans believe in an afterlife, they emphasize making the most of the present life in nature-based rituals. These include celebrations of the seasons, and rites of passage such as initiation, wiccaning (similar to baptism), and marriage or sexual union.

Because of some apparent resemblances to Satanism (the Horned God, for example), Wicca has often been confused with black magic cults, and has, until recently, suffered prejudice and persecution, especially in Christian countries. ■

I do not remember my past lives clearly; I only wish I did.
Gerald Gardner

See also: Animism in early societies 24–25 ■ Man and the cosmos 48–49 ■ The power of the great goddess 100

NEGATIVE THOUGHTS ARE JUST RAINDROPS IN AN OCEAN OF BLISS
FINDING INNER PEACE THROUGH MEDITATION

IN CONTEXT

KEY FIGURE
Maharishi Mahesh Yogi

WHEN AND WHERE
From 1958, Europe

BEFORE
From 1700 BCE Meditation techniques are found in early Indian Vedic practices.

From 6th century BCE Meditation is practiced in Buddhism in India and Confucianism in China.

19th century European intellectuals discover Eastern philosophy and arouse general interest in Buddhist and Hindu meditation and yoga.

AFTER
1967 The Beatles meet Maharishi Mahesh Yogi in London and visit his ashram in India for TM training.

1976 TM promotes its Siddhi program with the claim that it enables practitioners to levitate.

In 1958, Maharishi Mahesh Yogi traveled to the West to teach Transcendental Meditation (TM), with the original intention of founding a Hindu revival movement. His methods evolved from Hindu mantra meditation techniques, with the similar aim of transcending the confines of physical consciousness to tap into a creative force.

Cultivating inner peace
The practice of TM involves sitting in meditation for 20 minutes, twice a day, using a personal mantra. This is believed to result in improved psychological and physical well-being and increased potential for creativity, allowing the individual to experience "communion with the wellspring of life" and overcome negative thoughts, which become merely "raindrops falling into the ocean of your bliss."

At first, TM initiates were encouraged to give thanks to the Hindu deities for providing the knowledge behind the method and to study the Vedas and the

Maharishi Mahesh Yogi founded TM as the Spiritual Regeneration Movement. Today it is an organized international movement with its headquarters in the Netherlands.

Bhagavad-Gita. Today, proponents of TM offer it as a scientific method for self-development that is open to all. TM techniques have been adopted not only by individuals, but also by business institutions, and even in some medical practices, posing the question as to whether it should be considered as religion, or simply a form of therapy based on traditional Indian techniques. ∎

See also: Physical and mental discipline 112–13 ▪ Zen insights that go beyond words 160–63 ▪ Life-energy cultivation in Falun Dafa 323

WHAT'S TRUE FOR ME IS THE TRUTH

A FAITH OPEN TO ALL BELIEFS

IN CONTEXT

KEY MOVEMENT
Unitarian Universalism

WHEN AND WHERE
**From 1961, US
and Canada**

BEFORE
6th century BCE Confucius asserts that virtue is not sent from heaven, but can be cultivated in the self.

1st century CE Angering the Jews, who consider themselves the chosen people, Jesus asserts that God's kingdom is open to all who accept him.

16th century In Protestant Christianity, the authority of Rome is replaced by spiritual self-examination.

19th century The Baha'i Faith emerges as one of the first universalist new religions, open to all.

20th century Cao Đài is founded on the principle that all religions are equal.

The Unitarian Universalist Association (UUA) was formed in 1961 by the merger of two movements founded in the 19th century: the Universalist Church of America and the American Unitarian Association. Although it emerged from a largely Christian tradition, and some members have beliefs that are Christian in nature, the UUA aims to be a "non-creedal, non-doctrinal religion which affirms the individual's freedom of belief." Members acknowledge the need for a spiritual and religious dimension to life and believe individuals can learn from all the world's religions. They place more emphasis on a humanist search for truth and meaning in this life than on belief in a supreme being and salvation in an afterlife. Some followers are in fact agnostic or even atheist.

For the Unitarian Universalist, personal experience, conscience, and reason form the basis for religious faith; the opinions and beliefs of all men and women should therefore be respected.

This notion of respect runs through the UUA philosophy and its "Seven Principles": the inherent worth and dignity of every person; justice, equity, and compassion in human relations; the acceptance of one another and encouragement to spiritual growth; a free, responsible search for truth and meaning; the right of conscience, and the use of the democratic process within congregations and in society at large; the goal of world community; and respect for the interdependent web of all existence. ∎

The freedom of the mind is the beginning of all other freedoms.
Clinton Lee Scott

See also: God-consciousness 122–23 ▪ Why prayer works 246–47 ▪ The revelation of Bahá'i 308–309 ▪ Cao Đài aims to unify all faiths 316

CHANTING HARE KRISHNA CLEANSES THE HEART
DEVOTION TO THE SWEET LORD

IN CONTEXT

KEY FIGURE
A.C. Bhaktivedanta Swami Prabhupada

WHEN AND WHERE
From 1960s, US and western Europe

BEFORE
4th century BCE First evidence of worship of Lord Krishna, a key figure in the Hindu epics, appearing as an avatar of the god Vishnu in the *Mahabharata*.

6th century The bhakti tradition of devotional worship develops in Hinduism.

16th century The Gaudiya Vaishnava movement in India sees Krishna as the original form of God—the source of Vishnu, and not his avatar.

1920 Srila Bhaktisiddhanta Sarasvati Thakura Prabhupada founds the Gaudiya Math, an organization to spread the Gaudiya Vaishnava message around the world.

The Hare Krishna movement or International Society for Krishna Consciousness (ISKCON) is best known for the practice of chanting the Maha Mantra. ISKCON has its roots in the Gaudiya Vaishnava movement in Hinduism, founded by Chaitanya Mahaprabhu (1486–1534), in which believers use devotional practices known as bhakti to please and to develop a loving relationship with the god Krishna, believed to be the Supreme Personality of Godhead.

The Maha Mantra

The mantra is chanted as a means of clearing the mind and cleansing the heart. The repeated use of the holy name enables Krishna consciousness to emerge from the soul, free of the distraction of sensual or physical consciousness. The chant "Hare Krishna, Hare Krishna, Krishna Krishna, Hare Hare, Hare Rama, Hare Rama, Rama Rama, Hare Hare" calls upon the energy of God (Hare), the all-attractive (Krishna), and the highest eternal pleasure (Rama).

Chaitanya taught that by using this mantra anyone, even if born outside the Hindu class system, could achieve Krishna consciousness. In the 1960s, one of Chaitanya's followers, A.C. Bhaktivedanta Swami Prabhupada, traveled to the US and founded ISKCON. Its ideas dovetailed well with the hippie culture and a new interest in Eastern spirituality, and spread to Europe after being popularized by celebrities such as the Beatles. ∎

Lord Krishna provides everything we need to bring the spiritual world into our lives.
A.C. Bhaktivedanta Swami Prabhupada

See also: A rational world 92–99 ∎ Devotion through puja 114–15 ∎ Buddhas and bodhisattvas 152–57 ∎ The performance of ritual and repetition 158–59

THROUGH QIGONG WE ACCESS COSMIC ENERGY
LIFE-ENERGY CULTIVATION IN FALUN DAFA

IN CONTEXT

KEY FIGURE
Li Hongzhi

WHEN AND WHERE
From 1992, China

BEFORE
c.2000 BCE Various movement and breathing exercises are developed for meditation and healing in China, and are later collectively known as qigong.

5th century BCE Qigong exercises are incorporated into the philosophies of Daoism, Confucianism, and Buddhism in China.

1950s The Chinese Communist government adopts qigong techniques as part of a secular health-improvement program.

AFTER
1990s Li Hongzhi moves to the US; the Chinese Communist Party declares Falun Dafa a heretical organization, while in the West, the practice of qigong gains in popularity.

There was a revival of interest in the meditative exercises known as *qigong* (literally "life-energy cultivation") in China in the second half of the 20th century, and while the Communist authorities saw it as a way to improve public health, others found spiritual meaning in the practice. Among them was Li Hongzhi, who founded the Falun Dafa movement (popularly known as Falun Gong) in the early 1990s. He advocated the practice of Falun Gong ("Practice of the Wheel of Law") as not only a means of cultivating life-energy,

Qigong exercises aim to rebuild or rebalance *qi*, the essential life force or energy, through controlled movement, breathing, and mental awareness.

but also a way to put practitioners in touch with the energy of the universe in order to elevate them to higher levels of existence.

In his book *Revolving the Wheel of Law*, Li describes five core exercises to cultivate the mind, body, and spirit. He explains that the Falun (the law wheel) is situated in the lower abdomen, and its rotation—in sympathy with the revolving of the universe —rids the practitioner of negative influences, allowing access to cosmic energy. Complementing these exercises is a philosophy based on the virtues of *zhen-shàn-ren* (truthfulness, benevolence, and forbearance), similar to traditional Confucian, Daoist, and Buddhist ideas, which governs the conduct of Falun Dafa practitioners.

Viewed by some as a new religion, but by others as a practice continuing in the Chinese tradition of cultivation of the mind, body, and spirit, Falun Dafa has attracted many followers in China, where its religious overtones have, however, led to it being outlawed. ■

See also: Aligning the self with the *dao* 66–67 ▪ Physical and mental discipline 112–13 ▪ Escape from the eternal cycle 136–43

DIRECTORY

Despite the apparent prevalence of atheism in the West, the number of people professing some kind of religious belief is increasing worldwide. Christianity and Islam, both proselytizing religions, are now espoused by more than half of the world's total population. Other faiths, such as Hinduism, have also continued to attract followers into the 21st century. Religions spread for all kinds of reasons, such as the missionary activities of their adherents, population increases, and the need to fill "belief vacuums" that occur when primal or other local religions go into decline. So, while many people in Africa have left behind traditional beliefs to embrace new Christian churches, in Europe dissatisfaction with Christianity and interest in ideas from the East has led to a modest growth in Buddhism and other Eastern religions.

MAJOR WORLD FAITHS

NAME	FOUNDED	FOUNDER	GOD	ADHERENTS
Baha'i Faith	Tehran, Persia, 1863	Baha'u'llah	One God, revealed through various religions	5–7 million
Buddhism	Northeastern India, c.520 BCE	Siddhartha Gautama, or Buddha	Theravada is nontheistic; Mahayana involves devotion to the Buddha and bodhisattvas	376 million
Cao Đài	Vietnam, 1926	Ngô Van Chiêu	One God, and reverence for founders of other faiths (including Buddhism, Daoism, and Christianity)	8 million
Christianity	Judea, c.30 CE	Jesus Christ	One God, in the form of the Holy Trinity: Father, Son, and Holy Spirit	2,000 million
Church of Christ (Scientist)	Massachusetts, 1879	Mary Baker Eddy	One God, no Holy Trinity	400,000
Church of Jesus Christ of Latter-day Saints (Mormons)	New York, 1830	Joseph Smith, Jr.	Three separate beings: God the Father; Jesus Christ the Son; and the Holy Spirit	13 million
Confucianism	China, 6th–5th centuries BCE	Confucius	None, although Confucius believed in the Great Ultimate, or *dao*	5–6 million

NAME	FOUNDED	FOUNDER	GOD	ADHERENTS
Church of Scientology	California, 1954	L. Ron Hubbard	None	Not known
Daoism	China, c.550 BCE	Laozi	*Dao* pervades everything	20 million
Falun Dafa	China, 1992	Li Hongzhi	Many gods and spiritual beings	10 million
Hinduism	India, prehistoric	Indigenous	Many deities, all manifestations of one supreme reality	900 million
Islam	Saudi Arabia, 7th century CE	Muhammad, the final Prophet	One God, Allah	1,500 million
Jainism	India, c.550 BCE	Mahavira	No gods, but devotion to some divine beings	4 million
Jehovah's Witnesses	US, 1872	Charles Taze Russell	One God	7 million
Judaism	Israel, 2000 BCE	Abraham, Moses	One God, YHWH	15 million
Rastafari movement	Jamaica, 1930s	Haile Selassie I	One, Jah, incarnate in Jesus and Haile Selassie	1 million
Santeria	Cuba, early 19th century	None; a syncretic faith	More than 400 deities	3–4 million
Shinto	Japan, prehistoric	Indigenous	Many gods and spirits, known as *kami*	3–4 million
Sikhism	Punjab, India, 1500 CE	Guru Nanak	One God	23 million
Tenrikyo	Japan, 1838	Nakayama Miki	God the parent	1 million
Unification Church	South Korea, 1954	Sun Myung Moon	God, the heavenly parent of all humanity	3 million (official figure)
Wicca	Britain, 1950s, based on ancient beliefs	Gerald Gardner	Usually two: the Triple Goddess and the Horned God	1–3 million
Zoroastrianism	Persia, 6th century BCE	Zoroaster	One God (Ahura Mazda), but dualism embraced	200,000

BRANCHES OF HINDUISM

The Hindu faith is thought to have originated in the Indus Valley (Pakistan and northwest India) more than 3,000 years ago. Today, it has almost a billion followers, most of them in India. Hindus all worship a supreme being, though the identity of this deity differs according to sect. There are four principal denominations: Vaishnavites, for whom Vishnu is god; Shaivites, who are devoted to Shiva; Shaktis, who worship the goddess Shakti; and Smartas, who can choose their deity. These and other branches of Hinduism share many beliefs; the Vedas (pp.94–99) are their most sacred texts, and central to Hindu belief is the idea that a person's deeds affect their future in an endless cycle of birth, death, and rebirth.

VAISHNAVISM
c.600 BCE, India

The largest devotional sect within Hinduism, Vaishnavites focus on the worship of Vishnu as the one supreme god. He is seen as the preserver of the universe, a figure unparalleled in his divine benevolence. Vishnu is said to give life to the creator, Brahma, who sits in a lotus blossom at Vishnu's navel, and to sustain and protect all that Brahma creates. As well as inspiring devotion in his own right, he is also worshipped in the form of his avatars, Rama and Krishna. Followers, or Vaishnavas, emphasize devotion over doctrine. Their final goal is freedom from the cycle of birth and death, and spiritual existence in the presence of Vishnu.

SHAIVISM
c.600 BCE, India

One of the four major denominations, of Hinduism, Shaivism holds that Shiva is the supreme god. At the heart of Hinduism is the belief that dualities can be reconciled by a higher divinity. Shaivites (worshippers of Shiva) believe that Shiva embodies this coming together of opposites like no other deity. He embraces many dualities, such as life and death, time and eternity, and destruction and creation, and takes a multiplicity of forms. In one popular depiction he appears as Nataraja, Lord of the Dance. After destroying the universe, he dances its re-creation, carrying both fire (symbolizing destruction) and a drum (the first sound to be made at the beginning of creation). Shaivism encompasses many subsets, and is widespread in India, Nepal, and Sri Lanka today, and its influence is felt as far as Indonesia and Malaysia.

SHAKTISM
5th century CE, India

Shaktism is one of the main devotional branches of Hinduism. According to Hindu belief, Shakti is the divine power that creates and sustains creation; the great goddess (known as Devi or Mahadevi) embodies Shakti and is often referred to by the name Shakti; those who worship her are known as Shaktis (p.104). Although the roots of goddess worship in India extend to the earliest Indus Valley civilizations, Shaktism is thought to have arisen as an organized movement in the 5th century CE. The goddess of Shakti devotion has many names and can take many forms (fearsome, wrathful, benign, and homely), but all point to her as a manifestation of divine power and energy. The sacred texts of the faith are the Vedas, the Shakta Agamas, and the Puranas. Some devotees hope to come closer to the goddess by using yoga, puja, and tantra (pp.112–15).

THE DARSHANAS
2nd–13th centuries CE, India

While the followers of theistic sects, such as Vaishnavism, Shaivism, and Shaktism, worship deities, Hinduism also encompasses six schools, or *darshanas*, which focus on philosophy rather than gods. These schools emphasize the ultimate reality or Brahman, the great self who must be realized to attain liberation from reincarnation.

The *darshanas* follow sacred texts written in early Indian history, and each branch relates to a different sphere. The six *darshanas* are Samkhya (cosmology), Yoga (human nature), Vaisheshika (scientific laws), Nyaya (logic), Mimamsa (ritual), Vedanta (metaphysics and destiny).

SMARTISM
9th century, India

One of the four major sects of Hinduism, Smarta derives its name from the Sanskrit word *smriti*, which refers to a group of sacred Hindu texts. This orthodox Hindu sect draws from Advaita Vedanta philosophy, which propounds the unity of the the self and Brahman, and the teachings of the monk-philosopher Adi Shankara, who is thought to have founded the movement in India in the 9th century. Followers uphold the rules of conduct outlined in the ancient texts, known as the sutras, and worship the supreme god in any form (Shiva, Shakti, Vishnu, Ganesha, or Virya); for this reason, they are considered liberal and nonsectarian.

LINGAYATISM
12th century, southern India

Followers of the Lingayat sect take their name from the linga, emblem of the god Shiva, which devotees wear around their necks. The movement is thought to have been established in southern India in the 12th century by the teacher and religious reformer, Basava. Lingayats are distinctive for their worship of Shiva as the sole deity; in their monotheistic belief, Shiva and the self are one and the same.

They reject the authority of the Brahmin caste and of the sacred texts, the Vedas, promoting a message of social equality and reform. The movement retains a large following in southern India.

SWAMINARAYAN SAMPRADAY
Early 19th century, western India

Swaminarayan Sampraday was founded by the religious reformer Swami Narayan at the beginning of the 19th century, largely as a response to alleged corruption among other Hindu sects. Rituals, laws, observances, and prayers are based on Hindu tradition and the teachings of the movement's founder. By following these moral and spiritual codes in everyday life, the aim is to become an ideal *satsangis* (adherent) and thereafter attain ultimate redemption. The movement has several million followers throughout the world.

BRAHMOISM
1828, Calcutta, India

Brahmoism is a Hindu reform movement that can be traced to the *Brahmo Samaj* (Divine Society), founded by Ram Mohan Roy in Calcutta in 1828, which aimed to reinterpret Hinduism for the modern age. Brahmoism differs from orthodox Hinduism in its adherence to one universal and infinite deity. It rejects the authority of the Vedas (pp.94–99) and, in some cases, belief in avatars (incarnations of deities) and karma (effects of past deeds). One of its key features is social reform. Brahmoism has a following in Bengal, India, and in Bangladesh.

ARYA SAMAJ
1875, India

Arya Samaj is a modern religious and social reform movement founded by Swami Dayananda, a religious leader who sought to reaffirm the supreme authority of the ancient Hindu texts, the Vedas (pp.94–99). He built a number of schools throughout India in the late 19th century designed to promote Vedic culture. Similar projects continue today, including the establishment of colleges and orphanages, and activities that focus on social reform and the alleviation of injustice and hardship. The sect is opposed to the caste system, but has been criticized for intolerance of other faiths. Arya Samaj upholds the doctrines of karma and samsara and the centrality of rituals connected with major events in life. The movement is popular in northern and western India.

SATYAT SAI BABA SOCIETY
1950, India

Sathyanarayana Rajuin (born 1926) is thought to have performed numerous miracles. At age 14 he was stung by a scorpion and went into a trance. On waking he claimed to be a reincarnation of the guru Shirdi Sai Baba, and was henceforth known as Satya Sai Baba. His fame spread in the 1950s due to his miracles; he attracted several million devotees who are guided by four principles: truth, *satya*; duty, *dharma*; peace, *shanti*; and divine love, *prema*. Unlike many Hindus, he did not attach a specific dharma to each social class—all are said to be equal.

BRANCHES OF BUDDHISM

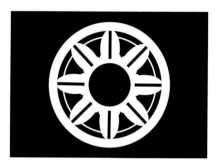

Now followed in many parts of the world, Buddhism originated in northern India over 2,500 years ago with the teachings of Siddhartha Gautama. Buddhism arose within Hinduism, which, at the time, was producing some of its most deeply philosophical and abstract texts, and Buddhism is dominated by ideas, not deities and doctrines. It has one aim—to guide each person on to the path that leads to enlightenment, or spiritual liberation from the worldly self. Buddha himself taught that any means by which this aim could be achieved was valid, and as Buddhism spread geographically, it also diversified to suit local traditions of worship. It now takes several forms, from the ascetic to the highly ritualized.

THERAVADA BUDDHISM
6th century BCE, Northern India

Theravada Buddhism is, with Mahayana Buddhism, one of the two main forms of Buddhism. The oldest surviving branch of Buddhism, it is generally considered the form closest to the dhamma—the original teachings of Buddha. It is practiced today in Thailand, Laos, Cambodia, and Burma. Central to Theravada is the concept of the *sangha* or monastic community. Theravada monks (and sometimes nuns, although they have a lesser status) have few possessions and live in basic accommodation. They follow the Eightfold Path and the Five Precepts (pp.136–43), travel around villages, and teach the dhamma and the scriptures of the Pali Canon. Their most important activity is meditation, which they practice to empty their minds of the self and move closer to nirvana (perfect enlightenment). Although a full-time monastic existence is the ideal, there is also a place in Theravada Buddhism for lay people. They play an important auxiliary role in helping to sustain the monks in their pursuit of an ascetic way of life; for example, supplying them with food in return for blessings and teachings.

MAHAYANA BUDDHISM
3rd–2nd century BCE, Northwestern India

Mahayana Buddhism, which, with Theravada Buddhism, is one of the two main forms of Buddhism, spread eastward from India and is today practiced in large areas of Asia, including China and Korea. Unlike Theravada Buddhists, who believe that total enlightenment represents a departure from this existence, adherents of Mahayana Buddhism believe that Buddha has remained eternally present in this world, guiding others to enlightenment. In this tradition, there is no purpose to enlightenment unless it is used to assist other people on their spiritual path. Mahayana Buddhists believe other people may become buddhas, and revere those who have come close to nirvana as bodhisattvas (wisdom or enlightenment beings), and who possess, in addition to their compassion, six perfections: generosity, morality, patience, vigor, meditation, and wisdom.

PURE LAND BUDDHISM
7th century CE, China

Arising in China out of the Mahayana tradition, Pure Land Buddhism now consists of several sects based in China and Japan. All are centered on devotion to Amitabha, the Buddha of Infinite Light, said to rule a paradise known as the Pure Land. By means of various spiritual techniques focused on Amitabha, the faithful may avoid the cycle of death and rebirth, go to dwell with him in the Pure Land, and thereafter achieve enlightenment. The main Pure Land text is the 1st-century Lotus Sutra, which states that devotion to Amitabha is the one true way.

TIBETAN BUDDHISM
7th century, Tibet

Buddhism was introduced to Tibet by Indian missionaries in around the 7th century CE. Although derived from the Mahayana tradition (see opposite), Tibetan Buddhism evolved quite differently from Buddhism in other countries. It has its own orders of monks and its own religious practices, including devotion to a guru and the use of mandalas, or symbolic diagrams, as meditation aids.

One of Tibetan Buddhism's most distinctive features is its nomination of lamas. These spiritual teachers are the most revered of all the monks, and several are believed to have been spiritual leaders in a previous life. Succession is by reincarnation. When a lama nears the end of his life, he gives a series of clues as to the identity of his next incarnation. His followers then search for the child who best matches these clues.

TANTRIC BUDDHISM
7th century, India

Tantric Buddhism takes its name from the texts known as Tantras, which became powerful tools in the quest for buddhahood. The texts describe how a person can realize their Buddha nature more quickly than in other forms of Buddhism. The techniques involved include the use of rituals, meditation, mandalas, and even magic. The Tantras seek to reconcile all states and emotions, recognizing that all are part of the essential Buddha nature of all people.

Tantric Buddhists revere many buddhas and bodhisattvas (including Amitabha, the Buddha of Infinite Light), seeing each as a manifestation of buddha nature. Today there are schools of Tantric Buddhism in Tibet, India, China, Japan, Nepal, Bhutan, and Mongolia.

ZEN BUDDHISM
12th century, Japan

The Chinese version of Buddhism (Ch'an) took root in Japan in the 6th century, where it became known as Zen. The religion has also had a significant impact in countries influenced by Chinese culture, such as Vietnam, Korea, and Taiwan. Zen Buddhism emphasizes devotion to meditation, the attainment of enlightenment, the value of experience over scripture, and the belief that human beings are identical with the cosmos and share an identity with all that is in it.

For its followers, Zen pervades every aspect of life—the physical, intellectual, and spiritual realms. Composing poetry and creating minimalist rock gardens are considered particularly expressive activities. The best-known schools of Zen are Rinzai and Soto.

NICHIREN BUDDHISM
13th century, Japan

The Japanese monk Nichiren founded this school of Buddhism based on the passionate faith he placed in the supreme spiritual power of the Lotus Sutra, a collection of Buddhist teachings from around the 1st century CE. He encouraged his followers to chant from the text: "I take refuge in the Lotus of the Wonderful Law Sutra." Rejecting all other forms of Buddhism, he believed that only the study of the Lotus Sutra could lead to buddhahood. Many Nichiren Buddhist sects still flourish in Japan and a number of new religious movements take his teachings as their basis, for example, Soka Gakkai (see right).

SOKA GAKKAI
1937, Japan

In 1937, two Japanese reformers, Tsunesaburo Makiguchi and Josei Toda, founded an education society inspired by the teachings of the Japanese Buddhist monk Nichiren. Following Makiguchi's death in 1944, Toda refounded the organization as a religious sect, naming it Soka Gakkai. Like Nichiren Buddhism, it places strong emphasis on the Lotus Sutra, and on the ritual chanting of the words of its title. The movement has attracted some 12 million followers in Japan and around the world, partly as a result of determined recruiting.

TRIRATNA BUDDHIST COMMUNITY
1967, United Kingdom

Formerly the Friends of the Western Buddhist Order (FWBO), the Triratna Buddhist Community was founded by the English-born Buddhist monk Sangharakshita. After studying in India he returned to the UK to form the movement in 1967, with the aim of explaining how Buddhism's basic teachings can be applied to life in the West today. Members are ordained, but may choose a monastic or a lay lifestyle. They commit to a number of core principles: taking Triple Refuge in the Buddha, the dhamma, and the *sangha*; the ideal of buddhahood; and belief in other teachings of the Buddhist tradition. These combine a balance of moral precepts, study, and devotion. The movement has affiliations with groups in Europe, North America, and Australasia.

BRANCHES OF JUDAISM

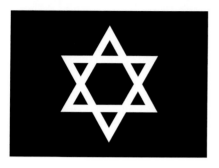

Judaism is the religion of the Jews. Dating back to around 2000 BCE, it is the oldest of the three main monotheistic faiths (the others being Christianity and Islam), all of which have roots in the Middle East. According to Moses, the patriarch to whom God revealed the tablets of the law, the Jews were God's chosen people and received his guidance in the form of the Torah. For much of their history the Jews were exiled from their homeland, so followers of Judaism may be found far beyond the Jewish state of Israel, giving rise to geographical branches of the faith. Jews interpret their faith in different ways, with varying emphasis on the centrality of the Torah and Oral Law to their beliefs and observances.

ORTHODOX JUDAISM
c.13th century BCE, Canaan

Orthodox Judaism sees itself as the continuation of the religious tradition developed in Canaan 3,000 years ago, and practiced by the Jews in the time of Moses. It is not a single movement, but is made up of many branches that share a set of core beliefs. At the heart of the faith is the belief that the Torah —the first five books of the Hebrew Bible—contains the actual words of God, and provides guidance on every aspect of life. From the Middle Ages, Orthodox Judaism was deeply rooted in Central and Eastern Europe. These communities of Jews were known as Ashkenazim, from the name of a patriarch. They were persecuted and frequently ghettoized over the centuries, and millions of Orthodox Jews in Europe died during the Holocaust. After World War II, many Jews traveled to the US, and later to the State of Israel, which was established in 1948, and where Orthodox Judaism is the state religion. More than 50 percent of practicing Jews consider themselves to be Orthodox.

SEPHARDIC JUDAISM
10th century BCE, Iberia

The name Sephardic Judaism refers to the Jews who lived in Iberia (modern-day Portugal and Spain) from as early as the 10th century BCE, and their descendants. Despite some restrictions, Jews coexisted peacefully for centuries with Christians and then Muslims in Iberia. However, following the Christian conquest of Spain in 1492, and of Portugal in 1497, the Sephardim who resisted conversion to Christianity were expelled by Christian decree and fled to North Africa, Italy, France, England, the Netherlands, the Ottoman Empire, and even America. Today there are thriving Sephardic communities in Israel, France, Mexico, the US, and Canada. Many of the fundamental beliefs of Sephardic Judaism are consistent with those of Orthodox Ashkenazi Judaism, though there is more emphasis on mysticism, and some notable differences in culture and practice, including those relating to language, diet, holidays, prayer, and worship.

HASIDIC JUDAISM
c.1740, Mezhbizh (now in Ukraine)

Hasidic Judaism (from *hasid*, meaning "pious one") is a branch of Orthodox Judaism that stresses a mystical relationship with God. Followers believe the Torah is made up of words that are in some sense realignments of the name of God, YHWH. A true Hasid is cut off from the world and meditates, prays, and studies the Torah to become closer to God. A core belief of Hasidism is that God is both the center of the cosmos and infinite.

NEOORTHODOX JUDAISM
Late 19th century, Germany

The Neoorthodox movement arose out of the persecution of Jews in the West in the late 19th century. It provided a middle ground for those who wished neither to withdraw completely into Orthodox communities nor to wholly renounce them. Although adhering to the teachings of the Torah, Neoorthodox Judaism attempted to accommodate, and adapt to, the demands of the modern world. Followers consider it vital that Jews engage with non-Jewish people.

REFORM JUDAISM
1885, Pittsburgh, PA

Popular in western Europe and North America, Reform Judaism has its origins in 19th-century efforts to update liturgy and worship in Europe. Reform Jews tend to see the Torah as written by a number of different writers inspired by God, rather than as God's actual words. They have adapted their beliefs and practices to be more consistent with modern lifestyles and are accordingly less strict in their observances than Orthodox Jews. For example, Reform Jews have abandoned many traditional dietary laws and adopted new traditions, such as the ordination of women rabbis.

CONSERVATIVE JUDAISM
1887, New York City, NY

Many Jews felt that the Reform movement in the late 19th century went too far in rejecting the traditional tenets of their faith. As a result, in 1887, the Jewish Theological Seminary was founded to foster a branch of the faith that preserved the knowledge of historical Judaism as exemplified in the Hebrew Bible and the Talmud. This form of Judaism, now known as Conservative or Masorti Judaism, holds that the Torah and Talmud do have a divine origin, and that their laws must be followed; however, rabbis have a freer hand in interpreting those

laws than their Orthodox equivalents. Many of the rulings of Conservative rabbis have been rejected by Orthodox Jews, but the movement has proved popular, especially in the US.

JEWISH SCIENCE
1920s, Cincinnati, OH

The Jewish Science movement was founded in the early 1920s in the US by Alfred G. Moses, Morris Lichtenstein, and Tehilla Lichtenstein. It is often considered to have been a response to the growing influence of Christian Science, as developed by Mary Baker Eddy (p.337) at the end of the 19th century. Adherents are encouraged to cultivate a sense of personal contentment and a positive attitude toward themselves and others. Rather than being regarded as a paternal figure, God is seen as an energy or force that permeates the universe, and as the source and restorer of health. Self-help, visualization, and affirmative prayer (focusing on a positive outcome) are central to the faith and are believed to promote both physical and spiritual well-being. Jewish Science acknowledges modern medicine and, unlike Christian Science, permits conventional medical treatment.

RECONSTRUCTIONIST JUDAISM
1920s–40s New York City, NY

The Reconstructionist movement was founded by Mordecai Kaplan, a Lithuanian-born American. He proposed a progressive approach to Judaism, which he regarded to

be an appropriate response to modernity. This branch of Judaism considers the laws of the Torah to be useful only if they have a clear purpose for the Jewish people, or for humanity as a whole, and that the laws therefore require continuous reinterpretation. Some of the changes that have been effected in Reconstructionist Judaism are quite radical. For example, their Sabbath Prayer Book includes no mention of the Jews as a chosen people, and does not look forward to the coming of a Messiah. In place of such doctrines, Reconstructionism strives for a better world for all, populated by better people.

HUMANISTIC JUDAISM
1963, Michigan

Rabbi Sherwin T. Wine founded Humanistic Judaism in the US in the 1960s to offer nonreligious Jews a nontheistic alternative to the traditional religion. Humanistic Jews hold that Judaism is an ethnic culture formed by the Jewish people, with no connection to God. The tradition's humanistic, egalitarian philosophy is reflected in its uplifting celebration of Jewish culture: nontheistic rituals and ceremonies are open to all, Jew and non-Jew, regardless of gender and sexual orientation. Participation in religious festivals is considered important, although all references to God are omitted from services, and religious passages have been rewritten from a secular perspective. Adherents are encouraged to focus on self-determination, self-help, and reason to shape their lives, rather than on the intervention of divine authority.

BRANCHES OF CHRISTIANITY

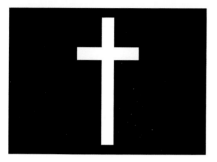

The world's largest religion, with more than two billion adherents, Christianity is based on the teachings of Jesus Christ, which are chronicled in the Gospels—four books in the New Testament of the Bible. Christianity is a monotheistic religion that has common roots with Judaism. However, Christians believe that Jesus was the Messiah promised in the Old Testament. Christianity spread around the world with European colonization from the 15th century. It diversified into Eastern and Western branches in the Great Schism of 1054, and then into many denominations after the Reformation in the 16th century. Since the 20th century, most Churches have engaged in the ecumenical movement, which seeks closer harmony.

CATHOLIC CHURCH
1st century CE, Rome, Italy

Catholics trace the origins of their Church back to Jesus of Nazareth. The Catholic Church, the largest of all the Christian Churches with 1.3 billion members, is governed by bishops, successors of the 12 apostles who were Jesus's close collaborators. The Pope, the successor to the apostle Peter, is the supreme authority within the Church. Baptism is the fundamental sacrament and Catholics live moral lives through the avoidance of sin and doing good works in the hope of immortality in heaven.

ORIENTAL ORTHODOX CHURCHES
3rd–4th centuries CE, various

The Oriental Orthodox Churches, which include the Coptic Church and those of Syria and Ethiopia, as well as Armenia (right), share the view that Christ has one nature (inseparably human and divine). All Oriental Orthodox Churches trace their origins directly to the early centuries of Christianity. The Coptic Church is Egypt's national Christian Church, dating to the 3rd century CE. The Ethiopian Orthodox Church was founded around 340 CE as a branch of the Coptic Church. It follows several Jewish-influenced practices, such as observing a day of rest on the Sabbath, circumcision, and dietary rules that link it to its Middle Eastern origins. The Syrian Orthodox Church has members in southern Turkey, Iran, Iraq, and India, as well as in Syria itself. The Syriac language is used in worship, and the liturgy is one of the richest of all the Christian Churches.

ARMENIAN CHURCH
c.294 CE, Etchmiadzin, Armenia

Armenia was the first country to make Christianity its state religion: St. Gregory converted its ruler, King Tiridates III, in the late 3rd century CE. The Armenian Church was at first close to the Eastern Orthodox Churches, but around 506 CE they split over definitions of the nature of Christ. Like the Oriental Orthodox Church, of which it is part, the Armenian Church sees Christ as having one nature, simultaneously human and divine. Armenian Christians worship in their own language using a 5th-century translation of the Bible. Their churches are plain and they have two kinds of priests: parish priests who, unless they are monks, must marry before ordination; and doctors, who are celibate and may become bishops.

EASTERN ORTHODOX CHURCH
1054, Constantinople (Istanbul)

Eastern Orthodox Christians, like Catholics, trace their origins to the person of Jesus of Nazareth, whom they venerate as truly God and truly human. For the first eight centuries, Orthodox and Catholics shared the same beliefs, but from the ninth century onwards there were subtle theological divergences. These were magnified by the political situation caused by a rift or schism in 1054. The schism continued until 1964. Eastern Orthodox Christians, like many other branches of Christianity, have developed a rich liturgical practice of prayer and celebrate the seven sacraments. Eastern Orthodox Christians have developed sublime art, especially in the form of icons, which assist them in private and communal prayer.

LUTHERANISM
1520s, Germany

The Lutheran Church traces its origins to German reformer Martin Luther (p.235). Lutheranism spread across northern Europe during the 16th and 17th centuries. Followers see the Bible as the only guide to doctrine and believe that people come to God through faith in Jesus Christ, not good works alone. There are now around 70 separate Lutheran Churches, all under the umbrella of the Lutheran World Federation.

ANGLICANISM
1534, London, England

The Anglican Church separated from the Catholic Church in the 16th century due to ecclesiastical and political conflicts surrounding King Henry VIII's petition to the Pope for a divorce from Catherine of Aragon. It retained many Catholic features at first, but was later influenced by Protestant reformers. Today, the Anglican Church embraces those who favor elaborate ritual, known as Anglo-Catholics, as well as those termed Evangelical who hold simpler services. The Anglican Church includes 40 autonomous Churches around the world, known as the Anglican Communion. All believe in the importance of Scripture, accept an unbroken line of bishops (traced back to the Apostles), and celebrate two sacraments: baptism and the Eucharist (p.228).

MENNONITE CHURCH
1540s, The Netherlands

The Dutch preacher Menno Simons, originally a Catholic who joined the Anabaptists—a radical Reformation group—in 1536, believed in Church reform, pacifism, and the baptism of adult believers only. His followers, known as Mennonites, spread throughout Europe. German Mennonites were among the early settlers of America, and many Russian Mennonites migrated to the US after World War II. Today, the majority of Mennonites live in North America and pursue a Bible-based faith. They anticipate the Second Coming of Christ and live a life of holiness and prayer. Missionary and relief work is important to believers.

PRESBYTERIANISM
16th century, Scotland

Presbyterianism originated with 16th-century reformers, such as French theologian John Calvin (p.237). As well as his influential ideas on predestination, Calvin believed Christian groups should be governed by elders. This appealed to church leaders in Scotland, keen to increase community involvement in religious affairs. Presbyterians are so named for being governed by presbyters (ministers or elders) and have no bishops. Congregationalism developed for similar reasons, especially in England, and was the religion of the Pilgrims who emigrated to America. In the late 20th century, the Presbyterians and Congregationalists joined to form the World Alliance of Reformed Churches, whose members see salvation as the gift of God.

BAPTISTS
Early 17th century, The Netherlands and England

The first Baptists were English Protestants; their Church was founded in England in 1612 by Thomas Helwys. Baptist beliefs include the primacy of the Bible and that baptism should be reserved for adult believers who can profess their faith. Baptist churches spread across the US and are especially popular with the black community there; they have gained ground internationally and are one of the world's largest Christian groups today.

QUAKERS
c.1650, Great Britain

The Quaker movement began in the 17th century, led by George Fox. The name originated when Fox told a magistrate to quake at the name of the Lord. Fox and his followers had no clergy, no sacraments, and no formal liturgy, believing that the Friends—as they called themselves —could communicate directly with God. They opposed warfare and refused to take legal oaths. Although widely persecuted, they are now admired for their campaigns for peace, prison reform, and abolition of slavery. Modern Quakers still emphasize direct contact with God, gathering together in silence until the Spirit moves a member to speak.

AMISH
Late 17th century, Switzerland

The Amish are members of a strict Protestant group that originated in Switzerland under the leadership of a Mennonite minister, Jacob »

Amman, but now mostly live in the eastern US. Of several groups of Amish that exist today, the most distinctive is the Old Order, who adopt traditional clothes, shun recent developments such as motorized transport, and run their own schools, preferring to help each other than to accept state funding. Worship takes place in their homes, with different homeowners taking turns to host the Sunday service.

MORAVIAN BRETHREN
1722, Saxony, Germany

In 1722, German Count Nikolaus von Zinzendorf invited a group of Protestants from Moravia (now in the Czech Republic) to form a community on his estate in Saxony. Owing their origins to the earliest Protestants, the followers of reformer Jan Hus, who was burned at the stake in 1415, they became known as the Moravian Brethren. Their Church looks to the Scriptures for guidance on faith and conduct, with little emphasis on doctrine. A key part of their worship is the sharing of a communal meal called a lovefeast. They are evangelical, sending missionaries throughout the world.

METHODISM
1720s–30s, England

Methodism was founded by John Wesley in England in the 18th century. It is now one of the four largest Churches in Britain and has more than 70 million adherents worldwide. Methodists believe that Christians should live by the method outlined by the Bible, and place major emphasis on Scripture and little on ritual. Preaching is considered especially important.

SHAKERS
c.1758, Great Britain

The Shakers' name is derived from the trembling experienced by members in religious ecstasy. Their founder, Ann Lee, claimed she had revelations that she was Christ's female counterpart. Persecuted in England, she and her followers emigrated to America, where they held their possessions in common and were celibate. Although the group was popular in the 19th century, membership declined in the 20th century, and today there are few members. However, the Shakers are still respected for their austere lifestyle and the simple furniture they created.

UNITARIANISM
1774, England

Unitarians believe in one God but not the Holy Trinity (pp.212–19), and they seek truth based in human experience rather than religious doctrine. Unitarian ideas began to emerge in Poland, Hungary, and England in the 16th century, but the first Unitarian Church was founded in England only in 1774, and in the US in 1781. Numbers declined in the 20th century, but there are still thriving congregations in the US and Europe. Congregations are independent of one another and there is no Church hierarchy.

MORMONISM
1830, New York

The Church of Jesus Christ of Latter-day Saints was founded by American Joseph Smith, Jr. He claimed to have been guided to a set of gold tablets bearing the word of God by an angel. He translated them as *The Book of Mormon* (1830), which, together with other Mormon texts, and the Bible, form the religion's writings. Smith claimed the right to guide the Church through further revelations, including permission for polygamous marriages and the possibility for all men to become gods. After his death in 1844, the Mormons followed a new leader, Brigham Young, to Utah, where the Church remains strong.

PLYMOUTH BRETHREN
1831, Plymouth, England

The Plymouth Brethren began as a group of Christians who rejected the sectarian nature of the existing Protestant churches, seeking a less formal religion. They believed that all should have equal access to their faith, and did not ordain priests. Enthusiastic preachers, they emphasized the importance of regular worship, Bible study, and missionary work. In 1848, they divided into two broad groups, the Open and the Exclusive Brethren, differing in their interpretation of certain theological issues and their attitudes toward outsiders. Today, there are an estimated two million members of the group around the world.

CHRISTADELPHIANISM
1848, Richmond, VA

The name Christadelphians ("Christ's brothers") reflects a desire of the Church's English founder, John Thomas, to return to the faith of Jesus's first disciples. He rejected the term Christianity, believing that the Christian Churches had distorted Jesus's true message. Followers adhere to Jesus's teachings but reject the doctrine of the Holy Trinity and look forward to the Second Coming of Christ. The Church does not ordain priests, and its members do not vote or take part in politics, and reject military service.

SEVENTH-DAY ADVENTIST CHURCH
1863, Battle Creek, MI

Adventists are Protestant Christians who believe in the imminent Second Coming of Jesus Christ. At this time, known as the Advent, Christ will return to earth, destroy Satan, and create a new world. The American Adventist William Miller claimed this would begin around 1843. When it did not, some of his followers, led by James and Ellen White, asserted that Jesus had begun a pre-Advent judgment in heaven. They founded the Church in 1863. Adventists follow the dietary rules of the Old Testament, eschew worldly pursuits (such as gambling and dancing), and observe the Sabbath on Saturday.

THE SALVATION ARMY
1865, London, England

Methodist preacher William Booth founded the Salvation Army in London in 1865. His beliefs were strongly influenced by his religious background, but the sect's organization was inspired by the military. The church leader is its general and its ministers are officers and wear uniforms. Booth's aim was to do missionary and social work on a large, organized scale, and the denomination gained a reputation for helping the poor.

JEHOVAH'S WITNESSES
1872, Pittsburgh, PA

The Jehovah's Witnesses (pp.312–13) have their roots in the International Bible Students' Association. They believe that Jesus Christ was not, himself, God, but God's first creation. They anticipate the coming of the kingdom of God, reject nationalism, and dispute doctrines such as the Trinity. The Church aims to convert others by door-to-door proselytizing.

CHURCH OF CHRIST (SCIENTIST)
1879, Boston, MA

Mary Baker Eddy dedicated her life to reviving the early healing ministry of Jesus after she was cured without medical treatment following an injury. Eddy claimed to be able to heal the sick, and believed that those who understand the link between God and love can also become healers. She founded the Church of Christ (Scientist) in 1879. Eddy's own writings and the Bible form the basis of the religion. Services feature readings from both, but have no sermons. Christian Science is today established in more than 80 countries.

PENTECOSTALISM
1900–1906, Topeka, KS; Los Angeles, CA

Pentecostal churches are prevalent in the developing world, and in poorer communities in the developed world. They take their name from the first Pentecost, (p.219) when the Holy Spirit is said to have descended on the Apostles as tongues of flame. The Churches' roots are in the work of the preacher Charles Parham. These Churches emphasize spiritual experiences, such as healing, exorcism, prophecy, and speaking in tongues after baptism in the Holy Spirit. Parham's student, William J. Seymour, founded the Apostolic Faith Gospel Mission in Los Angeles, which inspired the founding of Pentecostal Churches worldwide.

CHARISMATIC MOVEMENT
1950s–60s, various

The Charismatic movement is a worldwide movement of Christian revival. At its heart is the belief in the charismata, or gifts of the Holy Spirit (p.219). Worship tends to be informal and the Second Coming of Christ is often seen as imminent. The movement stresses the importance of the Holy Spirit, which is said to enter believers during baptism.

NEW AFRICAN CHURCHES
20th century, Africa

The last hundred years have seen the rapid rise of a specifically African form of Christianity south of the Sahara. In the late 19th century, Africans began to reject the Christianity imported by Western missionaries, creating independent African Churches. The largest include the Kimbanguists, founded in the Democratic Republic of the Congo, with some 10 million members; and the similarly sized Celestial Church of Christ in Benin. Many of these Churches arose in times of persecution and have a strong sense of sacred places.

BRANCHES OF ISLAM

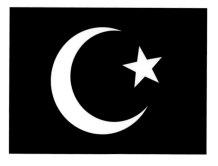

The most recently founded of the three great monotheistic religions, Islam spread quickly from its roots in the Middle East and has been hugely influential in scholarship and politics all over the world. The most significant division within Islam is that between Sunni and Shi'a, two branches that developed when the early Muslim community disagreed over who was to succeed their first leader, Muhammad. Later conflicts over leadership led to further subdivisions, but there are also groups within Islam that are set apart by doctrinal differences: Sufism, or mystical Islam, for example, is vigorously opposed by some more orthodox Muslim groups that consider its practices un-Islamic.

SUNNI ISLAM
7th century CE, Arabian Peninsula

More than 85 percent of the Muslim population of the world is Sunni. In most Islamic countries, the majority of Muslims are Sunni, with the exception of Iran, Iraq, Azerbaijan, and Yemen, as well as some of the Gulf States. The founders of this form of Islam were the group of Muslims who believed that Abu Bakr, Companion and father-in-law of Muhammad, should succeed the Prophet as the first leader or caliph (literally, successor). Sunni Muslims take the Sunna, or tradition of Muhammad, as the model for Muslim conduct and have a further allegiance to one of four schools that interpret Islamic law, or shari'a (p.273): Hanafi, Maliki, Hanbali, and Shafi'i.

SHI'A ISLAM
7th century CE, Arabian Peninsula

Shi'a Islam is named after the Shi'a 'Ali, or Party of 'Ali, the group within the early Muslim community that claimed that Muhammad had nominated his cousin 'Ali to lead the faith as his successor. Its largest branch identifies 'Ali and a continuous line of 11 descendants as the imams, or spiritual leaders, of Islam, whose authority is divinely sanctioned. This branch is known as Twelve-Imam Shi'a, or the Twelvers. Another group of Shi'a Muslims, the Seveners, does not recognize the last five imams in this lineage. Both groups also have doctrinal differences with Sunni Islam: for example, they hold that God may change his decisions (a concept called *bada'*).

KHARIJITES
7th century CE, Middle East

The assassination of the third caliph, 'Uthman ibn 'Affan, in 656 CE sparked a bitter conflict that split the Islamic world. At its center was a group of rebel Muslims responsible for the assassination, who later became known as the Kharijites, a name deriving from the Arabic for "to leave" or "exit." They did not believe that the position of caliph should be inherited, but rather that it should be won by election. The sect gained a reputation for their extreme militancy and opposition to established authority; however, some Islamic scholars have interpreted their actions as an attempt to uphold justice. The Kharijites maintained a literal and unswerving observance of the Qur'an, lived puritanical lives strictly according to Islamic rule, and held that anyone who committed a major sin could not remain a Muslim. The early Kharijites were almost wiped out in their frequent uprisings, but members of a more moderate group survive today in North Africa, Oman, and Zanzibar.

ISMAILISM
7th century CE, Arabian Peninsula

Ismailism is a sect of Shi'a Islam and itself has numerous subsects, including the Druze (see opposite). The movement has its origins in the late 7th century CE, following a conflict within Shi'a Islam over who should succeed Jaafar al-Sadiq as the sixth imam.

Those who considered his son Ismail to be the rightful successor established a breakaway group, and became known as Ismailis. Although there are variations within Ismailism, its followers generally uphold fundamental Muslim belief with respect to the unity of God, the Prophet Muhammad, the Qur'an, and shari'a law. However, among their principal doctrines is a belief that the religion has exterior and interior aspects, and that the exterior features hold hidden, inner truths that will be made clear via the imams. The imams' interpretations of the Qur'an's hidden truths are regarded as binding in the community.

DRUZE
11th century, Middle East

The beliefs of the sect known as the Druze developed out of Ismailite doctrine. This small sect is characterized by extreme secrecy: many of its teachings and practices have been withheld, not only from the outside world, but also from its own members. The Druze community is divided into the *ukkal* (initiated) and the *juhhal* (uninitiated); only the *ukkal* have access to the faith's sacred texts and may participate fully in rituals and ceremonies. The majority of Druze now live in Lebanon, with smaller groups in Syria and Israel.

SUFISM
13th century, Turkey

The mystical and ascetic branch of Islam is known as Sufism (pp.282–83). Devotees follow a spiritual teacher and seek a direct and personal experience of God, which is often characterized by intense, ecstatic experiences, including trancelike states. The spinning of the Whirling Dervishes, a Sufi order, is an expression of this attempt to experience God. Because Sufism involves such practices, which are thought to lead to the union of the individual with God, Sufis have been accused of turning their backs on Islam. However, they insist that their experience of the love of God is the anchor of their Islamic faith, and that adherence to shari'a law (pp.272–73) is as vital to them as it is to other Muslims.

AHMADIYYA
1889, Punjab, India

Controversy has surrounded the Ahmadiyya movement since its establishment in Punjab toward the end of the 19th century. The founder of the movement, a Sunni Muslim named Mirza Ghulam Ahmad, claimed not only to have been divinely inspired, but also to be a messiah figure (pp.284–85). This conflicted with the accepted idea of Muhammad as the last true prophet, and as a result most other Muslims regard followers of the Ahmadiyya movement as heretics. The movement does, however, share many traditional beliefs of Sunni Islam and accepts the Qur'an as its holy text. Adherents believe that the message about their version of Islam should be conveyed to non-Muslims as well as Muslims, and the movement has spread throughout the world, building centers of worship and learning in Africa, North America, Asia, and Europe.

SALAFISM
Late 19th century, Egypt

Salafism is a modern, conservative movement within Sunni Islam that looks to the Salaf, or predecesors, the earliest Muslims, for guidance on exemplary Islamic conduct. The movement is considered to have emerged as a reaction to the spread of Western, specifically European, ideology in the late 19th century; Salafists believe in eliminating foreign influence to ensure a return to the pure faith. They have a strict interpretation of the sins of shirk (idolatry) and *bida'h* (innovation), and reject *kalam*, or theological speculation. Followers uphold the precedence of shari'a law (pp.272–73) and the literal truth of the Qur'an. Salafism is said to be Islam's fastest-growing movement worldwide.

THE NATION OF ISLAM
1930, US

Arising out of the Depression of the 1930s in African-American areas in the US, the Nation of Islam was founded by Fard Muhammad, to whom some have ascribed divinity. Other key figures have included the civil rights activist Malcolm X and Louis Farrakhan. The theology of the movement combines core Islamic beliefs with a strong political agenda focused on African-American unity and rights. The Nation of Islam has been accused of being both black supremacist and anti-Semitic, but has nevertheless been effective in spreading ideas about faith and equality among black people, and upholds a strict code of ethics.

GLOSSARY

Key
(B) Buddhism
(C) Christianity
(D) Daoism and other
    Chinese religions
(H) Hinduism
(I) Islam
(J) Judaism
(Jn) Jainism
(S) Sikhism
(Sh) Shinto
(Z) Zoroastrianism

Adi Granth (S) See **Guru Granth Sahib**.

Advaita Vedanta (H) A school of Hindu philosophy developed in the 9th century, which gives a unified explanation of the **Vedas**, and focuses on the idea of **Brahman**.

Ahadith (I) See **Hadith**.

Ahimsa (B, H, Jn) A doctrine of nonviolence of both thought and action.

Akhand path (S) A complete and uninterrupted oral rendition of the **Guru Granth Sahib**.

Allah (I) The name of the one God.

Amrit (S) Sweetened holy water used in religious ceremonies; the specific Sikh ceremony of initiation.

Analects (D) The collected sayings of Confucius and his contemporaries, written by his followers.

Ananda (H) A state of bliss.

Anata (B) A state of freedom from ego to which Buddhists aspire.

Anicca (B) The impermanence of existence.

Arhat (B) A perfect being who has attained **nirvana**.

Artha (H) The pursuit of material wealth, one of the duties of a person in the "householder" stage of life, the second phase of the **ashrama**.

Ashkenazim (J) Jews from Eastern and Central Europe, and their descendants around the world.

Ashrama (H) The stages of life, of which there are four, in the Hindu social system: student; householder; retiree; and ascetic.

Atman (H) The individual self.

Avatar (H) An incarnation of a Hindu deity; especially the various incarnations of the god Vishnu.

Avesta (Z) The principle sacred texts of Zoroastrianism.

Ayat (C) The smallest entries in the Qu'ran, which are short verses or "signs."

Baptism (C) The sacrament that admits a person to the Christian Church in a ritual that involves being sprinkled with, or immersed in, water.

Bar/bat mitzvah (J) The ceremony marking a Jewish boy's or girl's admission to the adult religious community; the state of having reached religious adulthood.

Bhakti (B, H) An active religious devotion to a divinity leading to **nirvana**.

Bible (C) The collection of books that constitute the sacred text of Christianity. The Christian Bible comprises the Old Testament, which includes the Jewish books of the law, Jewish history, and the prophets; and the New Testament, which deals with the life and work of Jesus, his followers, and the early Church. See also **Hebrew Bible**.

Bodhisattva (B) Someone on the path to becoming a **buddha**, who puts off final enlightenment to help other people to reach the same state.

Brahma (H) The creator god, one of the Hindu **Trimurti**.

Brahman (H) The impersonal and unchanging divine reality of the universe. All other gods are aspects of Brahman.

Brahmin (H) A priest or seeker of the highest knowledge; the priestly class and custodians of **dharma**.

Buddha (B) An enlightened being.

Canonization (C) The process by which the Christian Church declares that a person is a saint.

Charismata (C) Spiritual gifts conferred by the Holy Spirit of God on believers, manifesting in forms such as the ability to heal, or speak in tongues.

Christ (C) Literally, "anointed one"; title given to Jesus.

Confirmation (C) A ritual in which those who have been baptized confirm their Christian faith.

Covenant (J) An agreement between God and the Jewish people in which the Jews are identified as the group he has chosen to play a special role in the relationship between himself and humanity.

Dao (D) The path or way that an individual aims to follow; the underlying way or pattern governing the working of nature.

Darshan (H) The worshipping of a deity by means of viewing an image of the god or goddess.

Dhamma (B) A variant of **dharma**, most commonly used in Buddhism.

Dharma (H) The underlying path or pattern that characterizes the cosmos and the earth; it also refers to the moral path that a person must follow.

Dukkha (B) Suffering or dissatisfaction; the idea that all life is suffering, the first of the **Four Noble Truths** defined by Buddha.

Eightfold Path (B) The path of disciplined living that Buddhists follow in the hope of breaking free from the cycle of death and rebirth. Followers aim to achieve correct understanding, intention (or thought), speech, conduct, occupation, effort, mindfulness, and concentration.

Enlightenment (B) Discovery of the ultimate truth, and the end of **dukkha**.

Eucharist (C) One of the main sacraments, involving the taking of wine and bread as the blood and body of Christ; it is known as Mass in Catholicism, Holy Communion in the Anglican Church, and the liturgy in the various Orthodox churches.

Fatwa (I) A nonbinding judgment on a point of Islamic law given by a recognized religious authority.

Four Noble Truths (B) A central teaching of Buddhism, explaining the nature of **dukkha**, its causes, and how it can be overcome.

Fravashi (Z) A guardian angel who protects the souls of individuals as they struggle against evil.

Gathas (Z) The most sacred texts of Zoroastrianism, supposedly composed by Zoroaster himself.

Gentile (J) A non-Jew.

Gospels (C) The four books of the New Testament of the **Bible**, attributed to the apostles Matthew, Mark, Luke, and John, which tell of Jesus's life and teachings; Gospel (good news) can also refer to the content of Christian teaching.

Granthi (S) An official who takes care of the **Guru Granth Sahib** and the **gurdwara**. A granthi is also a skilled reader of the sacred book.

Gurdwara (S) A Sikh temple; the place where the **Guru Granth Sahib** is housed.

Guru (H) Teacher; **(S)** One of the 10 founder-leaders of Sikhism.

Guru Granth Sahib (S) The Sikh sacred book, also known as the **Adi Granth**.

Hadith (I) Traditional accounts of the deeds and teachings of the Prophet Muhammad; the second source of Islamic law and moral guidance after the **Qur'an**.

Hafiz (I) A term of respect for a person who has memorized the **Qur'an**.

Haggadah (J) The body of teaching of the early **rabbis**, containing legends, historical narratives, and ethical precepts.

Hajj (I) The pilgrimage to Mecca, the fourth of the five pillars of Islam; all Muslims hope to make this journey once in their lives.

Halal (I) Conduct that is permitted; specifically, the correct method of slaughtering livestock, and the meat from correctly slaughtered animals.

Haram (I) Conduct that is forbidden; something sacred or inviolate.

Hasid (J) A member of a Jewish group founded in the 18th century that places a strong emphasis on mysticism.

Haskalah (J) The Jewish Enlightenment, a movement among European Jews in the 18th–19th centuries.

Hebrew Bible (J) A collection of sacred writings that form the basis of Judaism, including the **Torah**, revelations of prophets, and other sacred texts; the equivalent of the Old Testament in the Christian **Bible**.

Icon (C) A sacred image, usually depicting Christ or one of the saints, which is used as a focus for devotion, especially in the Orthodox Churches.

Imam (I) Leader of prayers in a mosque; or, one of the great leaders of the Muslim community in the Shi'a branch of the faith.

Incarnation (C) The belief that in the person of Jesus Christ, divine and human natures were made one.

Jihad (I) A religious duty to struggle against evil in the name of God, whether spiritually or physically.

Jina (Jn) A spiritual teacher. See **tirthankara**.

Kaaba (I) One of Islam's most sacred buildings, sited in Mecca inside the Masjid al-Haram mosque; a principal destination for those on **hajj**.

Kabbalah (J) An ancient Jewish mystical tradition based on an esoteric interpretation of the Hebrew Bible.

Kaccha (S) Long shorts worn under other garments by Sikhs; one of the distinguishing "five Ks" of Sikhism.

Kalam (I) Discussion and debate, especially relating to Islamic theology.

Kami (Sh) A spirit or deity in Shinto religion. There are many thousands of kami in the Shinto pantheon.

Kangha (S) A small comb worn in the hair by Sikhs; one of the "five Ks" of Sikhism.

Kara (S) A steel bangle worn by Sikhs on the right wrist. One of the "five Ks" of Sikhism.

Karma (B, H) The law of moral cause and effect that influences our rebirth after death.

Kesh (S) Uncut hair; one of the "five Ks" of Sikhism.

Khalsa (S) The community of initiated Sikhs, founded by Guru Gobind Singh.

Khanda (S) A two-edged sword of the kind used by Guru Gobind Singh in a ritual that marked the founding of the Khalsa; now a symbol of Sikhism.

Kirpan (S) A sword worn by Sikhs; one of the "five Ks" of Sikhism.

Kirtan (S) Hymn singing that forms an important part of Sikh worship.

Koan (B) In Zen Buddhism, a problem or riddle without logical solution, which is intended to provoke an insight.

Kojiki (Sh) The sacred text of Shinto.

Kosher (J) Sanctioned by religious law; especially food deemed fit to eat, according to Jewish dietary laws.

Kundalini (H) Life force or energy that is coiled at the base of the spine.

Lama (B) An adept spiritual teacher in Tibetan Buddhism, specifically one who has undergone particular **yogic**

or other training, or one who is considered to be the reincarnation of a previous spiritual leader.

Mandala (B) A sacred diagram, usually depicting a conception of the cosmos, used as a focus for meditation and in other rituals, especially in Tibetan Buddhism.

Mantra (B, H) A sacred sound or word used to bring about a spiritual transformation; in Hinduism, the metrical psalms of **Vedic** literature.

Matha (H, Jn) Monastic and similar religious establishments.

Matsuri (Sh) A festival or ritual in Shinto. Many feature processions of shrine-bearing worshippers.

Maya (H) The illusion of the world as experienced by the senses.

Mihrab (I) A niche in the prayer hall of a mosque, indicating the **qibla**.

Mishnah (J) The first major written redaction of the Jewish oral traditions and also the first major work of rabbinic Judaism.

Mitzvah (J) A commandment from God, specifically either one of the 10 principal commandments, or one of the 613 instructions found in the **Torah**.

Moksha (H) The release from the round of life, death, and rebirth; also known as mukti.

Mool mantra (S) A statement of Sikh belief in the oneness of god, composed by Guru Nanak; also called the mool mantar.

Mudra (B, H) A symbolic gesture, usually with the hands.

Mullah (I) An Islamic religious scholar, who may also preach and lead prayers in a mosque.

Murti (H) An image or statue of a deity, seen as the dwelling place or embodiment of the deity.

Nirvana (B) The state of liberation from the round of death and rebirth.

Puja (H) Worship through ritual.

Puranas (B, H, Jn) Writings not included in the **Vedas**, recounting the birth and deeds of Hindu gods and the creation, destruction, or re-creation of the universe.

Pure Land (B) The paradise where, according to some forms of Buddhism, the souls of believers go after death; known in Japanese Buddhism as jodo.

Purusha (H) The eternal and authentic self that pervades all things in the universe.

Qi (D) The life force or active principle that animates things in the world, according to traditional Chinese philosophy.

Qibla (I) The direction that a Muslim should face when praying—that of the **Kaaba** in Mecca.

Qigong (D) A system of breathing and exercise for physical, mental, and spiritual health.

Qur'an (I) The words of God as revealed to the Prophet Muhammad and later written down to form the sacred text of Islam.

Rabbi (J) A teacher and spiritual leader of a Jewish community.

Rabbinical (J) Of, or relating to, rabbis.

Ramadan (I) The ninth month of the Islamic calendar; a month of daily fasting from dawn until sunset.

Ren (D) Benevolence or altruism in Confucianism.

Sabbath (J) The rest day of the Jewish week, lasting from sunset on Friday to sunset on Saturday.

Sacraments (C) The solemn rites of Christianity. The Catholic and Orthodox Churches recognize seven: **baptism**, **Eucharist**, penance, confirmation, ordination, extreme unction (last rites), and marriage. Most Protestant Churches recognize only two: baptism and the Eucharist.

Sadhu (H) A holy man who has dedicated his life to seeking God.

Salat (I) Prayer; the second of the five pillars of Islam. Muslims are expected to pray five times each day.

Samsara (B, H) The continuing and repeating cycle of birth, life, death, and rebirth.

Samskara (H) Imprints left on the mind by experience in current or past lives; Hindu rites of passage.

Sawm (I) Fasting, especially during the month of **Ramadan**; the fourth of the five pillars of Islam.

Sangha (B) An order of Buddhist monks and nuns.

Satya (H) Truth, or what is correct and unchanging.

Sefirot (J) The 10 emanations, the attributes of God in **kabbalah**.

Sephardim (J) Jews who come from Spain, Portugal, or North Africa, or their descendants.

Seva (S) Service to others, one of the important principles of Sikhism.

Shahada (I) The Muslim profession of faith, translated as, "There is no God but God; Muhammad is the messenger of God"; the first and most important of the five pillars of Islam.

Shari'a (I) The path to be followed in Muslim life and, therefore, Islamic law, based on the **Qur'an** and on the **Hadith**.

Shi'a (I) One of the two main groups of Muslims, consisting of those who believe that Muhammad's cousin 'Ali was his rightful successor as caliph. See also **Sunni**.

Shirk (I) The sin of idolatry or polytheism.

Sruti (H) The **Vedas** and some of the **Upanishads**.

Sufi (I) A member of one of a number of mystical Islamic orders, whose beliefs center on a personal relationship with God. Sufi orders can be found in **Sunni**, **Shi'a** and other Islamic groups. Sufism is associated with the ecstatic whirling dances of the dervishes.

Sunna (I) Muhammad's way of life, taken as a model for Muslims and recorded in the **hadiths**.

Sunni (I) One of the two main groups of Muslims, followers of those who supported an elected caliphate. See also **Shi'a**.

Sutra (B, H) A collection of teachings, especially sayings attributed to Buddha.

Talmud (J) Text made up of a body of discussion and interpretation of the **Torah**, compiled by scholars and rabbis, and a source of ethical advice and instruction, especially to Orthodox Jews.

Tantra (B) Text used in some kinds of Buddhism (mainly in Tibet) to help users to reach enlightenment, or the practices based on such a text.

Tirthankara (Jn) One of the 24 spiritual teachers or **jinas** who have shown the way of the Jain faith.

Torah (J) The first five books of the Hebrew **Bible**, seen as representing the teaching given by God to Moses on Mount Sinai.

Trimurti (H) The trio of principal Hindu gods—Brahma, Vishnu, and Shiva—or a threefold image of them.

Trinity (C) The threefold god, comprising Father, Son, and Holy Spirit in a single divinity.

Upanishads (H) Sacred texts containing Hindu philosophical teachings; also known as the Vedanta, the end of the **Vedas**.

Vedas (H) Collections of hymns and other writings in praise of the deities.

Wa (D) Harmony, in which the group takes precedence over the individual.

Wuwei (D) Uncontrived and effortless doing.

Yin–yang (D) The two principles of the cosmos in Chinese philosophy, seen as opposite but complementary and interacting to produce a whole greater than either separate part.

YHWH (J) The four letters that represent the name of God in Judaism, considered to be too holy to utter, but pronounced "yahweh."

Yoga (H) A form of physical and mental training. One the six schools of Hindu philosophy.

Zakat (I) The giving of alms in the form of a tax to help the poor; the third pillar of Islam.

Zazen (B) Seated meditation.

Zurvan (Z) The God of time; in some forms of Zoroastrianism, the primal being, from whom were derived the wise lord Ahura Mazda and the hostile spirit Angra Mainyu.

INDEX

Numbers in **bold** refer to main entries.

F

G

H

D

ACKNOWLEDGMENTS

Dorling Kindersley and cobalt id would like to thank Louise Thomas for additional picture research, and Margaret McCormack for the index

PICTURE CREDITS

The publisher would like to thank the following for their kind permission to reproduce their photographs:

(Key: a-above; b-below; c-center; l-left; r-right; t-top)

21 Corbis: Anthony Bannister/Gallo Images (tr). **22 Getty Images:** Per-Andre Hoffmann (bl). **23 Corbis:** Ocean (tr). **25 Getty Images:** Time & Life Pictures (tr). **29 Corbis:** Michel Setboun (tr). **31 Alamy Images:** Horizons WWP (tl); Getty Images: Apic/Contributor (br). **33 Corbis:** Nathan Lovas/ Foto Natura/Minden Pictures (cr). **35 Corbis:** Giles Bracher/Robert Harding World Imagery (tr). **37 Getty Images:** Maria Stenzel (tr). **39 Getty Images:** Juan Carlos Muñoz (cr). **43 Alamy Images:** Pictorial Press Ltd (tl). **44 Alamy Images:** Emiliano Rodriguez (br). **45 Getty Images:** Richard I'Anson (tl). **47 Corbis:** William Henry Jackson (tr). **48 Getty Images:** David Sutherland (br). **50 Corbis:** Michele Westmorland/Science Faction (bc). **57 Alamy Images:** Imagestate Media Partners Limited - Impact Photos (tl). **59 PAL:** Peter Hayman/The British Museum (tr). **63 Corbis:** Kazuyoshi Nomachi (tr); Paule Seux/Hemis (bl). **64 Getty Images:** Religious Images/UIG (tl). **65 Corbis:** Raheb Homavandi/Reuters (br). **67 Fotolia:** Pavel Bortel (tl); Corbis: Liu Liqun (tr). **69 Corbis:** Werner Forman/Werner Forman (tr). **71 Alamy Images:** John Warburton-Lee Photography (bl); Stuart Forster India (tr). **75 Getty Images:** (bl); Keren Su (tr).

76 Mary Evans Picture Library: (tr). **77 Corbis:** Imaginechina (br). **78 Getty Images:** De Agostini Picture Library (br). **81 Corbis:** (bl). **84 Corbis:** Michael Freeman (bl). **87 Getty Images:** Universal Images Group (tl); Corbis: Kieran Doherty/Reuters (bl). **95 Alamy Images:** Franck METOIS (br). **97 Getty Images:** Gary Ombler (tr). **99 Corbis:** Nevada Wier (bl). **100 Corbis:** Godong/Robert Harding World Imagery (cr). **103 Getty Images:** Comstock (br). **108 Corbis:** Hugh Sitton (br). **111 Corbis:** Stuart Freedman/In Pictures (br). **112 Alamy Images:** Emanuele Ciccomartino (br). **114 Alamy Images:** World Religions Photo Library (cr). **119 Corbis:** Juice Images (br). **121 akg-images:** R. u. S. Michaud (tr). **123 Getty Images:** The Washington Post (bc); akg-images: R. u. S. Michaud (tr). **125 Alamy Images:** Lebrecht Music and Arts Photo Library (bl); Corbis: Bettmann (cr). **132 Corbis:** Pascal Deloche/Godong (bl); Pascal Deloche/Godong (tr). **134 Corbis:** Jeremy Horner (bl). **135 Fotolia:** Benjamin Vess (tr). **138 Getty Images:** Chung Sung-Jun (br). **140 Getty Images:** Oli Scarff (tl). **142 Getty Images:** SuperStock (bl). **143 Getty Images:** Earl & Nazima Kowall (tr). **145 Corbis:** Nigel Pavitt/JAI (cb). **147 Alamy Images:** Mary Evans Picture Library (bl); Corbis: Peter Adams (tr). **149 Getty Images:** DEA / V. PIROZZI (bl). **150 Getty Images:** Andy Ryan (tr). **155 Getty Images:** Godong (br). **156 Corbis:** Peter Turnley (tl). **157 Alamy Images:** Mark Lees (tr); Fotolia: Oliver Klimek (bl). **159 Corbis:** Alison Wright (bl); Alison Wright (tr). **162 Getty Images:** Kaz Mori (tl). **171 Getty Images:** DEA / G. DAGLI ORTI (bl); Corbis: Peter Guttman (tr). **172 Getty Images:** The Bridgeman Art Library (bl). **173 Corbis:** Christophe Boisvieux (bl); Getty Images: PhotoStock-Israel (tr).

174 Corbis: Nathan Benn/Ottochrome (tl). **177 akg-images:** Erich Lessing (tl). **178 Corbis:** Dr. John C. Trever, PhD (bl). **179 Corbis:** Richard T. Nowitz (tr). **183 Getty Images:** Philippe Lissac/Godong (tr). **185 Corbis:** NASA, ESA, and F. Paresce /handout (bl); Getty Images: Danita Delimont (tr). **186 Corbis:** Kobby Dagan/Demotix (bc). **188 Getty Images:** Uriel Sinai/Stringer (cr). **192 Alamy Images:** INTERFOTO (bl). **195 Alamy Images:** Israel images (tl). **197 Getty Images:** Steve McAlister (bc); Alamy Images: World History Archive (tr). **199 Corbis:** Silvia Morara (br). **205 Corbis:** Massimo Listri (cb); Chris Hellier (tr). **206 Corbis:** Francis G. Mayer (tl). **209 Corbis:** The Gallery Collection (tr). **211 Getty Images:** De Agostini Picture Library (tl); Universal Images Group (tr). **215 The Bridgeman Art Library:** Clement Guillaume (tr). **216 Getty Images:** Universal Images Group (tl). **218 Corbis:** eidon photographers/Demotix (tl). **219 Alamy Images:** van hilversum (tr). **221 Corbis:** Tim Thompson (tl); Getty Images: Mondadori Portfolio/UIG (tr). **223 Corbis:** Hulton-Deutsch Collection (br); Jose Nicolas (tr). **225 Getty Images:** Conrad Meyer (tr). **227 The Bridgeman Art Library:** AISA (br). **229 Getty Images:** DEA / VENERANDA BIBLIOTECA AMBROSIANA (bl); Scott Olson/Staff (tr). **233 Getty Images:** Lucas Cranach the Elder (t). **234 Corbis:** Alfredo Dagli Orti/The Art Archive (tl). **235 Corbis:** Bettmann (tr). **237 Getty Images:** (bl); Corbis: Paul A. Souders (tr). **238 Corbis:** Heritage Images (cb). **243 Alamy Images:** The Protected Art Archive (bl); INTERFOTO (tr). **244 Corbis:** Matthias Kulka (tl). **245 Getty Images:** Ron Burton/Stringer (tr). **247 Corbis:** (br). **253 Getty Images:** Muhannad Fala'ah/Stringer (cb); Alamy Images:

352 ACKNOWLEDGMENTS

Rick Piper Photography (tl).
257 Getty Images: Leemage (tl).
259 Corbis: Howard Davies (tr).
260 Corbis: Kazuyoshi Nomachi (tl).
261 Getty Images: Patrick Syder (bl);
Insy Shah (tr). **265 Corbis:** Alexandra
Boulat/VII (tr). **266 Corbis:** Christine
Osborne (bl). **267 Alamy Images:**
Philippe Lissac/Photononstop (br).
268 Corbis: Tom Morgan/Demotix (tl).
269 Getty Images: AHMAD FAIZAL
YAHYA (br). **271 The Bridgeman Art
Library:** Christie's Images (tl).
273 Corbis: Bertrand Rieger/Hemis
(br). **274 Getty Images:** Wathiq
Khuzaie (bl). **277 Corbis:** Owen
Williams/National Geographic Society
(cr). **278 Getty Images:** Rozikassim
Photography (cr). **281 Getty Images:**
Walter Bibikow (tl). **282 Corbis:** John
Stanmeyer/VII (cb). **283 Alamy
Images:** Peter Horree (tr). **285 Alamy
Images:** ZUMA Press, Inc. (tr).
291 Corbis: Hulton-Deutsch Collection
(tl). **299 Corbis:** ETTORE FERRARI/
epa (tr). **300 Corbis:** Christopher
Pillitz/In Pictures (bl). **301 Alamy
Images:** Art Directors & TRIP (tr).
302 Corbis: Christopher Pillitz/In
Pictures (bl). **305 Alamy Images:**
Alberto Paredes (tl). **307 The
Bridgeman Art Library:** (bl); Corbis:
James L. Amos (tr). **309 Alamy
Images:** Art Directors & TRIP (bl).

311 Corbis: Matthew McKee (bc).
313 The Art Archive: Tate Gallery
London / Eileen Tweedy (tl).
315 Getty Images: Ethan Miller (tl);
Henry Guttmann (bl). **317 Getty
Images:** travelstock44 (cl).
318 Corbis: Bettmann (cr).
320 Alamy Images: Pictorial Press
Ltd (cr). **323 Getty Images:** China
Photos (cl).

All other images © Dorling Kindersley.

For further information see:
www.dkimages.com